The Politics of Islamic Law

The Politics of Islamic Law

Local Elites, Colonial Authority, and the Making of the Muslim State

IZA R. HUSSIN

THE UNIVERSITY OF CHICAGO PRESS   CHICAGO AND LONDON

IZA R. HUSSIN is a university lecturer in the Department of Politics and International Studies at the University of Cambridge and the Mohamed Noah Fellow at Pembroke College, Cambridge.

The University of Chicago Press, Chicago 60637
The University of Chicago Press, Ltd., London

Printed in the United States of America

25 24 23 22 21 20 19 18 17 16   1 2 3 4 5

ISBN-13: 978-0-226-32320-6 (cloth)
ISBN-13: 978-0-226-32334-3 (paper)
ISBN-13: 978-0-226-32348-0 (e-book)
DOI: 10.7208/chicago/9780226323480.001.0001

Library of Congress Cataloging-in-Publication Data
Huzzin, Iza R., author.
The politics of Islamic law : local elites, colonial authority, and the making of the Muslim state / Iza R. Hussin.
pages cm
Includes bibliographical references and index.
ISBN 978-0-226-32320-6 (cloth : alk. paper) — ISBN 978-0-226-32334-3 (pbk. : alk. paper) — ISBN 978-0-226-32348-0 (e-book). 1. Islamic law—History. 2. Islam and politics. 3. Islam and state. I. Title.
KBP144.H88 2016
340.5'9—dc23   2015033818

⊚This paper meets the requirements of ANSI/NISO Z39.48-1992 (Permanence of Paper).

Contents

Acknowledgments

I have been fortunate, in the course of research, writing, and learning to rely upon a large community of scholars, friends, and family in many places:

At the University of Cambridge, my colleagues at the Department of Politics and International Studies provided valuable feedback during final revisions; Pembroke College and the Centre for History and Economics gave space and time in which to complete them. At the University of Chicago, my colleagues and students at the Department of Political Science, the Committee on Southern Asian Studies, the Chicago Center for Contemporary Theory, and the Center for Middle Eastern Studies provided invaluable critique and support. Lisa Wedeen and Dan Slater read the manuscript in its various iterations repeatedly and challenged me to make it the best book it could be; John Comaroff, Bernard Harcourt, and Gary Herrigel helped me remember what the book was about in the first place. My appreciation also goes to David Brent and David Pervin at the University of Chicago Press for their guidance, patience, and acuity, and to the press reviewers for their richly detailed and constructive comments.

At the University of Washington, Michael W. McCann, Joel S. Migdal, Ellis Goldberg, and Daniel S. Lev provided invaluable supervision, support, and mentorship from which I continue to benefit. Also at the University of Washington, many thanks are due to Gad Barzilai, Jessica Beyer, Ann Buscherfeld, Rachel Cichowski, Christine DiStefano, Steven Herbert, Arda Ibikoglu, Margaret Levi, Clark Lombardi, Arzoo Osanloo, Vicente Rafael, Susanne Recordon, Laurie Sears, Kristen Stilt, Allison Waggener-Boyd, Susan Whiting, and Farhat Ziadeh.

Shamsul A. B., Zainah Anwar, Laura Fan, Muhammad Kamal Hassan, Mulaika Hijjas and family, Muhammad Hashim Kamali, Clive Kessler,

Sumit Mandal, Norani Othman, and Dato' Seri Tunku Putri Intan Safinaz have my deepest appreciation for their support while I was in Malaysia. In the United Kingdom, the help of Annabel Gallop, Simon Over, William Roff, and William Gervase Clarence Smith was invaluable.

Many generous scholars have taken time to read and critique sections of this work in its various iterations, corrected some of its errors and supported its progress in varied ways: Leila Ahmed, Karen Barkey, Eve Darian-Smith, Michael Gilsenan, Tim Harper, Enid Hill, Elizabeth Hurd, Ayesha Jalal, Baber Johansen, Diana Kim, Brinckley Messick, Sally Merry, Michael Peletz, Barbara Powell, Justin Richland, Lawrence Rosen, Mitra Sharafi, Kristen Stilt, Charles Tilly (and the Contentious Politics Seminar at Columbia University), Christopher Tomlins, Frank Vogel, Susanne Wengle, and Malika Zeghal, as well as groups at Harvard University, Yale Law School (Critical Islamic Reflections), the University of Washington, the National University of Singapore, and New York University (Hagop Kevorkian Center for Near Eastern Studies). Robert Hefner, Saba Mahmood, Mahmood Mamdani, Tamir Moustafa, Justin Richland, Dan Slater, Lisa Wedeen, and other colleagues very generously gave of their time and expertise toward the final revision of this manuscript at a day-long workshop at the University of Chicago.

This project was supported at various stages by the National Science Foundation, the American Council of Learned Societies, the Council on Library and Information Resources, the Mellon Foundation, the University of Washington, the University of Massachusetts at Amherst, Harvard Law School, and the University of Chicago.

My parents, Salimah A. Samad and Hussin Mutalib, raised me in a household of ideas and of courage; my brother, Luqman, and my sister, Aziah, have been my teachers and fellow travelers. Cyndie McLachlan sheltered me; Devin McLachlan gave new meaning to the concept of home; Suhail and Maryam filled it with joy. To my family—gratitude beyond words.

Iza Hussin

PART I

Contexts

CHAPTER ONE

The Historical Roots of a Contemporary Puzzle

The Pangkor Treaty is just like the Koran, it is impossible to add a line to it, or to take a line from it.

The first British Resident in Malaya had neither a long nor a successful career. James Birch was appointed to the post in 1874, his task to raise revenue, abolish slavery, pacify a succession dispute among Malay nobles, and bring an end to war between Chinese secret societies. His position in the state of Perak, and the first achievement of British indirect rule in Malaya, was formalized by the Pangkor Engagement, signed in 1874. When one of the Malay chiefs in Perak attempted to negotiate a more advantageous position for himself through this newly signed treaty, Birch replied, "The Pangkor Treaty is just like the Koran, it is impossible to add a line to it, or to take a line from it."[1] The analogy was outrageous—the chiefs knew it, and his high-handedness and contempt for their authority rankled to such an extent that they organized his murder, not a year into his tenure. During that short tenure, however, Birch spent a great deal of effort attempting, on behalf of the British Crown, to make real what all around him were convinced was make-believe: he pursued elusive Malay nobles to secure the insignia of rightful office for the new sultan; he traveled the river courses, nailing proclamations about new tax laws to trees; he insisted that the sultan accept his authority and seek his advice as representative of the Queen of England, as the Pangkor Treaty dictated. To make real what all around him knew was make-believe, Birch attempted to make the law as fixed and as unassailable as the Qur'an—impossible to add a line to it, or take a line from it—an outrageous equivalence. Law in the early days of British colonialism in the Malay states was a thin fiction—the Pangkor Engagement itself signed on the deck of a British battleship by a shaky sovereign and reluctant chiefs, its English and Malay versions differing from each other, the reality it described only enforceable by war.

Yet within a few decades of this episode, it was the law of these same states that had come to deliver the law of the Qur'an—judges as employees of the state who interpreted its pronouncements, the administration of the state that enforced their rulings. Not just in Malaya, but across the Muslim world, by the end of the nineteenth century the equivalence between the law of the state and the law of the Qur'an was no longer a matter of outrage, but of steadily increasing acceptance and aspiration. In Malaya, all the Malay states delivered Islamic law through state administrative hierarchies within forty years of the Pangkor Treaty; in Egypt, efforts to make Islamic law stronger involved its translation into codes in the 1870s; in India a century earlier, the East India Company had decreed that the Qur'an would be the source of laws applicable to Muslims in matters of inheritance, marriage, and religion. Today, demands for Islamic states are articulated based on the assumption that in such states, the laws of the Qur'an and the laws of the state will be as nearly equivalent as modern man can manage. And for many Muslims today, the aspiration to equivalence works powerfully in both directions—just as the laws of the Qur'an should be expressed in the shape of modern state law, so should the laws of the modern state be as clear, as authoritative and as unassailable as the Qur'anic text. The demand for Islam is therefore very often expressed as a demand for state intervention, through law; contention over the place of Islam in the state is based on an assumption that it is the law of the state that will define, contain, and deliver Islam.[2] This remains so, even though our lived experience, as subjects of the law or as readers of sacred text, is that both are rarely as clear as we might wish.

This book began as an exploration of how Islam was transformed by the colonial encounter in Malaya, and seeks to understand the processes of that transformation and their political consequences. Instead of understanding these transformations as unavoidable outcomes of colonial and imperial dominance, I sought first to investigate how Muslim elites became invested in the translation of local norms, Islamic institutions, and varied structures of adjudication into the overarching logic of the colonial state. What combination of institutional arrangements, ideas, and interests made this transformation possible, and what accounted for its maintenance and growth? It became clear, as my research progressed, that the dynamics of this transformation in Malaya drew from the British experience in India and that, as the nineteenth century unfolded, changes in Malaya became increasingly connected to those in South Asia and the Middle East—Egypt, in particular. While Malaya remains the central case of this book, asking these questions within the empirical context of eighteenth- and nineteenth-century archives of Malaya, India, and Egypt allowed two analytic perspectives to emerge: first, instead of an overarching colonial logic, colonial officials and local elites conditioned each others' expectations of state capacity, the role of law, and the place of Islam. Second, "Islamic law" emerged as a central arena for politics out of the struggle between local elites and colonialism, first as a way to maintain a domain of local autonomy, and later as a basis upon which to build a challenge to colonial institutions and authority. To enter and leave the archives on any given day required passing through a world in which the space allowed to Islamic law—in Malaysia, in Egypt, in South Asia, in the United Kingdom—no longer seemed able to contain it, and as archival investigations encountered contemporary debates, other questions emerged: How has the contemporary institution of Islamic law been conditioned by its colonial antecedents? To what extent do structures of the modern Muslim state rely upon colonial-era frames, and to what effect? How have these institutional and theoretical frames shaped the future of Islamic law and what Muslims understand as its limits and possibilities?

"Islamic Law Happened to Me Yesterday . . ."

While traveling from one archive to another in Malaysia, I attended the installation ceremonies for a local notable in the state of Negri Sembilan. The rituals of this appointment carried all the markers of their multiple origins: yellow umbrellas nodded to the Hindu dynasties from which Malay rulers are descended; the assembled nobles wore Malay traditional costumes, augmented with British-style insignia on their sashes. Recitation of the Qur'an and prayers in Arabic punctuated each stage. The prominence of women in the ceremonies made evident that Negri Sembilan still held to aspects of *adat minangkabau*, the matrilineal customary practices of some Malays.

When the topic of my research arose, many of the men listening in would nod sagely and proceed to explain how—even though there might seem to be a number of matriarchal practices in Negri Sembilan—their *adat* (customs) really were all in accordance with Islam. At one of many meals shared after the ceremonies ended, one of the matriarchs of the clan raised her eyebrows at my research topic and said, "Yes, Islamic law happened to me yesterday [*memang, semalam makcik kena hukum Islam*]."[3] She then proceeded to relate her view that the matrilineal practices of *adat minangkabau* were Islamic, but that new interpretations of *hukum Islam* in the courts were beginning to erode her claims on land that had been passed from her grandmothers, favoring her male relations instead. "These men, they are taking ownership of the law," she said, and other women would nod in agreement, or sigh.

My research was mainly undertaken in archives, the voices of its major players muted by time and the constraints of the documents in which they were preserved. However, the driving concerns of my project came out of conversations and experiences beyond the archives. These conversations operated through two intersecting registers of debate and meaning, both of which have immediate political, economic, and social implications for many Muslims today, neither involving questions of political violence or the seizure of the state. For everyone I spoke with in this community in Negri Sembilan, it was important that Islamic law be obeyed, but each person spoke about Islamic law as if it were, at one and the same time, divine *and* vulnerable, immutable *and* contested, something in which they deeply believed *and* a pawn in a political game. There is the Islamic law of the shari'a, a matter for the judges to decide; but there is also the Islamic law of the community, passed down from their grandmothers. There is the Islamic law the state applies, but there is also the Islamic law that men and women call upon to critique the actions of the state. "Islamic law," however and by whomever it is invoked, seems to carry the shades of all these meanings and the gray areas between them. For the Muslims I spoke with in Malaysia, to speak of Islamic law was to make a claim about what is legitimate at the same time as to index what was possible, to refer to the past as well as to aspire to the future. Each marked a receding horizon and an immediate problem: the difference between what should be and what is, even though the extent and content of that difference is itself a matter for intense disagreement.

Debates about what "Islamic law" should mean are well worn, and it is not my purpose to define the term yet again. I wish instead to focus on the terrain of contestation that surrounds it, and the institutional foundations which undergird the limits and possibilities of debates about Islamic law in the Muslim world today. These foundations mean that "Islamic law," however it is defined, is deeply embedded in institutional and political parameters constructed within the last two centuries.[4]

To begin, my approach has been to look within historical sources for the ways in which Islamic law came to be defined by the multiple constituencies who invoked it—the genealogical tracing of a concept whose resonance has critical implications for Muslim life, state authority, and global politics. I understand Islamic law as multiple, slippery, and contested because for the resources I consulted in contemporary Malaysia, Egypt, India, and Pakistan, as well as for the actors I traced through the archives of colonial Malaya, Egypt, and India, Islamic law occupies a space of contradiction and tension. Three terms are commonly used to refer to the law of Islam, and all three represent that law partially: to say that Islamic law is shari'a, a divinely prescribed path of right conduct, effaces its ambiguities and its mutability in time and place; to parse it as *fiqh*, jurisprudential scholarship, allows for debate and difference, but minimizes the impact of institutional contexts and the embeddedness of jurisprudence within state and society; to read it as personal status or family law locates the law in its contemporary institutional loci, but diminishes its powerful symbolic and political appeal. The tensions and ambiguities among these coexisting definitions exist for most Muslims and Muslim states, and have for much of Islamic history, and they are powerfully productive of a range of meanings, discourses, and strategies for the conduct of Muslim life.

This project is particularly concerned with Islamic law as an arena for politics, a space whose scope, boundaries, rules, and content underwent a remarkable transformation during the late eighteenth and nineteenth centuries, throughout a large portion of the Muslim world. Of course, it is important to note crucial continuities, across borders and periods, in the relationship between Islamic law, the state, and Muslim identity. At the same time, the strategies, interests, and resources at each site of struggle made for important variations, and these dispel any preconception of Islamic law as monolithic or immutable. Therefore, my study seeks Islamic law not only in texts of *fiqh*, "Islamic" legislation or the courts that applied it, but through changing spaces of tension and struggle over Islam, law, and Muslim life during the colonial encounter. These spaces were marked not only by the workings of Islamic law, but often by its absence—after all, it was often not the provision of Islamic law but its diminution that catalyzed debates about the proper place and scope of Islam in state and society. Amid considerations of moral right, public good, social need, economic growth, and political power, which is the modifier in the phrase "Islamic law"? That choice is more important, analytically, than it may initially seem: if *law* is to be the modifier, then Islamic law is the application, in part or whole, of the legal aspects of Islam, which contains approaches to commerce, crime, and administration. If *Islamic* is the modifier, on the other hand, then there are other kinds of law, authorized by another source of organizational power: commercial, criminal, administrative, and Islamic law is one department among them, applicable in certain cases to certain people. The tension between these two understandings of Islamic law continues to drive many debates about the place of Islam in the contemporary state, and fuels much confusion on the part of external commentators. Broadly speaking, it is the historical shift from an emphasis on the first understanding of Islamic law to the second, and its attendant implications for state authority and power, that this book will trace.

At a time when the presence and absence of Islamic law is a matter not only of statecraft but of popular politics, I seek a way to look past questions of the accuracy or fidelity of any system of "Islamic law" to shari'a, *fiqh*, or modern state ideals, toward the politics that drive its appeal and the nature of its claims—to look for the political struggles and compacts that underlie it, to understand its assumptions and claims, its reliance on the past, and its vision of the future. Law continues to matter a great deal in the making of the Muslim state, and the dynamics of elite politics, institutional structures, and international interests continue to shape legal outcomes throughout the Muslim world. Current concerns about the future of Islam in the state, the prospects for reform, and the politics of Islamic legal change make an understanding of the local and historical conditions of the contemporary Muslim state even more critical. Given recent political and legal controversies in many Muslim states, the need for deeper understanding of the politics of Islamic law has rarely been greater; at a time when misunderstanding of the core dynamics of Muslim states and communities is prevalent, the need for systematic study of the underpinnings of contemporary Islam has rarely been more pressing.

This study should not be read as an argument for or against Islamic law, the shari'a, or the Muslim state. There are some readers who may infer that to say that Islamic law is political is to say that Islamic law is man-made—surely an argument that diminishes the shari'a. That is not my intention—surely the classical scholars of *fiqh* saw men and women to be crucial interlocutors for God's law. Certainly the history of the past two centuries shows that the struggle over Islamic law was fueled by piety as well as by polity, by the commands of Allah as well as by the power of men. Muslim societies today continue to struggle to define what is Islamic, what is possible, and what is appropriate: a better understanding of past struggles may help inform future movements, whatever direction they take. Neither is this project meant to provide a historical account of changes in the letter or institutional form of shari'a or *fiqh*: throughout this study, Islamic law will be explored as a contingent and constructed political space, through which historical processes work and through which state, society, and individuals in the contemporary Muslim world might be better understood.

Colonialism and Religion: The Making of the Muslim Present

Islam has been transformed in the last two centuries. The system practiced as "Islamic law" in every state with Muslim majorities or significant minorities has changed, from an uncodified and locally administered set of legal institutions and laws with wide-ranging jurisdiction to a codified, state-centered system with jurisdiction largely over family law. For Muslims, this change was monumental, relegating Islamic law to the private sphere and redefining the relationship between Islam and state authority. How did Islamic law become the state-controlled and limited province it now is in the majority of Muslim states? A parallel question accompanies it: Why, despite its ostensible subordination to the control of the administrative state, did Islamic law become such a powerful component of the modern state?

The first step toward answers to these questions is the acknowledgement that there is indeed a politics of Islamic law, that struggles over authority, legitimacy, and power link the institutions, agents, and ideas through which Islamic law functions and have done so throughout its history. This view of Islamic law as a product of, and a venue for, politics immediately sets this study apart from a view of Islamic law as divinely ordained, or as the repository of an unchanging Islamic "tradition" or "culture." Of vital importance to this study is the distinction between the divinely ordained path of right conduct for Muslims ("shari'a") and its manifestations in the historical, political, social, and legal experience of Muslims. We analyze the political life of Islamic law, but these struggles were important because of the conviction among both elite and ordinary Muslims that they were part of the path prescribed by God. The strategic making, unmaking, and remaking of Islamic law does not, in my understanding, run counter to deep and complex allegiances to shari'a.

Secondly, the institutional politics of contemporary Islamic law are inextricable from the historical conditions of their formation. It is important to stress at the outset that throughout Muslim history, the shari'a has never been universally applied by any state, and the relationship between shari'a, *fiqh*, and the state has always involved negotiating the line between the domain claimed by shari'a content, its institutions and its personnel, and its relation to the power and authority of the state.[5] During the colonial encounter, local and colonial elites negotiated the scope, content, and application of laws pertaining to Muslims and Islam, to their mutual benefit. In the process of making laws that defined Muslim life, religion, and relations with the state, these elites participated in a fundamental remaking of Islamic law in the evolving state, centered on family, personal status, ethnic identity, and the "private" domain. Islamic law was made, unmade, and remade through a series of political processes, and these processes were themselves shaped and reshaped by legal institutions, actors and rules. I compare these processes of making in three cases—Malaya, India, and Egypt—using documents of the British colonial period that have rarely been studied together, in order to undertake a cross-regional, networked study of sites of law and state making in the Middle East, South, and Southeast Asia. This cross-regional comparison allows the study of Islamic law as a transnational product, rather than an Arab export, shaped by local political networks.

Thirdly, despite clear power inequalities in the colonial period, local elites played critical roles in the making of Islamic law. The radical change in Islamic law—its codification and its consignment and limitation to the domain of personal and family law—in the modern Muslim state began in the colonial state. But the change did not simply occur as an imposition by the colonialists; it was the outgrowth of complex interactions and negotiations between local elites and colonial officials. Through processes of negotiation between colonial and local elites, Islamic law became a codified, state-centered system, limited to areas of personal and family law; the state became the final arbiter of Islam and Muslim identity; and Muslim elites became state elites. These changes have become the foundation of the modern Muslim state, and they marked a significant departure from the instance-based, judge-centered, and often diverse applications of Islamic law in these states prior to colonization.

Institutional Change and the Politics of Law

In India, Malaya, and Egypt, colonial and Muslim actors saw unprecedented opportunities for creating a new world, while at the same time their language and actions betrayed deep anxiety about a world changing beyond recognition all around them. While it is quite clear that the term "state" as we use it describes a set of institutional conditions that did not exist in early colonial Malaya, India, and Egypt, concepts such as "law," "religious," "secular," "public," "private," and "individual" were also only beginning to come into the meanings we tend now to take for granted. Law, in particular, tended to paper over the instabilities and incoherence of the state project; institutional analyses that track legal change purely on the basis of the pronouncement of law tend to miss the fact that law's proclamations—its treaties, its legislative pronouncements, and its judgments—worked to project its power and authority over areas where the dominance of the state was anything but assured. I pay special attention to processes and moments of the making, unmaking, and remaking of these foundational underpinnings of modern state power. The chapters that follow trace the winding and sometimes circular path that ideas about the proper place and meaning of Islam took through many domains and registers of law—from treaty text to policy and interpretation, conflicts and trials, judgments and their implementation, legislation and their public mobilization.

This book, therefore, looks past law's claims to continuity (often expressed as tradition or precedent) or change (often expressed as reform), toward the political pathways that legal struggles opened or foreclosed. As Thelen and Mahoney (2010) note, the "power-distributional" approach in historical institutionalist analysis provides a basis for thinking about institutional change, but "needs to be supplemented with attention to issues of compliance going well beyond the usual concern for *level* or *extent* of compliance . . . institutional change often occurs precisely when problems of rule interpretation and enforcement open up space for actors to implement existing rules in new ways."[6] In developing a theory of institutional change that incorporates institutional ambiguities, Thelen and Mahoney have pointed out that "lacking the capacity to destroy an institution, institutional challengers may be able to exploit its inherent ambiguities in ways that allow them to redirect it toward more favorable functions and effects."[7] Each treaty created a new set of opportunities and struggles for the many actors present at the formation of the colonial state; each trial removed the power of some actors and consolidated the influence of others; each text made authoritative lent itself to a new understanding of what Islamic law could be, and who Muslims should be. Each of these iterations featured changes in the rules of the game, but also in the preferences and understandings of its players.

Whereas historical institutionalists conceptualize institutional ambiguities as potential levers for institutional change, holding the preferences of variously situated actors constant as they challenged or accommodated the rules of the game, I detail how engagement with colonial institutions altered the preferences of Muslim actors and their conceptions of what was at stake.[8] As Talal Asad has argued, in exploring the relationship between the secular and the religious in the making of the modern state, "it is not enough to show that what appears to be necessary is really contingent . . . it is a matter of showing how contingences relate to changes in the grammar of concepts—that is, how the changes in concepts articulate changes in practices."[9] By tracing struggles between elites in multiple venues, in treaties, trials and texts of Muslim representation, I track how evolving concepts of law, religion, public, private, state, and individual came to become contingent upon each other.

Significant parts of the literature on colonialism and the construction of the modern state—its institutions, its power, and its discourses—approach processes of colonization as the sum of their component moments, such that colonization is seen as the upward progression of state centralization, colonial economic and administrative interests, and techniques of domination. Colonialism and the growth of the modern state are, in this view, locked in a zero-sum relationship with local institutions, varied normative structures and multiple arena for adjudication of disputes. As the expansionist colonial state advanced, so must these other forms of political organization and institution have receded. To a certain extent, these progressions are observable realities in the history of colonization in India, Malaya, and Egypt. However, connecting moments into processes in a linear fashion assumes unitary effects over a multiplicity of actors and motivations. As scholars such as Mahmood Mamdani, and Jean and John Comaroff have argued, the institutional impact of colonialism was often not the destruction of local institutions but their selective reification, not the removal of all local elites but their strategic redeployment in relation to the state coming into being.[10]

More often than not, moments of colonial encounter and struggle created contradictory opportunities, and were used by both colonial and local elites for widely divergent aims. Quite often, what seemed like a critical moment in the development of a new vision of state or religion never became significant, and the minor misunderstandings, or small agreements, could become major turning points for state and society. The failure to draw a line along neatly arranged points that indicate a uniform trajectory may not be a failure of either model or theory—it may in fact be a reflection of the real ambivalence and incoherence of the colonial state in formation, an incoherence that led to unintended and important consequences for state order, social power, Islamic legal scope and Muslim identity in the postcolonial period. Tracing the development of both colonial and Muslim ideas and institutions across two centuries shows that ambiguity and paradox have long been constitutive components of the politics of modern Muslim states and societies, and how these paradoxes have shaped their institutional arrangements and language as well as their trajectories of change. Mindie Lazarus-Black and Susan Hirsh (1994) advocate "reading for paradox," using methodologies that see law both as a force for institutional order and an arena to which actors bring their own resistance, strategies, and interests. Here, reading for paradox involves an understanding of contemporary Islamic law as carrying the colonial conditions of its institutionalization, at the same time as it is used today to stand for the rise of a particular vision of Islam and Muslims and for the increased involvement of the state in Islam. Following the work of Brinkley Messick, I have paid particular attention to the impact of transformations in law's textual forms—processes of textualization, codification, and officialization that were the hallmark of colonial state formation—on the ways Muslims negotiated authority, sought justice, and understood Islamic law.[11]

Law makes politics, and politics makes law.[12] To take this formulation seriously is to run counter to the view that law, especially religious law, is peripheral to the conduct of politics because it is residual (left over from historical antecedent or cultural tradition), formal (and therefore rule-bound, routine, and apolitical), or performative (an outcome or expression of politics rather than a determinant)—all assumptions that tend to underpin comparative political science studies of religion and the state, that may explain the relative lack of interest among political scientists in "religious" law, indeed in law more generally. It is also to run counter to the view, underlying some Islamic legal scholarship, that politics can be kept outside the legal domain by jurisprudence or by confining the interaction between law and power to the domain of administration and public policy, an assumption that makes possible a dismissal of analyses of power and politics in the making of Islamic law.

While early generations of legal pluralist analysis treated colonial legal hierarchies as preserving local law intact, legal pluralism scholarship has more recently become attentive to the problem of power in plural legal systems.[13] This problem of power, however, tends to be articulated in terms of the way that law embodies and maintains political hierarchies; we concentrate here on how the iterative process by which law was transformed under colonialism remodeled local political hierarchies, and then became part of new struggles for authority, meaning, and power. Transformations in local legal systems under colonialism profoundly altered local political hierarchies and institutions, so much so that a discussion of law in the contemporary Muslim world that ignores the political and historical contexts within which it functions would be incomplete.

In Islamic legal scholarship, the term "Islamic law" refers to both the shari'a (derived from divine and prophetic texts, the Qur'an, and *sunna*, the authoritative traditions of prior Muslim communities) and to *fiqh* (Islamic jurisprudence).[14] "Shari'a" as a word translates to "way," "path," and refers to a much wider body of authoritative guidance on all areas of Muslim life, only a small portion of it "legal" in nature. Islamic law is both a system of ideas and rules and a set of institutions and personnel: the beliefs of the individual Muslim about the path God has dictated are mediated through the authoritative interpretations of religious and secular powers, and acted upon through the structures of society and state, in conjunction with a range of other motivations, restrictions, individuals, and groups. "Islamic law" is not "shari'a" translated from Arabic into English, although its authority derives from the authority of the divine shari'a; Islamic law is not *fiqh* alone, although some of its content derives from the work of jurisprudents working in the classical *fiqh* tradition. In my project, Islamic law is understood to be a modern construction, inextricable from the state and its history, and therefore inextricable from colonialism and the influence of local elites.

A defining characteristic of contemporary Muslim states is the role played by Islamic law that is represented in the national legal system largely by Islamic family law, or personal status law.[15] Following this, comparative legal scholarship has tended to view "Islamic law" simply as the law, or part of the law, belonging to Muslim states. Shari'a jurisprudence of the classical schools, however, does not define a separate realm of law for the family; neither does it contain the notion of "personal status." Yet modern understandings of "Islamic family law" and "personal status law" are central to the identity of the contemporary Muslim state, as well as the societies and individuals that function around and within it. Personal status law is a particularly revealing site for the analysis of elite politics in the developing colonial state because, as the cases discussed here illustrate, it served as a new category of state intervention in the nineteenth century and functioned to delineate the boundaries of local elite autonomy in the state. This reformulation of the legal category of personal status—which came to mean family law, applied differentially based on religious affiliation—was a construction of the colonial encounter crucial to the creation of new understandings of Islam, law, culture, and ethnic identity.[16] Personal status law served as a critical venue for the articulation and resolution of disputes within the new state over these understandings, and this new centrality of family and personal status has had profound effects on Muslim life—especially the lives of Muslim women and families—in the last century.

Identification as a "Muslim state" is self-selective and shifting: in some cases a state may be "Muslim" in matters of public observances, such as the commemoration of state holidays, but not in others—for example, the recognition of the Qur'an as a source of legislation; in some cases both the state and the groups that oppose it claim to represent Islam. Both the categories of "Islamic law" and "Muslim state," therefore, revolve around understandings of authority, legitimacy, and jurisdiction. Who decides the meaning of Islamic law? Who judges where it begins and ends, and where the role of the state is in Islamic law? Is Islamic law a part of the state or autonomous from it? Key to understanding these questions is that Islamic law is a site of contest and a realm for the articulation of state-society relationships.[17] Law is not the sole province of the state: transformations in Islamic law marked a critical juncture for the articulation of autonomous regimes within the evolving colonial state, as well as new mechanisms for the inclusion of previously separate groups and institutions into the state.[18] While the traditional view of colonial law is that it was imposed by powerful imperial regimes on local colonial sites,[19] my study hypothesizes that legal change in the colonial period afforded local elites new opportunities and resources for increasing their power and realizing their visions of society and state. Law and its institutions are the product of negotiations among elites both colonial and local, elites whose motivations were varied and whose strategies and resources were unequal.[20]

I rely upon two theoretical conceptions of the term "state," and link their historical development through law's progressions. The first state is governmental: a complex of institutions, the network of cooperation, competition, and dispute through which official power aspired to govern in early colonial Malaya, India and Egypt. This governmental state was neither fully institutionalized nor entirely informal during the period of this study, but evolved gradually to an organizational structure with the British at its head. The postcolonial state inherited some of the institutional logic and bureaucratic order of its colonial predecessor and eradicated other legacies, but not along clear or predictable lines. The utility of this state concept is that it allows us to ask historical institutionalist questions of the state as a dynamic and varied component of governance and of society, promoting some institutions and elites over others, its principles at times divisive, and at others unifying.[21] The second concept of state has an individual and a social locus—a state as a "condition of being."[22] As the governmental state developed in the colonial period, it made increasingly expansive claims on the individual and social state; in turn, individuals and social groups came more and more to the governmental state to appeal, protest, and seek change.[23] For the modern Muslim state, as both institutional order and condition of being, law has come to connect and reinforce both dimensions, and law is often what has allowed alterations in one state to profoundly alter the other.

Comparative Politics and Islam: Malaya, India, and Egypt as Networked Cases

This project arose out of research in Malaysia, and it is cases from colonial Malaya and contemporary Malaysia that drive my central narrative. The contemporary Malaysian state presents a number of tantalizing paradoxes to scholars of Islam and Islamic law. On the one hand a secular multi-ethnic democracy, on the other a modern Islamic state; lauded as an economic and social success in the Muslim world, and as a moderate exemplar of a Muslim state in the West, Malaysia is a puzzle all on its own—perhaps the only Muslim state where Islam is constitutionally bound with ethnicity, language, and racial identity. In the Constitution of postindependence Malaysia, a "Malay" is defined as "a person who professes the religion of Islam, habitually speaks the Malay language . . . (and) conforms to Malay custom" (Federal Constitution of Malaysia art. 160, cl. 2). In Malaysia today, therefore, it is legally impossible to be Malay and not be Muslim. This racial and religious category of Malay confers particular rights and privileges involving land and business ownership, and having a privileged national language (Malay) and religion (Islam). Although the bulk of scholarship on the question of ethnicity and religion in Malaysia focuses upon the immediate pre-independence period to the present, my research shows that the roots of this conflation run deep.[24]

British colonial agents left India for Malaya and Egypt in the same period—the 1870s—and for the same reason: the need to protect British economic interests reliant upon shipping through the Suez Canal on one side of the Indian Ocean and the Straits of Malacca on the other. Having left the same site of colonial intervention, with the same broad mandate, how did these British agents fare once they arrived at their destinations? How was Islamic law, in practice in varied forms at each destination, changed by its encounters with British colonial power, its resources and the new challenges it presented to local elites and institutions? Finding answers to these questions requires an approach to explaining transformations that takes into account existing institutional constraints and pathways, as well as the rise of new resources, opportunities, and problems; it also requires an awareness that Islamic legal change took place across a number of sites of transformation across the Muslim world during the long nineteenth century. Developments in Malaya cannot be fully understood outside of their context within currents of change in Muslim societies undergoing colonization all across the Indian Ocean arena. Studies that cross established regional boundaries are rare when it comes to discussions of Islam and Islamic law, and the benefit of an inter-regional study of the politics of Islamic law is that it highlights the local conditions that shaped Islamic law and Muslim identity in each case, amid the global forces that connected each locality.

The approach to comparison here marks a departure from standard comparative political methods of parallel case studies, which would view India, Egypt, and Malaya as independent cases, and their independence from each other a key component of their suitability for comparison.[25] Here, the case of India serves to lay the foundations for understanding where British notions of Islamic law and the administration of Muslim societies might have come from, and to argue for a more central role for India in the history of modern global Islam.[26] The cases of Egypt and Malaya serve as contemporary juxtapositions, to elaborate how differences in colonial context, elite politics, and local Muslim institutions affected Islamic law. All three cases point to one broad reality: that a fundamental transformation in Islam took place in the midst of negotiations among local and colonial elites, and that a primary theater of this transformation was Islamic law. Also unlike some approaches to comparative study, the aim here is not to tell a causal story about the outcomes in each case. Rather, the aim is to identify the processes of making of a politics around Islam, Islamic law, and the Muslim state—about the apportioning of resources, tangible and symbolic; about the use of violence and force; about the systematic organization of language, discourse, and authority.

By studying three sites of British colonization, my study points to their historical interconnection, while also seeking out discontinuities and variations across states in the British colonial treatment of Islam. British officials often began their careers in India, where they also constructed a body of "knowledge" about Muslims, Islamic law, and the governance of Muslim societies. Building upon works such as Thomas Metcalf's *Imperial Connections* (2007), which details the "sub-imperial role of India," this comparison aims to underscore that networks of empire neither created this interconnectedness nor monopolized it: Muslim traders, travelers, pilgrims, religious orders, and family networks had long seen the Indian Ocean as an arena for exchange.[27] Further, both colonial and Muslim networks served to pass on experiences drawn from one place, to others; as the nineteenth century drew on, these dynamics of comparison, extrapolation, and translation would themselves play important roles in both colonial and Muslim strategies. Some of these strategies were convergent—for example, the broad movement for Islamic reform that emerged from sites across South Asia, the Middle East, and Southeast Asia from the mid-nineteenth century, provoking responses from the British to ascendant trans-imperial Islam, real or imagined. Some of these dynamics resulted in productive conflations of legal categories and concepts, premised upon efforts by both British and local Muslim elites to compare, translate, and make commensurable categories of British and Muslim law. Among the most important of these conflations was that between family law, personal status law, and Islamic law.

The commonalties among the three cases in this study provide a broad storyline: all focus on the construction of Islamic law within Muslim states under British colonialism. On the British side, personnel, strategic considerations, economic interests, and military constraints were shared in each case through the India Office, and, later the Colonial Office. British personnel brought their understandings of Islam and colonization from India into the Middle East and Southeast Asia in the same period, for the same strategic reasons, and were governed by the same considerations of limited resources, as well as an unstable domestic political climate. In India, Egypt, and Malaya, Muslim elites subscribed to many of the same tenets of faith, and, while schools of Islamic jurisprudence differed, the power of Muslim symbols and Muslim figures was a significant factor in all three cases. Finally, in all three cases, a legal code was produced between local and British elites, invoking Islamic law and incorporating elements of ethnic and Islamic identity: the content and form of these codes continue to represent Islam in the state in each case, and therefore studying them continues to be relevant.

In all three cases, these negotiated outcomes between local elites and the colonial state had lasting effects on Muslim religious and cultural identity. In each of these states, Islamic codes and legal institutions became quite different from anything that had existed in previous Islamic history. Religious laws, identity, and institutions began to play a new role in the state, and the state a new role in religion. The cases in my study revolve around Islam and Muslims, but these relationships were being negotiated with Hindus, Christians, Jews, Buddhists, and other religious groups as well.[28] This new relationship between state, society, and religion helped construct a new confluence of ethnic group and Muslim identity; a new vision of Islam that was more patriarchal and state-centered than in the precolonial period; and institutions and discourses of Islam centralized under the control of elites configured as "traditional" rulers.

There were also marked differences in the law-making and state-building processes in India, Egypt, and Malaya that we summarize here but will discuss in greater detail in chapter 2. The first set of differences derives from the chronology of colonization in each case, alongside which follow differences in imperial ideology, capacity, and the repertoires available for local elite response. British colonial formulations of Islam and Islamic law entered India in the late eighteenth century and form the context within which we begin to explore the making of Islamic law; our discussion of Malaya and Egypt centers on the period of British intervention beginning in the late nineteenth century. My study follows the transformations of Islamic law and British policy as they traveled from India into Egypt and Malaya. The second is institutional: varying institutional legacies, models of state and rulership, elite networks and political-economic structures led to variations in how the law was redefined under British administration, which local elites gained and lost from changes in jurisdictions, and how the Muslim state was reimagined and represented using new resources made available by colonial rule. In India, the British relied upon Mughal institutions, and personnel and symbols to govern, well into the nineteenth century. In Malaya, the British found a society not unfamiliar with colonialism but relatively autonomous from colonial centers of power, in which Islamic institutions were largely local in nature and, in comparison with Indian and Egyptian Islamic institutions, relatively weak.[29] In Egypt, the French colonial state, the Ottomans, and Egyptian elites themselves had already made critical inroads to the "modernization" of law and society by the time of the British occupation. The third is, broadly categorized, "cultural": while Egypt was close to the perceived center of Islamic culture and had elements of Arab culture and language to connect it closely with the Qur'an and Arabic-Islamic legal texts, Muslims in India and Malaya were removed from these sources of Islamic legitimacy by language and their more recent histories of conversion to Islam.

The sheer breadth of the transformations we discuss begs some big questions: are these changes merely side effects of the growth of the state, independent of colonialism? Can the story of these changes in Islamic law simply be told in the language of modernity, or capitalism, or secularism, or state building? Or perhaps this is another story about the unintended consequences of colonialism? These are not trivial questions, but, for the purposes of my argument, they are not central preoccupations. It is not my argument that colonialism caused these transformations in Islamic law, but that the specific opportunities and resources of the colonial encounter made room for the rise of particular local elites and a new dynamic of power, within which Islamic institutions—those of the shari'a in particular—played a critical role. Neither is it my argument that the transformations I track in India, Malaya, and Egypt are unique. Quite to the contrary, the patterns revealed in comparing these three cases can be extended to many other cases throughout Southeast and South Asia, as well as the Middle East and Africa.[30] The colonial story here is in large part focused upon the British Empire; while examples from the Ottoman case, and influences from French civil law, indicate that there are reasons to see some broad commonalities across imperial contexts, this study can only focus on encounters with the British. It indicates, however, a rich field for further comparative exploration of the effects of colonialism on local Muslim identities and networks and the construction of legal institutions.[31] Indeed, recent work has indicated that British India served as an important and inspiring example for other imperial projects in the Muslim world, such as French intervention in (and, according to Edmund Burke III, invention of) Moroccan Islam, at the same time that the British approach to Islam in India may have been at least in part a response to Napoleon's strategy in Egypt.[32] Among other lessons, commonalties and variation among the Middle East, and South and Southeast Asia show that Islamic law was not simply an Arab export, nor did it represent a particular shelter for local tradition or culture.

Archives and Artifacts: Definition, Jurisdiction, State Making

Teasing apart the multiple strands of state, society, and law that together constructed the category of Islamic law requires a methodology that looks for the making of law in multiple registers and archives. This book traces the making of Islamic law through the moment of colonial encounter, into the inevitable struggle over the meaning and extent of colonial intrusion, and through local strategies to capitalize upon colonialism, to translate and redefine "Islam" and "Muslim." This methodology treats archives as artifacts of the colonial encounter, the circumstances of their production contingent and strategic, seeing "documents . . . (as) mediations, their writers mediators, between the enduring text of shari'a law and the particular events of their world," and seeking out ways to make sense of "the problematic way documents fit the law to the world, and the world to law."[33] Following Messick, I seek to present a way of reading Muslim politics through a multiplicity of transformations in text, code, and discourse, tracking the dynamics of institutions and politics transformed alongside them.

Consequently, chapters 3 and 5 each revolve around a different set of artifacts—treaties, trials, and representations—each linking discursive, institutional, and legal changes in a chain of iterated processes that together produced these transformations. Chapter 3 uses treaties to discuss the wide-ranging ramifications of the division of jurisdiction in the state between local and colonial elites. Chapter 4 focuses upon trials in and of Islamic law to tease out the problem of defining "law," "Islam," and "Muslim" in the developing state; and the strategies and dilemmas of both colonial officials and their Muslim counterparts in the arena of formal adjudication. Chapter 5 takes texts of Muslim representation—portraiture, constitutions, and publications—to illustrate the ways in which the "Muslim state," as a condition of being and a governmental formation, elaborated upon and renegotiated the new discourses and institutions of Islamic law.

The emphasis on Malaya in this project is in part a consequence of the relative dearth of scholarly studies on the relationship between local politics and colonial power in the construction of Islam in the Malay states, certainly when compared to Indian and Egyptian studies.[34] My study is based upon original archival research conducted in Malay, Arabic, and English, in state archives, libraries, universities, and museums in the United Kingdom, Malaysia, Singapore, and the United States, beginning in 2002. Many of the documents used here have not been discussed by scholars working in English, and help to fill the silence previously left by British documents with the voices of local elites. As extensive scholarship in the documents of colonial India and Egypt has shown, records kept for the purposes of imperial administration and policy present an edited transcript of their exchanges with local actors. Documents kept by local elites, courts, and royal archives in India, Malaya, and Egypt allow us to hear a fuller version of those conversations, a version conducted in several languages, in a number of venues and registers, with multiple meanings and for the benefit of many audiences.

In combination, original archive research, interviews, local scholarship, and a wide range of secondary literatures inform each other: each helps fill the gaps and corrects some of the biases of the others. Archives in and of themselves, however extensive, present a partial picture, and require creative methods first to understand their political logic and material conditions, and then to fill in some of the gaps that remain. Historians have long had to grapple with the fact that most records available to scholars today were created and preserved as part of the business of government. The logic of these archives may have precluded much of the evidence of dissent against or within colonial governments, and many of the informal negotiations between colonial and local elites are lost to history.[35] Legal and institutional records of both Islamic and colonial systems have tended to present a vision of law's functions and developments as linear, intentional, and in full accordance with doctrine, regardless of the flexibility with which jurists, lawyers, judges, litigants, and administrators may have functioned. This has had implications not only for the academic study of Islam, but for how the tradition of Islamic jurisprudence and adjudication has been understood by contemporary Muslims. "That kept outside the letter of the law is lost to later generations who learn the law by letter alone," and so the written archive of law in the Muslim world emphasizes, more often than not, adherence to tradition rather than strategic negotiation of its components, a stricter obedience to the letter of the law than was the case in most Muslim societies, well before and throughout the colonial period.[36] Fortunately, the area of law is one of the most extensively documented of all areas of social and civic life, and actors at all levels of society appear in court records and within the law codes themselves.

The material of this book is based upon research conducted in court, administrative, and legislative records of the Malay States and Straits Settlements, Britain, India and Egypt; censuses; Parliamentary and Ruler

Council proceedings; minutes of meetings; and correspondence among colonial officials and local elites of the late eighteenth and nineteenth centuries. In addition to formal legal codes and documents, letters, treaties, travelers' accounts, and histories of many kinds provided information on how elites in each of these sites of law making interacted with the colonial state, what their interests and preferences were, and how they sought to achieve the outcomes they valued most. Whereas the official records of colonial and local elites provided one picture of the ways in which law was made and enacted, traveler's accounts, letters, news accounts, and other descriptions of social and political life during those periods helped create a picture of the performance of law and authority, and represent further evidence of the networks of power and symbolism that surrounded the enactment of law and the maintenance of legitimacy. Points of conflict and rupture in law and legitimacy—war, jurisdictional skirmishes, power struggles between colonial and local elite hierarchies—were particularly useful: they revealed not only what was at stake for the actors involved, but what was required to reestablish order and build new alliances.

The discussion of law in this study is in essence a discussion of elites—British colonial officers, prominent merchants, politicians, judges, and administrators; and local chiefs, religious leaders, traders, landowners, rulers, and strongmen. When ordinary men and women appear in these records, it is often as supplicants to the law, or as an imaginary public whose interests were to be protected or whose support was to be kept or lost through proper use of law and state instruments. As such, this is not a study of how the law worked in everyday life in India, Egypt, and Malaya—it is a study of how the law was conceived, bargained over, and used by powerful men and women involved in the workings of the colonial state.

The Making of the Modern Muslim State: Marginalizing and Centralizing Islamic Law

Current efforts to rebuild Muslim states in the Middle East and South and Southeast Asia have revolved around the issue of Islamic law. The "Arab Spring" was quickly followed by intense speculation about the possibility that authoritarian but secular regimes would be succeeded by "Islamist" regimes.[37] The postwar reconstructions of Iraq and Afghanistan handled the question of where, how, and to what extent Islamic law would figure in the law of the state with assurances that the religious sensibilities of the majority would be respected and that Islamic law would be assigned its proper place—and then faced deep disagreement about what that place would be. Would Islamic law be "the religion of the state," "a source of legislation," "the source of legislation," or "a principle of legislation" in Iraq? Would it be "the principles of the Islamic shari'a" or "Islamic law" or "the shari'a of Islam" that were constitutionally enshrined?[38]

Neither the questions in play in contemporary Iraq, Afghanistan, and elsewhere, nor the anxieties they reveal, are new—the phrase "Islam is the religion of the state" entered the legal discourse of the Malay states in 1895 (through the Constitution of Johor, see chap. 5), for example—and then as now they reflect a line of struggle between local and colonial actors. However, the assumption that the character of a Muslim state is determined by its ability to *deliver* Islamic law, and that Muslims themselves generally should look to the *state* for Islamic legal goods, is relatively recent and entirely modern. The connection of the Muslim state as a system of government and the Muslim state as a condition of individual and social being *through law* is a function of the complex interplay between the growth of state aspirations and abilities, the centrality of law in colonial administration, and the strategies of Muslim elites. After providing background to the study in part 1, each chapter in part 2 of my book focuses on a specific instance of this interplay—the division of jurisdiction within the state between local and colonial elites, the redefinition of "Islam" and "Islamic law" in courts, and the articulation of the Islamic character of the state in texts produced by local elites. Each of these chapters shows how the Muslim governmental state and the Muslim individual state became linked by law—how the Muslim state became increasingly defined through its delivery of certain kinds of Islamic law, and the Muslim subject became increasingly recognizable to the state through his (and, with increasing importance, her) subjection to Islamic law.

In comparative politics and comparative law, law is often seen as the exercise of power by a more or less unified state, as a policy instrument, a measure of state capabilities and development, as part of a progression toward modernity. In this view, legal formalism and developmentalism combine to paint a picture of law as comprised of codes and courts, and so the struggle over constitutional language that describes "Islam" and "Islamic" is diagnosed as a problem of institutional design.[39] Legal formalism has implications for the reading of history as well, casting the changes that took place with the growth of the state in the late modern period in terms of the codification of preexisting rules. A narrow focus on the letter of the law can lead one to imagine that little has changed about Islamic law through the growth of the colonial and then postcolonial state. Colonial state administrations were adamant that they would not interfere with the practice of Islamic law (or, in other contexts, Hindu, or Jewish, or Buddhist laws); local Muslim elites were equally adamant that it would be they who would control and administer the appropriate law.

The study of Islamic law has thus far been dominated by a legal formalist understanding of law as rules and institutions. This approach obscures the fact that the most significant changes that have occurred in Islamic law throughout the Muslim world are not to its substantive rules but to their application as part and parcel of the repertoire of the state, and that the embeddedness of shari'a principles in certain domains of state and not others has led to a fundamental alteration in what most Muslims perceive Islamic law to be. More significant than the transformation in law is the transformation in the relationship between Islamic law, state power and authority, and the Muslim subject—here again, a development that the most common understandings of law in political science fail to capture.

Having compared codes put into place in the Straits Settlements and the Federated States of Malaya governing Muslim marriage, for example, with the relevant Shafi'i texts, or their counterparts in India with Hanafi texts, I would posit that it is plausible to argue that Islamic law was "implemented" according to the teachings of the dominant school of the region. Indeed, this has been the assumption made by many scholars of the colonial state—that lack of interest and lack of knowledge among colonial officials left the province of Islam to Muslim elites, and that Muslim elites continued in their normal practices in adjudicating marriage, divorce, and the private religious observance of Muslims. Differences between the precolonial, colonial, and postcolonial position of Islamic law are, in this view, a matter of degree.

Many Islamic legal scholars hold to the formalist view of law as well, concentrating on the classical texts of *fiqh* and the relationship between these foundational texts and their formulations in the contemporary state legal system. This approach tends to lead to questions about the compatibility of Islamic jurisprudence with contemporary institutions of governance and the transfiguration of classical legal rules into modern codes.[40] However, personal status law is not the shari'a, and never has been: its content owes as much to British principles of law and cultural values, if not more, as it does to Islam and local values. How is the category of "Islamic personal status" or "Islamic family law" to be understood and studied? To assess the function and meaning of personal status solely through either Islamic legal principles or secular, national legal ideals would be insufficient, since it is clear that both sets of law were important to the colonial project.

Another common assumption among political scientists, drawing perhaps upon the influence of legal realism, is that these struggles over law are merely reenactments of larger struggles over the state, that law is an outcome of politics and legal struggle its symptom. Therefore, political positions on the constitutional placement of Islam map onto commitments to secularity, executive power, democratization, and the delegation of decision making in the new state. Those who argue for the implementation of more shari'a are "Islamists" by definition; their opponents, therefore, must be secularists.[41] Neither party disagrees that the locus of Islamic law is the state—the state initiates, legislates, and enforces the law by definition. According to this realist view, the more secularists in power, the less Islamic law; the more Islamists, the more Islamic law. Further, in this view, Islamic legislation has a generative effect and expands the power of Islamists.

While making opposite assumptions about law—that the words mean everything, and that the words mean nothing much at all—these formalist and realist treatments overlook the same important things. The first and most critical is that they both predispose an overly simple interpretation of change in Islamic law—that more Islamic law indicates more power for "Islamists" and that reductions in Islamic legal content indicate a move toward secularity. Recent history shows that when Islamist parties do come into power, they do not necessarily enact more Islamic legislation; when secularists rule, they do not always dial the content of Islamic law back.[42] Of course, the line between legislation and electoral politics is neither short nor direct—even the most formalist or realist of analyses does not discount the role played by political process and the need to satisfy multiple constituencies. However, the point extends further than recent history—the limiting of Islamic legal institutions, actors, and content during the colonial period in India, Malaya, and Egypt did not, by and large, result in the vanquishing of Islamic elites. On the contrary, the institutional marginalization of Islamic law led to the centralization of certain Muslim elites and the entrenchment of some areas of Islamic law, notably laws pertaining to family, marriage, divorce, inheritance, and matters of worship and ritual.

As a product of the colonial period, personal status or family laws that govern Muslims must be understood as part of the formation and maintenance of the colonial state. As negotiated outcomes between elites in the state, these codes and the practices, values, and institutions that developed alongside them must be seen in terms of the diverse interests and capacities of each of these groups. Legal pluralism as an analytic continues to efface, in critical ways, the transformations of law that were needed to construct legal pluralist regimes. Early works of legal pluralism, defined as "the presence in a social field of more than one legal order"[43]—while acknowledging the power differential between the different legal traditions practiced within an overarching, colonial national system—saw these legal traditions as separate and autonomous.[44] Islamic law was seen as an independent regime within the nation or part of a bargain between power holders within the state. More recent legal pluralists have studied multiple legal orders within the state—as part of the colonial project and as part of a system of culture, meaning, and power; and as part of the complex of knowledge, power, and resources upon which colonialism and the modern state are based.[45]

This development of the concept of legal pluralism does not, however, portray the ways in which multiple legal orders interacted with each other or how actors within this plurality chose among legal possibilities. By virtue of its existence among British and customary legal institutions, Islamic law itself changed, as did the strategies and identities of the people who now found themselves subject to several different legal traditions and powers. As yet, legal pluralism has not accounted for which laws were given over to Islamic personal status and which to the state or what effects this bifurcation of jurisdiction over Islam had. This project explores the formation of Islamic personal status law within the colonial state as a key part of the colonial project and an important component of the formation of Muslim identity. When legal systems, codes, and beliefs are brought together under conditions of colonial power, the system which results is not the mere layering of one system over another, or the mixture of Islamic family codes and British criminal codes. The system which results is fundamentally new: Islamic law and British law, as well as the practices, beliefs, and possibilities inherent in law, changed, and so did the strategies, attitudes, and aspirations of those who used this changing system.

The second important point that these views of law miss is that it may not be the outcome of struggles over Islamic law that matter for politics, but the struggle itself. Public contestation over the place, meaning and content of Islamic law makes room for old elites to regain prominence and new actors to rise. The jurisdictional politics of Islamic law are generative of new opportunities for participation and discourse, often regardless of the legislative outcomes, and so the analytic question when it comes to Islamic law in the state-building process is less *how much* Islamic law, but *who* may speak for the law? Who may interpret and change it, and along what lines? In this, the particular potency of law for both discipline and agency cannot be discounted: an understanding of law as discourses and struggles as well institutions, taken from law and society studies, is central to this study.[46] Law is a powerful disciplinary system for the state, but also opens the way for opposition to the state, and to contests within both state and society for resources, authority, and control over the state itself. State-in-society scholars have highlighted this permeability of state and society, and the mutual dependence and construction of states and social groups.[47]

This work also aims to contribute material from Muslim legal contexts to a growing body of interest in "juris-diction," as the speech of the law and the speaking of the law, as particularly revealing of the work that needs to be done in the everyday life of law to construct, repair, maintain, and mythologize law's workings.[48] Bradin Cormack's work on law and literature in the sixteenth century has helped show that legal proliferation, religious change, and jurisdictional crisis have had a rich and productive relationship in the history of English text. Jurisdictional crises—brought on by efforts at legal centralization but also by the challenges of new territory, new competitors, new subjects—helped elaborate the power and language of law. Cormack characterizes jurisdiction "as the administrative principle that orders power as authority by defining the scope of a particular power over a given matter or territory," seeking out "law's unstable practices rather than the image of its stability."[49] Cormack's detailed exegesis of English common law in the sixteenth century may seem a far stretch for a study on eighteenth- and nineteenth-century law, but there are two important reasons for its mention here. The first is historical, in that the moment of jurisdiction crisis Cormack explores is also a founding moment for the colonial imagination and colonial visions of law, which become critical frames for engagements with the Muslim world. The second is that this approach to law "as fundamentally improvisational, unfolding into doctrine only as and through practice," offers a way to rethink the development of Islamic law as part of the problematic of jurisdiction—as problematic, literary, performative, and contingent. Messick has underlined the productivity of "local bureaucratic and legal literatures" as "sites for the imaginative construction of a specific subjectivity," adding another dimension to the symbiosis of text, the administrative and material forms of the state, and subject formation.[50]

Chapters 3, 4, and 5 of this book present, as moments of the making of Islamic law and the Muslim state, several "moments of jurisdiction" in which "the law at once assumes its power to decide generally . . . asks after the limits of that power . . . and then elides the fact that in asking it is announcing that power anew."[51] Moments of jurisdiction are always, as Robert Cover would remind us, jurispathic and jurisgenerative, but these particular moments also make legible multiple, competing and often mutually exclusive jurisdictions—the speech and the logic of Islamic jurisprudence, itself entextualized and embodied in institutions, scholars, and discursive logics, against that of British colonial law, a variant of the common law particularly insistent on law's legibility, codification, and rationalization.[52]

Thirdly, political science's focus on institutions and states as the core actors in the drama of politics can overlook the fact that the debates about Islam, law, and the state that are taking place are fundamentally new in crucial ways. The period this study covers illustrates what both state in society and law and society scholars have often argued, that the conceptual categories we use—state, society, law, religion, politics—refer to realities in a state of constant making and remaking.[53] Both proponents and opponents of Islamic legislation accept that the unquestioned mechanism for the delivery of Islamic law is the state, through codified law, state institutions, state funding, and oversight.[54] This acceptance of state control over Islamic law, whatever its content and scope might be, was an outcome of the state-building processes of the colonial period, and postcolonial states have inherited the institutional outlines of the colonial state almost unchanged. Similarly, the space assigned to Islam in legislation has been inherited by the postcolonial state—family law, inheritance, ritual practice—and although this is a far more limited space than the shari'a assigns itself, most postcolonial Muslim elites confine their arguments for application of the shari'a to these domains.[55] The reasons why are neither obvious nor primordial, but political analyses of these struggles that fail to historicize them also fail to explain their endurance in contemporary politics.

Lastly, and following on this third point, local context matters a great deal for how law is made and what it can do. When the politics of Islamic law are cast as fundamentally about binary choices between democratization or secularization, authoritarianism or populism, tradition or modernity, wherever they occur, we miss out on significant variations between Muslim states that have little or nothing to do with these schema. Instead, these variations have everything to do with local responses to imperial pressure, strategic ambiguities intended to leave room for negotiations between elites, or the unintended consequences of legal language. For example, these dichotomies cannot explain why constitutional debate in Egypt revolves around the ambiguous phrase "the principles of the Islamic Shari'a are the principle source of legislation,"[56] whereas in Iraqi constitutional debates the final phrase that emerged was "Islam is the official religion of the state and is a basic source of legislation,"[57] and in Malaysia, "Islam is the religion of the Federation; but other religions may be practiced in peace and harmony."[58] Analyses that pay attention to the local particulars of struggle over the content, language, institutions, and agents of Islamic law pay a further dividend—they reveal the shifting contours of contested state authority and the processes by which "imported" institutions and rules become local norms and resources for further struggle over authority and power.

Marginalizing Islamic Law

What follows is a story of the institutional marginalization of Islamic law, but also of the productive political effects of that marginalization. Our comparison of British India, Malaya, and Egypt reveals a number of parallel processes at work. A dynamic of increasing centralization and bureaucratization of the law brought Islam under state control at the same time that it limited Islamic law to the areas of personal status: marriage, divorce, ritual practice, religious endowments. The rise of the governmental and administrative state was directly related to the rise of a version of Islamic law that was text-based, tied to a specific ethnic and national identity, and centered in state institutions and authority. As the power of some elites was consolidated in association with that of the administrative state, the nature of opposition to those elites and to the state had to change. Resources for the building of legitimacy and the control of justice and institutions of the state become concentrated in the hands of fewer elites, local and colonial. Similarly, the content of legal practices and community values became more unified. Those who resisted the state had to align themselves along these unified categories of race, religion, and subject, in order to be recognized by the state. In doing so, however, even the act of resistance against local and colonial elites helped reinforce the idea of a unified "Muslim" subject in India, Egypt, and Malaya.[59]

The argument that colonization marginalized Islamic legal institutions and Islamic legal content is not new, but scholars have differed on why, how, and to what effect this marginalization occurred. In addition to the formalists and the realists above, a large body of scholarship situates the marginalization of Islamic law as part of the rise of the modern state and the interventions of European imperial power.[60] In these accounts, processes of codification, institutionalization, and "etatization" conjoined to disempower Islamic institutions and the elites who benefited from them in favor of a new administrative and legal structure run by secular state and colonial elites.[61] For scholars like Bernard Cohn, colonialism was an ontological and epistemological project—its ways of knowing were its ways of governing—so not only was textualization and formalization of law critical for the imposition of colonial order, they were intrinsic to the colonial understanding of the territories and people they governed.[62] Law was not just a means of imposing order, but a means of knowing the colony; once in place, however, it served the purposes of both the colonizer and the colonized. Modernization itself plays a major role in the marginalization not only of institutions and groups, but of entire ways of being and modes of thought, the most critical casualty being what might be called normative pluralism.[63] For Thomas Bauer (2011), directly addressing the coming of Western modernity to the Near East, it was the pressure of imperial Western modernity that led Muslim states and elites to dispense with their long-held toleration of ambiguity in multiple institutions and modes of life in favor of more unitary and rigid Western-style institutions.

Scholars such as Wael Hallaq have shown that colonization's impact on the Muslim world lay not merely in its control over the state, but its impoverishment of an entire ecosystem of Islam, centered on institutions of learning and law. For Hallaq, the collapse of the "shari'a episteme" (2009, 15) carried enormous implications not just for institutions and elites in the Muslim world, but for the ability of Islamic institutions to harness the systemic pluralism of the shari'a. The entire epistemic economy within which the shari'a functioned in much of the Muslim world, from the mosques in which it was taught and debated, to the institutions of higher learning (*madrasa*) in which its practitioners and experts were trained and housed, to the religious endowments (*awqaf*) out of which they were supported, was crushed under the weight of the imported modern state.[64] The effects of jural colonization were indeed devastating for the shari'a episteme, but I will argue that it was critical to the colonial project that some domains of Islamic law were kept intact. These domains housed new and impoverished content, but through them Muslim elites continued to play a role in matters of Islamic law and governance, albeit a reduced and highly circumscribed one. This new space and function for Islamic law does not resemble the rich and perhaps idealized vision of intellectual and institutional symbiosis that Hallaq sees as the major achievement of the Islamic system.[65] Yet even this circumscribed arena provided room and resource for powerful challenges to the colonial state, for continued articulations of the meaning and utility of the shari'a, and in fact for new political and intellectual commitments to the shari'a in the modern period.

In James Scott's formulation, addressing the high modernism of a later period, state simplifications aimed at making the social and physical terrain legible for governance and order replaced "practical knowledge, informal processes and improvisation in the face of unpredictability" (1998, 6). For Scott, the high modernist vision of the state was such a juggernaut precisely because there was no social or civil society powerful enough to stop or even slow it.[66] The story of state making and consolidation here, however, is not one of collapse or supplantation, but of transfiguration and redefinition. The power of local elites during colonialism tends to be dismissed as symbolic, their presence as sovereigns a thin disguise for colonial mastery of economy, government, and the use of force. I explore the pivotal role of weakened local elites who capitalized upon the resources of the colonial encounter—its ambiguities, mistranslations, misunderstandings, assumptions, and omissions—to gain advantage for themselves. Given the realities of power asymmetry between local and colonial elites, the question arises: How did groups and individuals who perceived themselves to be less powerful achieve their aims? What strategies did they use, and how successful were they? How did these strategies themselves shape future choices, discourses and preferences?

The language of resistance goes only part way to explaining the range of decisions made by local elites during the colonial period in each of my cases: at times, local elites saw the resources and opportunities offered by colonial intervention to increase their own power over other elite groups; at other times, local elites chose negotiation in an effort to forestall colonial takeover. Some of these strategies resembled the "hidden transcripts" Scott has so acutely made visible, such as evasion, indirect refusals to comply, and misinformation.[67] Competition among groups of elites conditioned these strategies, as some groups of local elites rose to prominence over others through taking on "middlemen" strategies of translation, adaptation, and the emulation of colonial policies and Western culture, while others sought influence through diplomatic appeals to other imperial powers, or economic cooperation with colonial interests.

There is no doubt that colonialism altered power dynamics at the expense of local elites, but these elites continued to play an important role in governance, not least in cementing the ideal of a Muslim state authorized by its ability to deliver and control Islamic law in a limited domain—family law, personal status, ritual observance. In each of my cases, participation in the state often led to the increased power of some elites, at the same time that it allowed the state to define their roles; those who did not capitalize on the resources of the state found themselves out in the cold. The Malay sultans became heads of state in charge of religious and ethnic issues; in India, specific groups were incorporated into civil service and by doing so were associated with its interests; in Egypt ruling elites chose to "modernize" and "Westernize" in order to maintain their power in the face of colonization. For each of these groups, the institutional marginalization of Islam and its elites set into motion a new series of strategic negotiations that transformed Islamic law and made its delivery central to the legitimacy of the state.

Centralizing Islamic Law

The marginalization of the shari'a did not just eliminate Islamic law as a resource of power, but produced new technologies of power, new discourses of resistance, and new hierarchies of knowledge. Each of the processes by which Islamic law, and through it Islamic institutions and elites, was marginalized by the colonial state—its circumscription into the domains of ritual, personal status, and the family; its textualization and codification—also had the opposite effect of centralizing Islamic law. Its circumscription established for Muslim elites a domain of religion that they defended fiercely against colonial intervention (chap. 3). Its reification in texts gave Muslims in courts and in larger society concrete and legible references for litigation, appeal, and reform (chap. 4). The Muslim state that emerged toward the end of the colonial period was a contradictory phenomenon, its institutional Islamic content marginal but playing a central role in authorizing the state (chap. 5). The major institutional forms of this paradox were the categories of family and personal status law, the sovereignty of Muslim rulers, and the relationship between ethnicity and Islam.

For Foucault, this was not a contradiction but a concentration: modern law redefined and intensified the family by limiting, defining, and concentrating it: "Thanks to the civil code the family preserved the schemas of sovereignty: domination, membership, bonds of suzerainty, etcetera, but it limited them to the relationships between men and women and parents and children. . . . It constituted an alveolus of sovereignty through the game by which individual singularities are fixed to disciplinary apparatuses."[68] Asad takes up the role of law as the transformative link between the family and the disciplinary regimes of the state in his discussion of shari'a and secularization in Egypt: "The family is the unit of 'society' in which the individual is physically and morally reproduced, and has his or her primary experience as a 'private' being. The secular formula of privatizing 'religion' is adhered to by confining the *shari'a* to the family" (2001, 8). For Asad, the transformation of Islamic law into a province of state power amounts to the secularization of Islamic law.[69] Asad's view of secularization as a historically specific program of state power provides a theme that runs throughout this book. Alongside this theme are the questions, "How, when, and by whom are the categories of religion and the secular defined? What assumptions are presupposed in the acts that define them?"[70] Through the case studies in chapters 3, 4, and 5, I present a range of answers to these questions that suggest a modification of the theme of the secularization of Islam that underscores the peculiar power of Islam to reassert itself despite—or through—being co-opted into the state's toolkit for reading, reforming, and reproducing the Muslim subject.

By the end of the colonial period in India, Malaya, and Egypt, Islamic law was a state good: its elites paid by the state and arranged into the state hierarchy, its texts reified into state law or replaced by it, its rules circumscribed into state institutions governing the limited domains of family and ritual. Some elites who had played subsidiary roles in Islamic governance were now central to its authority, and others had been replaced—by texts, by colonial agents, by legal codes. At the same time, Islam had become a defining characteristic of the state itself, and the primary mode by which the state recognized its subjects, adjudicated among them, and authorized local elite power. The dichotomies of state sovereignty that we now tend to take for granted—public and private, secular and religious, administrative and political, and even the opposition between general state jurisdiction and the particularities of community or society—had come into much sharper focus, through struggles worked out in treaties, trials, and texts. In the transition toward nationhood, Islamic law would retain its colonial institutional forms, while Islam was poised to play a new role based upon its symbolic centrality.

The Politics of Islamic Law

I offer a genealogy of contemporary Islamic law or of "mixed" Islamic legal regimes; a political analysis of elite negotiations over religion, state, and society in the British colonial period; and a history of current Muslim approaches to law, state, and identity. The threads of secularism and colonial and Muslim modernities, as well as the rise of law as a mode of power, run throughout the project and link it to critical debates in comparative politics, history, comparative law, and Islamic studies—on how state power is constituted and maintained, on how law moves from one site to another, on whether the shari'a can be said to still exist in the modern Muslim state. A few other thematic threads run through my book, the first being that transformations on a global scale were always realized at the local level. The second is that the growth of the disciplinary capacities of the modern state was often accompanied by the destabilization of its bases of authority. Third, that the long life of institutions such as Islamic law contain a number of puzzles, most intriguing among them that its institutional marginalization at the hands of the colonial state in the long nineteenth century was accompanied by its symbolic centralization, a paradox that was not remedied by the achievement of postcolonial independence.

Chapter 2 establishes the contexts within which radical transformations in Islamic law took place in British colonial India, Malaya, and Egypt, laying out the chronologies and topologies of these changes. It outlines the precolonial conditions of state, society, and religion in India, Malaya, and Egypt; charts the chronological progression of colonialism and legal change; and discusses the territorial and historical scope of this comparative project. In all three cases, the shari'a was not the sole law of the land, and colonialism did not mark a change from a full "shari'a system" to an "Islamic law system"—rather, the colonial encounter set into motion the marginalization of Islamic legal content into a limited domain, presided over by local elites. This limited domain nevertheless also became a critical symbolic component of colonial legitimacy and of local elite authority.

Chapter 3 is organized around treaty-making moments in the colonial project, and the wider processes of jurisdictional division that they made possible. *Jurisdictional politics* proved to be immensely productive for colonial and local investments in the logic, the language, and the institutions of Islamic law. The treaties that form the archive of this chapter help clarify that the founding moments of the colonial state involved fundamental assumptions about religion, culture, and the place of law in the state and the state in law, as well as sovereignty, territory, and governance, and that these assumptions were often articulated as *denials of colonial jurisdiction* over Islam. The purpose of beginning with treaty moments to chart the development of the political space of Islamic law is twofold: firstly, treaties, far from establishing political order, represent evidence of the dividing line between the violence of the colonial state and its legitimations, between the chaos of colonial politics and the ordering imperatives of colonial rule. Treaties signed between the British and local rulers—as well as among local chiefs, merchants, and strongmen—laid the groundwork both for the division of jurisdiction and for struggles over these divisions and the power they represented. The crucial contribution of these treaties to the states which came to be built over them was *a new space in their politics*—a discrete space for religion and culture, for an "Islamic law" separate from the rest of the state. The first half of this chapter deals with the textual and conceptual bases of treaties that described the new spaces of Islamic law in the colonial state; the second details the multiple fronts upon which those spaces had to be constructed.

The material for chapter 4 comes out of an archive of conflict over the goods, the share, and the meaning of the Muslim state: legal trials that played an important role in ongoing processes of definition of Islamic law, local elite power, and Islam itself in the developing colonial state. Through trials of local and colonial elites, and trials in both Islamic and colonial courts, new elites replaced the old, new meanings of Islamic law and state power were made public, and new limits were placed on Islam and Muslim subjects. Alongside powerful and durable rearticulations of the multiple dimensions of jurisdiction—power, authority, territory, and administration—rose powerful articulators, local elites whose ability to capitalize on the opportunities of the colonial moment gave them great advantages over their competitors. This chapter asks, Having formally delegated jurisdiction over Islamic law in the colonial state, how did the colonial state apply Islamic law? The imperatives of colonial rule and the interests of certain local elite groups combined to define what Islamic law was, and which its authoritative sources and institutions; what the domains of religion, state, and society could be, and who their legitimate interlocutors; who Muslim subjects were, what recourse was available to them in the new state structure, and how those avenues could be used. I argue that there were two arcs of legal change that colonization brought to the transformation of Islamic law—the first, typified by cases tried in Islamic law under colonial administration, shows the *diminution* of the latitude of Islamic legal actors and their increasing reliance on the enforcement mechanisms of the state. The second arc of legal change describes less the content of Islamic law than its *place*, and as such is explored here through trials not in Islamic law, but of Islamic law: trials that helped—through their prominence, their political effects, and their rehearsal of new languages of elite protest and legitimacy—place *a newly limited domain of Islamic law at the center of the politics of the colonial state.*

Chapter 5 begins with moments of representation: portraits that reveal the multiple languages in which local authority was configured during the colonial encounter, as well as texts through which the growing power of the colonial state was imagined, extended, and challenged. This chapter details further the manner in which *local elites*, in response to the opportunities and hazards of colonial power, through networks that predated British colonialism, but whose interconnections were facilitated by empire, *transformed the Muslim state and were themselves transformed.* Here, we discuss the processes by which the Muslim state was remade: both as a political/institutional entity and as a condition of being.[71] In India, Malaya, and Egypt, both the Muslim governmental state and the Muslim individual state were transformed during the colonial period. The transformation of Islamic law during the colonial period bridged the governmental and the individual Muslim state in novel ways, tying the individual Muslim to the state through the delivery of Islamic law. Law's ascendance was facilitated and marked by its claims over the Muslim family and Muslim women, developments often welcomed by rising Muslim elites who sought Islamic law as part of a claim to represent the interests of a "Muslim community" in the colonial state. Changes in elite hierarchies and institutions brought about by the opportunities and pressures of colonial intervention contributed to the *institutionalization of Islamic law as private and personal law.*

Chapter 6 returns to the major analytic themes of this introduction, to bring the theoretical implications of this study into engagement with debates on secularism, Muslim modernity, Islamic law and the modern state, legal pluralism, law and power, and state and society. It begins by discussing what comparison between India, Malaya, and Egypt has yielded: a shift in the locus of sovereign power and the meaning of law in the development of the colonial and Muslim state. This chapter raises debates on secularism, modernity, and religion to make the case for continued attention to the diverse pathways by which Islamic institutions and actors came to occupy their contemporary places, in order to more rigorously question the conception that modernity rang the death knell for the shari'a system. In each case, the institutional conditions of the formation of Islamic law, even though they marginalized shari'a content and subjugated or eliminated Islamic legal elites, also constructed Islamic law as an entrenched and highly resonant resource for claims against the power of the state.

Chapter 7 concludes with the contemporary politics of Islamic law, focusing on recent court cases in Malaysia that illustrate the productivity of Islamic law's paradoxical status in the postcolonial Muslim state. Through a discussion of recent cases on apostasy in Malaysia, this chapter shows how colonial-era remakings of Islamic law matter for current Muslim politics, and grapples further with the analytic implications of paradox for comparative studies of states, religion, and secularism. The paradox of Islamic law is neither an analytic puzzle to be explained away nor a political problem to be solved, but an institutionalized historical outcome of the last two centuries that itself is now productive of a troubled politics in which the Muslim and the Muslim state are now enmeshed.

CHAPTER TWO

Mapping the Transformation

The study of Islam tends to contain an implicit spatial hierarchy in which Muslim legal and cultural production has been centered in the Middle East, spreading from the place and time of its beginning in Arabia and adapting to new locales and circumstances through the centuries. In this model, India and Malaya are part of a periphery, distant interlocutors with Islam in comparison to Egypt. More recent scholarship on Islamic law and society has gone a long way to dispel the model of a central Islamic core and a far-flung heterodox periphery.[1] Islamic law was not made in Arabia and "spread" but was carried in circuitous routes, through pilgrims and armies, merchants and marriage, scholars and saints, piecemeal and rendered through multiple layers of language, circumstance, and society, back and forth between territories, over the course of centuries. This study follows the transformation of Islamic law from India in the 1770s to Malaya and Egypt in the 1870s, further underscoring the problems of a center-periphery view of either Islam or empire. Where Islam and approaches to shari'a were concerned, India, Malaya and Egypt were at the time of mercantile imperialism already tightly bound by networks of mutual exchange—none of these sites can be understood to have been peripheral by any means.

Yet European colonialism had its own impact on the spatial and temporal networks of the Muslim world: in the eighteenth and nineteenth centuries, India became a new laboratory for ideas about religion, law, society, and governance; through the movement of British colonial officials from India to Egypt and Malaya and the vast acceleration in technologies of transport, print, and communication that made exchanges between Muslims across the world far more common, the reach of these new "Indian" technologies became global. While it may be easy to accept

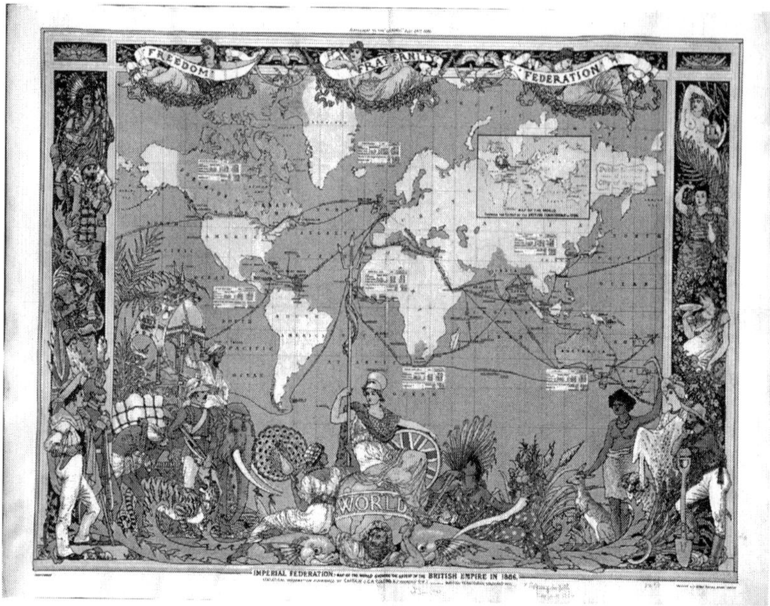

FIGURE 1. Imperial Federation map of the world showing the extent of the British Empire in 1886.
J. C. R. Colomb, 1886: originally published in *The Graphic*, July 24, 1886. Maclure and Company. Map reproduction courtesy of the Norman B. Leventhal Map Center at the Boston Public Library.

that it is no longer possible to think of peripheries, what this research makes even more striking is the impossibility of finding a center within which transformations in Islamic law might have been directed—Muslim sovereigns continued to hold titular authority over Islamic law but did not seem to control its administration; the British dominated state apparatuses for legislation, adjudication, and enforcement but denied any involvement in matters of religion; and Muslim judges and scholars continued to pronounce on specific matters of shari'a while bemoaning their growing incapacity over Islamic law. Yet between 1772 and the 1900s a new kind of Islamic law clearly did emerge, startling both in its departure from preceding practices and in the sameness with which it dealt with the lives of Muslims in India, Malaya, and Egypt. By the beginning of the twentieth century, this new kind of Islamic law had in fact spread all over the Muslim world; as Ottoman legal historian Haim Gerber points out, "the massive reforms carried out in almost all Islamic legal systems in the world left this law totally mutilated in comparison to its former self."[2]

Where chapter 1 presented the major questions of this study and the analytic language in which this narrative will proceed, I now set out the background against which these questions will unfold. Most critically, I posit a fundamental transformation that occurred in the scope, institutional context, and meaning of Islamic law during the colonial encounter in India, Malaya, and Egypt: the scope of Islamic law was gradually drawn tighter to encompass matters of the family and ritual; and the administration and interpretation of Islamic legal content came increasingly under the ambit of the growing colonial state. I have two aims: firstly, I provide a background against which to understand the nature and extent of these transformations. Secondly, I lay out pathways to navigating through these transformations to the fundamental puzzle they posit for our understanding of the later colonial and postcolonial periods, namely the increasing centrality of Islamic law in the symbolic repertoire of the Muslim state, both as a governing entity and a condition of being.

The map of the British Empire in 1886 above (fig. 1), showing British possessions throughout the world and the major shipping routes among them, illustrates a vision of the economic, political, strategic, and symbolic importance of empire in Victorian England, as well as the world being shaped around these imperatives. Britannia sits triumphant atop the world, trident held high, aligned with the Greenwich Meridian (made the Prime Meridian in 1884). The inset map illustrates the progress of the British Empire in a hundred years. The colonies are highlighted on the map in red along with their essential "facts": population, area, and trade figures. Each is also represented along the margins of the map by idealized figures, flora, and fauna, among which India is most prominent in the left corner: decorated elephant and native mahout, heavy-laden laborers and masterful British soldier, rifle pointed downward on his right arm, chained tiger held tame by his left. The rest of the world—Britain's imperial competitors, independent states—fades into the background in shades of watery yellow. The message is unambiguous: the hierarchy, order, and logic of this world system clear. We will from time to time return to the map above as a visual metaphor to discuss the contexts—ideological, economic, and geographic—upon which this comparative study is based.

The British imperial world, in this vision, is a colorful world, a progressive and expanding world, each outpost connected by trade routes. The imprint of British power is clear, the natives are identifiable by their color and their own traditional costumes, the sovereignty of Britannia is unquestioned, but the progressive principles of her empire uncompromised. Shipping lanes and trade routes crisscross the oceans, showing again the vital importance of the Suez Canal and the Straits of Malacca, at opposite ends of the Indian Ocean. As the boxes that enumerate trade figures for each colony show, the political-economic stakes of intervention in each of these states, and the maintenance of a viable and ordered connection between them, were indeed high. Colonial narratives of progress, embodied visually in the map above, tended to efface the local politics and histories with which British administrators had to contend. Here, India, Malaya, and Egypt are critical nodes of empire, but the map places the natives of these sites on the margins of its narrative, their role to provide local color.

As the materials that form the empirical core of each chapter of this book each represent a different material, social and political archive of the colonial transformation of Islam, the map above represents a specific worldview and one particular persuasive project. Made for the purposes of touting the project of an Imperial Federation, it is significant because it makes visible some important points in our discussion, and also because it is a reminder that the British Empire contained a range of politics and constituencies, and that these interacted with imperial competitors like France, Russia, and the Ottoman Empire, to create a dynamic polity rather than a static colonial monolith. To understand the significance of the worldview presented by the map above, we make a short digression to discuss the Imperial Federation idea. The Imperial Federation movement was galvanized as one answer to the growing questions about the place of Britain in the future of the world; proponents of the Imperial Federation, who were in Australia, Canada, New Zealand, Barbados, British Guiana, and in Britain itself, saw a powerful federal state made up of Britain and its English-speaking colonies as a large economic and political player on the world stage, where the United States, Russia, and Germany already loomed.[3] The Federationists in the colonies attempted to gain more say in domestic and economic affairs while still ceding defense and foreign affairs to London.

Debates about the meaning and future of the empire, the proper role of local elites in the government of the colonies, and the relationship between different states within the British Empire were part of the political context within which the dynamics I discuss in later chapters were unfolding. The example of the Imperial Federation, and the ways in which it used the language and symbols of empire to project a new vision of the world, is another case in which elites within British colonial possessions were attempting to negotiate a position for themselves at the imperial table. By the 1880s, the idea of the federation itself was on the wane, the world the map attempted to mold in its own image already changing almost beyond recognition. In later chapters, we will see that this strategy—trading influence in foreign affairs and external defense in exchange for domestic power—was also current among local elites in India, Malaya, and Egypt. However, these elites were not considered viable players by the Imperial Federation League, which saw the union of "English-speaking" colonies to be based upon cultural and racial commonalties.[4]

Zooming In: Three More Maps

> In years gone by flourishing cities and fields lined the great lakes where now dikes, brackish reedy pools, and desert tracts are all that strike the eye. Near Kantara, on the east, are the ruined towns of Tell-es-Smoot, and on the south those of Beer Migdol, on the sites of Migdol with its watch towers, erected by the Pharaohs as a protection against the Asiatic hordes. Suez, formerly a mere fishing town, has grown to be a flourishing seat of commerce.[5]

In the first decade after its opening in 1869, traffic through the Suez Canal went from 486 ships carrying 436,000 tons of goods and passengers to 2,086 ships carrying 3.1 million tons, a sevenfold increase. The canal linked Britain to India and Malaya through Egypt and raised the stakes for maintaining order and control at either end of the crucial India trade; and it is this link that provides the initial temporal frame for this study. On November 24, 1875, the day the British secured a controlling interest in the Suez Canal Company, Queen Victoria recorded in her journal:

> Received a box from Mr. Disraeli, with the very important news that the Government has purchased the Viceroy of Egypt's shares in the Suez Canal for four millions, which gives us complete security for India, and altogether places us in a very safe position! An immense thing.[6]

While the natives on the margins of the Imperial Federation map direct their gaze to Britannia alone, Britannia's gaze is turned toward India, colonizer and colonized in a relationship of mutual definition, contest, and anxiety. Most of our discussion of British India will focus upon the northern region of British India, between Bengal, the United Provinces, and Punjab, which provide us with the greatest coverage of contemporary nation-states, covering India, Pakistan, and Bangladesh. Bengal, in the northeast of British India (divided now between India and Bangladesh), was then and is still demographically the most "Muslim" region in South

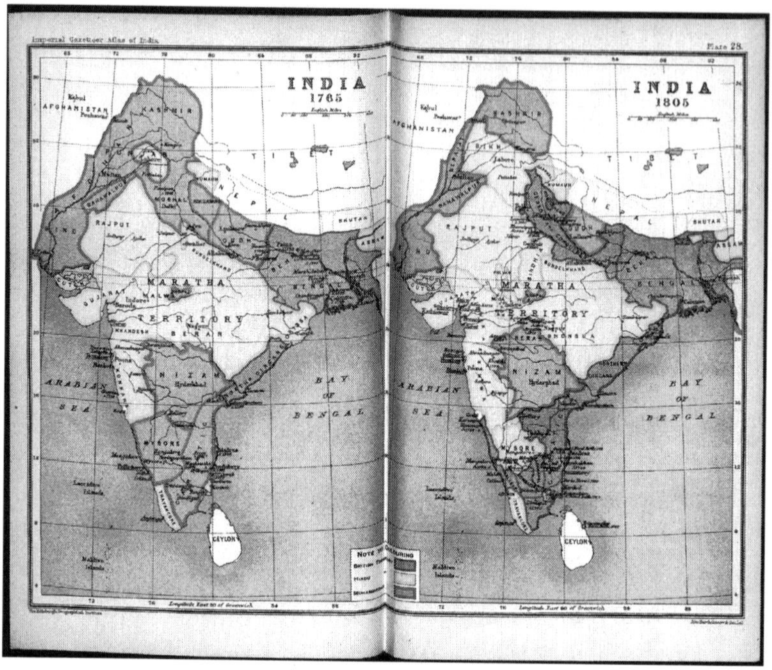

FIGURE 2. *Imperial Gazeteer Map of India, 1765* (left) and *1805* (right), showing "Muhammadan" areas in green, "Hindu" areas in yellow, and British Territories in pink.
Imperial Gazetteer of India, vol. 26, Atlas 1909 edition, *Historical Map* (1765) and *Historical Map* (1805), 28

Asia. Upon the assumption of the diwan of Bengal, Bihar, and Orissa by the East India Company in 1765, Bengal saw the first of British interventions in Islamic law in India, and continued to be an important site of legal change and "reform" by British administrators. The Punjab was also a significantly Muslim area, situated in the northwest of India (divided now between India and Pakistan) and among the last territories to come under British control (1847). The maps above and on the facing page, charting British colonial expansion from 1765 to 1857, show the growth of British colonial intervention from Calcutta north and west through Delhi (fig. 2) to Lahore (fig. 3).

The vast historiography of eighteenth- and nineteenth-century India has undergone a number of developments in recent years, the most pertinent for our purposes the waning of a once-dominant reading of the eighteenth century as a period of rapid Mughal decline whose anarchy paved the way for the rise of the East India Company, in favor of a more nu-

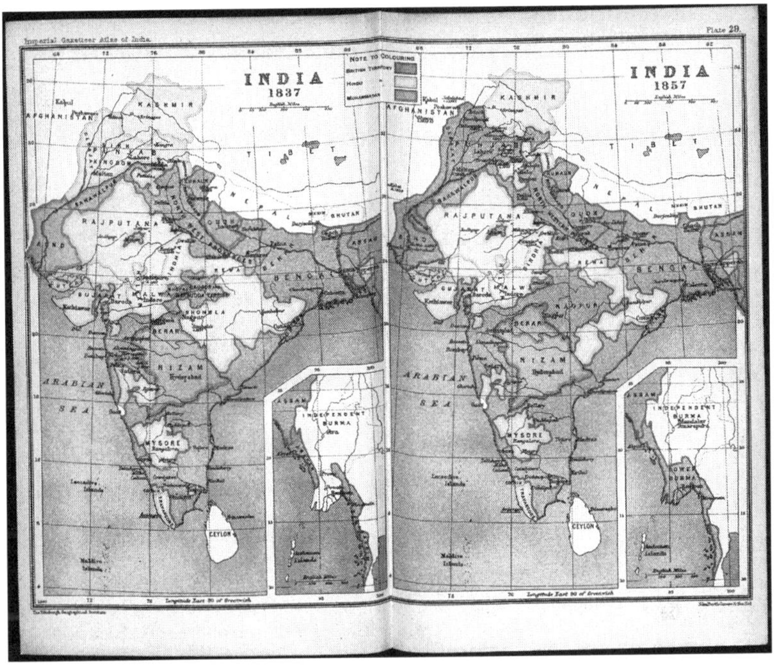

FIGURE 3. *Imperial Gazeteer Map of India, 1837* (left) and *1857* (right), showing "Muhammadan" areas in green, "Hindu" areas in yellow and British Territories in pink.
Imperial Gazetteer of India, vol. 26, Atlas 1909 edition, *Historical Map* (1837) and *Historical Map* (1857), 29.

anced view of the rise and fall of multiple groups of power holders in the face of new economic, political, and cultural opportunities and challenges. As Christopher Bayly notes,

> The receding tide of Mughal rule, as it were, revealed these slowly consolidating interests in Indian society. Yet at the same time Mughal decline was itself a result of the creation of new wealth and social power in the provinces where it could not be easily controlled by the distant monarch in Delhi. It was, after all, many of the areas and groups which had been most successful in the seventeenth century who revolted against or surreptitiously withdrew from under the Mughal umbrella in the eighteenth. The same areas and groups—Bengal, the commercial communities, the new gentry—in turn became the foundation of the British colonial regime.[7]

These foundations of the British regime continued to rely not only upon Mughal names and forms, but upon Mughal officials, texts, and in-

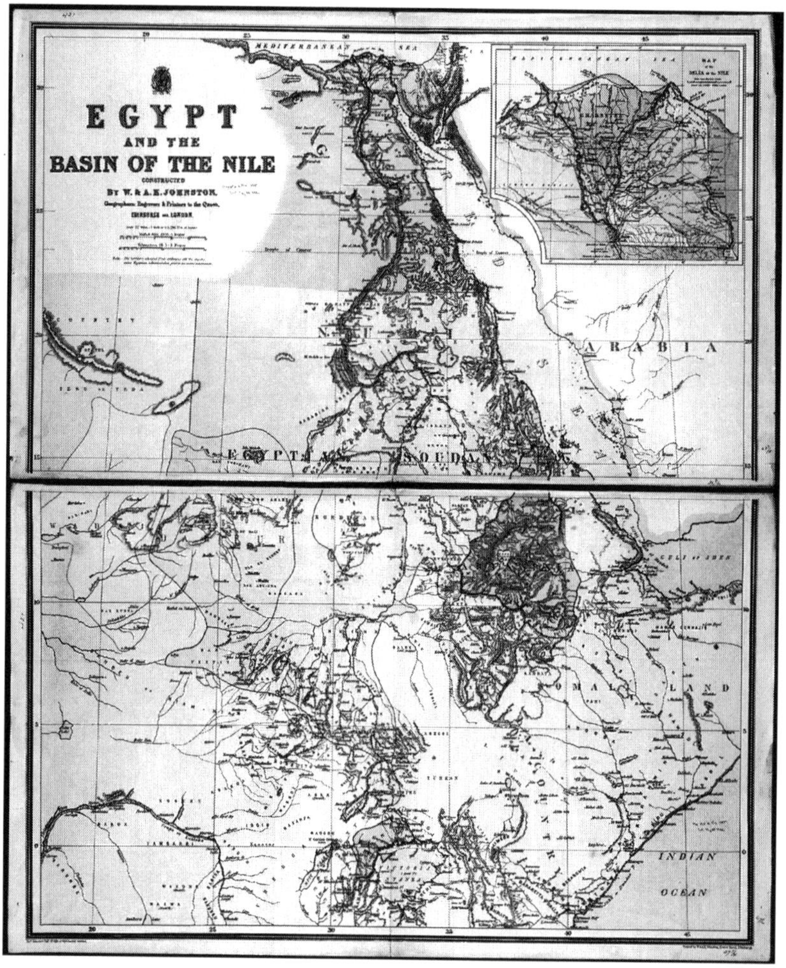

FIGURE 4A. Egypt and the Basin of the Nile, 1885. Johnston, W. & A. K. 1885. Map reproduction courtesy of the Norman B. Leventhal Map Center at the Boston Public Library.

stitutions. The East India Company took over the diwan of Bengal, Bihar, and Orissa in 1765, and in doing so maintained Mughal sovereignty as well as the divisions of the state under the Emperor Aurangzeb (d. 1707). The office of diwan was to collect revenues and oversee state expenditures, fit neatly into the economic interests of early British colonialism, and was conferred under a grant from the Mughal Emperor Shah Alam II (d. 1806), therefore conferring them legal rights under a Muslim state structure. Institutionally speaking, British rule preserved precolonial state

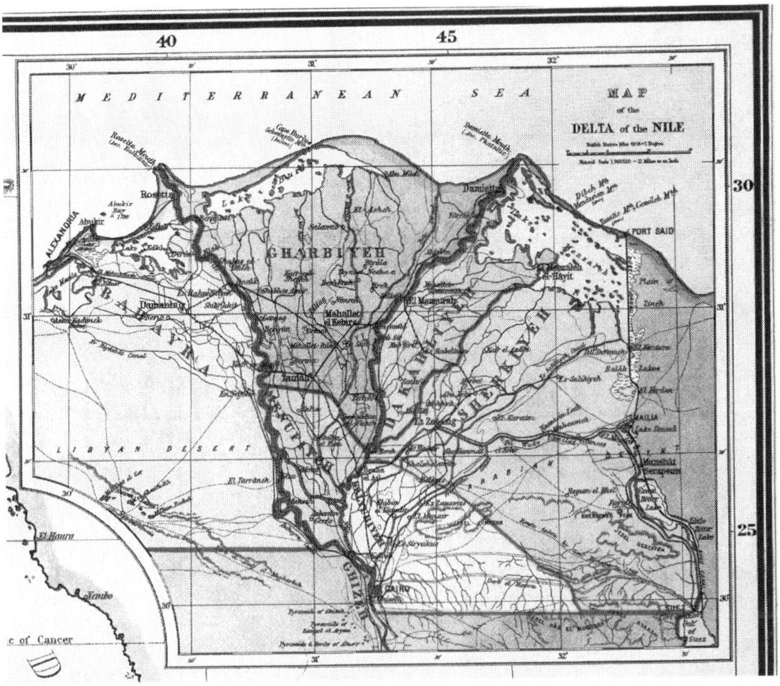

FIGURE 4B. Detail: Suez Canal. Citation: W. and A. K. Johnston. 1885.
Map reproduction courtesy of the Norman B. Leventhal Map Center at the Boston Public Library.

forms and legal structures into the nineteenth century, but put these institutions to new uses as the century wore on.[8]

India provided the impetus and much of the experience through which imperial Britain approached the project of governing in Malaya and in Egypt. India, and for the purposes of our study Bengal in particular, was the context against which imperial policies in Malaya and Egypt were articulated, and often the training ground on which officials of the colonial state gathered their experience for the governance and ordering of native states, Muslim subjects, and complex local hierarchies. The East India Company's efforts to govern Bengal laid the groundwork for the British understanding of Islamic law, Muslim governance, and the manner in which Islam might be handled by the British Empire. These lessons were extended through India, and, shaped by the particulars of the Indian experience over the course of a century, they were brought into play in British approaches to Islam in Egypt and Malaya.

Victoria's journal entry remarking on the purchase of a controlling interest in the Suez Canal Company continues with her marveling at the speed with which the whole thing occurred: "Only three or four days ago I heard of the offer and at once supported and encouraged him, when at that moment it seemed doubtful, and then today all has been satisfactorily settled."[9] British influence in Egypt continued to accelerate after this point, with British officials in key areas of Egyptian government by 1876 and the occupation of Egypt by Britain in 1882. Egypt remained under nominal Ottoman control until 1922, although it was de facto under British rule. Egyptian legal institutions had by the time of the British already undergone transformation, first under the Ottomans, then under Muhammad Ali. Muhammad Ali, in particular, in his efforts to extend independence from Ottoman rule, undertook wide-ranging changes to Egypt's administration, economy, military, and organization.[10] These transformations provided a model for the consolidation and modernization of Islamic law across the Muslim world; the increasingly close connection between India, Malaya, and Egypt after the opening of the Suez provided a way for this model and its discourses to find interlocutors across a wide range of Muslim and imperial networks. Elite Egyptian approaches to Islamic law ran the gamut from secularization and/or Westernization to a pan-Islamism based on "modernization" of the Islamic tradition. Egypt was an influential site for the articulation of Islamic law and Muslim responses to their times, and a hub for the exchange of ideas among several Muslim areas around the world: Mecca and the Arab world, the Ottoman imperial center, Iran, India, Malaya, Java, and Sumatra.

Formal British intervention in the Malay States also began in this period, with the first treaties signed between the British and Malay sultans in 1874. I focus on three states along the western coast of the Malay Peninsula: Perak (where formal British intervention began in 1874), Kedah to the north (on the border with Siam), and Johor to the south (the last state to come under British "protection" in 1914.) Each of these states represents a different set of elite strategies in response to British imperialism, and different institutional outcomes in Islamic law. Prior to British intervention, Kedah was a vassal state of Siam, and the development of legal/governmental institutions in the British period bore the mark of that institutional legacy, as well as the unusual strength of Islamic elites in that state. In Perak, issues of contested succession led to some local chiefs inviting British intervention in order to win advantage over others, and so the British role in this state was very often a balancing one. In Johor, vast resources and shrewd diplomacy on the part of one local ruler led to a high level of local autonomy that was used to build state institutions and

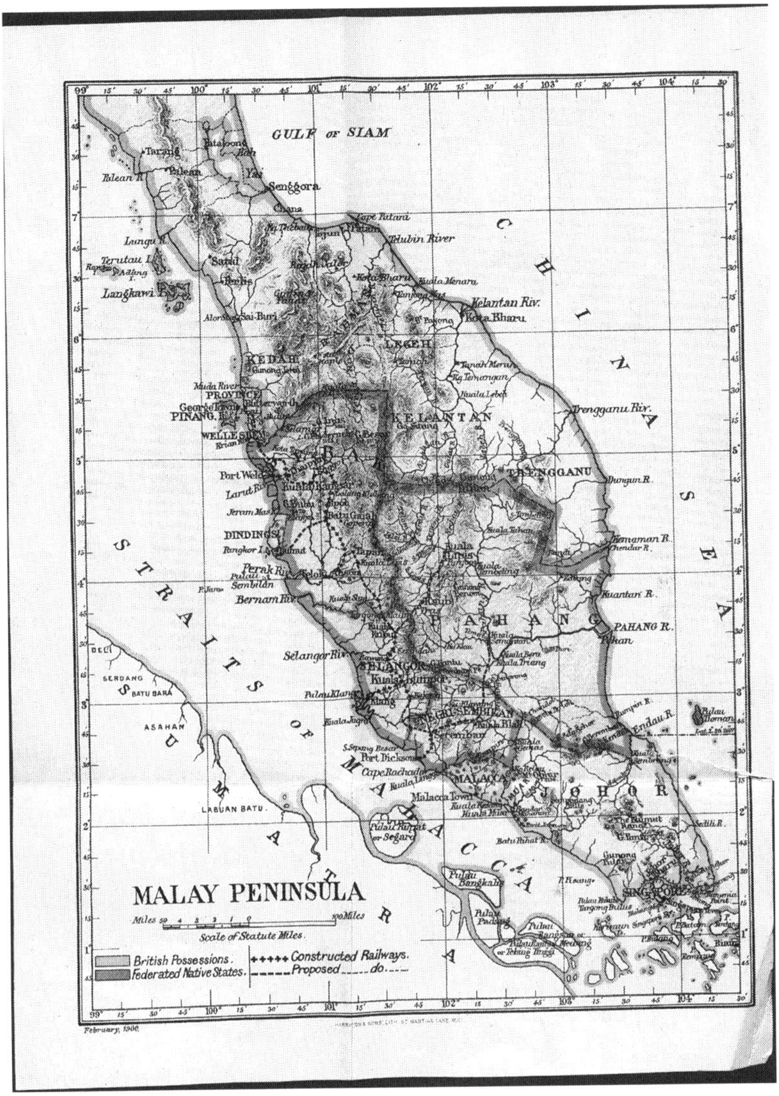

FIGURE 5. Malay Peninsula 1902.
H. C. Belfield, *Handbook of the Federated Malay States*. London: Edward Stanford, 1902.

enhance his own role. Johor, in particular, because it resisted formal colonial intervention until 1914, presents a striking case of the ways in which local ruler strategies converged with colonial logics, in an effort to preserve local sovereignty. In the late nineteenth century, as British imperial pressure increased, so did the opportunities available for the Sultan of Johor to travel, to negotiate multiple hierarchies of empire for his own advantage, and to encounter other, non-European resources for conceptualizing Islam and the Muslim state. These resources included ideas from India, the Ottoman Empire, and Egypt.

Imperial Legal Regimes: Shari'a, British Law, and the Problem of Local Authority

Both shari'a and British law developed in tandem with growing and expansionist empires; instead of seeing British and local authority as locked in a zero-sum game, this work traces the manner in which struggles over authority led to an increased role for the colonial state, while also enhancing the position of some local elites. Through these struggles, the relationship between the state and shari'a was—not for the first time in its history, but in critically new ways—renegotiated, and the category of "Islamic law" became a category of state practice. The problem faced by imperial regimes was how to facilitate the mobility and translatability of law while maintaining its order and logic. Having conquered and made possible the extension of empire, the challenge of embedding imperial law within the local context for both systems involved a careful balancing between overarching logics and local details, including the management of local sources and systems of authority.

Both the longevity and the stability of the Ottoman Empire were sustained, Karen Barkey argues, because "while accepting difference, they built their governance over similarities based on institutional structures and the shared understanding these generated."[11] Empire, for Barkey, is a "set of slow-moving, temporally based, entrenched, yet also changing political formations that need to be studied to understand how they change, adapt, and move on to maintain themselves, partly through reproduction and partly through innovation of their institutional structures."[12] Beyond the scope of this book, but an important area for further comparative research, are the ways in which the Ottomans present an antecedent to the kinds of imperial logics, jurisdictional politics, and state accommodations of Islam and shari'a we discuss here, with respect to British colonialism.[13] Certainly the detailed archival work of Ottoman legal historians indicates that some of the institutional developments we see under British colonialism—bureaucratization of law, including shar'i law; increasing reliance on text and legal categories in adjudication; expanding domains of state control—were also patterns in the development of Ottoman law from the sixteenth century on.[14] The Ottoman Empire cannot be understood to stand for all of premodern Islam, however, nor for a particular temporal stage in Muslim politics or states—in each of the cases in this book, colonialism came to different configurations of Islam, institutions, and law.

The vectors of modern legal development are many—similar logics of institutionalization and incorporation operated in the policy and ideology of the British Empire. Each of our three cases represents a different mode of British imperial rule—British India, first through Company rule and then formal dominion, Egypt through financial stewardship, military occupation and control while maintaining the formal sovereignty of the Ottomans, Malaya through indirect rule and residency.[15] As Ann Stoler has suggested, the ambiguity of these multiple forms of rule and the "graded variations and degrees of sovereignty and disenfranchisement" they represented were themselves key assets of imperial architecture.[16] The apparent continuity of legal forms from one system to another, and the manner in which categories of law seek to encompass contradictory and divergent forms of society and practice, resulted in formal continuity but substantive transformation—yet another reason this study seeks Islamic law both within its institutional domains and beyond them, in the wider contexts of law and society that define it.

While the dynamism of imperial law emerges quite strongly in my comparison of transformations of law in India, Malaya, and Egypt, the story of empire Barkey tells with respect to the Ottomans is a smoother and more consensual one. One reason for this is that Barkey's is a story told from the center of an empire, while mine is told from the vantage point of its outposts—a narrative of encounter and struggle from the start. Institutional innovation and "shared understandings" were indeed generated in British India, Malaya, and Egypt, and they did contribute to the maintenance of empire, but they also laid the groundwork for the undermining of key bulwarks of authority, legitimacy, and order. Therefore, I discuss the imperial logics of shari'a and British law in order to lay out some of the repertoire available to legal practitioners, scholars, and jurisprudents during the colonial encounter—the elements of imperial law intended to maintain its stability and flexibility in the face of new local challenges. Later on I explore the conditions on the ground in India, Malaya, and Egypt at the time of the colonial encounter, and the manner in which local politics, hierarchies, and institutions were poised to handle the problems and opportunities of imperial intervention.

The practice of Islamic law prior to the arrival of the British in India, Malaya, and Egypt was conditioned by two major factors: the presence of imperial governing institutions and systems of adjudication at the local level. Shari'a elements were present and authoritative at both levels—in India, the Mughal Empire, and in Egypt, the Ottoman, gave the state an overarching Islamic authority, and the person of the sultan had legislative rights in all matters. The role of religious authorities in sanctioning the religiosity of law and the correctness of the ruler remained an important feature of both Mughal and Ottoman political philosophy. In effect, this meant that the shari'a played a number of roles in the legal life of the state: by ruling in its name, the sovereign was authorized as a Muslim ruler and at critical moments could be judged by its standards. Secondly, various institutions and actors produced shar'i content in jurisprudence, theology, teaching, and adjudication in a variety of areas, including matters of statecraft, economy, and market; and penality, ritual, and family. Finally, local strongmen could adjudicate disputes and pronounce law at the local level based upon the rulings of the central state, upon the advice of *ulama*, and through the office of the qadi, and effectively balance the functions of the shari'a and other sources and systems of law.[17] As a matter of practice, and particularly for the Ottomans, where the shari'a was silent, rulers dictated *qanun* (derived from the Greek "canon," meaning measure, rule), roughly dividing the field of legislation into domains of shari'a and of administration. In time, these did come to circumscribe matters about which the shari'a was not silent, such as matters of property and penality; the extensive coverage of shari'a rules and the expansiveness of their theoretical reach was rarely, if ever, matched by their application in Muslim governance.[18]

While both the Mughals and the Ottomans subscribed to the Hanafi school of Islamic jurisprudence, both combined elements from other schools of law and from local customs in the practice of the law of empire, and the decline of the administrative power of the Muslim imperial state did not correlate with a similar decline in Islamic scholarship—evidence from India and Egypt indicates quite the opposite. In contrast, Islam was the predominant religion of the Malay Peninsula by the sixteenth century, but there was no overarching imperial or governing framework in Malaya comparable to the Mughal and Ottoman empires. This is not to say there was no legal system in place, nor that the shari'a did not have an important influence upon the workings of law—Islamic law and the customs of the Malays (*adat temenggong* and *adat pepatih*) were both in practice at the time of European contact, and the early texts of law, such as the Undang-Undang Melaka (or the Hukum Kanun Melaka, the Laws of Melaka), were strongly modeled after classical Islamic sources.[19] Throughout Malaya in the early nineteenth century, imams, muftis and qadis administered law and adjudicated disputes in accordance with shari'a texts and understandings.[20] Yet comparative scholarship on the development of Islamic institutions indicates that in Southeast Asia, by and large, authoritative Islamic institutions of learning and law were developing alongside European colonialism, rather than prior to them.[21] Even within Southeast Asia, variations were important and apparent—unlike neighboring Dutch-colonized Indonesia, for example, the elaboration of custom (*adat*) as a source of law was not extensive, nor was customary law seen as a system in competition with Islamic law. Comparing the systems of Indonesia and Malaysia, Roff argues that "the conjoint presence . . . of elaborate institutional structures for Islamic authority and of a related and growing corpus of positive law for Muslims, the whole coexisting with a secular civil and criminal law system derived from the British, has produced a legal dualism that is markedly different in many respects from that of Indonesia, though still very little described or studied."[22]

Islamic law and the states and societies into which it was constructed have been made, unmade, and remade repeatedly in their histories. My focus on the British colonial period does not imply it is the only, or the most important, making. Indeed, this period of making must be seen against the backdrop of layers unique to the history of each case, layers that do not lie inert beneath the surface of the politics of Islamic law but continue to exert influence upon it. In India, threads of Hindu (Brahmanic) legal practice intertwined with Muslim law texts in land law, for example, and the specific political-economic conditions under which land was held, used, and transferred, resulted in quite different land practices than in Malaya, where ancient maritime law and Malay land customs held sway, or from Egypt, whose British colonial experience interacted with not only French and Ottoman but pre-Islamic systems of agriculture, land ownership, and transfer.

The British colonial period does, however, go a long way toward explaining many features of Islam and the place of Islamic law in the contemporary state, and for this reason deserves special attention. For one thing, the conjunction of colonial knowledge and colonial interests lent resources, power, and institutional shape to groups that took this opportunity to advance visions of state, of social organization, of right, and of history—visions that may have otherwise remained merely one among a number of competing ideals, rather than primary inheritors of the state. The colonial period also inaugurated a new orientation to law, both as a mechanism for understanding colonized societies and for reimagining them. British colonial officials often acted as interlocutors of the layers of history beneath colonial law, pulling to the surface ancient texts and covering over oral traditions and contemporary local practice, prioritizing one class's interpretations of law over another's, extrapolating entire bodies of law out of snippets of myth, along contours drawn by the British imagination: of kingship, of sovereignty, of patriarchal families, and of Oriental despots. At times, the practices of Muslim empires and doctrines of the shari'a lent themselves to translation into British legal terms precisely because of shared imperial logics, and British officials learned in the classical texts of Islam made common reference to correlates between Islamic jurisprudential concepts and British common law.[23] In some cases, local ruling elites saw advantages to the codification of law and its administration by the state, since it centralized power and interpretation and emphasized their sovereignty. The emergence of the Anglo-Muhammadan corpus of law in India from the mid-eighteenth century is an example of a result of this process, in which British legal principles of hierarchy, equity, and precedent were combined with the use of Muslim scholars as expert witnesses in trials, and some texts of Islamic jurisprudence (in translation) were relied upon as authoritative.[24]

"If he is asked, any Englishman will say of himself and his fellow citizens that it is they who rule the East Indies and the oceans of the world, who dominate world trade, who have a parliament and trial by jury, etc. It is deeds such as these which give the nation its sense of self-esteem."[25] Hegel's observation in 1830 of the meaning of empire to the British public signaled a high point of the liberal ideal of empire, one characterized by the delivery of law, governance, and order to the colonized, wealth and dominion to the colonizer. Karuna Mantena characterizes this as the "liberal model of empire, in which imperial domination was argued to be an effective and legitimate tool of moral and material progress," one that was gradually supplanted after the 1857 Sepoy War (popularly called the Sepoy Mutiny) by a turn away from this ideal toward increasingly culturalist visions of the colonized that supported policies of indirect rule. The most salient characteristic of this turn away from liberal universalism to culturalism for the purposes of indirect rule was "the turn to a very different philosophy of imperial governance, one in which the native was thought to be best ruled through his/her institutions and structures of authority."[26]

Taking this view, the implications for law of such a monumental shift are clear in the contrast between the legislative efforts of Thomas Babington Macauley, whose Indian Penal Code of 1860 was to have been the first step toward total uniformity in the law, and the idea of indirect rule through preexisting native institutions, come to fruition in Egypt, Malaya, and Africa in the late nineteenth century. The problem with law, however, is that even after ideologies change, codification, court practice, and the actions of practitioners could continue to condition the action of the colonial state and serve as resources for a variety of practices reflecting a range of ideological positions and interests. The strategic use and interpretation of an archive of British legal practice and doctrine also served as a layer of law with which current colonial ideologies of rule interacted. Adding to Mantena's argument, this book presents evidence to suggest that the turn itself, from liberalism to culturalism based on a reading of tradition, community, and religion, was made possible by earlier definitions of law and the private domain.[27] The rigidity of law and its path dependencies means, however, that by the time this alteration in imperial ideology occurred, the meanings of law and its contents had acquired a particular cast—for colonial officials as well as for locals—that would be difficult to erase. These rigidities in the law produced incoherence and contention that would continue to dog the courts for decades, and that remain today to be activated by litigants seeking rights and advantage. Chapters 3, 4, and 5 will show that in each case it was the interaction of sources of law and practice at the local level that made the critical transformation in the content, scope, and meaning of Islamic law.

Local Legal Regimes: India, Malaya, and Egypt, and the Problem of Imperial Power

The view from the center of an empire allows for the sense of a course being steered, of the long-term evolution of institutions that maintain an essential character, indeed of empires as having the agency to "maintain themselves, partly through reproduction and partly through innovation" (Barkey 2008, 5). For Talal Asad, however, granting agency to imperialism presupposes that empires can be seen as actors who make purposive moves "in a game whose stakes are familiar to all participants." For both colonial and local actors in India, Malaya, and Egypt, the colonial encounter was a mixture of peril and opportunity, a game whose scope was unknown, whose rules were yet to be written, whose players were multiple and whose knowledge was highly contingent and conditioned. A different view of imperialism and empire emerges from the vantage point of these sites, "not as an already-constituted agent that acts in a determinate way, but as the diverse powers that converge to create a new political, legal, and moral landscape."[28] In fact the colonial state constituted a new field for both local and colonial actors, a field that shaped their actions and preferences as they attempted to influence its parameters, such that a particular definition of Islamic law to be defended or protected emerged in tandem with colonial attempts to change or preserve it.

The flexibility of the Islamic jurisprudential system and its ability to adapt to, and find accommodation with, the local systems of governance and law within which it functions, is well established.[29] Independent of Western colonial intervention and well before the period of this study, in the Mughal and Ottoman empires the diversity and heterodoxy of social and religious practice that came under the covering legitimacy of the shari'a made for a broad basis for loyalty to the state.[30] Pragmatic adaptations or divergences from shar'i legality did not generally detract from reliance on shar'i legitimacy for the state and its actions, a fact that Sami Zubaida points out cannot be held unique to the Muslim world.[31] As Roff, Eickelman, and Kessler, among others, have shown, the distance between the ideal and reality has acted as a dynamic force in many Muslim societies, "resulting in what can be seen as a dialectic constantly engaged in translating synchronic tension . . . the lack of fit at any given moment . . . into diachronic 'oscillation' (social, cultural, political or ideational change in one direction or another)."[32] The colonial relationship covered in the rest of my book documents one such period for these oscillations, and carries continuities from earlier shifts; yet the shift from the premodern to the modern, from Muslim governance to colonial, introduced a particular directional vector to these dynamics that has persisted into the current moment. Crucially, the locus of authority and legitimacy shifted away from those in charge of the state: whereas previous rulers, however distant their actions may have been from Islam, acted on behalf of a Muslim state, colonial administrators could not claim the same legitimacy and needed visible and recognizable signs of the state's legitimacy. These included the content of legislation and the involvement of local rulers and middlemen, both of whom came to stand for authoritative Islam in novel ways. The shift of shari'a from a "general societal discourse" to "Islamic law" carried implications not just for the content of the law, but in the processes, practices, and personnel through which government would be undertaken.[33]

The role of local elites and their strategies for making sense of, challenging, and capitalizing upon imperial intervention provides much of the interest in this narrative and a significant part of its variation across cases. Local elites often, for example, spearheaded certain kinds of "reforms" in order to resist and influence imperial intervention.[34] Hampered as they were on all fronts, local rulers, strongmen, and legal actors nevertheless often had the power to choose among colonial policy alternatives or thwart them. Local legal institutions and languages continued to play conditioning, if not always decisive, roles in the development of state law and certainly in their application and interpretation. During the colonial period, some elites rose in status and power, some traditional institutions and positions were elevated, and some visions of history, religion, and culture were advanced at the expense of others. As Table 1 below shows, the British period saw a consolidation of the power of some elites at the expense of others, leading to the emergence of a single head of state based on a monarchical model, with at least nominal oversight of both matters of state governance and religious and cultural interests of their subjects. These processes show a pattern of agreements among local and colonial powers which were followed by revolts and then the trials of local elites involved in the upheavals, which were then followed by the further rearrangement of local hierarchies and law.

Table 1 charts the broad contours of legal/institutional change across our three cases, allowing an overall view of the chronology of British interventions, Muslim elite action, and changes in Islamic legal institutions. In each case, the British period featured changes in who had jurisdiction over law and courts, how law and legal institutions were configured, where Islamic law would fit in this new system, how much of it would be allowed, and whom its main arbiters would be. In India, we focus on the period beginning with British intervention in the state in 1765, when the East India Company (EIC) was granted diwani status, allowing it to act as a state first in the area of tax collection and then in state administration as well. During this period, local elite hierarchies shifted—the "scribal gentry," "martial communities," and aristocracy became dominant and capitalized upon colonial institutions to maintain that dominance, reinforcing colonial assumptions about community, religion, caste, and race.[35] The process of colonization and elite involvement in the codification of Islamic law resulted in an entirely novel body of law, the Anglo-Muhammadan corpus, whose influence filtered into the legal systems of Egypt and Malaya through British judges and officials.[36] The shari'a was gradually displaced by the Indian Penal Code, Evidence Act, Contract Act, and Transfer of Property Act, at the same time that Muslim litigants who came to the courts for issues of family relations and succession came to be judged solely under shari'a laws, applied and interpreted by Mughal emperors and the East India Company, and later by British judges.

In Malaya, beginning in 1874, Islamic law was contained, redefined, and legislated in ways that radically altered its position on the peninsula. Islamic institutions, just beginning to gain prominence in the region, rose in competition and concert with the colonial state. Within three decades of British intervention in the government of Malaya, the structure of state power had gone from many local centers of power and adjudication, organized among chiefs who exercised power almost as equals to the sultan, to a bureaucratized, state-centered, and controlled pyramid, with the sultan at the top, and a government below him that included state councils, salaried ministers, district officers, land officers, and an Islamic bureaucracy.[37]

In Egypt at the time of British occupation, Islamic law competed with French, Ottoman, and English systems of law against the backdrop of a contest among Egyptian, Arab, and Muslim identities.[38] The Ottoman system of law, and then the French, was institutionalized in Egypt in ways that customary practices and Islamic law were not in Malaya, or for that matter in India, and the predominance of Islamic institutions of learning and law made them an obvious target for state attacks. The Mixed Courts (1876) and the Native Courts (1883), and later the Civil Code (1948), all carried within them the struggle among these strands of law in Egypt, and among the groups represented by these various systems of law. The place of the shari'a in Egypt became part of this struggle; the case of Egypt calls into question a number of assumptions about Islamic law, among them the adherence to shari'a being stronger in "central" (Arab) than in "peripheral" (non-Arab) Islam. The Ottomans, the French, and the British all oversaw important and lasting changes in Islamic law in Egypt, changes which continue to have unexpected consequences even today.

The literature on legal and social change in the British imperium has tended to understand these changes as "reforms," as the growth of the colonial and modern state, as the rationalization of systems of law. Like the narrative of change that is visible from the map of the Imperial Fed-

TABLE I. **Timeline: Tracing Legal Transformations in India, Malaya, and Egypt, 1765–1948.**

	India	Malaya	Egypt
1765–1799	1765: Allahabad Treaty 1772: Hastings Plan: "Muhammadan" law based on Quran/classical texts		
1800–1899	1858: British sovereignty over India 1858: Last Mughal emperor in India tried for sedition 1864: "Native advisors" in courts abolished 1875: Colonial codes cover all except family and some property cases	1874: Pangkor Treaty 1876: Perak Malay elites tried for Birch murder 1895: Johor Constitution, first in Malaya 1896: Judicial Commissioner replaces Sultans as final court of appeal	1839: Tanzimat reforms begin in Ottoman Empire 1874: Administrative independence from Ottomans 1875: Britain buys Ismail's Suez shares 1881: Urabi revolt 1882: British Occupation 1882: Urabi trial/exile. 1875: Egyptian civil code 1876: Mixed Courts removes "foreigners" from Egyptian jurisdiction 1882: British occupation of Egypt 1883: Native Courts 1893: M. Qadri Pasha's "Personal Status Law"
1900–1948	1937: Shariat Act 1947: Partition	1904: Separate administration for Islamic law 1914: Johor joins Federation and accepts a British Resident 1946: Malayan Union	1914: Protectorate status for Egypt 1948: Civil code

eration, this vision of history sees processes of codification, textualization, and secularization in law as part of a linear progression whose major motive force has been Western Europe. Studies of colonialism that understand colonial intervention as a zero-sum game, and the increase over time of European colonial power at the expense of local power, miss the fact that while many groups in the colonized regions did lose power, some made use of the opportunities colonial powers presented to increase their own status and resources at the expense of those of their competitors.

Islamic law and legal institutions became entwined in the evolving bureaucratic state in all three cases, such that Islamic law during the British period came to be understood as part of the domain of the central state in ways it had not before. One of the state's new functions became the articulation and maintenance of institutions, posts, and populations for the administration of Islamic law: courts, judges, muftis, qadis, imams, all in the employ of the state or acting under its authority. The form and content of Islamic law itself underwent changes: its regional and interpretive diversity was reduced, and a much more unified legal system introduced within the boundaries of the state; customary local practices and orality were replaced by authoritative texts, codes, and precedents. The unification of Islamic laws and Muslim legal institutions occurred alongside changes in how Muslims were defined, by the state and among themselves, as a political category. As regional institutions and variations diminished, so did the power of elites who used to be involved in them, and in their place rose a national class of bureaucrats and power holders who began to be identified with the newly redefined Islamic law. In Malaya and India, this unified Muslim identity also carried ethnic meanings that would play increasingly important roles. As we shall see, the British did not achieve these changes alone—local elites, historical legacies, and global forces played major roles in shaping the politics of Islamic law, the Muslim state, and Muslim identity in the colonial period.

PART II

Treaties, Trials, and Representations

CHAPTER THREE

The Irony of Jurisdiction

Whose Law Is Islamic Law?

Every denial of jurisdiction on the part of a court is an assertion of the power to determine jurisdiction and thus to constitute a norm.[1]

Law is a process . . . shaped by rules and a cultural logic, and here I add that it is also a discourse fought over by very real agents with different political agendas. The outcomes of earlier struggles over state law may have consequences for officials and ordinary people many decades and even centuries later. Yes, law matters, which law matters, and especially whose law matters.[2]

In the contemporary Muslim world, jurisdiction has become perhaps the most critical issue in Islamic law and society, as both states and social actors battle over what the proper scope of Islamic law should be, and in whose voice it may speak.[3] Put another way, the problematic of jurisdiction poses the question: *whose law* is Islamic law? The first formal answer provided to this question during the colonial encounter was often the text of a treaty that divided jurisdiction among local and colonial elites. I examine those formal declarative moments as part of wider processes that bifurcated public from private, law from custom, religion from the secular, and the state from society, during the British colonial period. Treaty moments set into motion elaborate processes of social and legal division, reassigned political and economic resources, and set the stage for a new politics of Islamic law. These moments generally allowed the fiction of the preservation of both local elite authority and of Islamic practices in law and state to continue, while making critical redistributive changes in elite hierarchies and roles, legal content and institutions, power distribution and legitimacy.

This chapter begins with the formal colonial moments that divided jurisdiction over the colonial state: in India, the Treaty of Allahabad in 1765, which established East India Company jurisdiction in Bihar, Bengal, and Orissa; and the Victoria Proclamation in 1858, which announced Britain's assumption of sovereignty over East India Company territory in India. In Malaya, the Pangkor Engagement installed a British Resident in the state of Perak, the model for indirect rule in the Malay states from 1874. The crucial contribution of these treaties and proclamations to the states that came to be built over them was a new space in their politics—a discrete space for religion and culture, for an "Islamic law" separate from the rest of the state. This new, and newly privileged, space became an arena for the making of new local elite hierarchies, new claims upon and against the state, and new visions of the relationship between Islam and the state.

These colonial attempts to impose a divided jurisdictional order were often articulated as *denials* of jurisdiction over religion: the Victoria Proclamation of 1858 disclaimed the "right and desire" to impose Christianity upon Indian subjects, and charged agents of the Empress to "abstain from all interference with the Religious Belief or Worship" of her subjects.[4] The Pangkor Treaty of 1874 excepted matters relating to "religion and custom" from the authority of the British Resident.[5] The title of this chapter is drawn from Robert Cover's characterization of "the irony of jurisdiction," in which the denial of jurisdiction is itself a profoundly authoritative and generative act. Cover's work on the productive tension between *nomos* and *narrative* also provides the backdrop against which this chapter's discussion of law will unfold—treaties whose meanings are embedded within contexts and discourses and whose workings in the world depend upon "the force of interpretive commitments . . . (that) determine what law means and what law shall be" (1983, 7). By tracing the multiple fronts upon which colonial jurisdiction was built, contested, and reconstructed, I reveal the multiple interpretive commitments that animated struggle over Islamic law. I follow the polyvalent and often contradictory nature of jurisdictional claims—in which proclamations and treaties bridged divergent political projects—and, rather than seeing these contradictions as impasses, trace through them the development of new political relationships and institutions.[6] In another sense, moments of *juris-diction*—of the speaking of the law, and of law's speech—in treaties, in proclamations, in plans and doctrines that seem at first glance not to have much legal impact at all, reveal at once the discursive, the ceremonial, and the mundane work that must be done to construct, maintain, and elevate law.[7]

While the general shift of jurisdiction from the local to the state level is key to understanding the radical change which occurred in Islamic law during the colonial period, even more crucial was *which* part of the state, *which elites* took hold of the reins of jurisdictional change. The processes by which the division of jurisdiction in the early period of colonization took place allowed local elites to choose among various fora for dispute resolution and legality and therefore position themselves more favorably with regard to resources, institutions, and political networks. The analytic utility of a focus on jurisdictional politics is that it helps emphasize that struggles over control of the state were fought over both discursive and material resources, and multiple orders of conflict and accommodation.[8] India, in particular, served as an important field for the articulation of British notions of legality, legitimacy and administration, so important that the *Oxford English Dictionary* definition for "jurisdiction" tracks its usage through colonial India.[9] Whereas in India the colonial division of jurisdiction resulted in a transformation of "little kings to landlords" (Dirks 1986), the local dynamic of power, interests, and political context in Malaya resulted in a shift from chiefs to sultans. In Egypt, jurisdictional politics operated against the backdrop of Ottoman imperialism prior to the French and British imperial presence, extending our discussion beyond Western and non-Muslim colonialism to the dynamics of empire more broadly defined. A brief discussion of these politics shows that the division of jurisdiction between local and imperial institutions and elites, there too, mobilized new categories of autonomy and identity. There was a transfer of power, in many colonial situations, from one set of local elites to another, but each of these cases shows that there was also a shift in the identity and preferences of the elites themselves. The transfer (or appropriation) of power, authority, territory, and administration—of jurisdiction—depended upon the dynamics of local elite competition, upon the new resources and opportunities provided by colonial intervention, and upon existing institutional and economic configurations (which included enduring and powerful Islamic institutions and networks).

Each treaty was a moment in a wider patterned process: while ostensibly defining the terms of relationship between British and local parties, they mainly established the grounds upon which further debates about the extent and nature of the state would occur. Performances of justice and order in their own right, each of these treaties occurred against the background of wars and threats of war, which themselves featured struggles between competing local rulers and struggles with emergent British power. As historical documents, treaties like Allahabad and Pangkor communicate the political conditions of moments whose social details may no longer be available to researchers, and therefore serve as powerful embodiments of historical struggle. As political documents, they reveal the elements of balances of power at the moment of colonial encounter—they name key actors, lay out the stakes, lend explicit value to intangibles, and define penalties. They also sketch out a framework within which future negotiations might occur (e.g., the treaties which followed Pangkor and Allahabad in other colonial states) and through which previously excluded groups might contest the status quo (e.g., opponents of local rulers often saw these treaties as carving out areas of influence which they could contest). By beginning with treaties, we can chart the path dependencies of colonial states and their inheritors, their contingencies, and unintended consequences.

Religion and custom, previously matters embedded within a broad social and cultural arena, during the colonial period became defined as domains of local elite autonomy.[10] This suggests a fundamental dynamic in the making of the colonial state, in which the delegation of a domain of local autonomy—a productive denial of colonial jurisdiction—made possible the incorporation of religion and custom into the overarching umbrella of the colonial state, and helped identify high stakes for the local elites who would accept this new bargain. Interpretive commitments could be induced to change, and here we see the beginnings of an answer as to why some local elites might have agreed to participate in a system whose definition of their religion and custom was so unlike their own. In each of the treaty moments below, the division of jurisdiction between colonial and local domains was predicated upon concepts of religion and custom whose definitions were unspoken at the moment of treaty. British understandings of what religion and custom meant, and to what extent they mattered for the governance of the colonial state, would shift in the years between the Treaty of Allahabad (1765) and the Victoria Proclamation (1858). By the time of the Pangkor Engagement of 1874, in Malaya, these terms would also take on the cast of race, relating the religion of Islam to Malay custom and delegating both to the rule of local Malay sultans. As such, these treaties set into motion forces which would initiate new struggles within the law, and would form the basis for one of the puzzles raised in the introduction of this book—the conflation of Malay ethnicity and Islam in contemporary Malaysia.

As the details and processes of treaty making and jurisdiction building demonstrate, however, local elites who were willing to sign a treaty with the British did not always accept the terms of the colonial state's authority. Struggles between local rulers and colonial officials, at many levels and in many arena, reveal the multiple fronts upon which jurisdiction over the state had to be built during the colonial period. They reveal a rich seam of material about how authority, sovereignty, territory, and power were understood at the moment of the colonial encounter, and help establish the extent and nature of the changes that were about to take place: in the location of Islam, its relationship with society and political institutions, its level of articulation with concepts of race, custom, and legitimacy. The answer to the question, "whose law is Islamic law?," needed to be articulated across multiple venues and to multiple audiences—as an expression of who had the *authority* to pronounce on matters of Islamic law; who could *control* its application and enforcement; in whose purview the everyday *administration* of law lay; and across what scope of *territory* these would all extend. In India and Malaya as elsewhere in the British Empire, these struggles often led to violent confrontation, and to the replacement of elites most resistant to the terms of colonial authority.[11]

Yet the work of establishing jurisdiction, even as it disrupted the business of the state and eliminated a number of its agents and actors, gradually elevated the position of law within the evolving state order. Lauren Benton has argued that the construction of colonial state sovereignty had long relied upon the assumption that multiple claims to authority, and multiple jurisdictional orders, required the intervention of the state.[12] In this chapter and the next, we see this process of law's ascendance through jurisdictional politics, one outcome of the "jurisdictional politics" Benton traces—"a juridical space for the state that was historically novel" and "legally dominant" (2002, 259). Formal declarations of divided jurisdiction left open an arena of local autonomy over religion, and by doing so set off patterned processes of political negotiation, rather than marking their resolution. Treaties attempted to define the scope and content of jurisdiction, struggles over these delineations between the colonial state and a range of local elites would eventually lead to violence and warfare; and the aftermath of this violence would involve new performances of law, establish new hierarchies of local elite authority, and elaborate a revised language of colonial legality. Colonial legality became dominant in part through prescribing an order to the legal pluralism of the colonial state, an order embedded in institutional and interpretive hierarchies. However, this pluralism, with a claim to Islamic legitimacy and authenticity at its core, time and time again would serve to contest the authority of the colonial state and undermine the bases of its stability.

Divided Jurisdiction I: The Treaty of Allahabad (1765) to the Victoria Proclamation (1858)

The partitioning of state and society in India began with treaties to establish the British presence, the relationship between colonial and local elites, and the relations between local elites. The Treaty of Allahabad marks the moment when the East India Company (EIC) was first granted the right to act on behalf of the state in India, setting into motion further processes of jurisdictional division between colonial and local elites. It is best known for formally recognizing the diwani status of the EIC, the right to collect taxes on behalf of the state in Bihar, Orissa and Bengal, the richest sources of revenue in India. The treaty was also a peace accord, a defense pact, a trade agreement, and an announcement as to which local figures could legitimately govern.

The Treaty of Allahabad was signed on August 16, 1765, between the nawab Sujah al Dowlah and Robert Lord Clive (Governor of Fort William), acting on behalf of the East India Company and Nabob Najim al Dowlah, Subahdar of Bengal, Bahar, and Orissa, with the approval of Mughal Emperor Shah Alam II. The battle is widely seen as the military apex of EIC power in India, and the treaty as putting the Mughal seal on its dominance over the Eastern subcontinent. At the height of its power, the EIC sought legal means to secure influence in India, and it sought this security through cooperation with some local elites at the expense of others. These local elites: the Mughal Emperor Shah Alam II, the nawabs Sujah al-Dowlah and Najim al-Dowlah, gained not only British military backing through the Treaty of Allahabad but the resources and support of a new colonial machine.

Nicholas Dirks is sceptical of the power of local elites in these negotiations, calling them "treaty kings . . . for the imperial fiction of indirect rule."[13] For Dirks, the treaties were more performance than substance and served to limit local power rather than to establish cooperation: "The 'traditional' agencies of maharajas and chiefs were to be incorporated into the empire through a political economy of honor (displayed in gun salutes and durbars) and isolation (the 'foreign' policies of these states were to be managed by the British)."[14] This is an important challenge to the argument that treaties establish a playing field for negotiation, especially since similar treaties and patterns emerge in the other cases: Were these treaties in fact mere shams, designed to keep local rulers irrelevant to the actual business of governing in India? While treaties like Allahabad were indeed conceived amid power inequalities between colonial and local figures, these inequalities were not absolute, and the actions, networks, and interests of local rulers were in no way irrelevant. "Imperial fictions" were potent fictions, and the discourses they enabled through law had important and far-reaching legislative, political, social, and religious effects on the Muslim state.

The durbars and ceremonials of the colonial state were not only significant demonstrations of both sides' economic, symbolic, and political commitment to the performance of legitimacy as defined by treaty, but figured prominently in British reports from India, as well as in metropolitan discourse about empire. Even if we accept that the role of local rulers was as mere "treaty kings" in a colonially orchestrated balancing act between honor and isolation, this minimum level of influence had significant effects on Islamic law and Muslim identity. Treaty kings were often granted a level of sovereignty they did not previously hold, precisely in order to sign some of it away; in doing so, the treaties did not merely divide power but created it, and in doing so reified a vision of state and rulership new to the local context. They also created a new category of law and state—a province of autonomy left to local rulers. This province of autonomy would continue to shape the politics, society, and identity of its subjects—in this case the Muslims of India—in more far-reaching ways than could be imagined in 1765.

Further Jurisdictional Changes: The Hastings Plan and Its Effects

The East India Company assumption of the diwani in Bengal, Bihar, and Orissa, and the Hastings Plan which followed it (1772), established a dual system: British colonial administration alongside Mughal laws and institutions. The Hastings Plan represents possibly the most explicit British colonial attempt to define Islamic law, and it set the stage for the trials that follow in this chapter. British judges and EIC courts had jurisdiction over British subjects and EIC employees, while Muslim and Hindu law would continue to have jurisdiction over native subjects. In civil law, Muslims would be governed by Muslim law and Hindus by Hindu law, in courts presided over by company officials, with Muslim and Hindu advisors under the employ of the company. In criminal law, Muslim law was applied to all by Mughal officials.

The Allahabad treaty, unlike the Treaty of Pangkor, did not explicitly address the matter of religion and culture: what it did, in the main, was establish a domain of autonomy for the colonialists, a domain which in 1765 excluded the local state from the business of revenue collection. In 1766, the nawab's troops were demobilized and the EIC took over the functions of defense and order in Bengal, ceding yet another area of jurisdiction. In 1772 sweeping reforms of Bengal law were undertaken within the Hastings Plan, and these reforms did what the Allahabad treaty did not: defined the scope and target of religious law for both Hindus and Muslims and set into motion a new system for the governance of matters of religion and culture.[15] This system was based on a view of India that was comprised of great traditions or civilizations marked by the religious binary "Hindu/Muslim," rather than a diversity of overlapping linguistic, confessional, or customary groups.[16]

As the colonial state grew in both scope and influence, its institutional claims over Islamic law also grew, and the need for a rationalized bureaucracy of Islamic law, a common vocabulary of legal terms and references, and a unified administrative approach to Islam also developed. One of the first and most ambitious steps in this direction was the Hastings Plan. The Plan was based, in Hastings's own words, on a sense that the British were to act as far as possible as local rulers, basing their order on

> principles of experience and common observation, without the advantages which an intimate knowledge of the theory of law might have afforded us: We have endeavored to adapt our Regulations to the Manners and Understandings of the People, and the Exigencies of the Country, adhering as closely as we are able to their ancient uses and Institutions.[17]

The Hastings Plan defined both Islamic and Hindu law in a specific, text-based way, basing it upon Sanskrit, Persian, and Arabic texts.[18] However, "colonial administrators may never have changed Islamic legal arrangements quite so profoundly as when they were trying to preserve them."[19] "Muslim law" was defined in the Hastings Plan as "indigenous norms" to be derived from the Qur'an "in all suits regarding inheritance, marriage, caste, and other religious usages or institutions."[20] These were distinguished from "Hindu law," which would be derived from the "Brahmanic Shasters." The selection of these norms tended toward the conservative and patriarchal, and served to further emphasize divisions among Hindu and Muslim by perpetuating that division institutionally.[21]

This new reliance on ancient texts and written rules reduced the fluidity and adaptability of Islamic legal practices to a rigid and archaic formalism, which then served as proof of the unchangeability of Islamic law and its unsuitability for a modern legal system. "Backed by the literalist legalism of colonial administration, 'Hindu' and 'Muslim' became an important part of a new bureaucratic vocabulary of colonial control—a vocabulary that drew upon indigenous terms, but imbued them with a Procrustean quality as they were deployed in governance."[22] These legal redefinitions would be accompanied, as we will discuss in greater detail in chapter 4, by new technologies of colonial administration.[23] Civil and criminal courts were set up for Bengal, Bihar, and Orissa, in accordance with the East India Company's role as diwan, standing in for the local ruler.[24] The district collector administered civil law through a court council called the Mofussil Diwani Adalat, applying Hindu for Hindus and Muslim for Muslims in the civil arena alongside Muslim criminal law, as was the practice in Bengal.[25]

The Plan must not, however, be mistaken for a full description of reality. Even though the Hastings Plan was an ambitious and ultimately far-reaching one, colonial administrators could not and preferred not to become too involved in the internal affairs of the rural areas, and their relative lack of interference allowed more freedom for communities further removed from administrative centers. While the functioning of Islamic law in the everyday lives of Muslim subjects is beyond the scope of this work, it is possible to say (based on a sampling of local documents) that the actual administration of justice was a mixed affair, dependent both upon existing local practice and the power-sharing arrangements of local elites. In fact, "in urban as well as rural areas, local bodies had acquired privileges of legal autonomy under Mughal rule that persisted during the colonial period. The autonomy of legal arrangements sheltered a diversity of legal norms, even among peoples professing a strict adherence to the same orthodoxy."[26]

Further, given that the major goals of the East India Company were economic extraction and political control, it can be said that most colonial administrators chose not to rock the boat, and relied upon a strategy of co-opting local elites backed by military and police power. Throughout the subcontinent, the British exercised power by adapting themselves to the contours of precolonial political systems, including law. The result was that in many of its structural features, as well as its substantive policies, the colonial state sustained what were essentially precolonial political forms until well into the nineteenth century.[27] Zamindars were allowed jurisdiction over local disputes, as they did under the Mughal system. At the same time, the British Parliament created a Supreme Court of Judicature at Fort William, in response to political pressure in Britain for checks to be established against the EIC.

By dividing jurisdiction among local and colonial elites and by attempting to define the domains of religion, custom, and culture in India, both local and colonial elites contributed to the reshaping of these domains in the modern state. While it may be argued that the initial negotiations over jurisdiction in the colonial state were based upon calculations of economic and political interest, the process of jurisdictional change led to the redefinition of the domains of Islamic (and Hindu) law, of the realm of local elite autonomy, and, in the end, of the very identity of the local elites and the Muslims they governed. Bernard Cohn observes that this new definition of Islamic law, which privileged written sources and evidence, and limited even these sources to their ancient texts, when put to the service of a colonial administrative and governmental agenda, had enduring consequences. He described these consequences in terms that merge the language of government and policy with the language of science and causality:

> By the middle of the nineteenth century these were conceived to be the very embodiment of an authentic India—becoming the determinant of action, policy and structure, not only for the rulers but for many of the ruled. What had been fluid, complex, even unstructured, became fixed, objective, tangible . . . what had been a decision taken at a particular time, for what the actors thought to be pragmatic reasons . . . had a consequence which wholly transcended its origins. What had been a dependent variable—the result of an action through time—became an independent variable and the determinant of action.[28]

By the time of Victoria's Proclamation, therefore, British categories of religion and society, their assumptions of Indian "sensitivities" and identities, had become part of colonial knowledge about India and were themselves constitutive of the rules of engagement with regard to the empire. The Proclamation also charted a change in the ideology of late colonial rule, building on Victorian understandings of the privileged position of "tradition" and "culture" in Indian society to formulate a vision of empire based on indirect rule.[29]

Events such as the Sepoy War of 1857 in India further raised the association in the British colonial consciousness between interference in the religious sensibilities of native subjects and violent rebellion.[30] The war had military, economic, territorial, and political causes as well: dissatisfaction among sepoys (from *sipahi*, referring to Indian soldiers in the British East India Company Army) over pay and treatment, economic hardships caused by punitive tax regimes, cash cropping, and British imported goods, the increasing alarm among native rulers over their dispossession of titles and land, and abuses of power among EIC officers.[31] The spark, however, was widely seen as religious: in the spring of 1857, cavalry and infantry in the Bengal Army—both Brahmin and Muslim, angry at the command to bite into rifle cartridges coated in beef tallow and pork fat and at increasing Christian evangelization by British officers—revolted against British command. The rebellion quickly spread beyond the army, through the north and center of India, rallying under the symbol of Mughal Bahadur Shah, who was proclaimed Emperor of India.

British troops managed eventually to quell the rebellion starting in early 1858 but not without much brutality and loss of life. The aftermath of the war further rearranged the political and dynastic landscape of India: the army was reorganized, the ratio of British to native troops increased; the East India Company lost its governance of India to the Crown in 1858; Bahadur Shah was tried for treason and exiled, dying in Burma in 1862, the last of the Mughal emperors; the title of Empress of India was assumed by Queen Victoria in 1877. The Sikhs and Pathans of the Punjab and Northwest Frontier, the Aga Khan, and other groups loyal to the British were rewarded, and reprisals in Delhi and the princely states which backed the rebellion were, by most accounts, bloody and thorough: "Following the 1857 conflict, the British and most of India's remaining Princes reached general agreement on the mutual benefits of stability in their relationships."[32]

Proclamation by the Queen in Council to the Princes, Chiefs and People of India, November 1, 1858

> Firmly relying Ourselves on the truth of Christianity. . . . We disclaim alike the Right and the Desire to impose our Convictions on any of Our Subjects. We declare it to be Our Royal Will and Pleasure that none be in any wise favored, none molested or disquieted, by reason of their Religious Faith or Observances; but that all shall alike enjoy the equal and impartial protection of the Law: and We do strictly charge and enjoin all those who may be in authority under

> Us, that they abstain from all interference with the Religious Belief or Worship of any of Our Subjects, on pain of Our highest Displeasure. . . .
>
> We know, and respect, the feelings of attachment with which the Natives of India regard the Lands inherited by them from their Ancestors; and We desire to protect them in all Rights connected therewith, subject to the equitable demands of the State; and We will that generally, in framing and administering the Law, due regard be paid to the ancient Rights, Usages, and Customs of India.[33]

Victoria's proclamation in 1858, which assumed Crown sovereignty over India and relieved the East India Company of its governance of India, guaranteed noninterference in religion.[34] This guarantee was underwritten by an emphasis on "the Law" as a critical component of British rule in India—we will explore the rise of "the Law" in chapter 4, in the trials that followed the violence necessary to securing the colonial state, at home and in the colonies. Here, the law of empire was seen to be a crucial defense against empire's excesses, and a protection for Indian subjects; it also reified the relationship between Indians and their "Ancient Rights, Usages, and Customs." The Proclamation also affirmed the role of native princes in British India: "After 1858, the British devoted much effort to creating new rituals and symbols which would both display and affect the incorporation of the Princes into the British 'feudal' political order."[35] These took the form of preserving Mughal ranks, honors, rituals, terms; yet "it is clear that colonial rule brought a host of entirely new political institutions, and that when indigenous mechanisms were adapted to colonial purposes, they were incorporated within new institutional fora."[36] One of these was the colonial law court, which used British models of law but employed Muslim *maulavis* and Hindu pandits to advise on matters of religion amid a new system of courts, a growing legal profession, and a developing body of statute and court practice, about which more will be said in the next chapter.

The Proclamation charged colonial officers to "abstain from all interference with the Religious Belief or Worship of any of Our Subjects, on pain of Our highest Displeasure," but by the time this guarantee was made, religious belief or worship had been redefined to refer to a small substantive domain of social and individual life, and the institutions administering these domains had been, by and large, brought under the interpretive and bureaucratic control of the colonial state. A colonial code replaced much of Anglo-Muhammadan law with British law in 1875. By then, the only province left to "Islamic law" was what we now see as Islamic law in most postcolonial Muslim states: family law, inheritance, and religious endowments. By the end of the nineteenth century, therefore, large areas of Islamic law in India had been placed under the jurisdiction of the colonial state or replaced by British law, "native advisors" whose role had been to advise British judges in Islamic law had been phased out, and institutions and local elites involved in the administration of Islamic law and local custom were increasingly under the aegis of the colonial state.

The denial of jurisdiction over matters of religion in India was premised, by the time of the Victoria Proclamation, upon a conceptual, sociological, and institutional definition of religion built over almost a century of British rule since Allahabad. In Malaya, contemporaneous to the development of Anglo-Muhammadan law in India, the Pangkor Engagement reiterated an understanding of native sensibilities that privileged religion and custom, and in the case of indirect rule in Malaya delegated authority over religion and custom to the Malay sultan.

Divided Jurisdiction II: The Treaty of Pangkor, 1874

On January 20, 1874, the Pangkor Engagement was signed between a number of Malay chiefs and Sir Andrew Clarke, the Governor-General of the Straits Settlements, installing a new Sultan of Perak and alongside him a British Resident, whose advice the sultan was to seek on everything except matters of religion and custom.[37] Within twenty-five years of Pangkor, four Malay states had Residents, and, by 1914, all of peninsular Malaya was part of the British Empire.[38] Told in this way, the progression from autonomous Malay states to colonial territories ruled by a sultan and his British Resident "advisor" seems relatively straightforward.[39] However, viewed from a different angle the story seems quite different. Each state which came under the rule of the British did so through its own struggles. I now elaborate struggles over the scope, meaning, and content of jurisdiction in the first Malay state to come under British indirect rule.

Engagement Entered into by the Chiefs of Perak, January 20, 1874

> Whereas, a state of anarchy exists in the Kingdom of Perak owing to the want of settled government in that Country, and no efficient power exists for the protection of the people and for securing to them the fruits of their industry, and . . .
>
> Whereas, certain Chiefs for the time being of the said Kingdom of Perak

> have stated their inability to cope with their present difficulties, and together with those interested in the industry of the country have requested assistance . . .
>
> His Excellency Sir Andrew Clarke, K.C.M.G. C.B., Governor of the Colony of the Straits Settlements . . . has proposed the following Articles of arrangement . . .
>
> I. First.—That the Raja Muda Abdullah be recognized as the Sultan of Perak . . .
>
> VI. Sixth.—That the Sultan receive and provide a suitable residence for a British Officer to be called Resident . . . whose advice must be asked and acted upon all questions other than those touching Malay Religion and Custom . . .[40]

The chiefs in Perak, a state on the western coast of the Malay Peninsula, could not come to agreement over who was to become a Sultan, and their disagreements were bringing the state to civil war, thereby disrupting the lucrative tin trade. Raja Abdullah, an aspirant to the Perak throne, invited British colonial officials into the dispute. The British were anxious to broker a peace which would make the region safe for trade, at the same time seeing an opportunity to install a sultan who would be receptive to British interests. The treaty carved out a role for the British Resident that included revenue collection and "the general administration of the country."

The Treaty of Pangkor reflected a negotiation about which actors in Malaya had jurisdiction in each area of law, and under which terms British participation would be possible. Careful to establish their legitimacy as commercial and secular "advisors" to Malay and Muslim rulers, British officials in Malaya kept the arena of religion, custom, and traditional practice explicitly out of their scope of authority. In dividing territories of governance among themselves and the Malay rulers, however, religious and racial identity, not previously a major part of Malay elite legitimacy or discourse, became the center of the Malay elite domain and the key to their survival. Here, as in Allahabad, a moment of treaty making served as a point of departure for new conflicts and processes—what might be seen as an opportunity seized by one group of Malay elites to use British influence to broker a favorable succession established legal British interference in the state, inviting new state actors at the same time as it excluded others. The treaty also brought into play new resources for negotiation—an area of autonomy for Malay rulers, "matters of religion and custom," as well an area of colonial control: revenue and general administration.

While they were themselves compacts between local and colonial elites, albeit often on unequal terms, treaties marked off a space of struggle. They reveal that the relationship between local and colonial elites, and among elites, was a matter of constant contention: of negotiation, cooperation, historical accident, uncertainty, misunderstanding and cross-communication. As the Pangkor Treaty and its aftermath shows, each treaty was a moment of loss for some elites, and of gain for others; each agreement sparked off new rounds of competition. Even the parties to these treaties themselves did not wholly agree on their meanings and scope—as was the case with the Treaty of Pangkor. Perhaps the fact that the treaty was signed on the deck of a British ship (the H.M.S. Pluto) amid British arms discouraged the chiefs from openly disagreeing to resolve their succession dispute in quite the way the British had arranged.[41]

Treaties speak in multiple languages—the British believed that the wording of the treaty meant that the Resident's advice had to be acted upon by the raja, whereas the raja's interpretation leaned more heavily on the notion that the Resident's role was consultative rather than executive. The Malay rulers found later that the English version of the treaty documents was far more assertive about the rights and powers of the Resident than the Malay version. The treaty documents in Jawi (Malay in Arabic script) that bear the "chops" (seals) of the chiefs of Perak articulate the powers of the Resident as such:

> Fasal yang ke-enam—arakian maka ada-lah Yang di-Pertuan Perak itu mahu terima dan buat sa-buah rumah yang layak bagi tempat duduk suatu tuan yang di-bawah perentah British Gobermen gelaran-nya Tuan Residen Negeri Perak menjadi orang kerajaan governmen. Akan Yang Di-Pertuan itu *mahu-lah menempah dengan-nya dahulu daripada fasal sekalian perkara dan pekerjaan Negeri Perak itu melainkan tiada boleh ia masuk daripada fasal Ugama Islam dan Adat Melayu itu ada-nya.*[42]

The key Malay phrase that defines this relationship (italicized) begins with the phrase "mahu-lah menempah dengan-nya dahulu," which carries the meaning that the ruler of Perak "will desire to consult with him first," "him" here referring to the Resident. The contemporaneous English version translates this phrase to "whose advice must be asked and acted upon."[43] To get a sense of the vernacular understanding of this phrase in its time and place, the Malay translation of the English text of the treaty, published in the Singapore Daily Times shortly after the signing, reads: "*hendaklah di-tuntut apa-apa nasihat daripada-nya mengikut ajaran-nya pada membuat apa-apa*" [(the sultan) shall ask his (the Resident's) advice and follow his direction before undertaking any action]. When the sons of Sultan Abdullah in 1915, in an attempt to contest British control in Malaya, raised the issue of these uneven translations, they presented their own reading of the same clause, which read:

> Clause 6—the Sultan of Perak shall receive and make a suitable house for a residence for the officer who is under the British Government called the Resident of Perak and is accredited to the Sultan's Court. The Sultan shall consult with him first on all matters and administration in the State of Perak except that he, the Resident, may not intervene in matters of the Mohammedan religion and Malay customs.[44]

Whereas the English version went on to define the zone of the sultan's autonomy as "questions . . . touching Malay Religion and Custom," the Jawi version demarcated a space of autonomy into which the Resident could not enter, and defined this space as "matters of the religion of Islam and Malay custom." The British understanding of religion and custom, articulated in the Victoria Proclamation and in the development of Anglo-Muhammadan law in India as a limited domain largely involving the family and ritual worship, conflicted with that of the Malay chiefs in Perak, in substance as well as in procedure. Yet, as they did in India, struggles over the domain that "the religion of Islam and Malay custom" would occupy in Malaya would further reshape not only the space of religion and custom and its autonomy, but its content and its position in the social and political fabric of the Malay states.

Building Jurisdiction: Authority, Territory, Administration

Having denied jurisdiction over matters of religion and custom and defined those terms narrowly, the colonial state had to govern and administer across a wide range of issues and spaces in which religion and custom mattered locally: in elaborating the authority of colonial institutions and actors, in adjudicating matters of land tenure and usage, in administering courts and institutions of everyday life. Cover's "irony of jurisdiction" takes on yet another dimension, here, in which the very terms by which the colonial state appropriated its legitimacy and sovereignty became part of its daily struggle to govern. As divided jurisdiction was built upon multiple fronts in Malaya, it brought in elements of colonial administration developed in India, and incorporated a symbolic as well as a bureaucratic language for governance. The symbolic authority of local rulers was performed as part of the justice of the colonial state and its noninterference in religion and custom, yet these symbols had a way of complicating the work of colonial administrators and officials. The administrative needs of the colonial state continued to rely upon older institutions and actors, often incorporating precolonial elites into the machinery of colonial administration.

These incorporations both aided the workings of the colonial state and frustrated them, by legitimizing the state and allowing precolonial institutions to continue to function, but at the same time fueling further conflicts about the meaning of justice and authority, and the bases of colonial governance. The functional and symbolic necessity of relying upon legal actors from the precolonial period for the everyday administration of the colonial state also drove these conflicts into a quotidian register, so that instead of remaining a matter of proclamation and treaty, issues of the proper place and meaning of religion and custom percolated into negotiations between colonial elites themselves, as well as between colonial officers and their local counterparts.

As chapter 2 discusses in greater detail, broadly speaking, before the colonial period, authority over Islamic law—the right to pronounce the law—was exercised by religious figures at the local level; these figures also administered the application of Islamic law alongside other sources of law and custom at the local level, such that Muslims went for adjudication of disputes and determinations of shar'i rulings to the figures whom they associated with authority over Islamic law. The enforcement and control of these rules depended in part upon these religious figures and in part upon the interests and capacities of local rulers—in many parts of precolonial Malaya, for example, there were few enforcement mechanisms to which local religious authorities could turn. In Mughal India, however, local Islamic authorities could and sometimes did depend upon the state for enforcement; however, this also meant that the state could exercise a certain degree of control over the administration and content of Islamic law at the local level. The capacity of the state to administer the law was, therefore, related to the ability to extend its control over matters of the content and application of law; the discourse of authority, however, depended less upon capacity to administer and more upon the ability of the rulers to capture the loyalty or obedience of local religious figures.

During the British colonial period, local religious figures lost much of their control and administration over Islamic law to state rulers, bolstered by the colonial state and its administrative hierarchies. This process had important effects for the form, content, and meaning of Islamic law and for the political dynamics of Muslim communities, whose particulars in each case we will discuss. The concept of territory captures the scale on which changes in Islamic law occurred, as well as who controlled land: whereas before the colonial period changes mainly took place at the local community level, during and after the colonial period changes in Islamic law were most often aimed at the state level. This change in jurisdiction—a spatial change—also had important effects on the content and meaning of Islamic law, effacing the local character of Islamic legal practices and institutions and replacing them with a new, often more authoritarian and patriarchal, state-administered system.

Symbolic Performances of Authority

Lack of agreement on the terms of the treaty were not the only stumbling blocks to achieving its goals. Having appointed a new Resident by treaty, the new sultan had to be confirmed by coronation.[45] A coronation required the objects of Malay rulership (the Perak regalia—ceremonial weapons, musical instruments, and the royal elephants) and these, the spurned heir to the throne refused to give up to the British and their new sultan. With twists, turns, and absurdities worthy of a Gilbert and Sullivan operetta, the soon-to-be Resident Birch and his aide Swettenham traveled in a small boat (captained by a man named Speedy) up and down the waters off the western coast of Malaya chasing after Raja Ismail and the instruments of rightful rule. At every port of call, they were told that they had just missed him.

For these British officers, the regalia were instruments of power, objects to be handed from ruler to ruler:

> As regards the regalia, the country can get on very well without it, or, as soon as it can afford it, a new set can be procured, but it is difficult to convince these native chiefs of this. . . . It is not the possession of the regalia, therefore, that need give any anxiety, but the fact that Ismail still holds it leads the people, or many of them, to believe the assertions of Yusuf and other interested persons that Ismail is still, and ever has been, Sultan de facto. . . . Whenever Ismail

joins the Treaty and receives his money, all difficulties in the Government of the country will disappear.[46]

For the Malay rajas, the regalia did not just represent power; they were powerful in and of themselves and required careful treatment.[47] As Birch himself acknowledged, whatever the British believed, the Malay rulers themselves saw the regalia at the least as holding immense importance for proving the legitimacy of a ruler and, perhaps even more so, as objects of power.

> Not even the Sultan could safely walk in front of these instruments . . . and that they should be moved only on the rarest occasions, such as when the Sultan had to meet another ruler of higher rank than himself. . . . They should not be moved when the Sultan was travelling alone, almost as if it would be lese-majeste [an offense against dignity/majesty, usually of a sovereign/state] to disturb them for so little: they were the servant greater than the master. To ignore these conditions . . . could prove speedily fatal. . . . On no account should one come too near them. A Chinese . . . who had gone up the stairs in spite of all warnings . . . had swollen up like a puffer-fish, and died, bloated (it was said).[48]

Raja Ismail refused to pass the regalia to his rival through British officers. Without the ceremonial instruments, the weapons of precious metal, or the royal elephants, there could be no coronation for Abdullah. Without a coronation, the Treaty of Pangkor and the world it envisioned, an orderly regime of obedient monarchs and benevolent British advisors could not be maintained even performatively. While they may have conducted treaty negotiations at a military and economic disadvantage, local chiefs and rulers were more than equal to the task of avoiding, resisting, and deliberately sabotaging the agenda of their colonial counterparts.

The Pursuit of the Perak Regalia and several incidents of its kind during the first three decades of British indirect rule serve to underline the fact that while treaties between the British government and the sultans concentrated Malay elite power in the specific domain of religion and custom, this domain was not what the elites themselves considered their natural and proper jurisdiction.[49] It is quite clear that both the British and the new sultan in Perak saw the importance of fulfilling the symbolic and ceremonial requirements of rulership over Malays, as did their opponents. At the same time, new power configurations and players resulted in ruptures in this symbolic discourse, whose order often required the use or threat of violence in order to restore. The history of accommodations between local rulers and British colonizers during this period is full of episodes in which the rulers relied upon their ceremonial forms to avoid compliance with British demands, then capitulated under British military force. This rupture of ceremony was often followed by a different ceremonial performance, with some rulers attending, often with drawn British arms behind them. [50]

Within months of the Pangkor Treaty, major conflicts between local Malay and British colonial elites occurred over issues outside the British definition of religion and custom: taxation and slavery, whose unsatisfactory handling led to the killing of the first British Resident in Malaya and the Perak war, the aftermath of which gave rise to yet another legal conflict—the trial of most of the major figures in the Perak ruling class for conspiracy to murder the British Resident.[51] British reprisals during the Perak War of 1875 included the exile of Sultan Abdullah to the Seychelles in 1877 and Raja Ismail and a number of others to the state of Johor, clearing the Perak Malay hierarchy of its most visible opponents to the colonial order. The aftermath of this conflict helps illustrate further articulations of the relationship between local elite visions of the state and the place of Islam within it, and will form the basis of our discussion in chapter 4.

Administration: The Bureaucratization of Islamic Law

The battle over authority in the colonial state was fought through discourse and symbol, and, on this playing field, local elites held the advantage. Colonial interventions into Islamic law on the basis of Victorian morality, the civilizing mission, and other claims to justice may have been made possible by growing control over the resources of state power, but these claims were ultimately based upon the discourse of right, of moral authority. Local rulers and other elites held authority based upon their control of religion, of symbols and rituals, and of indigenous discourses of divine right, primogeniture, and sovereignty. As the colonial encounter progressed, these competing notions of authority began to change, feeding off each other and creating new debates about just rule, morality, and rights.

The authority of Islamic law was closely tied to the power of Islamic elites traditionally independent of the state: qadis, *shaykhs*, muftis, imams, religious teachers, and leaders of mosques and institutions of Islamic learning (*pondok*). Among the first acts of the colonial state, with the cooperation of the sultan and local rulers, was to begin to regulate the abilities of these Islamic elites to adjudicate the law, arbitrate local disputes, teach religion, and earn money from their usual duties. For example, among the first regulations passed by the new Perak State Council in 1880, prior to the registration of marriage and divorce (1885), prior to the prohibition against slavery (1882), was one prohibiting qadis from collecting *zakat* (an amount paid by each Muslim for charitable purposes).[52]

British intervention introduced the colonial state as a prize to be captured at the same time that it dictated the conditions under which power taken from the state would be exercised. With the help of devices such as treaties, trials, and texts, the colonial state raised some issues to prominence (like the need to protect "matters of religion and culture" in realms of personal law) while making other issues disappear (including the presence of religion and culture in areas of revenue and trade). In doing so, the colonial state made opportunities for struggle over resources, power, and legitimacy at the same time as it ordered the manner and realms in which those struggles would be conducted.

After the Perak War, it became even more important for both British and Malay elites that Malay autonomy over matters of religion and custom be preserved and that the terms of the Pangkor Treaty be upheld, despite the gradual erosion of elite control over the state. In India, too, the symbolic role of local rulers was upheld and made even more visible, while their presence in state policy began to diminish. This had unexpected consequences for the politics of Muslim identity, well into the postcolonial period in many Muslim communities: as Michael Anderson says of India, "The Anglo-Mohamedan law seems to have contributed to an environment in which a new politics of Muslim identity could flourish" (1996, 8). In Malaya, for example, the protection of Malay interests became a key factor in the survival of Malay sultans and in the rise of a new Malay civil service class, whose interests became intertwined with those of the bureaucratic state, so that being Malay and being Muslim started to become mutually defining identities.

Islam had a powerful role in conferring authority upon local rulers and religious elites—their functions in upholding religious practice, maintaining Islamic institutions, and allying with Islamic elites both at home and globally gave them a core of local support the British were wary of disturbing. British Residents, whose roles were growing in a number of

Malay states, took great care to cultivate the sultans and to incorporate the chiefs into the civil payroll, if not into key roles in government. The sultans and the chiefs voiced their opinions more often in the domains of the colonial state: State Councils, consultations with Residents and British officials, and correspondence with the Colonial Office in London. The formation of stable institutions allowed (and in many cases required) opportunities for local elites to make claims and adjustments, which were significant for the shape of the Malayan state. Some areas of Malay life became more institutionalized, such as the Councils of Muslim Religion and Malay Custom, and the sultans' independence over these areas of governance was made more prominent while their actual decision-making power over other areas was diminished.

The compromise reached between British Residents and Malay sultans managed to benefit both sides substantially. The area of policy overlap between them was large, and, as personal status legislation continued to be elaborated in the early twentieth century, the number of Malay elites who were encouraged to take advantage of allying with the state, therefore capturing its language and identity as well as economic benefit, increased significantly. While negotiations at each level of law resulted in varied outcomes, the overall pattern within personal status codification in the first three decades of the colonial state in Malaya was an increase in the degree to which laws and legal institutions appeared to conform to traditional forms of authority under the leadership of the sultans and while both law and the sultans were being incorporated within an ever more encompassing state.

In India as well as Malaya, as more local elites were incorporated into a growing state system and public opinion about colonial policies changed, conflicts among British officials over the proper conduct and aim of colonial policy were common, as notorious public events such as the Hastings trial show (see chapter 4). In the daily implementation of both Islamic and secular matters, these disagreements had important effects. Underlying these conflicts, though, were two broad facts. The first was that British officials on the ground had both the institutional and the physical resources to control the enforcement of laws, Islamic and English: "The autonomy of intermediaries operated in the context of state patronage and the ever-present threat of armed intervention . . . if Company courts lacked the moral qualifications demanded by orthodox theories to interpret and enforce legal norms of Islamic inspiration, they carried the threat of a military power that . . . could effectively put down any serious resistance."[53]

Secondly, along with this institutional and military superiority came the power to impose overarching ideas of British justice over even areas of law where the British has ceded authority: "Company administrators were increasingly able, as the nineteenth century wore on, to intervene in areas of Anglo-Muhammadan law that most threatened their authority. At the same time, they were less hesitant to prohibit practices which offended their sense of morality."[54] Chapter 4 will discuss these concrete interventions in Islamic law in more detail and explain how colonial control over the resources of the state led to selective changes in the content and forms of Islamic law, eradicating practices like sati in India and slavery in Malaya while vehemently defending others.

Even within the initially limited scope of the East India Company, changes were made, many with unintended and complex consequences. Anglo-Muhammadan law, the hybrid product of Islamic legal content (defined in the Hastings Plan and taken from a small number of translated jurisprudential texts)[55] and British common law principles and institutions, was an example of this. New content was placed into old institutions and laws; formalization and regularization became priorities in the implementation of law in novel ways; oral traditions and local practices tended to be neglected in favor of written texts. In 1864, the Muslim advisors in the courts—native law officers, or *maulavis*—were no longer a part of the judicial system, and textbooks of Anglo-Muhammadan law and compilations of fatwa (legal opinions, often abstracted from a body of cases) replaced their advice. Indeed, "the immediate purpose of these translations was to make Islamic law directly accessible to British judges who deeply mistrusted the native maulvis advising them on points of law."[56] By replacing the multiple and messy opinions of jurists with a brief and translated code of Hanafi law on personal status, the British attempted to limit the discretion of Muslim legal professionals, allow British judges to pronounce on Islamic law using an authoritative code, and subject the content of Islamic law to the forms and logics of British judicature.[57]

In Malaya, Islam was neither an imperial religion nor a totalizing one. Carried by Muslim traders and mystics from the Indian subcontinent and the mercantile centers of the Middle and Near East, it was adopted by rulers and incorporated into the existing body of Malay traditional practices, itself based in part on Buddhist and Hindu influences.[58] Referring to "native" or "local" practices invokes the whole body of these influences, meanings, and practices.[59] Malay rulers were Islamic rulers, but until the colonial period their governance over Islam was not a central part of their authority.[60] The concentration of Malay ruler power in the domains of religion and culture had unprecedented effects on Islamic law and Muslim legal institutions, resulting in the unification of Islamic legal authority, the reification of Islamic legal content, which took on many of the specifics of elite interests and worldviews, including its patriarchal elements.

As in India, in Malaya, the new versions of Islamic law enshrined in positive law and sponsored by state institutions tended to be elite law.[61] This law helped rearrange hierarchies of elite groups and persons, and set up "a new framework for disputes among the local and regional elite, who were able to use courts to mediate disputes among themselves and to reinforce their dominance over agrarian producers."[62] They also began to rearrange hierarchies of legal sources and systems: as Malay identity and Muslim legitimacy became more unified, traditional customary practices which did not align with the dominant interpretation of Islamic law began to be replaced with Islamic legal practices codified by British elites. The matriarchal laws of the *Minangkabau* of West Sumatra began to be replaced by more patriarchal *adat temenggong*, and British interpretations of Islamic law from India came to be accepted legal practice for some areas of Malay religion and custom: marriage and divorce, for example.[63]

In the precolonial Malay state, jurisdictional authority was granted by the sultan in the form of *surat kuasa* (letters of authority), and these continued to be conveyed after the British arrived, as an outward sign that ultimate authority was still vested in the sultan.[64] In practice, however, Islamic religious elites had significant autonomy and exercised considerable authority over the rulers.[65] The bureaucratization of Islamic legal institutions allowed for gradual consolidation of control over Islamic law—for example, through pronouncements made by the Sultan in Council, which dictated that only approved religious teachers and judges could work within the state and could only teach the Qur'an or approved subjects.[66] The first meeting of the sultans of the Federated Malay States addressed matters of the appointment of qadis and the effort to standardize some elements of Islamic law such as *zakat* (tithing).[67] The Malay States began to establish state councils on Islamic matters (e.g., Mesyuarat Ulama, Majlis Agama Islam in Kelantan (1915) and Majmuk Ulama in Kedah 1904) and appoint Chief qadis and Shaykh ul-Islam (state muftis and chief jurisconsults, often trained in the Hijaz).

The centralization of jurisdiction over Islamic law was often accompanied by an attempt at the unification of its content. In Kelantan, a legal "notis" issued by the Sultan in Council in 1917 "provided that no fatwa on any question of fiqh might be given by anyone without the prior approval of the Majlis Agama, and that all fatwas issued to applicants of the Shafi'i school must follow Shafi'i doctrine, save when given by the mufti." *Surat kuasa* issued to the jurisconsult (mufti) and chief judge (qadi) at about the same time charge them with "following the Muhammadan shari'a or administrative regulation [siasat shariah], in accordance with the most approved Shafi'i opinions [*qaul yang mu'tamad pada madzhab Shafi'i*], and in the interests of the governance of the state [*yang jadi maslihat bagi perentahan negeri*]."[68] By the early twentieth century, the concepts of *siyasah shar'iyyah* and *maslaha*, referenced here as administrative regulation and the interests of the governance of the state, were key components of a new discourse of Islam and politics across the Muslim world.[69] We will discuss the wider concept of *siyasa shar'iyyah* and its development within the discourse of Muslim state politics in chapter 5.

This principle of "the interests of the state" opened the door to debates about innovations in law which included the enactment of positive laws on Islam and their enforcement by state agencies, as well as new rules about how to arbitrate Islamic disputes. According to William Roff, these were conflicts over "authority, tribunal and decision . . . an argument about how to argue," (336) in which the shari'a played a central role. The key questions in Kelantan and in other Muslim states in the early 1900s, as pressure grew from inside and out to modernize and define, or redefine, Islam, were from what should the shari'a derive and who should decide its content and form? In Kelantan, the debate took place between parties which saw the need to allow some deviation from one school of Islamic law for the public good, invoking principles such as *talfiq* ("patching," taken from Deobandi teachings) and other groups such as the state Majlis Agama Islam (Islamic Religious Council),

> the new validator of authority and source of writ in Kelantan . . . embodying a restatement of two essentially Islamic constituents—temporal authority (sultan) over a Muslim community in conjunction with proper consultation (shura) with the learned—the Majlis nonetheless partook also of bureaucratic and legal forms borrowed from the British. Established in the name, and ostensibly as the delegate, of the sultan's vice-caliphal responsibility, it reflected primarily the patronage interests of the state's ruling aristocracy and those of the ulama allied with them.[70]

The structure and administration of Islamic and customary law continued to be an area of contestation between Malay sultans and British colonialists during the period under discussion. Whereas before 1896 the sultans were the final court of appeals in the Federated Malay States, after 1896 they were replaced by a judicial commissioner. The judicial commissioner presided over a court hierarchy which placed qadi (*shari'a* judges) and penghulu (village chiefs) at the bottom of the system and which gradually removed rights of appeal and oversight over capital crimes from both the Resident and the sultan. In 1904, Malay rulers wrested back some of these rights by claiming a separate institution for the implementation and adjudication of Islamic law and arguing that Islamic law could not rightly be administered by non-Muslim, non-Malay judges.[71] Islamic courts were to answer ultimately to the sultan, as head of Islam in each state. Local Muslim qadis and other Islamic officials were brought back into the justice system, this time under the umbrella of the state, and positions in administration given to members of the Malay elite who now demanded a place for themselves in the new order as chiefs, penghulus, local Islamic figures. The British encouraged the training and deployment of this new Malay civil class.

By 1904, the sultanate and most other Malay elite positions had become incorporated within a British colonial state structure. As J. M. Gullick (1992) describes, "The Ruler now stood at the apex of a system of government which included State Councils, a salaried administration of ministers . . . , district officers and sub-district headmen (penghulu), land officers to regulate the use of agricultural land as a transferable form of property, and an Islamic bureaucracy" (333). The Muhammadan Laws Enactment in the four federated states was both a significant achievement and a recognition of the limitations of the rulers' power, making the rulers' authority over matters of religion and custom into a matter of law but at the same time severely limiting the position and application of Islamic and customary law within the overall jurisdiction of the colonial state. In 1905, the rulers suggested that the chief qadi hear appeals instead of British magistrates with no training in Islamic law, with the rulers themselves hearing final appeals. The rulers' recommendations were heard, but then a Supreme Court was established for appeals. Just a year later the final appeals option was given to the Privy Council, finally uniting the legal system in Malaya under British authority.

In Malaya, elites were allowed autonomy over matters of religion and culture, and because of this became guardians *solely* of religion and culture, at the expense of the multiple roles they had previously played. Changing *what* Malay elites represented ultimately changed *who* these elites were in relation to state and to society, and focused their interests on preserving this domain of religion and culture. The forms and powers of the colonial state had come to be seen as the legitimate domain of Islam. The position of sultan was not only imbued with ultimate authority over Islam and culture, but was now combined with the power and resources of the state to set the institutional agenda for several decades. The centrality of Islam and Malayness to the authority of the sultans meant that when challenges to their authority did come, they came precisely from old and new Islamic elites.[72]

Having become central to the power and authority of local rulers, whose jurisdictions in other areas of state and law were shrinking, Islamic law began to take on great political significance and to become an important part of the struggle between local elites for authority. The conflict between local groups over the meaning, content, and direction of Islam and Islamic law would continue into the postcolonial state. It is ironic, perhaps, that the attempt by the colonial state to buttress the authority of local rulers by basing it upon Islam, would in turn give new impetus to opposition by other groups—religious elites paramount among them—with competing claims to that same power base.[73] This battle continues to rage in the postcolonial state.

Territory: Land and the Reconfiguration of Local Authority

The two prevailing explanations for British noninterference in Islamic law are, first, that it was less useful for economic extraction and therefore not worth the trouble and, second, that Islamic laws of personal status in particular were left aside because they are detailed and well-defended by local Muslims. Neither of these arguments is adequate to the task of explaining how control over Islamic law was divided during the colonial period. Research into the records of the everyday manifestations of this struggle indicates that the situation went beyond a zero-sum struggle between local and colonial elites for control over the law—local elites often attempted to use the power and institutional resources of colonial officers to achieve their own ends, and colonial officers were at times reluctant to venture into the realm of local religious affairs, regardless of the explicit instructions of their superiors. Particular institutions of Islamic law and the elites who controlled it came under close colonial scrutiny and control and in the process were significantly altered.

Jurisdiction in the early days of the colonial state was not delegated—it had to be built, and the building of a system of divided jurisdiction resulted in the reorganization of territory and land tenure. This in turn had critical effects upon local hierarchies of Islam, the adjudication of disputes, and the distribution of authority over Islamic law. The definition of jurisdiction as territory links space and power, and in the colonial project control over territory was at the forefront of the colonial agenda. Treaties like Allahabad and Pangkor were part of the effort to secure control over a discrete space (Bengal and Perak), for economic reasons first and foremost: the rich resources of these states and the opportunities they presented for British trading interests. A major consequence of both treaties was a redefinition of borders (through military and administrative means) and land ownership (both philosophical and legal): "As surely as the mercantilist logic of imperial trade yielded to the bureaucratic imperatives of the imperial state, land became what the colonial state was all about."[74]

In Malaya, changes in territorial jurisdiction upheld the power of local rulers while at the same time allowing colonial expansion into the interior and the securing of private property for colonial economic interests. There was a rapid and comprehensive change in land law, and a more gradual but no less wide-ranging change in the roles of some elites at the expense of others. Both the sultans and the British upheld the traditions of Malay agrarian life, emphasizing the virtue of Malay pastoralism while isolating most Malays in villages. Very often, both change and conservation were legitimated through appeals to Islam and to "tradition."

In 1883, W. E. Maxwell, Colonial Commissioner of Lands, sent a letter to the colonial secretary proposing a bill for the consideration of Parliament,

> under which it will, I believe, be possible to systematise the administration of the Land Department of the Colony, and to organise a system of district government through native headmen. The two subjects are inseparably connected, and while, on the one hand, no land revenue system can possibly work without the intelligent employment of local native officials, so, on the other hand, the employment of native headmen as a rural police will be of little avail unless they have a local influence founded upon their position as land-owners and land revenue collectors.[75]

Maxwell, who had been Assistant Resident in Perak after Birch's death, was a vehement proponent of land reform in the Malay States, and his campaign to achieve this illustrates another kind of colonial legal process in Malaya: the compilation and construction of "indigenous law" for the purposes of administration. The major problem for Maxwell was that it was close to impossible to gain a coherent understanding of current Malay practices or customs relating to land tenure. He attempted to solve this problem by himself publishing an account of Malay land tenure based on Malay literary sources and his own observations (Maxwell 1894).

Maxwell pointed out that rights to land, separate from ownership of land, were conferred by continuous usage of the land and that the laws put in place in Malaya by British authorities ignored this in favor of English land law based on medieval concepts. Maxwell's desire to combine Malay customary land practices with a "modern" system led to his investigation of the possibility of adapting the Torrens system, developed in Australia, to the Malay States.[76] His solution was entirely novel to both colony and metropole: a combination of the Torrens system, with an adaptation of what he called a "tithe," an assessment on land allowable under Islamic law. Frank Swettenham, who was then Resident in Selangor, disagreed, arguing that the tithe was not part of Malay custom. Maxwell's reply argued in essence that this new method of taxation was in essence upholding Malay and Islamic ideals, something the current Malay rulers could not do without the colonial state:

> Because Mr. Swettenham and Mr. Rodger have not seen in the Malay Peninsula a Mohammedan government sufficiently civilized and well-organized to collect its taxes properly, they have assumed that the recognized Mohammedan taxes are not leviable. This is an entire mistake. It is also an error to suppose that the Malay cultivator is a serf with no proprietary interest in the land he cultivates, merely because a Malay Raja may be a tyrant. . . . Mr. Swettenham in his description of the uncertainty of rights under Malay Government . . . has mistaken these exactions and this oppression for the law, instead of regarding them, as Malays do, as invasions of it, to be submitted to of necessity when the perpetrator is the supreme ruler, and this is all the more remarkable because, under some circumstances, he finds that their interests and feelings are too important to be disregarded.[77]

Alongside the construction of "indigenous law" and the elaboration of a system for its application was the construction, in the British colonial mind, of the "native ruler" and of Malay/Muslim aspirations. The product of these processes of construction may have been entirely novel, as the application of the Torrens system in Malaya was, but it was couched in an appeal to Islamic law and an ideal of Malay governance. This remark above, made in a heated exchange between two colonial administrators, reveals a connection between two elements of policy the British were generally careful to keep separate: the reconfiguration of Islamic authority and systems of land tenure. This may be one reason why the transformation of land tenure systems, such a crucial development in the colonial period, is so rarely given its due as a critical factor in the history of Islamic law.[78] Changes in ownership and control of land had immense implications for elite authority and power, colonial and local.[79]

Concepts of ownership and control over territory changed dramatically during the colonial period in both Malaya and India. First, the meaning of land itself and its relations of ownership, use, production, sharing, and transfer were transformed through an attempt to standardize and regularize land law throughout the state: "Codification distorted social life by way of selecting and interpreting material. The issue of land tenure, for instance, was a complex matter involving reciprocal rights and duties in a number of relationships; it could never be contained adequately within the simple question that preoccupied many British administrators—that of who would inherit the land."[80] Where land was not generally thought of as something to be "owned," much less bought and sold, in the precolonial period, the economic imperatives of colonialism brought private property relations to the forefront of land law. Dirks argues that

> personages who held political office in the pre-colonial regime often thrived under the law of private property, exercising political control by virtue of their new legal rights . . . (using) Company courts when it suited their purposes, but (exercising) . . . extra-judicial power when the law was inconvenient or contrary to their interests.[81]

In India, some local elites working in conjunction with the colonial state "were frequently able to appropriate considerable amounts of land under their political control and then have themselves recorded as the proprietors under British legal authority."[82]

Land law is a good example of the ways in which British techniques of definition and codification of Islamic and local practice combined with local elite networks and new institutions of administration to transform the content, scope, and meaning of Islamic law. In 1875, for example, Malay titles to land were acknowledged by the government only as long as leases remained unissued by other parties, a law which facilitated the dispossession of Malay peasants and ran counter to Malay customary law. The 1891 Selangor Land Code assumed that all land belonged to the sultan, despite no evidence for this claim, and labeled Malay smallholdings "Mohammedan customary land" in order to register these smallholdings and claim taxation from them. "Customary land" encouraged the Malay peasant to stay on one piece of agricultural *padi* (land) instead of grazing and shifting, a change which was important for the stability of the colonial state; once a peasant had held the land for a decade, it could be sold (ostensibly to allow for Muslim inheritance practices). The right to hold customary land was changed in 1892 to allow all persons regardless of race or religion to hold and sell it, substantially increasing its value.[83]

Colonial intervention in land tenure and expansion into new areas of the state also involved the attempt to normalize the colonial presence, both in colony and metropole.[84] Taxation and land tenure was also meant to solidify the new colonial regime as stable, peaceful, productive, and legal (as opposed to volatile, military, extortionate and corrupt, as some Indian and British critics of British India asserted, for example, at the Hastings trial).[85] One of the ways this was done was by presenting British intervention as the return of order and peace to the colonized society so that "traditional" rulers could truly govern. This language was used differently in India and Malaya, since Malaya was governed under the doctrine of indirect rule, but in both cases the upholding of "custom" and the rulership of "traditional" elites was a key component of the British legitimization of colonialism. These traditions and customs were in many cases constructions of the colonial period, or redefined and given new significance and political meanings by colonial and local elites; in both India and Malaya, "traditional" systems of land tenure were newly defined and used for the purposes of colonial legal reform.[86]

Scholars of colonial Indian political economy have argued that the colonial project represented two broad categories of economic interest: that of British colonialism and that of the land-owning elites of India. Changes in the legal system with regard to land in both Malaya and India are clearly representative of this. Ulrika Freitag points out, however, that "the implications of this amalgam proved more complex than they may at first appear": local elites may have participated in British colonial land reforms, but they did so for their own interests, and their participation in the colonial state altered their positions in Indian society.[87] As in Malaya, land-based elites became increasingly important to the colonial state at a time when other elites (in India, urban and often Western-educated) were rising as potential opposition figures. The identification of land-based elites with the colonial state and the exclusion of other local groups created their own local political dynamic, much of which the colonial state could neither define nor control.

In both India and Malaya, preexisting groups with close ties to local land and law were incorporated into the colonial state in novel ways: in the case of India, I focus upon the zamindar; and in Malaya, the penghulu. The Zamindari system was a pre-Mughal institution of hereditary land holding which underwent several alterations during Mughal and British periods in India. In the pre-Mughal period, zamindars were hereditary land holders, and, under the Mughal rulers, they were defined as land holders who collected rent (distinguishing them from cultivators), and who also came to hold administrative, military, and social powers. Their courts, called the *zamindari adalat*, presided over the administration of justice at the local level. The Mughal emperors and nawabs came to depend upon this class of land holders. Zamindars were not considered to own land or inherit it automatically and did so only by grant of the ruler, and so the relationship of interdependence between local land holders and imperial/aristocratic elites was kept in balance.

The diwani of the East India Company (achieved through the Treaty of Allahabad) turned the zamindars into tax farmers or replaced uncooperative hereditary land holders with new tax farmers. Under Hastings, zamindars were offered a carrot (ten percent of revenues) and a stick (replacement by the EIC,) and, while many zamindari families chose to take their demotion along with its revenue guarantee, discontent continued to percolate. The Permanent Settlement of 1793, brokered by Cornwallis, altered the position of zamindar again, making them landowners, giving them further ownership of public land, allowing them to sell and inherit both these categories of land and therefore giving the zamindars more control than ever over land, its resources and the people who cultivated and depended upon it. However, Cornwallis also permanently removed the zamindars' judicial and administrative functions, assigning them to district collectors in the employ of the EIC and relegating local officials to the smallest of jobs. The civil services were effectively "Europeanized" by restricting any post whose salary was over five hundred pounds to Englishmen.[88]

The Permanent Settlement Act of 1793 was seen by many in the British colonial administration of India as a way to stabilize Indian society by creating a class of intermediaries whose interests were allied with the economic and administrative interests of the British.[89] India was to remain an agricultural stronghold, as was Malaya, in its turn. In both cases, British policy encouraged the growth and entrenchment of a class of landholders who would uphold the "traditional" nature of the peasantry and its relations to land and at the same time facilitate British interests. The Permanent Settlement entrenched a particular definition of the zamindari land system into the social, economic, and political fabric of Bengal, pushing aside other systems of land and neutralizing a powerful base of opposition by striking at its economic foundations. In other parts of India, too, local elites took advantage of the new laws and different land regimes such as *ryotwari* and *mahalwari*, in ways which perhaps the British had not envisioned: the Punjab Alienation of Land Act of 1900, for example, which defined "agricultural tribes" for the purposes of land distribution, became an important step in the rise of an "Islamic gentry" which would, by the early twentieth century, play an important role in the articulation of Indian Islam.[90]

As in India, in Malaya, changes in the administration of territory and in land law had significant repercussions for local elite hierarchies. For some British officials, the need for a new Malay administrative class was inseparable from the further reform of law in the Malay States. The gradual diminishment of power among chiefs, who had before held major military, economic, political, and regional roles, and the rise of the relatively humble village headmen (penghulu), illustrate this phenomenon in Malaya. While most Malay chiefs were given titles and pensions in the new state organization, their actual role in politics diminished during the early period of British Residency. These chiefs, who had previously held power over the sultans through their control of local territory and resources and whose rivalries constituted much of the dynamics of Malay politics, found themselves increasingly isolated from the sultans by the Residents and from their local domains by individuals and institutions given prominence by the colonial state.

Conversely, the traditional Malay position of penghulu, the village headmen who played important roles prior to colonial intervention, became a central part of the daily local administration of the colonial state: they performed the functions of police, collected taxes, kept the peace and resolved disputes, and reported to the Residents on local conditions and the feasibility of colonial policies. They played, in fact, much the same role they had in Malay society prior to the arrival of the British and the growth of a bureaucratic state, but at the same time their appointments were made official, their salaries were paid by the state, and their duties multiplied. So essential were they to the colonial state, in fact, that Residents began to seek ways of establishing a class of Malay administrators and local agents through a new system of education and through encouraging able Malays to enter government service.

Legal Pluralism and Legal Transformations: A New Space for Islamic Law

The irony of treaty moments is that colonial powers had to recognize the position and rights of local rulers in order to disempower them, and these moments of formal recognition had consequences long into the postcolonial state.[91] Colonial interventions in law reordered the political relationship between local elite authority, colonial state power, and society. As Mahmood Mamdani has shown in the case of Africa, indirect rule combined techniques of institutional incorporation, legal dualism, and the reorganization of local elite territory and hierarchies to produce "communities," "tradition," "custom": "The form of rule shaped the form of revolt against it. Indirect rule at once reinforced ethnically bound institutions of control and led to their explosion from within. . . . (Ethnicity) . . . defined the parameters of both the Native Authority in charge of the local state apparatus and of resistance to it."[92]

The process of jurisdictional change did not just transfer control over Islamic law and Muslim life to local elites; it transformed the meaning and content of Muslim law and culture. Early scholars of legal pluralism (e.g., M. B. Hooker, 1975) saw in this division of jurisdiction the beginnings of legal pluralism: the overlay of colonial law over indigenous law, within the power dynamics of the colonial state. Later legal pluralists argued that even local legal systems are plural, and jurisdictions were divided independent of colonial policies. Exploration of the multiple fronts upon which colonial legal plurality was built helps show that the character of law itself changed when jurisdiction was divided among local and colonial elites: its content, its scope, its philosophical claims, its institutional and social power, and therefore its ability to maintain hold over even the limited areas of its influence. Chapter 6 of this book further details how the concept of "pluralism" may be descriptively accurate, but is not analytically sufficient to explain the effects of this process on Islamic law and Muslim society.

Emergent from colonial treaty makings such as that at Allahabad and Pangkor was a new category of law and state—a province of autonomy left to local rulers, based on the understanding that religion and culture could be separated out from the business of running a government, that Islam could be separated from law, and law from Islam. Each of these treaties, while ostensibly defining the terms of relationship between British and local parties, mainly established the grounds upon which further debates about the extent and nature of the state would occur. In both India and Malaya, the early period of colonization saw a bifurcation of the state, dividing jurisdiction between local rulers and colonial officials. A crucial part of the compact between these elites was that Islam, Islamic law, and Muslim "culture" would remain under the control of local Muslim elites. However, the definition of Islamic law, of Muslim culture, and, as we shall see in the next chapter, of Muslims themselves, was a matter for continued negotiation and redefinition in the workings of colonial justice and the adjudication of Muslim disputes.

We have so far traced the manner in which the formal agreements of colonial rule set into motion processes that divided jurisdiction over critical elements of Muslim life in India and Malaya—in the way that land was owned and managed, in the foundations of local elite legitimacy, in the structures by which Muslim subjects were governed and the daily logics by which they were administered. British claims to disinterest in matters of religion may be judged as more or less true, according to the historical record, but regardless of intent, colonial attempts to answer the question of who could speak for Islamic law called forth a variety of new answers. Whereas sultans in Malaya had been one voice among a few powerful articulators of Islam and Malayness, colonial treaties raised them to sovereignty just as they limited their power; similarly, the need to define the rights of the East India Company required the recognition of a domain for local ruler autonomy. In both these cases, the new centrality of Islam as a basis for local elite authority gave rise to new pressures to define, locate, and isolate Islamic law into a discrete arena. Next, we turn to Egypt to show how these divisions of jurisdiction gave rise to a new domain of law that would occupy the center of Islamic legislation and politics for the next century.

Jurisdictional Transformations without Colonization? The Case of Egypt

There was no equivalent treaty in the case of Egypt—in fact, even though the British invaded and occupied Egypt in 1882, Egypt remained officially a part of the Ottoman Empire until 1922. However, divisions of jurisdiction between imperial and local orders, in this case the Ottomans and the Egyptians, and then between the Egyptians and the British, allow us to discuss the varied ways in which imperialism and colonialism mattered for the transformation of law in the Muslim state. In Egypt, the question with which we began, *whose law is Islamic law?*, was answered as part of a struggle for autonomy between the rulers of Egypt, Muhammad Ali paramount among them, and the central state apparatus of the Ottoman Empire. So here, too, jurisdictional struggle was a way to assert sovereignty over the logic and system of the state, and here, too, jurisdictions were being built along axes of territory and administration, authority and control. The innovations of the Ottomans in the matter of codification, textualization, and bureaucratization of all domains of law also indicates that the story of this chapter is not one of simple European intervention, but of the appeal of legal reform as a method of early modern statecraft. The problem of the imposition of alien forms of law by a foreign imperial power was, in the case of Egypt, mitigated by two factors: first, the claims of the Ottoman imperial state to be conducting reform compliant with the applicable *fiqh* rules, and with the approval of *fiqh* authorities; second, the justification of a reform program in order to strengthen the state against incursions by an even less desirable foreign empire—first the French, then the British.

The Ottomans undertook a centralization of the legal system in Egypt from at least the beginning of the eighteenth century, appointing a chief judge, the *qadi 'askar*—from Istanbul and placing him in charge of a hierarchy of qadis across the state. During Muhammad Ali's rule as the semiautonomous pasha and viceroy of Egypt (1805–48), he undertook further changes to the Ottoman system to centralize and regularize the application of law, including the appointment of *ulama* from each of the four *madhahib* to a council (Diwan al-Wali) that administered the law in Cairo and other major cities. In 1848, a Judicial Council, Majlis al-Ahkam, was established, to adjudicate in matters of criminal law, with two muftis attending the cases; matters of civil law were left in the jurisdiction of the shari'a courts.[93] The first decree of the Tanzimat era (1839–76), the Gülhane Rescript of 1839, emphasized the importance of legislation and code: "In order to better administer the Sublime Empire and the Well-Protected Dominions, it is deemed necessary and important to enact some new laws. The most important provisions of these indispensable laws consists of more personal safety, of a better protection of honour, decency and property, of fixing the taxes and specifying the way of drafting the required soldiers and the period of their service."[94]

Processes of codification both brought Western-style commercial and penal codes (1850 and 1858) but also reformed the content and scope of existing law in areas of criminal, land, civil (the Mecelle of 1868–76), and family law (1917). The *nizamiyyah* courts, an Ottoman institution, were introduced to Egypt in the 1860s, and began to erode the domain of shari'a jurisdictions, such that French and British incursions seemed an extension of the process, rather than its root cause. Egyptian law reform proceeded alongside that of the Ottoman Empire in some areas, such as the Penal Code of 1876, but also in implicit distinction to the legislative choices being made in the central Ottoman state. For example, the Egyptian Civil Code of 1875, "to a high degree a copy of French law, was passed at a time when the Ottoman legislators in Istanbul were preparing the Majalla, an attempt to codify a synthesis of the major Islamic madhahib" (Skovgaard-Petersen 1997, 59). In other words, in Egypt, the overarching concern to keep both the Ottomans and the British at bay gave the model of the French code a decisive edge.

The Capitulations allowed European states jurisdiction over their citizens residing in Ottoman territory; the Mixed Courts, established in 1876, extended the legal protection of European states to non-Muslim and minority Ottoman subjects. The Mixed Courts applied the reformed laws of the past few years, were staffed by judges from a number of countries, and paralleled the Native Courts (*al-Mahakim al-Ahliyyah*) established in 1883. These applied a parallel set of codes based upon those of the Mixed Courts, with a few exceptions. Scholars of Egypt in this period have argued that these reforms represented an attempt to strengthen the shari'a system within a wider body of reform, and that changes in the form of Islamic legal institutions should not be easily dismissed as the denuding of Islamic content and logic from the Egyptian system (Fahmy 2008; Brown 1995).

Fahmy argues that although prevailing scholarly wisdom on nineteenth-century Egypt has tended to be seen "as having followed a similar pattern of teleologically unfolding European-inspired ideas and institutions . . . (where) Egypt, for the most part, appears as a stage on which these ideas were tried out, enacted, and refined," this view is both Eurocentric and ahistorical.[95] The creation of the Mixed Courts, for example, is seen as an important development in the construction of a "modern" legal system in Egypt. The separation of jurisdiction over "natives" and the subjects of European powers has been interpreted as further eroding the power of the local state. However, scholars like Brown and Fahmy argue that the Mixed Courts brought Capitulatory subjects back into the fold of the Egyptian legal system, and were a measure to limit European control and to create a judicial system that was independent of the administration:

> Contrary to the repeated claim that the Mixed Courts were imposed because of the capitulations . . . the Mixed Courts were a means by which the Egyptian government sought to limit the capitulations. This motivation . . . should be attributed to the entire movement of legal reform along European lines because the latter can be seen as a tool for resisting direct European penetration.[96]

While these moves may have resisted direct interventions by European powers, they proceeded along similar lines to the jurisdictional divisions undertaken by colonial governments in India and Malaya, suggesting that it may have been the struggle over jurisdiction itself, rather than the struggle against Western colonialism, that was most significant for the continued diminution of Islamic institutions of law. For Islamic legal institutions, the effects were in many ways the same: while the khedives of Egypt had initiated the narrowing of jurisdiction of the Islamic courts, both the Mixed Courts and the Native Courts contributed to the process, "entrenched it, and stamped it with the imprint of British power and French law"; "in past times, Islamic courts had been competent to handle the full scope of civil cases, as well as many types of tort and crime. As of the 1880s and beyond, anyone in Egypt who wanted to claim a broader jurisdiction for Egypt's Islamic courts was essentially proposing to claim some aspect of jurisdiction enjoyed by the Native and Mixed Courts."[97]

The 1880 Law of the Shari'a Courts placed the courts within a national hierarchy of courts overseen by the Ministry of Justice. By 1883, the shari'a courts had been "reduced in scope and importance to third place after the Mixed and National Courts" (Skovgaard-Petersen 1997, 60). They were the only courts that applied uncodified law, and their domain had been reduced to matters of personal status, *awqaf* and gift (*hiba*). Further ordinances in 1890 and 1910 reduced the competence of the courts strictly to matters of personal status and introduced procedures and evidence in keeping with those of the secular national courts. After the British occupation in 1882, the jurisdiction of the shari'a courts began to be limited to matters of personal status law and some matters of land. Further reorganizations of shari'a courts brought them closer to the national hierarchy of courts, until in 1897 their scope was formally limited to matters of personal status law.[98]

Conclusion

Islamic history shows that Muslim states have, more often than not, been mixed in their legal systems and in their jurisdictional politics, and certainly this was the case in Malaya, India, and Egypt even before the era of European imperialism. However, what was novel was the particular character of this bifurcation of law and its effects on Muslim politics and identity. Rather than Islamic law applied in multiple areas—commerce, statecraft, crime, family, and so on, as it had been by multiple authorities in the past—the law was divided into two domains: local (matters of religion and custom) and British (all else). Henceforth what would make law *Islamic* was *who* authorized it, and to whom it could be applied. Postcolonial legal plurality has a deep, complex, and violent history, that continues to shape current struggles over Islam, law, and state.

The overwhelming majority of modern Muslim states practice a form of Islamic law within a national legal system whose origin (or model) is European and colonial, and in these states similar patterns of struggle and accommodation occurred.[99] The "relegation" of Islam and Islamic law to matters of personal status, however defined, and the institutional takeover of the administration of such laws by the state did not in any case spell the end of the story. The involvement of local elites in authorizing the law, and in cooperating in the continued rearrangement of territory and resources that were central to the colonial project, meant that struggles over Islamic law would continue. In the following chapter, I follow another stage of these struggles through trials in and of Islamic law, which provide a clearer picture of the processes which defined Islamic law in the new colonial state.

CHAPTER FOUR

Trying Islamic Law

Trials in and of Islamic Law

The founding documents of the colonial state in India and Malaya involved a denial of British interest in religion and culture as well as a deep investment in delineating their limits and content. The treaties and proclamations of chapter 3 neither cemented British power nor established the colonial state; instead, they set the scene for new struggles over Islam and law in the evolving state. I trace these new struggles through the venue of trials in India, Malaya, and Egypt—in trial transcripts from 1777 to 1882, the multiple implications of increasing state encroachment on matters of Islam become increasingly clear. These trials illustrate, in ways that legislation and doctrine cannot, how contentious the process of legal transformation was in the colonial period, and how many issues were at stake in struggles between local and colonial elites, such that the position of Islamic law emerged almost as a byproduct of other struggles. The colonial state was often at war with itself; local elites used colonial courts to jockey for dominance and wealth; Muslims found themselves appealing to British courts and judges for confirmation of their right not to be adjudicated by British law.

Having formally delegated jurisdiction over Islamic law in the colonial state, how did the colonial state apply Islamic law? Further, what was understood by Islamic law, to whom would it apply, by whom, and in what areas (issues, locales, and people) did it not apply? And what happened to Islamic law (and Muslims) when the law was applied by the colonial state? Through a discussion of trials as an arena of struggle, I first address the argument that the coming of colonialism to the Muslim world tolled the death knell of the shari'a. I argue that there were two arcs of legal change that colonization brought to the transformation of Islamic law—the first, typified by cases tried *in* Islamic law under colonial administration, shows the diminution of the latitude of Islamic legal actors and their increasing reliance on the enforcement mechanisms of the state. Here, the "juridical death" argument, made most persuasively by Wael Hallaq (2009), rings true: with the coming of the colonial state, both the interpretive architecture and the institutional foundations of the shari'a episteme were greatly undermined. The second arc of legal change describes less the content of Islamic law than its place, and as such is explored here through trials not *in* Islamic law, but *of* Islamic law: trials that helped—through their prominence, their political effects, and their rehearsal of new languages of elite protest and legitimacy—place Islamic law at the center of the politics of the colonial state.

The role of the law in colonial projects of the modern period has often been characterized as the leading edge of state rationalization and modernization, with the law itself a powerful tool in the repertoire of the state. In what Wael Hallaq describes as "a policy of demolish and replace" (2009, 376), the rooting out of shari'a institutions, actors, and knowledge was followed by the instituting of newly translated colonial texts and codes, a process that he argues ultimately led to the death of the shari'a system. Just as treaties alone cannot cover the complexity of colonial rule but are often taken to stand for the advent of colonial control, legislation is an incomplete record of the colonial implementation of legal change. Translated texts and codified laws represent the trace of the beginning of a struggle rather than its completion, and the arena of law offered not just a tool for state domination but an opportunity for multiple kinds of protest, appropriation, and performance—perhaps less "demolish and replace," and more "occupy and renovate."

As a building block of the colonial state, Islamic law in particular served as a key factor in its legitimacy and at the same time generated struggles which regularly threatened its authority. This chapter begins and ends with cases of the *application* of Islamic law in the colonial state, which reveal the complex and frequently contradictory logics that underwrote the work of actors in the colonial justice system. In India shortly after the Hastings Plan, the application of "Muslim law" required the presence of a qadi, a mufti, and a fatwa acting in accordance with the texts of Hanafi *fiqh*, within the overarching administrative and judicial context of colonial institutions, resulting in tragedy for the qadi in particular. In Malaya under British Residency rule, a century later, the qadi's dependence on the colonial state for enforcement of his rulings resulted, in this case, in demands from both Colonial Office and the qadi that the local British official to apply Islamic law, against his own wishes. Further, I chart a complementary series of changes in the legal context within which Islamic law functioned—trials that broadcast the paramountcy of law as the central principle of the British Empire, that defined religion as a problem of public order that could only be contained by colonial law, that removed local elites who opposed the logic of colonial rule. Together, these trials in and of Islamic law show that law is neither an outcome of politics or its reflection, but instead that law generates its own dynamic of struggle, transformation, and challenge, that the spectacle and performance of trials served to dramatize law's growing indispensability for the state and project this message from metropole to colonies and back.

Applying Islamic Law: India, 1777

After the Treaty of Allahabad (1765) and the Hastings Plan (1772), the East India Company was said to have applied Muslim and Hindu law in Bengal, Bihar, and Orissa. "Muslim law" was defined in the Hastings Plan as "indigenous norms" to be derived from the Qur'an "in all suits regarding inheritance, marriage, caste, and other religious usages or institutions."[1] This statement is often taken at face value in histories of Islamic law and it is often repeated that the realm of Islamic law in the modern state has been reduced to the areas of family law, without a sense of how this limitation functioned within the legal system, and how the limitation of Islamic law itself produced its own politics, its own meanings, its own struggles. What did it mean for a British Company acting on behalf of the Mughal emperor to "adhere" to "the laws of the Koran"?[2] We begin our discussion of trials with a case that took place soon after Allahabad to index the ways in which even the adherence to the law of the Qur'an had deep and far-reaching consequences for what Islamic law would become in the colonial state, for colonial legal officials applying the principles and procedures of Islamic and British law, for the politics of empire itself.

The case revolved around matters of inheritance and intestacy. Shahbaz Beg, a wealthy rent farmer from Patna, had died in 1776 without a male heir. His nephew, Bahadur Beg, petitioned the Court of the Provincial Council in Patna to claim the estate. Bahadur also complained that Shahbaz's widow, Naderah Begum, was taking property from the house.

He asked for a qadi to investigate and secure the estate.[3] The Court, presided over by an official of the East India Company, directed its qadi and mufti to inventory the estate and report upon its proper disbursement under Islamic law. The widow, Naderah Begum, was in residence and in possession of her husband's seal and the documents that proved his land grant from the Mughal emperor. She claimed that her husband had left her his estate and produced documents in support—a deed of gift and a deed of transfer. The qadi and mufti's report pronounced them forgeries. They issued a fatwa—in this instance, a specific determination based upon the case at hand, a verdict rather than a juristic opinion—arguing that the nephew should be awarded the bulk of the estate and that the widow could not inherit more than a quarter under Islamic law.[4]

In the enforcement of this ruling, the Court's men moved through the house, forcing the widow to seclude herself in one room after another, and imposing a search of her person. Naderah Begum fled and took refuge in a local shrine, a move calculated to garner her pity and a measure of political support. By no means a helpless woman in her own right, even guarded by Company soldiers who prevented her from leaving the shrine, she managed to get a message to Governor General Hastings at Fort William, after which the soldiers were removed. In the meantime, a charge of forgery was brought against her and five others in the Foujdari Adalat, the criminal court. In retaliation, Naderah Begum appealed for aid to the Supreme Court of Judicature at Fort William. Using a British lawyer to argue her case, she leveled a charge at Bahadur Beg, the qadi, and the mufti, accusing them of assault and battery, false imprisonment, and causing personal injury, demanding monetary restitution. This act had the effect of sparking off a turf war between the Supreme Court and the governor general, already at odds.[5] The Supreme Court ordered the defendants' arrest. Hastings, outraged at what he saw as the Court's undermining of the Company, posted their bail. The Supreme Court decided in Naderah Begum's favor and awarded her half her claim; in response, Hastings ordered the four defendants detained, in case they fled and the Company be made to foot the enormous bill.

Of all the outcomes of the conflict, the plight of the qadi—the central figure in Islamic legal cases, but in this system one of a number of Company functionaries—seems a fitting allegory for the situation of Islamic law in the British colonial state. The Company qadi, who had performed his functions within the Islamic legal system redefined by the Hastings Plan and his employers, who had then been accused of thwarting justice, who had been imprisoned by the Supreme Court, bailed out by the Company and then rearrested by them, died between Patna and Fort William, while in Company custody.

For many Islamic legal scholars, the colonization of Muslim states by European powers was a disaster for the shari'a system. Wael Hallaq characterizes the combination of codification, limitation, and bureaucratization that took place in the modern period as "jural colonization" that took place throughout the Muslim world and led to the "structural death" of the shari'a.[6] For Hallaq and for many others, the shari'a, its institutions, its personnel and its cultural and social contexts constituted an entire "episteme"; the maintenance of the letter of Islamic law in the area of family law and some matters of ritual observance, however faithful to the original texts—without the epistemic infrastructure to sustain teaching, commentary, debate and interpretation—spelled the death of the shari'a in the modern state. Certainly, the colonial period did much to impoverish Islamic law, erode its epistemic integrity, and rob its scholars of their protections and dignity. The imprisoned qadi, dying while in colonial custody having attempted to perform his duties in the new system, would serve as a dramatic illustration of this argument; the fatwa, denuded of its dialogical relationship with juristic debate and exchange and reduced to a formulaic determination of doctrine and fact, typified the nature of the change—Islamic jurisprudential terms applied to cover new and impoverished institutional practices.

While the prognosis for the shari'a in this period remained grim, there are reasons to be cautious about calling it moribund. The system of knowledge and practice to which Hallaq refers may for large periods and regions of the Muslim world have existed only in parts, and its theoretical wholeness served then, as it does now, as a yardstick against which the government of the day could not but fall short. The case of Bahadur Beg, and many like it, does show that Islamic legal elites were hemmed in from all sides by the dictates of a law that denied its interference in their work while at the same time placing them at the bottom of an increasingly complex chain of jurisdictions and authorities. Yet from their positions within colonial legal institutions, Muslim legal officials would participate in the remaking and reordering of Islamic law, at times in unexpected and enduring ways. Mughal legal officials remained indispensable to the everyday functioning of the courts of the colonial state, and Muslim and Hindu legal scholars were retained as Company employees to serve as experts in both local legal practice and religious law. As in the case of Bahadur Beg, these levels of adjudication remained somewhat intact in the matter of inheritance—a matter explicitly left in the Hastings Plan to "the laws of the Koran"—but whatever these laws may have been, their application and enforcement depended upon the mechanisms of the colonial state. In this case, political friction between powerful parties in the colonial state placed Islamic legal officials such as the qadi and mufti of the Company in an intractable position—they were representatives of British justice at the same time that they were proof of the inadequacies of the local system.[7] The broader backdrop to this drama of adjudication was that the colonial state's structures of authority were being hotly contested, and competition among key institutions of policy, legislation, and adjudication would engender frequent rearticulations of what colonial justice should mean, to whom it should be applied, and to what extent the law could deliver it.

Trials of Islamic Law: Moments of Struggle, Processes of Definition, Civil Rituals

The trials below chart an arc in the emergence of new discourses of Islam and state authority between the late eighteenth and late nineteenth centuries, across our three cases. The first was a trial in the metropole, perhaps the most famous of all, of Warren Hastings and the conduct of colonialism in India. During the course of this trial (1787–1795), law was recast as the core civilizational heritage of India, and law as the path by which the colonial project could be reformed. The second was the 1858 trial of Bahadur Shah, King of Delhi, after the Sepoy War; both events served to emphasize the role of religion—Islam, in particular—as a political incendiary. The third, the 1876 trial of the Perak chiefs accused of conspiring to assassinate the first British Resident in Malaya, helped cement both the newly circumscribed content of "matters of religion and custom" and removed local elites who resisted this interpretation. The fourth and final trial, that of Ahmed 'Urabi, shows that Egyptian elites had by 1882 taken on many of the logics of European law, including the codification of Islamic law and its incorporation into a unified state legal system.

"The law," while it was coming into being as the bedrock of imperial efforts to rationalize, regularize, and order the states they governed, was also a deep wellspring of instability for these states. The trials show how deeply the colonial state had penetrated into the content the reasoning and the personnel of Islamic law, and how imperative the acceptance of British rule was even for those who defied it. But they also put on display the inextricability of British authority from elements of Islamic legitimacy. Even as the trials removed dissenting local elites and institutionalized a cadre of new Islamic legal elites in the employ of the colonial state, state encroachment into matters of Islamic law spurred Muslim production of texts, arguments, and strategies for countering and capitalizing upon colonialism. The trial of Hastings made clear the need for colonial law that unified the control of the state over its subjects, yet the conduct of the trial also emphasized for many the need to maintain discretion and difference within the application of colonial policy. The trials of local elites Bahadur Shah, the Perak chiefs, and Ahmed 'Urabi allowed for the airing of grievances against the colonial state, and also for the publicizing of a nascent language of protest and resistance against colonial rule.

Trials such as these allow access to local rulers in Malaya and India, to British colonial officials and politicians, to ordinary men and women in court rooms, and to judges, witnesses, and local advisors. Trial transcripts contain voices which have otherwise been silenced, edited, or remained unrecorded, and they often allow those voices to speak for themselves in ways that other kinds of colonial records did not. Because they occurred at the center of the colonial state, court trials are at one and the same time a testament to the power of that state and its institutions, and evidence of the lines of struggle which continued to crisscross through state authority and control. And because each moment of struggle sparked new contests and opportunities, trials were often followed by legislation, protest, violence, and changes in administrative and political strategy. This chapter reflects that dialectic in its structure, discussing trials amid the wider repertoires of governance and contestation within which they functioned.

These trials were performances of justice and authority, rich in symbolism and productive of new rituals of power and legitimacy. Michael Fisher (1990) has characterized them as "civil rituals," and shown that both colonial and local elites participated in highly symbolic and elaborate ceremonials, in legal courts and in the courts of local rulers. Both these courts were a venue for contention as well as for performances of authority, reflecting changing political dynamics and reshaping the relationships between local rulers and their new colonial counterparts. They were performances in that they played to a wider audience, in the colonial state and in Britain, sending signals about the relative power of each actor, the wealth and splendor of the state, and the legitimacy of the system.[8]

I. Colonialism on Trial: Warren Hastings and the Need for Law

> (He) declared that the people have no laws, no rights, no usages, no distinctions of rank, no sense of honour, no property—in short, that they are nothing but a herd of slaves, to be governed by the arbitrary will of a master. On the other side, we assert that the direct contrary to this is true . . . we have referred you to the Mohometan law, which is binding upon all, from the crowned head to the meanest subject—a law interwoven with the wisest, the most learned, and most enlightened jurisprudence that perhaps ever existed in the world.[9]

In his final speech at the trial of Warren Hastings, Edmund Burke sought to indict the man as well as the practice of colonialism in India, to put forward a portrait of Indian society and a platform for the reform of British imperialism. The Hastings trial began with an impeachment in 1787 and ended with an acquittal in 1795, quite likely the most extensive and spectacular of British political trials in history. Hastings, who had been instrumental to the establishment of the East India Company in Bengal first as governor and then as British governor general, was accused by prominent British figures, Burke foremost among them, of corruption and tyranny. Burke excoriated the East India Company for its rapaciousness and calculated destruction of India: "There is not a single prince, state or potentate in India with whom they have come into contact that they have not sold. There is not a single treaty they have made which they have not broken."[10]

Even though he was eventually acquitted, Hastings's trial may be read as a trial of the East India Company representing the conduct of British Empire, which prompted closer British governmental control over the Company, as well as heightened efforts at the "reform" of India. A large component of the language of these reforms involved rule of law and a concern with the state as responsible for the delivery of justice, rather than merely as a revenue generator. The trial offered law as the redemptive hope for the future of India and of the British Empire itself. Against a portrait of Hastings and the Company's representatives in India as little more than pirates and privateers, Burke presented a picture of a society whose natural order was reflected in the law of Islam, "a law interwoven with the wisest, the most learned, and most enlightened jurisprudence that perhaps ever existed in the world," an order destroyed by the rapaciousness of the East India Company's rule.

Stephen Browne characterizes Burke's participation in the trial against Hastings as "the staging of public virtue," a performance whose drama included lessons on the proper ordering of society, the defense of valued principles, the protection of trustees and the prosecution of criminals.[11] British virtue, both at home and in India, was cast in Victorian terms as delicate and easily damaged by the actions of a few rapacious men. The Indian nobles themselves were portrayed as trustees whose trusts had been violated, and Hastings the ringleader, committing "monstrous acts" upon the homes of "Mohamedan nobility,"[12] a "vulture" who facilitated the dissolution of their schools and estates, who ignored the rule of law, who debauched noble women and denigrated the fair sex. Hastings's extensive and intimate (perhaps over-intimate, some of Burke's comments suggested) knowledge of local customs and institutions, far from instilling in him a desire to protect and preserve, had been used for the furthering of his own interests.

Not only did the conduct of empire abroad threaten India, however—of critical concern was its effects on Britain itself. The trial itself is believed to have been instigated by widespread public suspicion of the vast wealth being made by British "nabobs" returning from India, and the resulting changes it wrought on elite society and public culture: these new rich were now competitors with the old aristocratic elite for political power. Their incursions into Parliament were raising concern among both Whig and Tories, and their corrupt, Oriental ways were rumored to be infiltrating English society: "What is England now? A sink of Indian wealth, filled by nabobs and emptied by Maccaronis! A senate sold and despised! A country overrun by horse-races! A gaming, robbing, wrangling, railing nation without principles, genius, character, or allies."[13]

The trial of Warren Hastings was, in this respect, a struggle over British elite power and an attempt by elites in the center of empire to maintain control of the political and social structure of Britain, against what they saw as outside contenders. It was also a struggle over British colonial policy; many scholars have seen Burke's campaign against Hastings as having succeeded because although it failed to secure an impeachment, it resulted in enduring changes in the discourse and character of British policy in India and the empire at large.[14] However, these changes were not simply in the line of a kinder, gentler empire; they were also aimed at colonial consolidation—both governmental and ideological.[15]

The trial, therefore, served as a pedagogical exercise, a morality play in which British Parliament could teach Hastings, the Company, the British people, and the world at large about the duties incumbent upon a responsible empire, the need to protect the welfare of British India and its people. Accompanying the moral drama was an object lesson in the laws and systems of India, portrayed as a noble civilization which Hastings had brought to its knees: "In theory, Hastings' prosecution would send a message that the natural laws of imperial justice knew no artificial bounds, and that all of Britain's subjects would be protected by the mobile 'rule of law.'"[16] The underlying lesson was that it was neither colonialism nor Britain that was flawed, but the all-powerful agents of the Company, aided and abetted by "Black Dewans" (native tax officials), who had abused their power and neglected their duties in the pursuit of self-aggrandizement and personal gain. Burke's mission was that the trial would have shown that "it is not the rights of the people which are nothing, but rather the rights of the sovereign which are so. The rights of the people are every thing, as they ought to be in the true and natural order of things."[17]

Before the military expansion of the Company across India in the late eighteenth century, the East India Company's agents came to local rulers as supplicants. Afterward, the presence of British Residents and Company officials in local courts, and the power granted by British military and economic resources, saw a new kind of ceremonial interaction develop.[18] British colonial officials used the titles and wealth gained from local rulers in the colonies and at home, displaying a level of ostentation on the level of "native" nobles, and at great expense.[19] The impeachment trial of Hastings was also a trial of British imperial mores and culture: "By the mid-nineteenth century, and addressing European audiences in India or Britain, the British symbolically contrasted their honest, plain black frock coats with the pretentious glitter of the oriental monarchs they controlled."[20]

The trouble was that a sizeable portion of the British public agreed with Hastings's argument that Burke's principles were laudatory, but the reality was quite different, and that successful policy in India depended upon the ability of its agents to maneuver with discretion[21]: "Burke brought articles of impeachment against Hastings for what everyone knew was business as usual. In Burke's obsessional litany of Hastings's excesses, what was embarrassing was neither Hastings's greed nor his methods so much as his manifest success in making the horrors and the pleasures of empire realisable." [22] Even after it became clear that an impeachment would not be forthcoming, Burke delivered a speech intended for posterity, which could be used by reformers to continue to "enunciate a vision of what empire might be, were it to be based on justice."[23] This new colonialism, buttressed by its credentials for justice and probity, would extend even further into the realms of state and society through the actions of the governors general who followed Hastings, like Cornwallis, who negotiated the Permanent Settlement Act with the zamindars (see chapter 3), altering the structure of property and the hierarchy of justice administration in India and paving the way for the colonial consolidation of Islamic law:

> In the wake of Burke's attack, a colonial bureaucracy was established to monitor the greed with which all Britons went to India from the late eighteenth century on. Burke shifted the balance of power to the state rather than the mercantile elite, and it was under his scrutiny that the colonial state was born. . . . British rule represented its interest in securing steady revenue through a language of improvement predicated on the rule of property and the benevolent intent of a new "postdespotic" state.[24]

For Karuna Mantena (2010), the changes in doctrine and attitude that Burke signaled were followed by a series of waves of ideological change and reaction that dictated both the extent and the spirit of British imperialism. Mantena distinguishes between early and late imperial ideology—whereas the early period saw the need to reform and reconstruct colonies in the image of the metropole, the later imperial period saw a shift away from interventionism:

> Rather than eradicated or aggressively modernized, native social and political forms would now be patronized as they became inserted into the institutional dynamics of imperial power, most notably in the theory and practice of indirect rule in colonial Africa.[25]

In Malaya and in Egypt, regimes of indirect rule such as Mantena posits in colonial Africa did, by the late nineteenth century, rely upon local social and political forms at the same time as they inscribed these societies with the marks of ineradicable cultural difference from the metropole. For the purposes of this project, however, it is important to distinguish between the elites that the British relied upon, and those they eradicated: between native forms that were determined to be incommensurate with colonial rule, and those that found institutional and political support from the colonial state. Further, elements of reform, reconstruction, necessity, and cultural difference remained embedded in legal institutions, doctrines, and practices well after their initial ideological context had changed. Once the colonial state had intervened in native state, society, and law, it was neither able nor willing, in most cases, to actually disengage.

The trial of Warren Hastings revealed that the imperial project, and British colonial government more specifically, embodied two contradictory impulses—unification and diversification. The unifying policies of the state included an insistence on rule of law; on the maintenance of order; on clear agreements over trade, taxation, land ownership, policing—one law, one government, one regime of private property. However, within that unifying policy was a logic which depended upon divisions based upon difference: here, the law worked to distinguish Hindu from Muslim, British from native, men from women, public from private. The law would embody both these impulses in the conduct of empire—in India after Hastings, in Malaya, and in Egypt. The trial of Hastings helped to position law as an instrument not only for the ordering of empire but for its rectification, the delivery of law a key rationale for colonial intervention and the enforcement of law the guarantor of the dignity and protection of its people.

Trial documents reflected not just the complex processes of colonization in the metropole but the contradictory and competitive politics of imperial elites, politics that had implications beyond India. By the 1870s debates in England over the proper conduct of British policy had important repercussions on indirect rule in Malaya as well as the vexing question of Egypt, and these debates built upon the foundations laid by earlier struggles, such as that between Burke and Hastings.[26] The tension between British reluctance to engage in imperial expansionism in India, Egypt, and Malaya, and British commitment to a vision of glorious empire based upon ideals of justice and progress, was not a zero-sum interaction. It produced, for example, the policy which justified the colonization of Egypt in 1882 by a Liberal British government.[27]

In the discussion of trials of local elites in India, Malaya, and Egypt over the period 1858–1882, during which Mantena sees a period of "liberal retrenchment," there was indeed a sustained attempt by British officials to pay more than lip service to the ideals of indirect rule. The most extreme of these examples may be that seditious sovereigns were tried in their own names, brought to justice on their own authority, as it were, instead of by British arms and power. Yet the archive of these trials also reveals conflicts between the extent and reasons for intervention between colonial officials in the colonies and at home, with officers on site far more ready to take drastic steps than their superiors would allow; a continued reliance on the language and ideals of universal justice alongside pragmatism bordering on the cynical; the insertion *and* excision of native social and political forms by both colonialists and native elites. Ideology writ large may indeed have moved on, but in the struggles we see below, old and new ideas combined with current concerns to produce highly ambiguous and ambivalent discourses on empire, authority, and the meaning of Islam for the imperial project.

Local Elites on Trial

The colonial project managed to achieve radical transformations in law and society, including in the area of religion and culture, because it either made accommodations with local elites or removed them. The assertion of new bases of authority for the state was made through their removal in more ways than one—the trials by which these elites were removed were themselves rehearsals of new discourses of authority, and they made possible the insertion of Muslim elites whose political expression would thence have to occur through engagement with the colonial state and the unstated assumption of its authority. The trials we will discuss below mark a progression of ideas and discourses about authority, sovereignty and justice—in India in 1858, Islam was recast as the incendiary core of native Muslim identity, something to be protected and feared; in Malaya in 1876, the definition of religion and custom was denuded of its political and economic content; in Egypt in 1882, British occupation was justified in the name of law and order and the preservation of khedival authority, and proto-nationalist elites had taken on assumptions about the need to reform Islamic law into their programs against colonialism.

Trials of local elites during the early colonial encounter show that Islam and Islamic law were rarely directly mentioned as stakes in the conflict. Instead, both local and British actors dwelt upon local power networks and the proper hierarchy of the new state; on state ceremonial and ritual observances; on taxation, labor, land and military matters; and on the use of force to achieve those aims. In India, Malaya, and Egypt, these trials show that local elites considered the British to have far overstepped their bounds, to have strayed deep into domains local elites considered their own. They also show an insistence on the part of the British on law and justice, albeit justice specially defined. Looking into the history of struggle between local and colonial elites reveals something which is not, from our current vantage point, always clear: Islam and Islamic law were not at the center of either colonial or local elite concerns in India, Malaya, and Egypt at the start of the colonial encounter, but became so. If we look at the process of definition of Islam and Islamic law through eyes conditioned by current global politics, it is possible to forget that there was a time when Islam was neither the only tool in the local arsenal, nor the main prize to be won. However, it is also quite difficult to look at trials of local rulers in Malaya and India, and drama of justice and force which surrounded them, and not see similarities in recent events.

These trials, through their intervention into elite power and hierarchies, helped rearrange the political landscape in such a way as to facilitate radical changes in Muslim life and identity. In their aftermath, local elites who could not navigate the new waters of colonial negotiation—in matters of religion and culture and beyond them—were no longer able to dictate Islamic law or influence Muslim society. Having established the central place for law in the reform of the colonial project, from the mid-nineteenth century on, the politics of law and justice in the colonial state helped define Islam and Islamic law as the core of Muslim sensitivities, determined that Islamic law would be a special preserve for local authority and legitimacy, and that, as such, reform of the state would need to come from outside Islamic sources and systems.

II. Trial of Bahadur Shah II, 1858: Problematizing Islam

By 1858, politics between local and colonial elites had taken on a well-established public pattern: after the signing of treaties, a rebellion against colonial intervention, then a war of retaliation, and the trial of prominent local figures in the aftermath.[28] In India, the trial of Bahadur Shah and the trial of Sultan Abdullah after the Perak War, twenty years after, followed this pattern. As with Perak, the trials became an opportunity to publicly air elite discontent with what they saw as the overstepping of British bounds. For the British, a key issue in the staging of both trials was the problem of trying a sovereign. At issue for both sides was the proper understanding of previous treaties with the British, and the rights and duties of each party—in other words, these trials became a venue for the redrawing of lines between local and colonial sovereignty and the content thereof. Where the Hastings trial centered on the conduct of empire and the redemptive possibilities of law for the imperial project, the trial of Bahadur Shah was a venue for making sense of the Sepoy War. While Burke's indictment of the conduct of Company rule hinged upon his characterization of India as a noble civilization of laws and learning, the lessons drawn from the Sepoy War and the trial of the king of Delhi depended upon the centralization of Islam (and native religion more generally) as a political motivator and the volatile core of the native character.

The primary narrative of the Sepoy War has in fact been that the religious sensibilities of the Sepoys, Hindu and Muslim troops who had become accustomed to high standards of religious and ritual purity in the Indian Army, were violated when their officers ordered them to bite into cartridges greased with beef tallow and pork fat. Both the analysis of British colonial officials and of historiographers have tended to dwell upon religion as the root cause of the Mutiny, and of the war which followed, and this fit with the development of an image of Islam as a religion of fanatics, and of India as a population which needed to be pacified and made rational through British control.

Recent analysis of the events which led to the Sepoy War has shown that while the initial spark may have been provided by the cartridge incident, the wider conflict of the war also had to do with the internal politics of British officers and local soldiers, as well as elite discontent over the usurpation of their lands, titles and power. In Bengal, the coming of British colonial intervention brought about a massive change in the organization and power of Muslim elites. Once rulers of the Mughal Empire, Muslims—who made up a third of Bengal's population—occupied only a small handful of positions in government. Their judicial positions had been abolished, the Islamic laws upon which they relied set aside for British rules, and Persian was abandoned as the court language. These "demotions" to the level of Hindus and native subjects was, for the British, enough to assume Muslim hostility and sensitivity, according to Thomas Metcalf: "Whether firmly grounded or not . . . this anti-Muslim sentiment left its mark upon British policy for several decades."[29] This sentiment seems to have had deeper roots than the Mutiny itself, however, and the administrative and policy reactions of British officials reflected a debate which had been part of British rule in India already: how to appropriately govern a native population, how much autonomy and power to allow individual Indians in government, and what relationship there should be between the governed and the governors.

At the time of the war, this debate took the form of a conflict between those British officials who favored semi-independent presidencies, and the "reformers" who felt that the Company would be better served by unified, centralized rule with firm control over local actors.[30] This debate was conditioned by the racism prevalent among British planters, businessmen and colonial officials, a racism the Company used to rationalize in order to keep Indians out of the higher echelons of government, and which in effect administered a dual government and legal system in which "Europeans" were never to be subjected to Indian authority.[31] After the Mutiny, the opinions of those who had all along argued that the Muslims "have been too much trusted, and must be watched carefully hereafter," prevailed, and those who argued that the revolt had not been a religious one, or a Muslim one, could not prevent the massive retaliation against Muslim communities and institutions which followed.[32]

The British were not the only ones to see, in the turmoil of the early colonial period, a religious conflict. The rise of "foreign" influences and the growing presence of colonial norms and institutions gave rise to a number of responses from a number of quarters. While those who saw accommodation of the new regime a sign of the times were growing in numbers in government and positions of prominence among the elite, other groups based their responses within the language and networks of Islam. Even among these groups, responses to colonialism and change differed. Islam was central to Mughal authority, but under Bahadur Shah, Sufi philosophy and poetry flourished, and the life of the Mughal court was one where Hindu and Muslim influences both played a role. The Sepoys themselves were Hindus and Muslims, with Hindus in the majority: the Mutiny was rallied in part through the language of religious resistance to British/Christian incursion—by both Hindus and Muslims—as a jihad.[33] Once taken on, though, this language began to carry its own weight, and some Muslim groups attempted to turn against even the Hindus.

The 1857 War involved several Muslim factions: Bahadur Shah represented the focus of a faction allied around sultans, the authority of whom relied to an important extent to an Islam conjoined with state power and ruler legitimacy. There were, however, other groups which rejected Bahadur Shah as a focal point, challenging ruler authority as well as British colonialism by an appeal to jihad. The Wahhabis, for example, rejected the authority of Bahadur Shah because of what they read as his heretical tolerance of Hindus and his Sufism; they may also have taken advantage of the weakness of local rulers to make a claim based on a new kind of Islamic legitimacy. The Wahhabis helped fuel the assumptions of British colonial officials that the Sepoy War was a religious war, and after the war was over, their struggle against both British and local rulers continued. There were a series of high-profile trials till the 1870s, accompanied by the assassination of a British judge (Chief Justice John Norman, 1871) and a viceroy (Lord Mayo, 1872).[34]

Bahadur had asserted his claims, as Mughal emperor, to superiority over the governor general, to dictate the succession, and to maintain his claims and rights over the Company. By the time of his reign, the Mughal Empire had by and large been overtaken by its British administrators. Successive governors-general and secretaries of state for the colonies had thwarted these claims: Lord Minto described the British attitude to Mughal kingship "as a complementary recognition of a nominal sovereignty," and Lord Amherst was even more pointed: "Your kingship is but nominal; it is merely out of courtesy that you are addressed as king."[35] When Bahadur insisted on maintaining the same rights and claims as his father before him, the British retaliated with economic sanctions as well as ceremonial ones, discontinuing gifts and removing from him the privilege of awarding honors, of holding durbars and sitting upon the throne.[36] The throne itself was taken to an underground cell until it was "liberated" by the Indians who re-crowned Bahadur the King of Delhi in 1857. The trial was held in the same audience room, the Diwan-i Khas, where Bahadur Shah had stood and been proclaimed king of Delhi.[37]

During the takeover of Delhi by Sepoy troops in 1857, Bahadur Shah was made the figurehead of the revolt, appointed its leader and Emperor of India. He declared his support for the rebellion, his sons were implicated in the siege of Delhi, and he was tried for aiding the mutineers, for treason, and for murder on multiple counts. The prosecutor accused him of engineering the revolt as part of a wider conspiracy on behalf of fanatical Islam: "To Musalman intrigues and Mahommedan conspiracy we may mainly attribute the dreadful calamities of the year 1857 . . . the prisoner, as the head of the Mahomedan faith in India, has been connected with the organization of that conspiracy, either as its leader or its unscrupulous accomplice."[38] Bahadur Shah denied all charges, arguing that he had been a prisoner of the rebels. After a forty-day trial, he was sentenced to transportation, and died four years later in Burma.

The inquiry was meant more to discover the causes of the Mutiny than to convict Bahadur Shah: the commission did not have the authority to deliver a conviction, and whatever the outcome of the trial, Bahadur's life had already been granted. Even though they saw Bahadur Shah's status as a monarch as merely nominal, the British were reluctant to put a monarch on trial. Bahadur Shah was tried for sedition as a "subject and pensioner" of the East India Company in a trial conducted by a military commission under Sir John Lawrence, Chief Commissioner of Punjab. The judge-advocate's address to the court acknowledged that "the scope of the investigation [was] not in any way confined by the observance of technicalities, such as belong to a more formal and regular trial." The prosecution, however, argued that in order that "the verdict, whether one of conviction or acquittal, will have the stamp of authority," a trial must be held. [39] The finding of the trial, therefore, was the determination that the Mutiny was a conspiracy against the British on behalf of Islam.

The logic of colonial control contained an unlikely pairing of tradition and reform—both of which were defined in ways specific to the imperative of the colonial project. Since the Mutiny was defined as a revolt against British interference in the traditionalist tendencies of Indians, especially Indian Muslims, these parts of Indian society and life were to be left alone:

> Above all else the Mutiny brought home to them the strength and tenacity of the traditional institutions of India. . . . It was far safer and more sensible, they [the British] decided, to take Indian society as it was, and to concentrate upon the provision of sound efficient administration.[40]

But the methods and content of this administration were far from unobtrusive, and certainly benefited from the removal of the most troublesome of local elites from their positions of power, in the violent aftermath of the Sepoy War. "Sound efficient administration" was portrayed as a neutral policy choice, even though it involved

> the abandonment of social legislation, the introduction of taluqdari settlement in Oudh, Canning's gentry-magistrate system, the conciliation of the princes, the reform of the Legislative Council. . . . The British wished to buttress the traditional institutions of India, to minimize social change, and to soften the impact of Western rule.[41]

Yet British policies which were aimed to "soften the impact of Western rule" were also strategies which would pacify Indian elites and bring Indian government under firm British control. One outcome of the war and the trial of Bahadur Shah was the sense among British officials that the old system of paternal government in India was no longer sufficient;

what was required was full reform, which would install a unified authoritarian government in Bengal, give sweeping powers to the executive, and wipe the judicial system clean. If anything, the British concluded, the war showed that locals were frustrated by the current system of judicial and governmental procedure, which was slow, corrupt, and decentralized. In this opinion, then, both Indian subjects and British officials seemed to agree: reform was necessary, and it would take the form of a unified state, tight control over local elites and functionaries, and a specifically colonial form of government: "We cannot . . . any longer try to rule Asia on the constitutional principles of Europe." [42]

The Government of India Act of 1858 was a victory for the reformers who wanted authoritarian control over British India, and represented a consolidation of colonial power. The East India Company was removed from its governmental role in India, and this role was passed to the queen, whose representative would be the secretary of state for India, who had wide powers with few checks. This new system of government included the passing of laws (Acts, as opposed to Company Regulations) which were to unify India under a single legal system, beginning with the replacement of Islamic criminal law and procedure (with the Code of Civil Procedure 1859, Code of Criminal Procedure of 1861, and the Evidence Act of 1872). High courts were instituted in all the provincial capitals, and the local administration of justice was taken into the ambit of the increasingly centralized state.[43] At the same time, by the time of the Victoria Proclamation of November 1, 1858, assuming Crown sovereignty over India, religion had been clearly marked as an area requiring special treatment.[44]

"Henceforth, the British in India would always walk in fear . . . now the British stepped back permanently to their neat little compound, fenced and right-angled, of facts and rules."[45] In combination with a new conviction of the centrality of Islam to native concerns and sensitivities and the need for sweeping reforms to the governance of India, the protection of "the Law" took on a specific meaning for British India. The law, as articulated by legal figures such as Henry Maine, while treating groups in Indian society as part of a plural order, also standardized the relationship of this plurality to the central state, "(moving) legal pluralism outward and upward from the diversely constituted periphery toward a more uniform national level."[46] By 1875, the year of the Perak War in Malaya, Anglo-Muhammadan law in India had been replaced with British law in all areas of law except those of the family and some property law.

III. Trial of the Perak Chiefs, 1876: Rationalizing British Justice

> 5.6.1876. Testimony of Pangulu Mat Akib: When the Sultan showed reluctance at approving further delegation of his authority, Birch sent a messenger to say, "Mr Birch directs me to tell you to consider well. If you do not put your chop, you will become simply Abdulla." Birch also considered replacing Abdullah with the deposed Sultan, Ismail, but when Ismail suggested that the Pangkor Treaty be re-negotiated in his favour, Birch replied, "The Pangkor Treaty is just like the Koran, it is impossible to add a line to it, or to take a line from it."[47]

The Pangkor Treaty allowed for a British Resident to be installed in Perak, whose advice the sultan was to seek and follow on all matters except those of religion and custom. The Treaty was signed on January 20, 1874, and by November 2, 1875, the first British Resident in Malaya was dead, from numerous spear wounds inflicted by a group of locals who attacked him while he was bathing in a river in Pasir Salak, Perak. The attack on Birch, and the swift and brutal reprisals by British troops (shipped in by the thousands from India and the Straits Settlements), are together called the Perak War.[48] Soon after the attack, British investigations and eye-witness accounts revealed that the assassins were closely associated with key Malay elites in Perak. The aftermath of the war gave rise to yet another legal conflict—the trial of most of the major figures in the Perak ruling class for conspiracy to murder the British Resident. Correspondence among British officials reveals that they were unsure if the British had the right to prosecute a trial of local rulers.[49] Despite this, extensive testimony was taken and a trial held in order to establish the guilt of a number of Malay chiefs, as well as Sultan Abdullah, in the Birch killing. The demonstration of British justice was seen as vital to the continuance of order and control in Malaya, especially after a demonstration of British force.[50] During the course of these trials, a clearer sense emerged of how both sides perceived their rights and power, and these trials laid the ground for further definition of treaties and terms of agreement between local and colonial elites.[51] The trial made clear what was at stake under the term "religion and custom" for both Malay elites and colonial officials, and to what lengths each party would go to protect their definition of this concept.

Whereas the aftermath of the Sepoy War established the sovereignty of Victoria over India, the Malay States were not direct colonies of the United Kingdom. They were ruled indirectly, as protected states, technically sovereign countries even though their part in the British Empire was clear in London as well as in Malaya. Trial transcripts show that even in the later period of British imperialism, in a state where the policy of indirect rule seemed well understood by its colonial administrators, both regimes of direct and indirect rule operated on the ground. In these conflicts, the seeds of the political valence between rights and race, culture and ethnicity, were being sown, tying elite sovereignty to religion and custom and the legitimacy of the state to the protection of these. As Mahmood Mamdani argues, "indirect rule never entirely displaced direct rule: the two co-existed as two faces of power, direct rule a regime guaranteeing rights to a racialized citizenry and indirect rule a regime enforcing culture on an ethnicized peasantry."[52]

The trial of the Sultan of Perak indicates that the importance of maintaining both the image and practice of British justice often led to tensions at all levels of the colonial project. A stated mission of the colonial government was to bring British methods of government and practices of civilization to native states under British protection; however, maintaining ruler control over religion and custom was a pillar of the policy of indirect rule and seen as representing British imperial regard for rule of law: "The contradiction inherent in these aims, the one impossible of realization in terms of existing Malay institutions and the other dedicated to their preservation, led to a fundamental dichotomy in British policy seen at every turn in Malaya's colonial history." [53]

These fundamental dichotomies arose as key questions in the trial—in struggles over the proper definition of local sovereignty, over whether slavery was an issue of public morals, business or local custom, over the proper bases of state authority, over the manner in which law should be enforced and interpreted. Hastings's deployment of the Islamic concept of *siyasa* and Birch's assertion of the equivalence of the Pangkor Treaty with the Qur'an may be read at one glance as facile attempts to translate foreign intervention into a more acceptable local idiom. However, the statement that "the Pangkor Treaty is just like the Koran, it is impossible to add a line to it, or to take a line from it" exemplified the heart of the conflict at the trial—where the British proposed the extension of legal order, the chiefs saw usurpation of sovereignty; where the British claimed preservation of local religion and custom, the ruler saw radical diminution of both; what for the British was a trial of sedition and treason against the state, the Malay chiefs saw as the legitimate removal of an arrogant interloper.[54]

While the treaties between the British government and the sultans concentrated Malay elite power in the specific domain of religion and custom, this domain was not what the sultans themselves considered their natural and proper jurisdiction, nor did they agree upon what the terms religion and culture encompassed. Within months of the Pangkor Treaty, major legal conflicts between local Malay and British colonial elites occurred over issues outside the British definition of religion and custom—taxation and slavery/debt bondage—which were at the core of local elite power, and critical to the functioning of their households and their patronage systems. For example, the elimination of slavery as an issue of justice came before the maintenance of Malay rulers' prerogatives over religion and custom, just as the British judicial principle of repugnancy allowed British judges working in Malaya to disregard any local legal practices they found to be contrary to the values of British justice, subjecting even matters of religion and custom to the forms and language of Crown law. The nature of the relationship between the Malay sovereigns and Britain was the subject of a number of trials in the late 1800s. British businessmen were eager for Britain to assert authority over the Malay States, for trading advantage, but also for the enforcement of English law in matters of contract and business transactions more generally. This was something the British courts tended to refuse to do, regardless of economic pressure or colonial policy.[55]

The political objectives of the inquiry were clear, but even so, the character of the investigation and the care with which the evidence was arranged before Parliament and the Colonial Office indicate that the trial of Sultan Abdullah and the Malay chiefs was being conducted in at least a pseudo-judicial manner. Even after the British were convinced of the sultan's complicity in the killing, in fact, they continued to hold the trials of the conspirators under his name.[56] Jervois's opinions on the matter were plainly stated, but he was at pains to show that the proper forms of judicial inquiry were observed:

> It had to be considered whether, after having summoned Abdullah to Singapore, in order that he might give an explanation of the charges against him; after having furnished him with a written statement of charges; after retaining counsel for him, and after receiving his reply, the inquiry should be conducted before the Council as before a legal tribunal, viz., to allow Abdullah to appear before that body by counsel; to take the evidence before him afresh; to call and examine witnesses for his defence, and then decide whether he should be re-

tained or dismissed from the Sultanship, upon the question whether the charges against him were, or were not, susceptible of legal proof.[57]

The war, and the trials which followed it, had a number of effects on British perceptions of the colonial project in the Malay States: keeping local elites content became a major part of the Resident's job description, but at the same time British policy would also become more interventionist in local affairs because of how clearly the Birch killing illustrated that local affairs, and titulary rulers, were under the control of local chiefs. Correspondence between London, Singapore, and the Malay States indicates that the space of colonial policy was a flexible one, at least from the viewpoint of the Colonial Office: in times of crisis, the autonomous Malay States came under the supervision of the Straits Settlements, a colony. In times of peace, indirect rule was still the policy, although this was not always to the liking of British officials and businessmen on the ground, who used their opportunities in times of crisis to expand British power over the local sphere. Both the Colonial and India Offices would protest too late, and at times too much, over the use of violence and the extension of British power, all the while legitimizing imperial influence and rearticulating British policy.

First a commission was appointed, consisting of three British colonial officials ("Mr Justice Phillippo, the Hon. C.B. Plunket, and Mr Paul") who examined witnesses and established a strong prima facie case for the complicity of most of the Malay chiefs and Sultan Abdullah in the killing of Birch. Mr Plunket then was left to conduct further examinations and lay the evidence before the Executive Council in the Straits Settlements.[58] The transcripts of the evidence taken by the commission are themselves valuable for what they reveal about the chiefs' views on British intervention, their own positions in the state, and their understanding of the avenues open for their response.[59] At first, the British assumed that Abdullah, who had become sultan as a result of their intervention, was ignorant of the plot to kill Birch, and so the initial investigation and appointment of judges was done under Abdullah's name.[60] It turns out, however, that Abdullah was still deeply embedded in the power structures which preexisted British intervention, and that even he who stood to benefit most from the British system wished to overthrow it. The chiefs and sultan met on several occasions, and made a compact to dispose of Birch in a number of ways: by supernatural intervention (*bermain hantu*), by poisoning, and by attack.

The trial transcripts show that even after the Pangkor Treaty, the chiefs continued to perform consultative functions with the sultan, and that he continued to see himself as first among equals. At every step, the chiefs and sultan discussed how to handle the British, shared intelligence, and perceptions of British actions, and made plans for taking action against Birch. Some chiefs made their own determinations as to which treaties and agreements they would follow, not ceding this authority to the new sultan:

> Maharaja Lela came to see the Sultan, and the Sultan told him, "I have given Mr Birch full powers to govern the country in my name and all you Datos (chiefs) must obey his orders." Maharaja Lela responded, "the other datos may obey Mr Birch's orders if they like, but I never will. I will follow the agreement we formerly made, and I will not allow Mr Birch to put his foot on my grounds."[61]
>
> Documents submitted as evidence at the trials of the chiefs also indicate keen understanding of British officials among some local actors and of the hierarchy of relationships they held with each other. The chiefs prepared a list of potential questions and their answers in the event that one of them would be arrested under suspicion of the crime: "Draft catechism drawn up by the Mantri, and found in Raja Yahya's possession."[62]
>
> Q: If the Governor asks you why do you (Tuan Rajah) not follow the Treaty of Pulo Pangkor made by Sir Andrew Clarke?
>
> A: We know nothing about it.
>
> Q: How is it that you do now know about it?
>
> A: We said that we do not know about it, because we thought the Governor was a sensible man, and clever, and if he intended to do anything to a stranger's place, of course he would ask the Master of the place first, and consults (*sic*) and examine privately the stranger's place, and then he will do it, in order that what he does may not seem foolish. The Malay custom is that every country has its king. . . . If you want to help us, you may assist to make our kingdom perfect and turn out whoever denies our authority.
>
> Q: Who denies your authority?
>
> A: You know better than we do who denies us.

The chiefs and the sultan saw Birch's actions as being tantamount to "taking over the country for the Queen," and used the language of the Pangkor Treaty to keep Birch in a consultative function.[63] Contrary to their understanding of the treaty, he prevented them from collecting the taxes they saw as their due for governing and protecting the country, he attempted to pressure the sultan into giving up more and more power, he encouraged slaves and especially the women of the chiefs' households to escape and would not return them if they sought shelter with him, he gave them away in marriage without consulting the chiefs, and he was rumored to have relationships with one or more of these women.[64] The sultan's assessment of Birch's attitude was borne out by reports sent by Birch himself to the Colonial Office: "It really concerns us little what were the old customs of the country, nor do I consider they are worthy of any consideration in dealing with the present taxation of the country."[65]

Finally, the accounts of the killing itself show that the Malay public may not have been particularly receptive to the new British laws either. The riverine state of Perak was ruled by chiefs in a clientage system, and when Birch came upriver to deliver the news that a new law was now in place, he was met with a number of responses. As he attempted to nail the new laws and proclamations to trees along the trade routes, people tore them down, and said they had not heard of the new sultan: "We don't understand this, we only know the Malay law and custom."[66] This said, the Malay accounts of the killing also show a population whose lives were ruled by powerful chiefs who considered their own word to be law, and who did not see the coming of the British to have wrought a change in that. Another person told Birch's men they had orders from the Maharaja Lela to kill anyone trying to put up the new laws. Se Putum, who was arrested and charged for the murder of Birch, said in his last testimony: "I have nothing more to say about this except to complain of the big men of Perak who led me to this. I am a poor man and they arrested me, and let the big men off."[67]

Indeed, both Malay elite and British colonial treatment of the sultan indicate that Se Putum was right, to a certain extent: different kinds of justice were meted out to different classes of people. Three of the conspirators, themselves elites, were hanged, and a further number exiled. Whether the sultan's trial was to be a judicial trial or not was itself a matter of doubt among British officials. Jervois commented that, at that point,

> it is sufficient, in order to deal with such a case politically, that all the parties dealing with it should be able to justify themselves in their own consciences, and if necessary to the world at large, on the ground that the evidence was so strong and so supported by documentary testimony that it appeared conclusively, that whether a conviction could or could not be obtained from a judicial tribunal, yet that abundant evidence would remain to justify the Government

> in removing the Sultan from Perak, and in taking such other steps as might be necessary to prevent his being an obstacle to the peace of that state.[68]

Trial documents and the correspondence among colonial officials after the trial show that the Executive Council which appointed the Commission of Inquiry, and the Colonial Office itself, took it as their jurisdiction to discover whether Birch himself had provoked the chiefs' actions. Both Birch and the policies of the British Residency in Malaya were being evaluated alongside claims of guilt and innocence in the killing, and the Executive Council did in fact find that Birch had provoked the attack against him. The report to London argued on his behalf: "This provocation was to a great extent caused by his zeal in carrying out proposed reforms and by his feelings of humanity in the protection of slave women and, on the other hand, he was greatly provoked by the impracticability of the Sultan; he was constantly thwarted by the Sultan and his Chiefs, and thus placed in a position of considerable difficulty from the commencement."[69]In other words, the attack and the war were cast as the unfortunate result of the overzealousness of one colonial official faced with a particularly recalcitrant local cabal—not the outcome of lasting contradictions within colonial policy and its conduct on the ground.

The history of struggle and accommodation between Malay rulers and British colonizers during this period is full of episodes in which the Malay rulers relied upon their ceremonial forms to avoid compliance with British demands, then capitulated under British military force. New power configurations and players brought about by colonial treaties and alliances resulted in ruptures in this symbolic discourse, whose order often required the use or threat of violence in order to restore. This rupture of ceremony was often followed by a different ceremonial performance, with some Malay rulers attending, often with drawn British arms behind them.[70] After the Perak War, both sides carried with them the memory and the threat of violence into negotiations, leading a British official to comment, "By the action which his [Birch's] death made necessary, the State of Perak gained in twelve months what ten years of "advice" could hardly have accomplished."[71] By October 1876, almost all the major Malay figures in Perak, including the sultan, had been replaced, paving the way for new relationships between elites in the state. Religion and custom would henceforth be understood to exclude matters of slavery, taxation, finance, and public administration, and was increasingly administered as the law of marriage and divorce, as the next trial demonstrates.

IV. Trial of Ahmed 'Urabi, 1882: Resistance and Incorporation

The 'Urabi revolt has been read as a proto-nationalist uprising against the European and elite Turco-Circassian rulers of Egypt, represented by the khedive. In Egypt, nationalism and anticolonialism took expression not only through revolt but through multiple kinds of administrative and organizational changes meant to forestall Ottoman and then European intervention without opposing it outright. Yet, often, attempts to keep these imperial powers out of the governing of Egypt meant taking on reforms that resembled those of the imperial center. The trial of Ahmed 'Urabi provides insight into the dangers of multiple sovereignties over Egypt; both the trial and the strategies of Egyptian elites in its aftermath show that resisting imperial intervention could also involve taking on imperial logics. Ahmed 'Urabi, graduate of al-Azhar, former military officer and minister of war, was tried for treason against the khedive of Egypt. The formal British occupation of Egypt in 1882 occurred in the aftermath of the revolt of 1881–1882 and at the invitation of the khedive, "but if England was to assume control of Egypt, " 'Urabi and his followers had first to be dealt with." This too meant a trial, which came under the jurisdiction of an Egyptian court; as with the Malay and Indian elites, "it was perhaps not just the man but his example that needed to be disposed of."[72] What this example consisted of represents a departure from the Malay and Indian cases, and an illustration of how far changes in aspirations for the law had come.

The 'Urabi trial itself, in December 1882, gave no opportunity for a public airing of grievance nor for debate, unlike earlier trials in India and Malaya—firstly, 'Urabi did not have the status of a sovereign, and was being tried by court martial in the name of the Ottoman Empire and the khedive of Egypt; secondly, Britain did not have formal status in Egypt and could not afford the political risk that a long trial would incur. By arrangement with the British, 'Urabi pled guilty, was sentenced to death, and had his death sentence commuted to exile in Ceylon.[73] While the trial itself was brief and uncontested, it provided the occasion for a controversy both in England and Egypt about the justification for the revolt, and by implication the justifications for the British occupation of Egypt. Whereas the British government and the Egyptian court (comprised of Khedive Tawfiq and Cabinet members) which tried 'Urabi saw him as a mutineer, Blunt and 'Urabi's supporters saw his struggle as one which sought to unify Egypt under the slogan "Egypt for Egyptians," and which also sought to limit European intervention and presence in Egypt.[74]

Cole (1999) argues that the 'Urabi revolt was not an elite-led uprising, but a wider social movement which was cut short by British force. By the 1880s, Europeans were playing visible and decisive roles in the Egyptian courts, bureaucracy, finance, and politics; the Ottomans and Circassians held the reins of power; the "intermediate strata," for whom the identity of "Egyptian" had taken on increasing political salience, saw these two groups as the critical obstacle to be overcome: "Policies that might once have simply elicited popular hatred of the viceroy now conjured up anti-European protestors."[75]

Wilfred Scawen Blunt, the British poet, one-time diplomat, and political writer, opposed what he characterized as the British government's attempt (led by Lord Cromer) to criminalize Ahmed 'Urabi, and arranged a British defense team for him. This team, fearing the partiality of the khedival Commission of Inquiry, pled his case in the court of British public opinion as well, in language that affirmed the paternalism of empire but appealed also to its sense of honor. In a letter to the *Times*, 'Urabi's defense counsel argued that the charge of treason could not stand:

> A feeling seems to have somehow or other arisen in England that the rebellion itself admits of no denial, and that the only difficulty is the ultimate disposal of the persons of its leaders. We regret that our duty does not allow us to hasten the very necessary settlement of Egypt by accepting this conclusion. The prisoners deny there has been any rebellion in its legal sense. They say, and will prove if time is allowed them, that the Sublime Porte from first to last approved their action . . . we chiefly rely on our proofs that Arabi, rightly or wrongly, really headed a National movement, that he received the moral and material support of nearly the whole of Egypt, and that he was only deserted when he failed to secure success. These facts we feel sure of establishing . . . we submit it is quite as important for those with whom the responsibility for the future of Egypt mainly rests to know the whole truth as to recent events as to hurry over a merely formal trial simply because Arabi Pacha blocks the way.[76]

Colvin, the chief European financial advisor to the khedive, while sympathizing with the "liberal" elements in Egypt argued that the problem was 'Urabi's insistence on reclaiming financial control by Egyptians: "The European interests engaged in Egypt were far too various and important to permit of the engagements contracted by the Khedive being placed at the mercy of Egyptian soldiery or of an inexperienced native administration."[77]

British arguments supporting the occupation and control of Egypt based on these arguments also cast "'Urabi himself as an 'illiterate fanatic' incapable of absorbing Western discipline."[78] This characterization lent credence to Lord Cromer's view that Islam itself was part of the problem in Egypt:

> If a religious belief cannot adapt itself to the requirements which are constantly cropping up as the world grows older, one of two things will probably happen. Either society advances and the religious belief is stranded and eventually forgotten, or the creed holds society in its grip and bars the way to advancement. It is the proud boast of the Christian religion, and more especially of the Protestant version of that religion, that it is not obliged to choose between either of these alternatives. It possesses sufficient elasticity to adapt itself to modern requirements.[79]

'Urabi himself, having pled guilty before the court martial, argued a different case to his audience in the *Times*:

> I know that my future treatment will depend on England and the generosity of the British people, I leave Egypt with perfect tranquility and confidence in the future, because I know that England cannot any longer delay the reforms which we have struggled for. In a short time the Anglo-French control will be abolished; Egypt will be no more in the hands of a myriad of foreign employees filling every available post, to the exclusion of the Egyptians; our native courts will be purified of abuses; codes of law will be enacted, and, which is more important, carried out; a Chamber of Notables will be instituted with a voice and a right of interference in the affairs of the Egyptian people; the swarm of usurers in the village will be driven out. The English people, when they see all these things, will then be able to realize the fact that my rebellion had a very strong justification.[80]

'Urabi's list describes an ideal state quite different from those imagined by Muslim elites even a generation earlier, a state defined by the its ability to represent a nation and its people, legitimized by the delivery of law, "codes of law" the guarantor of the purity and effectiveness of the courts. 'Urabi's arguments as to the validity of his claims against the khedive contained reference to Islamic law, the *ulama* and to classical Islamic concepts of just rule, but the state he and many Egyptians were fighting for by the end of the nineteenth century was a state based on codified law.

The ongoing effort to maintain Egyptian independence from the Ottoman central state as well as from encroaching European powers played a critical role in the direction of legal change in Egypt from the 1870s on. Ottoman efforts to adapt Islamic law to European positivist models resulted in the Mecelle, applied as an Islamic civil code in lands under direct Ottoman rule. Muhammad Qadri Pasha, Egypt's minister of justice, drafted a similar code for Egypt but was stalled by those who argued that legal change along European lines would be better suited to the project of Egyptian autonomy—both from the Ottomans and the Europeans. The aftermath of the revolt and the British occupation for the shape and content of Islamic law was to persuade Egyptian governing elites of the administrative and political wisdom of adopting codes based on French models. The promulgation of a civil code in the French model in 1882 was aimed at halting the incursion of British officials into Egyptian administration at the same time that it made the formal incorporation of Egypt into the British Empire seem less likely. It also was a step toward the equalization of Egyptians and Europeans before the law, since this code meant that both populations (in the Mixed and Native Courts) would be governed by the same bodies of law.[81]

In India in the late eighteenth century, the performance of British justice included the centralization of Islam as a problem of governance: religion was essential to the native character, and any interference in religion an incendiary to native revolt. In Malaya by the late nineteenth century, British efforts to extend imperial control sought a solution to this problem through a keen sensitivity to the need to keep religion and custom apart from matters of colonial government, a concern local elites were quick to capitalize upon. Yet at around the same time in Egypt, "the adoption of 'secular' legal codes in the 1880s made clear that changes in Egyptian society had loosened the grip of classical Islamic legal theory on the hearts and minds of Egyptians, particularly those in the elite."[82] When, as we will discuss at length in chapter 5, Islamic elites sought to find a way to strengthen Islamic law as an institution, they did so through the vehicle of codification.[83]

In Egypt, Malaya, and India, local elites who rejected the bases of British authority were removed from the political scene by a combination of force and judicial process. Their trials reflect the attempt to redefine authority in the new colonial state and a rejection of independent bases of local authority, be they royal sovereignty, witchcraft, popular representation, or chiefly collaboration. In Malaya, decisions were no longer to be made by a conclave of chiefs whose reliance upon local networks was buttressed by the ceremonial, symbolic, and supernatural instruments of rule: seals of office (chops), regalia, magic. In India, titular monarchs were stripped of the ceremonials of their status and brought firmly into line with the new unified structures of the British Raj. In Egypt, the start of British occupation was accompanied by the trial and exile of a nationalist icon. In all of our cases, the language and semiotics of the colonial state relied heavily upon rule of law, upon administrative imperatives, and upon colonial aspirations for control.[84]

In this new regime, areas of law which local elites had reserved for themselves—like slavery and taxation, as well as religion and culture—were no longer sacrosanct. Violent and extraordinary suppression of civil rebellion brought to the forefront the imbalance of military power in favor of the British, and in doing so made opposition over the content of treaties much riskier for the elites who remained. However, the high cost of such suppression, in both material terms as well as in terms of political opinion in both colony and metropole, made British officials, especially in the Colonial and India Offices, more sensitive to the need to keep these newly pacified elites compliant. Therefore, the ceremonials, titles, and pensions continued; their importance and their expense caused many complaints among British administrators, and any attempt to reduce them raised local elite protest to such an extent that they were often quietly reinstated. The image of local rulers, diminished in power but insistent on their ceremonial dignity and their wealth, served to bolster the colonial state's belief in its own legitimacy and incorruptibility, but also undermined the project of indirect rule among its subjects.

In the absence of a clear locus of local power, a more popular politics began to emerge; the publicity of British trials often excited public debate about justice and imperial power. For example, the trial of Bahadur Shah and of the Wahhabi leaders for separate attacks against the British in the 1860s and 1870s provoked a debate among Muslims in India—in the press and the mosques—about where their first loyalties should lie. Ordinary Muslims, who had already experienced the harsh military backlash against the Mutiny, saw these trials and their verdicts as further victimizations of Muslims by an increasingly evangelical Christian colonial power. Muftis met in Calcutta and Delhi to discuss the matter of rebellion, and came to different conclusions: in Calcutta, British India was seen as *Dar al-Islam* (domain of Islam), within which rebellion was not permitted by Islamic principles. In Delhi, the jurists felt differently: British India was not part of the domain of Islam, but nevertheless outright rebellion could not be advocated.[85]

In Egypt, the 'Urabi revolt of 1881–82 held some parallels with that of the Sepoy Mutiny—discontent within the ranks of native soldiers, the sense of a religious contest between Islam and the encroachment of Christianity—and had some similar effects: the consolidation of British rule in the aftermath of violent conflict and occupation, and the further colonization of local life and institutions. For some observers in England, the 'Urabi revolt spelled even more for the future of Egypt:

> Cairo has now declared itself as the home of progressive thought in Islam, and its university as the once more independent seat of Arabian theology. Secured from Turkish interference by the national movement of the Arabs, the Ulema of the Azhar have joined heart and soul with the party of reform. The importance of this event can hardly be overrated; and if, as now seems probable, a liberal Mohammedan Government by a free Mohammedan people should establish itself firmly on the Nile, it is beyond question that the basis of a social and political Reformation for all Islam has been laid.[86]

Both the Sepoy Mutiny and the 'Urabi revolt continue to be remembered in India and Egypt as nationalist and anticolonial movements. These debates were being followed in Malaya as well as in other parts of the Muslim world, all of which were formulating responses to the encroachment of colonial power within their states. These discussions yielded a rich vein of resources for the articulation of Islamic law and the role of Muslim judges, jurists, and elites in the new colonial state.

The trials we have discussed above mark particular processes in the transformation of the relationship between law, Islam, and the state during the colonial period. The trial of Warren Hastings failed to secure an impeachment, but succeeded in articulating a new vision of imperialism, a vision in which law would play a critical, purifying, and emancipatory role in India and in the British Empire. Moving away from trials in the metropole to those in the colonies, the trials of leading elites in India, Malaya, and Egypt functioned to underscore the importance of law and justice in the self-perception of British governance in the colonies, while at the same time serving as a mechanism for removing troublesome and uncooperative elites and clearing the way for new hierarchies of rule. The civil rituals of these trials show a complex interplay of multiple claims to justice and order, playing to many audiences, representing changes in the meaning of Islam; its place in the state; the role of Muslim elites; the rights of the governing power; and the manner in which interpretive control over matters of religion, custom, and local practice would be controlled.

Redefining Islamic Law: Inclusions, Exclusions

Textualization, codification, and the rigidification of the interpretive framework of shari'i jurisprudence had many implications for state power, for Islamic institutions, and for the shape and function of law, but these interlocking changes also carried with them substantive transformations for the lives of ordinary Muslims. In India, Egypt, and Malaya, a move away from local customary practices toward standardizations along the lines of one jurisprudential tradition often led to the favoring of a more patriarchal set of interpretations of the laws of marriage, inheritance, divorce, and child custody. Allied with European understandings of the nuclear family and the place of women in marriage and public life, the courts and the codes of colonial India, Malaya, and Egypt tended to work against the interests of Muslim women in new ways.

Centering and Engendering Family Law

If the shari'a is seen to have survived anywhere in the modern state, it is in the area of family law, and in this area, both colonial administrators and the postcolonial governments that succeeded them are widely understood to have left Islamic family law intact. Yet the process by which disparate practices governing matters of marriage, divorce, inheritance, and child custody became the core of Islamic family law in the modern Muslim state was itself part of the politics of Islamic law, in which ideologies of British protection and liberalism combined with the patriarchal ideals of both elite Muslims and Victorians to produce a new legal structure and logic. This logic was comprised of three powerful streams of thought: the first was that the role of British law in the colonies was to deliver a new standard of humanitarianism and protection to the weak in native society, women and girls in particular. The second stream of thought was Victorian patriarchy, whose ideals applied broadly to the imperial project itself, casting England in the role of protector over the colonized, and more specifically to the projection of Victorian ideas of gender, family, and public sphere onto native societies. In combination with the third stream of thought, elite Muslim patriarchal ideals, these allowed for the construction of a private sphere that served as the proper locus for women, at one and the same time a key target of colonial improvements through law and a sanctified domain needing to be preserved according to local sensitivities.

While the stated policy throughout much of the colonial period was noninterference in matters of religion and culture, the core of which were assumed to be matters relating to the family and women, laws regulating marriage and divorce were routinely passed by the early colonial state, requiring registration of marriages and divorces, dictating the age of marriage, punishing adultery, regulating polygamy, and laying out rules for husbands, wives and children.[87] These were often provoked by high-profile cases and trials (for example, the Rukhmabai case in Bombay in the 1880s and the Phulmoni case in 1890 in Bengal, both on the subject of child marriage).[88] In Egypt, the codification of family law also involved the selection, by Muhammad Qadri Pasha, of particular doctrines and opinions within the Hanafi school that often worked against the interests of women litigants in matters such as the right to contract marriage on her own behalf.[89]

In the courts, these streams of thought often met with the tactics of litigants, many of whom were women, to produce a variety of results. Some judges argued that British law was inapplicable to the adjudication of marriage, divorce, and inheritance because these belonged to the domain of the private and the local. In the 1867 Malayan case of Chulas and Kachee v. Kolson bte Seydoo Malim, the court argued that "the general principles of English law cannot be applied to locals who have their own distinct social and religious institutions. The application of these principles will result in injustice and cruelty."[90] The inapplicability of common law then required a decision as to what law should apply in each case, and required the interpretation of shari'a jurisprudence and its incompatibility with common law by British judges. In 1869, the question arose in the Malacca courts as to whether a married Muslim woman had the ability to undertake a contract. The court decided that the basis of the decision must be the law which governed her marriage contract—Islamic law—the judge commented that under common law, man and wife were considered one person, whereas under Islamic law they were separate legal persons, so a married woman's property did not come under the jurisdiction of her husband.[91]

The freedom of British judges to interpret justice and equity for themselves according to Victorian principles, though, meant that such instances were rare, and that even where Islamic law or local matrilineal customs allowed more equitable treatment of women, British judges would limit the application of these rules. In Malaya, for example, Malay customary practice (*adat*) which was more equitable to women, such as the concept of *harta sepencarian* (joint marital property), allowed a wife to claim a portion of property gained during the course of a marriage, even if it was earned by the husband. A 1907 Perak ruling limited *harta sepencarian* to divorce proceedings, meaning that the concept could not benefit women except in a divorce.

Women who appealed to the British courts had to contend with both the potential for advantage in a new jurisdiction, and the likelihood that British judges would choose to adjudicate based upon Victorian assumptions about marriage, women, and local practice. Indian patriarchy was admired in some circles, precisely because of the high profile of feminist activities in England. Leila Ahmed has commented on the reverse phenomenon in Egypt, where feminism among British politicians appeared to be fueled by expediency and internal political motives more than ideological commitment. Ahmed points out that Lord Cromer, a vehement proponent of gender reform in Egypt, was also a leading figure in the fight against women's suffrage in England.[92]

Even the patriarchy of the court could work in the interests of a strategic litigant, though: in the 1777 Bahadur Beg case with which we began, for example, "the Patna widow mirrored the actions of many other Indians who discovered in the fragmented and complex architecture of colonial rule an opportunity to defeat local representatives of rule by appealing to more distant authorities."[93] British legal officers at Patna complained that the widow Naderah Begum had manipulated public opinion and court proceedings to appear much more pitiable than she really was; at the same time they could not quite bring themselves to believe such a disadvantaged person as a Muslim woman in India would have the capacity to manipulate a British bench[94]:

> The Women of this Country and particularly the Musulman Women, are, from their confined Situation, bred up in too much Ignorance and Subjection to be capable of Judging or acting for themselves: they become in consequence merely Tools in the hands of their Vaqueels, and neither fare better or worse, which ever Side Succeeds in the Contest. On this account there seems much reason in the Customs of their being required to live under the Protection of the next Male Heir.[95]

The language of "protection" was a recurrent component of the pattern of British intervention in the area of women and gender, areas generally considered to have been part of the realm of local elite autonomy. But the imperative of the colonial government to "protect" allowed incursions into that territory, although not always in the direction of more liberal policy. In fact, the colonial state more often than not took conservative and patriarchal positions in law and policy, despite a rhetoric of progressivism. In India, for example, the 1891 Age of Consent Bill was pushed forward by reformists to change the legal age of consummation of marriage from eight to twelve. In balancing the weight of political opinion between the feminists, reformists, and missionaries on the one hand and religious traditionalist elites on the other, the colonial government was far more concerned that the bill not raise the hackles of religious groups, and so limited the scope of the legislation's implementation while it established a further foothold into the realm of family law.[96] Here, colonial control tended in fact to limit the extent of reforms: in comparison to states such as Bengal, which were under direct British rule, the Indian princely states—subject to the same reformist pressures but not the same British control—generally took more progressive stances in legislation on issues such as gender, women, and family law. While Bengal could only change the age of legal consummation, and then limit its application in 1891, the Infant Marriage Prevention Regulation in the princely state of Mysore (1893) made child marriages themselves (not just their consummation) illegal.[97]

Often, the colonial state and existing local (elite and patriarchal) institutions worked together to govern women and the family: "Women became subject to dual authority structures: their everyday lives continued to be subject to the social power of the community, while property-related disputes made them subjects of the state. An interlocking structure came into place, with both sets of laws upholding male-dominant family forms."[98] As local and colonial elites negotiated family law, upper-class norms and institutions came to govern all Muslims. Through laws on the family, local and colonial elites also governed land and inheritance, labor and peasant/working-class relations[99]: "The colonial state in fact helped constitute the private domain that Indian nationalists later cherished as free from colonial interference. It was precisely during the colonial period that a clear demarcation between a public and private sphere was achieved by the colonial state."[100]

Exclusions from Islamic Law

Having equated the family with private law and made it a special protected domain for Islamic law, further distinctions were made during the colonial period to assign Islamic law to the domain of private law. What did exclusion from Islamic law entail? Given that the initial mandate to govern was narrow and hemmed in by claims to the sovereignty of native rulers, the areas that could clearly be excluded were few; when intervention was to be rationalized, it was done so on grounds that the matter at hand was so morally urgent as to require the contravention of established practice. Otherwise, the extension of British legality proceeded along multiple sidelines: through the rearrangement of hierarchies of doctrine and adjudication, through the gradual replacement of Muslim legal personnel with texts whose interpretation was left to British judges, through legislation where Islamic law was understood to be silent, through the expansion of the category of custom and the identification of populations to be considered exempt from Islamic law. The fundamental achievement of these exclusions was to articulate a divide between the public and administrative law of the state and the private and particular law of Islam; this was rationalized through an increasingly powerful image of Islamic law as ossified in its functions, limited in its scope, and unable to cope with the demands of the new state.

Firstly, the most important changes occurred less at the level of legislation than at the level of adjudication and personnel: the gradual replacement of Islamic legal elites with codes and texts should be seen in this light: not only the need to regularize and codify the law, but the need to remove an entire powerful class of Muslim elites from the business of adjudication, of politics, and of court ritual. When the British arrived in India, the dominant language of court and civil ceremonial was that of the Mughal Empire. India's regional courts each had their own "expressive sacred and political traditions . . . which identified and linked it with the people of the region it ruled . . . (and) further signified its relationship to its particular sources of authority."[101] The British adopted some of these rituals and symbols in order to signal their connections to the Mughal court and its legitimacy, and in doing so relied in large part upon the same corps of local elites as the Mughals—*munshis*, "ritual specialists retained by its Ruler and drawn from the Islamicized service elite that dominated the administrative and diplomatic world of India for centuries before the intrusion of the British."[102] The British in Malaya also relied on munshis as translators, scribes, guides, and informants, and these Muslim interlocutors were important local actors in their own right.

Symbol and ceremonial were part of the compact between local and colonial elites, and the civil rituals of the state were important components of local elite maintenance of their authority and stature, and therefore important components of British influence over local rulers. Both local and British public support depended upon a balance between colonial control and local authority, but the appearance of local sovereignty had to be preserved in order for indirect rule to conform to British ideals. Among the most powerful of these appearances were the symbols and performances of ruler authority, in which both the Company and the ruler invested. Rites and symbols of rule became increasingly important under indirect rule precisely because they occupied the intersection of what the British imagined local sovereignty and authority to be, what local elites could control and define, and what colonial publics could openly demand: "Beyond this, many of the Indian Rulers were able to use their court rituals as a political device in order indirectly to control their Residents."[103]

Secondly, another principle of law which allowed the gradual increase of English legal content in the legal systems of India, Egypt, and Malaya was the sense that Islamic law simply did not cover all eventualities, and where the Qur'an and classical texts were silent, English law or British judgment could fill in the blanks. The reliance on textual forms of law and the rise in codification of Islamic law, as well as the concomitant reduction in Islamic legal interlocutors working in the courts who could interpret new cases in light of Islamic legal principles, or using shari'a jurisprudential techniques, contributed further to the sense that Islamic law was a finite and fixed resource. Such was the understanding of Judge Benjamin Malkin, who decided as early as 1835 in Penang (in the Straits Settlements, from which large bodies of precedent were taken for law in the Malay States) that the laws of England had been introduced to Penang by the 1807 Charter. Therefore, the English law of estates allowed a Muslim to distribute all his or her property in a will, regardless of the fact that Islamic law forbad such a will. This judgment had much to do with the territorial status of Penang as a Crown Colony, which the Malay States were not, but it also reveals an assumption on the part of British legal actors that prior to the coming of British law, the Malay Peninsula was a blank slate, upon which English law could be written and then altered as the need arose.[104]

By the late 1870s, British principles of law and methods of administration had clearly begun to make an impact on the legal system in Malaya, and by the 1880s Malays were administering British policy in some areas of law, while upholding Malay custom in others, and more often than not using legal reasoning and tools from British, Malay, and Islamic legal systems on a daily basis. In 1891, the Perak State Council looked into the implementation of Islamic punishments for adultery, commenting that they were "not such as can be carried out in the present day," deciding through this that some areas of Islamic law could not be applied even within the family laws. That same year, "traditional" principles of land tenure were invoked and land codes were drafted which fundamentally changed the structure of landholding and inheritance in many Malay states, while claiming to protect them.[105]

Thirdly, principles such as equity, repugnance, and good conscience established a hierarchy of law within the colonial justice system, whereby British judges could override even that which they were meant to uphold as representatives of a state where the law was Muslim law for Muslims, Hindu law for Hindus. Here, there were some issues so important to the British understanding of morality that they were by that fact taken into the ambit of British courts, where English law superceded any other.[106] A stated mission of the colonial government was to bring British methods of government and practices of civilization to native states under British protection; however, maintaining ruler control over religion and custom was a pillar of the policy of indirect rule and seen as representing British imperial regard for rule of law. The elimination of slavery as an issue of justice overcame the maintenance of Malay rulers' prerogatives over religion and custom, just as the British judicial principle of repugnancy allowed British judges working in Malaya to disregard any local legal practices they found to be contrary to the values of British justice, subjecting even matters of religion and custom to the forms and language of Crown law.

Slavery is an example of an area of law where the autonomy of local elites in matters of religion and culture was overridden by British legal and moral principles. Whereas the chiefs clearly considered slaveholding a matter allowed by both their religion and custom, and in fact a matter of their households, British public opinion and policy required its prohibition, and the British legal principle of repugnancy facilitated this. After the Perak War, however, this policy was couched in more careful terms: slavery was to be eliminated "with as little delay as is consistent with the necessary caution which is to be observed in the new relations with Perak."[107] The practice was officially ended with the emancipation of all slaves in Perak on the last day of 1883.

Whereas the Hastings Plan provided that when local laws provided no rule for a case, "justice, equity and good conscience" would rule, by 1887 this meant the rules of English law.[108] British judges deciding Muslim cases were also to apply the principles of equity and repugnancy, thereby introducing themes of natural justice in a context where they may not have delivered the intended outcome, and imposing British ideals of justice upon a population which may not have interpreted them as such. Eventually, even the substance of British laws gradually replaced areas of Anglo-Muhammadan law.

These understandings of law and the administration of justice over Muslim subjects carried through to other parts of the empire such as Malaya and Egypt. Ahmad Ibrahim, the jurist primarily responsible for the Administration of Muslim Law Act in Malaysia, argued that the British understanding of religion was conditioned by the relationship between Christianity and the state, and when applied to Islam and the state, not only failed to capture the wider scope which Islam claims over Muslim life, but gave the British colonialists more scope for their own policy actions. The use of British judges not trained in the application of Islamic law, or the application of British laws to Muslim subjects, led to criticisms of the administration of justice in the Malay States. These judges would apply equity and tort principles, or English law, in cases where no written provisions were deemed to apply.[109]

Fourth, religion and culture, custom and Islamic law, once defined as areas within which local elites had at least a nominal claim to autonomy, also became political categories in more ways than one. We will discuss Islamic law in the context of the formation of local Muslim identity later in this chapter, and more extensively in chapter 5. Here, we will explore the ways in which "custom" and "Islamic law" were defined first to be distinct from one another, and then as exclusive and competing sources of law. The Hastings Plan set aside the local practices of Hindus and Muslims in Bengal, which were mixtures of religious, customary, group, caste, class, and regional norms and institutions, in favor of the laws of the Qur'an and the Shasters. In doing so, British officials and courts significantly reduced the realm and status of custom and customary law, privileging the classical texts of gradually homogenizing religions. However, "frustrated by the inadequacy of religious texts and native law officers, British administrators in the latter half of the nineteenth century began to focus upon custom as a source of law."[110]

Custom, too, went on trial, appearing in courtroom tests in 1868, when judges ruled that custom could override Hindu law, and later, Muslim law.[111] In the Punjab in 1872, for example, revenue officers were sent to record customary land-holding practices in order to better the system for collection of revenue. These attempts at collecting, standardizing, and then codifying custom functioned along the same principles as the Hastings Plan of a century earlier. That they were put in place is a sign firstly that the Plan had not managed to achieve its aims solely through the unification and definition of Islamic law, but also that native law officers were becoming an obstacle to the administration of colonial policies, perhaps in part because of the fact that a strictly defined Islamic law gave them a measure by which British actions could be judged and potentially found wanting. The choice of custom, then, was a new political strategy, but it encountered some of the same problems as that of the Hastings Plan, reifying otherwise varied and contingent practices into fixed and flattened codes. Whereas customary practices "necessarily entailed a reinterpretation of community standards and the interpreter's position within them . . . very real struggle over what the standards were in the first place . . . what the British called 'customary law' was inherently incompatible with the epistemological dictates of codification."[112]

Codification was a tool in the colonial administrative repertoire, and so it is unsurprising that the codification of custom and the codification of Islamic and Hindu laws occurred along the same principles—as clear solutions to discrete problems. It is also unsurprising, then, that the failures of codification were similar in all these realms of law. In the area of land tenure, for example, the solution the British were looking for was the answer to the problem, "who inherits this land?" They looked first to Islamic law and then to customary land tenure systems to provide the answer, but found instead that land was held in reciprocal relationships, involving rights and duties rather than title.[113]

The British understanding of custom required that it be "enforceable, reasonable, and existing from time immemorial"—this test was applied to many areas of law and custom was found wanting, and therefore inapplicable.[114] As with Islamic law, the use of customary law by the colonial state was subject both to the imperatives of colonial policy and the judgment of British morality. Some aspects of social life were recognized as part of the realm of customary law, "above all, the codification and judicial application of custom supplied administrators with a set of devices for incorporating diverse practices within the political recognition of the colonial state."[115] Its availability as state law, however, allowed claimants to use custom to their advantage, as in the case of *adat pepatih* (matriarchal customary practices in certain Malay state). The Perak State Council recognized Malay custom as a "part of the public law of the country": "It is the custom of the Perak Malays in the matter of property division after divorce, when the said property has been obtained by one or both parties during the marriage, to accept the division of two parts to the man and one part to the woman, and that gifts between married people cannot be taken back even after divorce."[116] In Malaya, women used (and continue to use) custom to claim rights in courts, where prevailing Islamic law and Victorian ideals provided them little recourse.

Finally, as in Egypt, the introduction of the Mixed Courts under the Capitulations system in 1875 acted to remove entire populations, mostly European, from the province of local law. In this case, the commercial and strategic importance of the Suez allowed extraordinary uses of law to secure state and local elite debts, to protect European business interests, and to preserve order. However, the exclusion of certain subjects and populations from Islamic and local law were made for strategic reasons by local elites as well. Brown argues that "contrary to the repeated claim that the Mixed Courts were imposed because of the capitulations . . . the Mixed Courts were a means by which the Egyptian government sought to limit the capitulations."[117]

While it cannot be denied that in this case Egyptian elites sought to limit their losses while in a position of power disadvantage vis-à-vis European powers, the limiting of Islamic law was not universally opposed by local elites. In fact, in the area of land law, where local elites had much more leverage in relation to colonial powers, codification and the registration of land often benefited local elites to a very great extent, allowing them to own, sell, and inherit land over which they would have had no such right under previous systems of law. Even where the expansion of colonial law at the expense of Islamic and local legal systems seemed to have reduced the scope of local elite power, therefore, it benefited some of them in particular ways and thereby ensured their support. chapter 5 discusses in further detail the way in which "reform" of the legal system was part of elite strategies to limit colonial intervention where colonialism was indirect.[118]

Applying Islamic Law: Malaya, 1885

More than a century after the case of Bahadur Beg with which we began, this time in Kuala Selangor, Malaya—having determined that the proper domain of Islamic law was the adjudication of matters of marriage, divorce, and inheritance; having delegated jurisdiction over these matters to qadis (*kadi*) within the hierarchy of the colonial state; still the project of containing Islamic law within the powers of modern colonial legality could not be completed. As Samera Esmeir has argued, "Far from indicating a failure, this incompleteness provide(d) at once an occasion to intensify these powers and a space for competing ones" (2012, 5). In the Bahadur Beg case, the qadi, having completed his task according to the demands of the East India Company, died while in Company custody, a victim of the conflict between multiple orders of colonial law. In this Malayan case, the conflict among multiple orders of law provided a space of ambiguity within which the qadi could press for the enforcement of his judgment, despite the adamant refusal of his colonial superior. At the same time, the process by which the judgment was carried out further underlined the new hierarchy of adjudication within which Islamic law in Malaya would function.

The correspondence below records the conflict among parties with jurisdiction over the administration of the law in the colonial state: the British official in charge of executing policy in Kuala Selangor (in the Federated Malay state of Selangor)—the district collector—his superior (the Selangor Resident), and the local qadi/kathi (Islamic judge), in a case of adultery. A man named Rantow was divorced from his wife by an Islamic judge and proceeded to leave the state. He returned unexpectedly a few weeks later and "straightaway proceeded to the house of his former wife whom he found sleeping with a man named Dowd upon whom he at once committed an assault." Dowd and the woman were called before the qadi, who sentenced them to three months imprisonment on the grounds that the woman could not remarry until the period of her "Edda" (mandatory waiting period for a woman after divorce, in this case three months and ten days) had passed.

A close reading of this exchange shows how Islamic law might actually have been implemented in Kuala Selangor, given the bifurcation of the state between "matters of religion and culture" (in the jurisdiction of the sultan, and by extension his deputies and judges, including the local qadi) and all other matters (the jurisdiction of the British Resident and his deputies, including the district collector). The qadi went first to Rajah Mahmud (the sultan's delegate in Kuala Selangor and a member of the ruling Malay family) for the execution of his sentence; Rajah Mahmud declined to do so because the district collector was not present and "he could not himself do so," and the *kadi* then amended the sentence to "forty blows of the stick." [119]

Once incorporated into the colonial state, local Muslim elites attempted to use its resources, its power, and even its personnel toward the furtherance of their own ends. Even among British officials, the definitions of proper jurisdiction was contested and took complex and contradictory forms. The district collector's initial complaint was that "the Kathi has called upon me and requested that I will help him to carry his sentences into effect by which I understand him to mean that the police force is to be put at his disposal and I am to imprison anyone whom he thinks well to name and supervise the flogging of other individuals which I have told him distinctly that I cannot do or in any way mix myself up with religious matters." He wrote to the Resident to ask "whether the Kathi has power to pass sentences of this description and if the Gaol here is to be open for the execution of the same."[120]

The correspondence which followed between the two colonial officials demonstrates the deep ambivalence even within the colonial state when it came to jurisdiction over Islam and local Muslim life. While we often discuss the negotiation of jurisdiction among local and colonial elites as a zero-sum struggle, this exchange shows that negotiations over Islamic law occurred at different levels, and in surprising directions. The British official on the ground was adamant that his office not be involved in the application of Islamic law ("by so doing I should take upon my own shoulders . . . the justice of any argument the kadi chooses to enunciate but from this I trust it will be possible for you to exempt me") while his superior's instructions were woven through with English and Islamic legal comparisons and fraught with the potential contradictions of trying to apply both[121]:

> I told you that cases connected with the Mahomedan religion will be decided by the Kadi, and that in cases tried by you, you will be guided by the provisions of the Penal Code in criminal, and the English law in civil cases. . . . You are however an official in a native Mahometan state. . . . Instead of ignoring Mahometan law and customs, you should endeavour to become conversant with them, and obtain such a knowledge as is required from any collector and Magistrate in India.

While the Resident's instructions appeared, up to this point, to uphold the separation of jurisdictions, his next requirements highlight the essential problem of British intervention in the Muslim state and the conditions under which Islamic legal matters were conducted in Selangor:

> If the Kadi imposes a sentence which either because of recalcitrance on the part of the person sentenced, or otherwise, he requires your assistance to enforce, you must satisfy yourself on these points before assisting him (1) that an offense against Mahomedan law has been committed (2) that the person sentenced is guilty, (3) that the sentence is just.[122]

The resources of the state could be deployed only with the colonial official's approval, which laid the justice of Islamic law not, finally, at the hands of the *kadi* or sultan, but in the judgment of the Collector and/or Resident. The judgment of the *kadi* now depended upon the jurisprudential, legal, and moral determination of British officials. In this case as in many others, the British officials themselves could not come to agreement about the justice of Islamic law. The case ends on a discontented note from the Collector: "The man shall be fined or imprisoned and the woman allowed to go at large, according to the instructions contained in your minute of the 21.7.85 but I do not think that I should be acting rightly to myself if I did not state that have respectfully to differ entirely from you on this subject."[123]

Conclusion

The trials we have discussed were arena of struggle, within which colonial elites, local elites and local subjects grappled with the new realities of state and society. However, they were arena controlled in large part through the resources of the colonial state, peopled with its officials, run by its logic, and in the language of colonial authority. As such, these trials were mechanisms of control as well as arena of struggle: in that, they helped define the colonized state and its subjects in much the same way as other technologies of rule introduced by colonialism—maps, census, and scholarship. In India after the Sepoy War, the trial of Bahadur Shah served to reestablish a language of justice and order after brutal British reprisals, and to cast religion as the catalytic agent among easily incited natives. Whatever the complex of motives and politics that initiated the Mutiny, thereafter religion would be seen as what defined the Indian subject, and its protection and preservation critical to the maintenance of peace. By the time of the Perak War, this lesson was being repeated among British officials in Malaya, and matters of religion and culture clearly marked out as sensitive territory. Yet trial documents also reveal that British intervention required a redefinition of this marked-off territory, and that British officials routinely intervened in what Malay chiefs considered to be matters of religion and culture.

By the end of the nineteenth century, British colonial officials were no longer using the language of *siyasa* to justify their intervention in matters beyond their original scope. The conduct of Islamic law as part of the administration of the colonial state was by then a matter of common knowledge, and Muslim legal elites worked within a plural system whose hierarchy of law and enforcement was clear. Scholars of comparative legal history such as Lauren Benton have commented that the use of law for administration and "forced acculturation" was a common feature of European imperial expansion, and that jurisdictional complexity was the norm rather than an exception:

> The shift to territorial empire, the changing economic relation of Europe to its colonies, Enlightenment-inspired projects of reform, and widespread concerns about the growing costs of empire simultaneously sustained legal administrative expansion and recommended building on rather than abandoning the fluid order of early colonialism.[124]

The colonial state made use of jurisdictional ambiguities and confusions to establish itself as a sovereign arbiter, to deliver order and to adjudicate among multiple litigants, varied levels of enforcement, incommensurable languages of justice and legality. In doing so, the British courts became a necessary venue for the delivery of Islamic law, even for those who denied the right of the colonizers to administer shari'a. Jurisdictional tension and confusion cut both ways, however, and these courts also became venues where subjects of colonial rule pressed their advantages: "Through such conflicts . . . the 'rules about rule' that had always formed the subtext of the colonial legal order were simultaneously challenged and reified as part of a state-centered institutional structure."[125] By the time of the 'Urabi trial and the British occupation of Egypt, these rules about rule had become part of the parlance of anticolonial nationalism, and the language of Muslim politics had taken on new bases of legitimacy.

All three trials removed local elites who had been figureheads of revolt and resistance, and whose bases of authority were located beyond the evolving colonial state. In doing so, they cleared the way for new kinds of elite leadership, but increasingly within the idiom and ambit of the colonial state. The resolution of these trials cleared the way for a new kind of Muslim elite to exert influence, and new techniques of colonial governance. Local rulers, officials, and new elites were becoming adept at using the opportunities and structures of the colonial state in order to redefine themselves, their power, and Islam itself. The Muslim state was being shaped in India, Egypt, and Malaya, both as a political and administrative entity and as a social and individual identity. The processes by which both these states were constructed were profoundly implicated in law and legal institutions. The next chapter discusses the growing body of legal text and scholarship on local law, practice, and society, and a growing state machinery of knowledge, numbers, and policing. Through these, the "native" and his laws were defined and governed, and Islamic law and Muslim identity were transformed.

CHAPTER FIVE

Making the Muslim State

Islamic Law and the Politics of Representation

So long as the link between power and identity is obscured, we remain ignorant about how power reproduces certain identities and erodes others. The result is a notion of politics that focuses one-sidedly on aggregating given preferences, but not on politics as the changing of preferences. It is the creative dimension of politics—politics as the changing of preferences—that highlights the relationship between power and responses to it, between power and consent, and teaches us that these are not simple opposites, but that power can and does generate its own form of consent.[1]

Politics as the Changing of Preferences

Recent scholarship on the concept of the Islamic state has highlighted the fundamental incommensurability between Islamic models of governance and the nation-state (Hallaq 2012), and between shari'a prescriptions and modern state law (An-Na'im 2008). Running through these debates are struggles to map the lines of tension between Muslim aspirations toward the shari'a and the institutional and political pathways available for the realization of these aspirations. For Hallaq, processes of modern state formation and "jural colonization," including the codification, reification, and bureaucratization of Islamic law that have been central to the narrative of this book, were impositions that destroyed the epistemic unity of the shari'a by separating the content of law from the universe of interpretive, institutional, and social dynamics within which it was meant to function. Thus, contemporary Muslims face a "dissonance between their moral and cultural aspirations . . . and the moral realities of the modern world . . . realities with which they must live but that were not of their own making" (2012, 3). This epistemic transformation, and the dissonance it engendered, cannot be discounted; however, Muslim perceptions of the colonial encounter, and their strategies for making meaning and authority within these realities, depended on their positions in relation to the colonial state, Islamic, and other local institutions. This chapter begins with an example from nineteenth-century Malaya to suggest how a different reading of the relationship between jural colonization and Muslim agency—one that seeks out the ways in which Muslim elites capitalized upon, negotiated, and reinterpreted the realities of colonization—also might provide a way to understand contemporary Muslim investments in Islamic law *as* state law.

I begin with elite representation in Malaya as a way of understanding the remaking of Islamic law and the Muslim state: the Sultan of Johor (d. 1895) made strategic use of local, regional, and imperial institutions to signal his legitimacy at home and abroad, in the service of the consolidation of his authority and his dynasty.[2] Faced with the increasing inevitability of British colonial intervention, in the last years of his life the sultan adopted both the Ottoman Mecelle and a constitution that proclaimed Islam the religion of the state. This model was a persuasive one for other states in the Malay Peninsula, and an important precursor for constitutional monarchy in Malaysia. The example of Johor represents an increasingly common pathway for the institutionalization of Islam by local elites in the late nineteenth and twentieth centuries, many of whom faced similar imperial pressures and domestic concerns, and some of whom looked increasingly beyond their borders for solutions to the problem of imperialism. Here, Mamdani's characterization of "politics as the changing of preferences" provides a way of interpreting Muslim responses to colonial interventions in Islam and Muslim society neither as submission to inexorable colonial domination, nor as unidimensional Islamic resistance.

Instead, in Malaya, India, and Egypt, we see a wide range of local strategies and logics for addressing colonial intervention, all of which acknowledged the fact of colonial power but saw in Islam and Islamic institutions multiple ways of responding to their challenges. The sultans of the Malay States and the Ottoman Empire, the *ulama* of Deoband and al-Azhar, Muslim lawyers working within the British system, did not share a unified understanding of Islam, nor did they occupy similar positions with regard to its place in politics and statecraft. Yet we see, particularly in the late nineteenth and early twentieth centuries, increasing similarities in the strategies of Muslims with regard to the colonial state's incursions into the domain of Islam. These strategies often included the continuation of colonial relegation of Islamic law to limited domains of family, "personal status" and ritual worship, alongside renewed efforts to theorize and institutionalize the proper division between matters of Islam and matters of the state. These similarities mark an increase in exchanges between South Asia, the Middle East, and Southeast Asia, facilitated by technological change and the colonial peace, but also by the opportunities these afforded to existing Muslim networks of learning, pilgrimage, and trade. They also mark a certain convergence between previously quite separate logics and institutional bases, in part resulting from the assumption by colonial officials that the principles for governing Muslims in India would translate to the Muslims of Egypt and Malaya, and in part a consequence of an increasing interest among varied Muslim elites to articulate Islam in ways that would be legible to the colonial state and translatable across multiple domains.

The transition between the precolonial state and the postcolonial involved, as I have shown, profound changes not only in governmental structure but in elite identity and hierarchy, providing elites a stake in the new state order grounded in the language of tradition and custom. For Mamdani, while direct rule aimed at the assimilation of a small local elite into imperial culture, indirect rule allowed for local elite autonomy and precisely because of this was the more hegemonic of the two systems.[3] The role of custom in this hegemony was crucial, and the task of defining custom was "to identify the authoritarian strand so as to sculpt it and build on it, sanctioning the product officially as customary law. This sculpting and building, in turn, was done less by colonial administrators than by their 'native' allies (called 'chiefs') whose agency indirect rule did much to unleash."[4] The organization of power was marked by the binaries of the modern and the customary, the civil and the traditional, rights and customs, citizens and subjects. "It is by institutionally undergirding the reproduction of political identity that power also shapes the identity of those who respond to power."[5] Elite investments in colonial categories of Islam and Islamic law in turn conditioned the politics of Muslim anticolonialism and Islamic revival in the late nineteenth and early twentieth centuries. British conceptions of "communities" divided by religious affiliation after 1857 in India, for example, fueled law reforms based on legal pluralism; after the 1880s, in particular, claims for political representation by Indians came to be articulated in terms of communal representation.

The processes discussed in chapters 3 and 4, the division of jurisdiction among local and colonial elites, and the redefinition of law and legal institutions that governed Islam and Muslims, linked these transformations of institution and identity. Here, I detail further the manner in which local elites, in response to the opportunities and hazards of colonial power, transformed the state and were themselves transformed. Where the central archive of chapter 3 was treaties, and the core of chapter 4 was trials, here I use archives of representation—portraits that provide evidence of the way in which local elites chose to represent themselves to multiple audiences, and texts by which Muslim populations were represented and governed, both by British colonial officials and by rising Muslim elites.[6] In these portraits and texts, representation served both to define and to translate the Muslim state—to project images of sovereign rulers recognizable in a Western and regional idiom, to articulate Muslim practice and shari'a texts in the language of British law, to identify strategies for Islamic revival that acknowledged the reality of the colonial state while at the same time asserting alternative bases for authority within Muslim societies worldwide.

The Muslim state we discuss here was both a set of institutions and a network of relationships: rulers presiding over hierarchies rearranged by the colonial encounter, institutions that collected taxes, counted people, assigned land title, adjudicated disputes, educated children, issued proclamations, and—in the colonial period—aspired to govern through an increasingly long list of functions. For purposes of clarity, I label this the "governmental" state, based more on its aspirations than its reality, perhaps. However, the Muslim state was also a condition of being: individuals or groups who were strategic, resistant, active, mutinous, quiescent, sensitive, ethnicized, isolated, unified, oppressed, independent, religious, secular, and again the list goes on.[7] I have labeled this the "individual" state, although it should be understood that "the Muslim" refers to both a collective and an individual subject.

The transformation of Islamic law during the colonial period bridged the governmental and the individual Muslim state in novel ways, tying the individual Muslim to the state through the delivery of Islamic law. What began in India as the colonial attempt to define jurisdiction over the revenue of the state proceeded over the course of the next century to redefine the content, scope, and meaning of Islamic law. By the end of the nineteenth century, Malay and Egyptian elites were speaking of Islamic law as codes rather than as the jurisprudence of a class of *ulama*, delivered, administered, and paid for by the state alongside multiple other kinds of law. Across our three cases, Islamic law was by the nineteenth century seen as occupying the domain of the private, itself a category in the process of being formed. The religious and the private realm were co-constituted over the Muslim family, in the institutionalization of personal status law. In India in the 1770s, personal law referred to differential jurisdictions—laws applied depending upon membership in religious communities, Hindu laws for Hindus, Muslim laws for Muslims.[8] By the time the formulation was instituted in Egypt as *'al-Ahkam al-Shar'iyya fi al-Ahwal al-Shakhsiyya*, the "personal" in "personal law" carried two meanings—the first tied to communal affiliation, the second to the individual as a unit of administrative control.[9] We trace here how changes in elite hierarchies and institutions brought about by the opportunities and pressures of colonial intervention contributed to the institutionalization of Islamic law as private and personal law.

Further, this transformation of Islamic law became a central basis for local Muslim elite authority and a critical resource for mobilization vis-à-vis the state, meaning that Muslim elites became invested in the new institution of Islamic law and its attendant implications. Timothy Mitchell's work on Egypt has demonstrated how European imperial powers represented Egypt through exhibitions, maps, and plans, and in doing so rearranged the order of Egyptian life; our exploration of representation here—in portraiture, text, and legislation—draws from this concept of representation to "study . . . the power to colonize."[10] A central space for this imaginative and creative project was the Egyptian body and, by extension, the Egyptian family and the society of which it was a part. The revisioning of the Egyptian state from an earlier metaphor—the body politic as a body composed of differentiated organs—to the colonial metaphor of state, of a machine distinct from its operator and its subjects, facilitated French and British colonial rule. Mitchell argues that it also gave rise to visions of self-government among Egyptians who saw in the machine metaphor the potential autonomy of the ruled from their rulers, a potential Muslim elites in India and Malaya were also exploring.[11]

It is to this new politics of Muslim preferences that we now turn: to the ways in which different groups of Muslim elites in India, Malaya, and Egypt strategized reform, used the multiple languages of the colonial period, and participated in the development of the Muslim state even as they attempted to navigate its colonial character. While drawing upon Mitchell's concept of representation, I emphasize that Muslim elites first represented *themselves* in strategic, multivalent, and effective ways to resist and use European imperialism. Insofar as the transformation of

Islamic law can be said to have been a colonial project, it was a project with multiple authors, including local elites, who used the European and local vernaculars of power to appeal to their many audiences. Rather than reading the dissonance that Hallaq diagnoses as a silencing of the shari'a system, I suggest that it might be analytically productive to think in terms of polyphony: as an outcome of Islamic law's transformation through the colonial process, the Muslim state represents itself through a number of symbolic registers, projecting its authority and authenticity to multiple audiences in multiple languages.[12] As elites who worked to stave off imperial intervention by taking on imperial institutional forms well understood, this polyphony contained the possibility of both mutual reinforcement and contradiction. When this polyphony was embodied in legal institutions, as we will discuss in the case of the state of Johor, it extended the reach of the state at the same time that it made new spaces and opportunities for contesting that state.

Making the Muslim State: The Sultan of Johor, 1868–1895

The state of Johor is an important example for this analysis because it illustrates the multiple ways in which colonialism mattered for the Muslim state. Johor did not accept a British Resident until 1914, and so it did not properly come under the category of a colonized state until the last decades of British imperialism in Malaya. The Federated States of Malaya were in fact never direct colonies of the British Empire, coming instead under the category of "indirect rule" and protectorate. Yet the shadow of British power and influence loomed large over Johor, hemmed in as it was between the Straits Settlements (colonies from the beginning of the nineteenth century) and the Federated Malay States (beginning with Perak in 1874). The case of Abu Bakar of Johor is that of a local ruler who used the opportunities provided by competition among imperial powers in Southeast Asia to rise to prominence within local elite hierarchies (from Temenggong, to maharaja, to sultan). In Egypt and India as well, rulers often took on reform projects and Western forms of government precisely to avoid colonization, and in doing so both forestalled imperial intervention while advancing the transformation of Islamic law along imperial lines.[13]

Abu Bakar began as one chief among many in the state of Johor, a crucial trading gateway on the southern tip of the Malay Peninsula.[14] He requested the title Maharaja of Johor in 1873—a title unknown in Malaya previously—and although the British were reluctant to allow it, he succeeded because his support was crucial to British strategic and economic interests. Once at the apex of his power, he wrought radical changes in the state, changes that reflected imperial influences at the same time that they worked to limit colonial intervention. These included the codification of Islamic law in the form of the Ottoman Majalla (1885, within the Ottoman Empire), the promulgation of the first Constitution in Malaya, whose provisions cemented his dynasty, established Islam as the state religion, and opened up a space for consultative functions within the monarchy.

The portraits below, a selection of many posed in Abu Bakar's lifetime, show him using a wide symbolic repertoire in his formal portraits—in figure 6, a number of elements of dress from the Malay world worn along with Arab/Ottoman elements; figure 7 shows the sultan in British military regalia, but with Islamic/Ottoman insignia; figure 9 is a painted rather than photographic depiction of the sultan combining Malay, Ottoman/Islamic, and British elements of dress. These images (figs. 6–9 below) are posed portraits whose exact contexts are now unclear. However, as representations of Abu Bakar (1833–1895) at various stages of his career, they show that like many Muslim rulers during the colonial period, he had as part of his repertoire a number of methods of signaling his identity and, by extension, the identity of his state. These visual representations of the sultan's choices as to public image, the presentation of his persona as sovereign at various points in his ascent through the hierarchy of Johor, and the elements of dress and insignia referring to his place within other global hierarchies serve as a reminder of the diversity and breadth of his political repertoire. Together with other texts, they present a picture of a ruler who used the opportunities of the colonial relationship to consolidate his authority and to remake the state over which he ruled. Images such as these have been used by scholars of the colonial period to argue that rulers were slowly "Westernized" through their contacts with, and dependence upon, colonial power. Indeed, Sultan Abu Bakar was among the most "Westernized" of the Malay rulers, if his travels in Europe, his social activities, and his marriages were any indication. [15] However, Abu Bakar's influence among the Malay rulers, his economic power, and his diplomatic acumen, indicate that his success was far more than a measure of his Westernization.

The politics of representation manifested themselves in the ways that rulers presented themselves to their constituencies, the languages in which they chose to communicate their authority and legitimacy, and the laws and institutions they put into place. In an article that discusses the portraiture of Muhammad Ali of Egypt, Emily Weeks argues against the Saidian vision of Orientalism as a unidirectional relationship featuring the power of the West to represent the East.[16] Muhammad Ali commissioned his 1841 portrait by the artist Sir David Wilkie and is known to have made changes and represented himself in such a way as to "project an image of diplomatic authority to both British and Egyptian audiences."[17] Indian princes, too, were keenly aware of the need to project images of themselves as progressive and Westernized reformers in order to be recognized politically by the British.[18] Rulers' use of overt and covert signals of their amenability to Western ideas had to be balanced—especially where imperial interest was high but its authority still a matter for negotiation—alongside their need to assure their local constituencies of their continued allegiance to existing hierarchies, practices, and religious mores. The extent to which this balancing act constituted strategy, mimicry, collaboration, or cooptation has long been a matter for scholarly debate.[19] For the British in their empire, too, elements of the local and the British were brought together to project an image of authority and authenticity and to broadcast through architecture, portraiture, dress, and ceremonials manifold messages both at home and abroad.[20] When these messages were deployed by local sovereigns and elites, they played to a range of audiences, some of them colonial, and some comprising of local constituencies. The use of multiple kinds of evidence—here, representations of state and sovereign in portraiture and in legal texts—helps show that rulers such as Abu Bakar calibrated their signals according to their political needs, and that their repertoires involved complex vocabularies in multiple vernaculars.

Both visual and textual evidence indicate that Abu Bakar's political repertoire consisted of symbols from multiple sources, including Britain and its imperial system, the Ottoman Empire, and Muslim networks in the Indian Ocean. The Johor Sultanate itself was one of the most diversely constituted of the Malay States, comprised of multiple fiefdoms on the Malay Peninsula as well as in the Riau and Lingga islands, combining elements of culture from centers of power in Minangkabau, Bugis, and Malacca. The Malays of Abu Bakar's generation, sons of the aristocracy and the "first Malay salarymen . . . clerks, interpreters and printers," knew that colonialism offered gains as well as losses, and they often learned early on that new kinds of repertoires would be needed to handle "living between

FIGURE 6. Abu Bakar of Johor
Arkib Negara Malaysia: http://hids.arkib.gov.my/doc/jilidiii/julai/18_07_1895_1980.htm. Accessed November 28, 2007.

worlds."[21] On the streets of Penang and Singapore, young men of Abu Bakar's generation, educated as he was by Europeans in schools whose aim was to raise the sons of the Malay ruling class, adopted the "trousers, socks, shirts and boots of their teachers, and to show that they are not completely converted, they wear the *kebaya*, a rather loose Arab cloak and turban."[22] In the figure above (fig. 6), Abu Bakar is shown posed in a Malay *kain samping* around his waist and a folded cap; his jacket appears to be influenced by Ottoman styles and his sword and stance are common to photographic and painted portraits of both Western and Ottoman rulers (Maxwell 2003). Abu Bakar's costume signaled his Malay and Islamic allegiances while his stance echoed Western conventions of state portraiture; the braiding on his jacket, and possibly the textiles of his garments, were imported from India and Britain.[23]

In 1868, Abu Bakar, then Temenggong of Johor, requested the title maharaja, an Indian title unknown in Malaya previously. Abu Bakar's father, Temenggong Daing Ibrahim, had gained control over the state under the terms of a treaty signed in 1855 between the British in Singapore and Sultan Ali of Johor. The position of Temenggong, initially one of the *Majlis Orang Kaya* (lit., Council of Rich Persons) who held geographic fiefdoms within the Sultanate of Johor, rose to preeminence in Johor under Temenggong Ibrahim, but its claim to the Johor succession was still a matter of contest among Malay nobles. A central preoccupation of Temenggong Ibrahim and Abu Bakar after him was the consolidation of their dynastic claim, and British imperial power lent itself to this aim (Winstedt 1932).

In this endeavor, Abu Bakar's Westernization was viewed as an asset by his colonial observers, perhaps the most widely cited—and, later, perhaps most damning—being from Sir Harry Ord, Governor General of Singapore, who characterized him in 1868 as

> in his tastes and habits . . . an English gentleman, as a ruler is anxious to promote in every way the advancement and civilization of his people, and he is the only Rajah in the whole Peninsula, or the adjoining States, who rules in accordance with the practice of civilized nations. He is deeply attached to the British Government and nation, and feeling with their support and encouragement he is most likely to benefit his country he takes no steps of importance in administration without the advice of the local government, whilst he is ready at all times to place the whole resources of his country at our disposal.[24]

Johor was a trading gateway on the southern tip of the Malay Peninsula crucial to British strategic and economic interests, and although the British were reluctant to grant Abu Bakar's unprecedented request to be titled maharaja, they did so.[25]

A decade later, in August 1878, the maharaja requested British support for a change in his title to sultan. The governor of the Straits Settlements' reply was swift: "Most undesirable to recognise Maharajah as Sultan it would be an incendiary to the whole Peninsula and following closely on the question of the Moar succession would greatly complicate our position." However, the maharaja's cooperation was needed against Dutch and French interests in Southeast Asia, his own vast landholdings throughout Malaya would supply a route for the Malayan Railway, and his influence among the Malay rulers was unparalleled. His continued goodwill remained so important for British political and economic interests that in 1885 he was granted his request. The wording of the Treaty of 1885 that made the maharaja a sultan reveals what was at stake for both parties, and the means by which they sought to legitimize their actions:

> Whereas His Highness the Maharajah of Johore has made known to the Governor of the Straits Settlements that it is the desire of his chiefs and people that he assume the title of Sultan, it is further agreed that, in consideration of the loyal friendship and constant affection His Highness has shown to the Government of Her Majesty the Queen and Empress, and of the stipulations contained in this Memorandum, he and his heirs and successors, lawfully succeeding according to Malay custom, shall in future be acknowledged as His Highness the Sultan of the State and territory of Johore, and shall be so addressed.[26]

As in the change of title to maharaja, the combination of local legitimacy and imperial recognition was key to his success. By this treaty, two sets of relationships were cemented: the first between Abu Bakar, previously not in line for the throne of Johor, and "his chiefs and people"; and the second between the sultan and the British. The treaty proclaimed Abu Bakar Sultan "by the desire of his chiefs and people," consultative language that until then had not been part of the rationales used by Malay rulers to legitimize their positions, but that now was used to appeal to British ideals of just rule as well as to key constituents within the state of Johor. At the same time, the treaty inserted Abu Bakar's line into the succession of rulers of the state of Johor and into the company of other sultans in the Malay States: the phrasing "he and his heirs, lawfully succeeding according to Malay custom" worked to legitimize an action that was far from customary, and then to insert it into a chain of tradition, made anew by colonial power and elite stratagems. The phrase "loyal friendship" and the reference to "stipulations" referred to the economic and strategic considerations of British policy in the Straits—the sultan ceded the conduct of foreign policy to the British, and made promises not to interfere in the Malay States.

Not only was Abu Bakar made Sultan of Johor, his treaty was signed in London, not in Malaya as were all other treaties with Malay sultans. Not only was he made sultan, he was made Sultan Sir Abu Bakar, Knight Commander of the Order of St Michael and St George. Figures 7 and 8 below show the sultan and Prince George, Duke of Cambridge, in similar stances and costumes: Prince George was Grand Master of the Order St Michael

FIGURE 7. Sultan Sir Abu Bakar of Johor, K. C. M. G.
"The Sultan of Johore," *Illustrated London News* (London, England) February 28, 1891: 271. *Illustrated London News*. Web. December 8, 2014.

and St George during Abu Bakar's appointment and commander-in-chief of the British Army from 1856 to 1895. Appointments to the Order were made in recognition of service in the colonies and in foreign affairs. Both the sultan (fig. 7) and the prince (fig. 8) were depicted in official portraiture wearing emblems of the Order, whose traditional image is St Michael subduing Satan, often depicted as a Moor (St. Aubyn 1964). The Ottoman crescent and star figure in the sultan's embroidered coat and on his headwear; in these and other portraits of the period, the sultan also wore newly

FIGURE 8. Prince George, Duke of Cambridge (1819–1904).
Prince George William Frederick Charles, Second Duke of Cambridge. By Walery, published by Sampson Low & Co. Carbon print, published July 1888. National Portrait Gallery of the United Kingdom, NPG x9114.

minted decorations of his own royal family, which resembled British and Ottoman decorations.

This portrait below (fig. 9), almost certainly the latest in our series of representations of Sultan Sir Abu Bakar of Johor, appeared in *Vanity Fair* in 1891. It illustrates the symbolic parallels of legal and political decisions made by the sultan in his attempt to balance the reality of British colonial power in the region with his own sovereignty over Johor, as an independent Malay monarch and a Muslim ruler. He wore the Maltese Cross with black tie, headwear akin to that worn in the Ottoman empire and decorated with a crescent and star, and a *kain samping* (traditionally worn by Malays with *baju kurung*, the Malay shirt and pants) at his waist. This series of posed portraits indicates a keen and dynamic awareness of multiple languages of fealty and authority, and they also indicate that for rulers like Abu Bakar, these languages might have been used simultaneously, despite of, or because of, their ambiguities and contradictions. The translation from symbolic to legal and political performance is, of course, neither linear nor seamless, but self-representation and the projection of authority to multiple audiences relied upon similar techniques, for similar ends.

Local elites who are now seen to have benefited from colonial interventions have generally been cast either as collaborators or as fathers of the modern state. However, the legacy of figures like Abu Bakar was far more ambivalent, and continues to have unexpected impact on the states they helped shape. In Malaya, for example, British intervention seems to have facilitated the institutionalization on the Malay Peninsula of far more Islamic legal content over far greater territory than before. Islamic law and British institutions of law also adjudicated among customary practices and the elites who had controlled them, often favoring *adat temenggong* (in which Malay customary practices mixed with shari'a content, applied variably by local chiefs) over *adat pepatih* (in which matrilineal and matriarchal principles governed local communities). The patriarchy of Victorian values, carefully chosen customary practices, and shari'a content combined with a nascent nationalism to produce Muslim elites—Anglophiles, resisters, patriarchs, democrats—who were themselves hybrids, and whose impact on the Muslim state can be read in multiple ways.

As in India, where the application of Anglo-Muhammadan law brought into being an entire system of law based upon a small slice of Islamic jurisprudence, "the original settlement with the Malays, based on the conciliation of the ruling class, had a somewhat ironic effect of rendering de facto a system of authority which had previously existed de jure."[27] Seeking sovereign monarchs in the image of Victoria, British practices of indirect rule in Malay raised sultans to the pinnacle of state hierarchy, replaced or eliminated independent chiefs and demoted strongmen, and installed a locus of power in each state around a royal palace. The sultans accepted state allowances and disbursed state funds and titles, thereby cementing their newly elevated position as the locus of state authority.

FIGURE 9. Sultan of Johor, 1891.
Vanity Fair print: "HH Tunkoo Abubeker Ben Ibrahim, Sultan of Johore 1891," *Vanity Fair Album*, 23 (1891), pl. 19. (London: Vanity Fair, 1869–1912).

Said's model of Orientalism, an important and productive starting point for this study and many others, does not account for the actions of local elites whose independent strategies and interests in the face of colonial power made for unexpected alliances, new cultural constructions and new discourses of power. The power to represent, as both Said and Mitchell have argued, has been a critical component of the imperial project. While we could read the actions of the Sultan of Johor as a kind of self-Orientalism, and certainly this too has its conceptual appeal (cf. Tageldin 2011), local elites represented themselves using multiple and flexible repertoire to a number of audiences, in order to achieve ends quite apart from those of the imperial project. The Sultan of Johor and ruling elites like him—nawabs in India (both in the princely states and in British India), the khedives of Egypt—were "creole pioneers" (Anderson 2006) in their own right.

If by invoking this phrase we also invoke Anderson's trajectories of nationalism and state formation, this is apposite: it was during the latter half of the nineteenth century that the story of ruling elites and the narratives of nascent popular national consciousness began to respond to each other. Ruling elites represented themselves to their imperial interlocutors as Westernized, cosmopolitan, progressive, and loyal, and by doing so achieved a measure of autonomy and retained elements of their sovereignty. By the late nineteenth century, these same elites were also keenly aware of the need to be seen to represent their people, a people whose national consciousness had been sharpened by the experience of being oppressed by both colonial and native rulers, and hastened by the rise of print media, travel, and state institutions. The standardization of law, the removal of Islamic jurisprudential elites and institutions, and the processes of textualization and codification described in the last few chapters, played two roles—they helped consolidate some elements of conservative rule while serving as the foundation for the building of a nation along more populist lines.

The sultan's efforts to represent himself, and his state, as being capable of self-government: as modern, wealthy, efficient, rational, and enlightened, took place in the areas of law and administration in particular. They culminated, during the last year of his life, in the promulgation of the Undang-Undang Tubuh Negri Johor, that detailed Johor's autonomy, the duties of Cabinet and Legislative Council, established Islam as the state religion, and placed the sultan as head of state—in effect a constitution, the first in Malaya. The document was drafted by the sultan's legal advisors in Singapore (C. B. Buckley chief among them, from the firm Messrs. Rodyk and Davidson) and his ministers (Chief Minister Dato Jaafar bin Haji Mohamad and Dato Abdul Rahman Andak, Setiausaha Kerajaan [State Secretary].) It comprised four parts: the position and powers of the sultan; the Council of Ministers; the State Council; and matters of justice, nomenclature, and Islam.[28]

Given its timing (the sultan was ill, and died that same year), the 1895 Constitution can also be seen as an attempt to formalize state structure and the position of the sultan and his descendants, until then guaranteed only by treaties signed with the British. A constitution had more legitimacy than treaties, and could not easily be revoked or altered, especially by the British, who presented the biggest challenge to Johor state autonomy at that point. The language of the document supports this argument. Part 1.1 states: "The Raja rules and owns this State of Johor and all territories in its dominion . . . with the agreement of all the members of Our Council of Ministers and Council of State." At the same time, the language of the constitution also left open the possibility of interpreting the power of the sultan to be contingent upon the consent of the Councils. Part 2.2, though, allows for penalties against those who challenge the position and power of the sultan, with penalties for treason at the sultan's discretion.

> It is clear that His Majesty saw the Constitution as a device for strengthening his position through the co-optation of the state's elites in government. When there were no internal threats it was thought that the independence of the state of Johor could be preserved. The formalisation of the Sultan's rights over Johor and the legitimisation of the current government was considered paramount at the time because of the growth of British influence in the Malay States.[29]

A few years after the last portrait in our series, the Sultan encouraged the adoption of the Ottoman Majallah (the 1885 codification of Hanafi commercial laws: Majallah al-Ahkam al-Adliyyah), promulgated in 1913 as the Undang-Undang Sivil Islam: Majalah Ahkam Johor (Code of Islamic Civil Law.) [30] In 1895, the sultan promulgated the peninsula's first constitution, both enshrining Islam as the religion of the state and redefining that state in a political vocabulary thus far unknown to Johor. Legal pluralism is often explained in terms of the colonial state, in which European laws are imposed upon a system of local laws; here, the adoption of law was not undertaken by force, and neither was the plurality of that law derived only from European sources. Johor was not governed under the system of indirect rule as the Federated Malay States were; neither the reports of colonial officials nor Malay historical accounts indicate that these changes were anything but a voluntary policy decision by the sultan and his advisors. In fact, these changes were more far-reaching than any in the Federated States, and to some degree the Straits Settlements, which were under direct rule of the British. A few caveats are necessary, though, to make clear the type of pluralism these adoptions constituted: firstly, the Ottoman Majalla was itself an attempt to modernize some components of Islamic law in the face of European pressure; secondly, these changes may have been undertaken without colonial coercion, but they were clearly made in the shadow of colonial power. By focusing on the figure of the sovereign at the moment of adoption, however, it is possible to see the law as the sultan and his advisors may have in the last years of the nineteenth century—as part of a strategy for maintaining and consolidating sovereignty, using global resources made available by the sultan's diplomatic and political networks. It will then be possible to see the manner in which these logics were later adapted and transformed in accordance with other political and strategic needs.

The Ottoman effort to codify and regularize certain matters of Islamic law through the Majalla was itself undertaken in the shadow of European imperial pressure. The Majalla codified rules relating to commerce, although it also covered matters of witnessing (*baiyyinah*), oaths (*tahaluf*), and judging (*hukum qada*). [31] The effort to reform the Ottoman economy by placing Hanafi jurisprudence on market transactions within the realm of modern, codified, regularized, and "rational" law created a divide between these "rational" laws and the unreformed shar'i rules relating to other areas of law—notably family, marriage, and inheritance. Jane Collier points out that reforms undertaken with the explicit rationale of regularizing the economy had perhaps unintended, but ultimately far-reaching, consequences:

> "Rationalizing" market exchanges established other types of property transfers, such as those involved in marriage, inheritance, succession, and adoption, as governed by "irrational" (i.e., emotional or religious) principles. The Ottoman reformers who subjected commercial transactions to the requirements of modernity, reason, and law thus unwittingly established family life as a realm governed by tradition, sentiment, and biology.[32]

These portraits represent a source of information on the ways in which concepts of authority, legitimacy and authenticity were represented in nineteenth-century Malaya that allow us to read in a different way how these concepts may have been projected to multiple audiences, and how they may have changed over time. They make immediately clear what readings of law and memoir may not—that ruling elites were adept at simultaneous translation between multiple symbolic languages. As Weeks argues in discussing similar elites (the Ottoman Sultan ʿAbd al-Majid (reigned 1839–1861) and Muhammad Ali of Egypt (ruled 1806–1848), portraiture was a recognized part of international diplomacy and a carefully managed component of the exchange between East and West (Weeks 1998.) As Michael Laffan argues, the translation of political concepts into Malay expanded the range of meanings available to Muslim elites, who chose among multiple registers and genres of text from which to draw their vocabularies (Laffan, *Malay Concordance Project*).

Legal texts represented state authority and legitimacy to multiple audiences in a similar manner, serving a critical role in the sultan's public diplomacy as well as his internal statecraft, and building a discourse from which many of the peninsula's monarchs would draw. The adoption of the Ottoman Majalla and the Undang-Undang Tubuh Negri Johor in the last years of the nineteenth century illustrates patterns of borrowings, translations, and projections. Just as the portraits above were authored by their sitter as well as their artist, and draw upon a complex lexicon of symbol and affect, the adoption of legal instruments from both "Islamic" and "Western" canons helped represent the state of Johor and its monarch as modern, progressive, authoritative, and authentic. They also served to cement a new succession and forestall direct British intervention. The institutional ramifications of law, however, had far-reaching and longer implications for the future of the state of Johor, its ruling elites, and Malaysia itself.

The Sultan of Johor's efforts to maintain the independence of his state from British encroachment involved judicial and administrative reforms, including a Constitution that defined and legitimated his position, but also limited its scope to functioning in tandem with a state government and its officers. In the decades that followed, these measures resulted in changes in the relationship between sultans and the other elites—like the Mufti—in the state. So, while it is insufficient to equate reform with Westernization and modernization—these steps were often taken to preserve the power of local elites and maintain the position of precolonial laws—it is also inadequate to see them as purely conservative measures. They may have been intended to consolidate the sultan's power, but they also made possible the re-entry of elites who had previously been excluded from the sultans' compacts with the British.

Among the Malay states, Abu Bakar's reputation for closeness to the British, and the autonomy provided by his strategic adoption of the constitution, provided yet another set of models. In 1911, when the state of

Terengganu adopted a constitution, the document explicitly proscribed the sultan ceding the state or any part thereof to a foreign government or European power, and labeled as traitors any ministers or State Council members who acted in this direction.[33] The Terengganu constitution drew heavily from the Johor model, including in its overall strategy to consolidate the power of the sultan against British (and in the case of Terengganu, Siamese) intervention. However, its strictures on the actions of ruling elites, especially in the area of foreign policy and territorial sovereignty, were much stronger. Even though the ruler was valorized in the document as sovereign, by 1911 the law was also being used to circumvent potential British demands for influence by removing the authority of ruling elites to grant such influence.

The centrality of Islamic symbols and language also varied within the Malay states according to the relative position of Islamic institutions and elites, and increased in the early twentieth century.[34] In the state of Kedah on the other end of the Malay Peninsula, the sultan's autonomy was hedged on the northern border by the Siamese (to whom they sent tribute) and the British to the south (Penang had become a Straits Settlement in 1786, the first Malay state to do so) the first. Here, Kedah used close relationships with the British to keep the Siamese at bay, and vice versa, but internally, Islamic elites were a key constituency and close to the sultan's court. Therefore, in Kedah and Terengganu, to a greater extent than was the case in Johor, Islamic elements of governance—such as a powerful *ulama* presence in courts, administration, and advisory capacities—continued to be a part of strategies to maintain state autonomy. Whereas the Johor constitution made mention of Islam and made space for Islamic institutions, the sultan's limited dependence on Islamic elites and institutions, and his interest in placing these institutions within the ambit of the state, meant a somewhat minimalist use of Islam in the text.

In Terengganu in 1911, the use of Arabic, reference to Islam and Islamic institutions in its constitution was an explicit move to highlight Terengganu's Muslim character, against Siamese and British imperial pressure. The Sultan of Terengganu, Zainal 'Abdin III (1881–1918), was reputed among Malay and British contemporary sources as a pious man, and undertook the pilgrimage to Mecca shortly after the constitution was promulgated.[35] The Sultan of Terengganu's travels, constituencies, and context, therefore, lent themselves to a politics of representation of himself, and of the state of Terengganu, in explicitly Islamic terms that owed much to the language of an Arabicized Islam. The constitution itself was formally titled in Arabic and Malay *Itqan al-muluk bi ta'dil al-suluk: Undang-*

Undang bagi diri Kerajaan Terengganu [The constitution of the way of illustrious sovereignty: The laws of the Constitution of Terengganu].[36] The official printing of this document includes an Arabic statement that the law was proclaimed by the sultan, referred to as *Syed al-Mursalim al-wathiq billah al-Qawi al-Matin al-Sultan Zainal Abidin III*, and the text itself contains many Arabic and Islamicate terms.[37]

The equation of Islamic law during the colonial period with one portion of its former functions was a feature of the modernization of the Johor state as well. In this case, however, the modernization was undertaken by a local ruler, and the bifurcation of the state into "matters relating to the law of Islam" and matters beyond it followed different lines. Whereas in the Ottoman case the reform of the Majalla separated it from other realms of shari'a, defining the Majalla as modern and areas such as family law as traditional, in Johor, the adoption of the Majalla was seen as proof that Islamic law could be modern, and could therefore be a part of the infrastructure of a modern Muslim state. Other states in the Malay Peninsula, such as Selangor, had undertaken revisions of Islamic legal practice, but the state of Johor, by adopting the Majalla, brought commercial transactions into the domain of Islamic law in a novel manner. Here, context matters: in the Johor system, where Chinese mercantile practices, British contracts, and Malay maritime rules commingled, the codification of Ottoman Hanafi jurisprudence was both an Islamizing and modernizing move.

Whereas this modernization and bureaucratization has been read as the effective end of the shari'a system, tracing the details of these processes as they unfolded in Malaya as the nineteenth century became the twentieth makes clear that new kinds of politics were being built into the institutions of state Islam and Islamic law. Legislation by the sultans of Malaya may have been initiated to capture Islam and its institutions for the state, but the inclusion of Islamic institutions and vocabulary into the repertoire of state administration in documents such as the Majalah and the Constitution also constructed a new kind of relationship between the state and Islam. For Islamic legal elites the tradeoff was complicated—it limited the power and autonomy of Islamic institutions, but it also made them a key source of the state's legitimacy and ensured these elites a place at the table. Here again, processes of jural colonization that severed shar'i content from adjudication and legislation also resulted in the elevation of selected Islamic elites into positions of government, and paved the way for their investment in the new state order. Administrative bodies like the Department of Religion and Education were established that bureaucratized Islam and Muslim life further, and brought it under the formal purview of the state. To underscore further the extent by which religious authority had been incorporated into the state, whereas in the first document the Mufti of Johor (the highest Islamic official in the state) signed himself "al-Haqir" (*Yang Hina; the Base/Humble*), by the time of the second printing of the Majalah, he signed "under Orders" (*dengan perintah.*).

During this time, the Majalah was also being inserted into a hierarchy of state law, within which the secular state constitution became paramount. The sultan was asked for, and granted, permission for it to be used as one source for the Hukum Syara' (Islamic law of the state), excepting that the Johor Constitution superceded the Majalah.[38] By the time of its second printing, the relationship between Majalah and Constitution had been clarified to allow "all officers, magistrates and judges in the state of Johor" to use the Majalah "in matters relating to the law of Islam." [39] This latter phrase had, since the Treaty of Pangkor in 1874, a specific connotation for the Malay States, tying Islam to matters of culture and religious observance, in contrast to matters of state, finance, administration, and the like. However, the Majalah was not a legal text for public consumption, remaining in Arabic for two decades before being translated into Malay. While it was adopted in 1893, the first printing of the Majalah in Malay was in 1913. This text begins: "This book contains discussions of the fiqh rulings which are derived from the shari'a of Islam which have been in use in the past by the government of Johor in the Arabic language."[40] This helps explain how a Hanafi text could have been adopted into a Shafi'i context with so little initial adaptation or attempt at justification: the lack of translation of the text into the vernacular allowed interpretation to remain a matter for the Mufti and a select few Islamic elites. The translation of the text into the vernacular marked, therefore, not only a potential pluralization of its audiences and interpretors, but a certain measure of assurance that future interpretive struggles would take place under state supervision and jurisdiction. Tradeoffs between state and Islamic elites would further shape Islamic law in India and Egypt, as it had in Malaya, as the next section details.

Jural Colonization? *Siyasa* as Administrative Law, Discretion, Politics

> *Siyasa*
>
> (a.), verbal noun from the root *s-w-s* "to tend, manage," etymologically connected with Biblical Hebrew *sus* "horse," originally used in Bedouin society for

the tending and training of beasts, hence *sa'is* "manager or trainer of horses, camels, etc." (this last appearing, via Hindi, in the Anglo-Indian word *syce* "groom," Fr. *çais*; see Yule-Burnell, Hobson-Jobson, a glossary of Anglo-Indian colloquial words and phrases 2, London 1903, 885–86).

1. In the sense of statecraft, the management of affairs of state and, eventually, that of politics and political policy.[41]

Here, we turn to debates and changes in the use of the concept of *siyasa* as a way of tracking the politics of representation in the domain of Islamic law. For both Muslim and British colonial governments, *siyasa* was a concept that bridged the reality of plural legal orders with the ideal of shari'a governance, and as such offered the possibility of claiming authority along a sliding scale of Islamic legitimacy. The meaning and content of *siyasa* depended upon the power balance between the state and Islamic institutions, and changed with time: in India, the Mughals relied upon *siyasa* to order relations of plurality between state, society, and law.[42] In the Ottoman project to reform law, *siyasa* functioned as administrative discretion in accordance with the shari'a. For the Malay sultans, the concept of *siyasa* rested upon this Ottoman usage but later also responded to a wider sense of *siyasa* as politics, taken on from the discourse of twentieth-century Muslim politics. Here I explore the concept of *siyasa* as it entered the lexicon of colonial governance and emerged in the early twentieth century as a way for Muslims to talk about, to, and against the state, for by the twentieth century, *siyasa* had also come to refer to the conduct and content of politics across a worldwide Muslim discourse on modernity, Islam, and the state.

As Muhammad Khalid Masud observes, "Between training a horse and punishing the criminal, *siyasa* finally emerged as a term meaning art of governance . . . an overlapping principle that kept the pluralist system of laws operating in the Muslim societies."[43] Masud points to the tendency of *siyasa* to be invoked at times of "political crisis" in Islamic history, from its elaboration in the eighth century to delimit the ruler's discretion in matters of adjudication, in the tenth century to defend the public interest against schism, in the fourteenth century to maintain order in the face of political and social disarray, and in the period of the rise of great Muslim imperial regimes (the Ottomans and the Mughals) as public policy to maintain balance amid plurality.[44]

Once the British took on the mandate to administer the state in India, *siyasa* was deployed to cover a similar realm of statecraft, namely the public policy discretion of the ruler. In colonial India, the initial grant by the Mughal emperor to the East India Company merely to collect revenue in Bengal in 1765 was followed, in 1772, by Hastings's claims to govern in both civil and criminal matters. As Nawab Governor General, Hastings made this claim based upon the Islamic doctrine of *siyasa*, understood in this case to be the prerogative of the ruler to administer justice. By invoking *siyasa*, Hastings was claiming temporal authority for governing, as opposed to the spiritual mandate of earlier Muslim rulers, but doing so within an idiom of Muslim political philosophy and history. British colonial *siyasa* relied upon a series of assumed equivalences: shari'a was in essence what the British system thought of as "law"; the Qur'an and the sunna were its "sources"; classical *fiqh* would be understood as jurisprudence and its major figures "legal authorities," producers of "doctrine" and "legal textbooks"; *fatawa* were understood as "precedent." Qadis would be "judges," and the *ulama* who appeared in the court system would function as "lawyers" or "experts."[45] The British concept of "justice, equity and good conscience" figured at first within the Company concept of *siyasa*, through a sense that British judges would apply the law in cooperation with qadis and with due consideration of conditions and understandings on the ground—a necessity in any case given the small body of substantive law from which the British initially had to work. However, justice, equity, and good conscience gradually became a catchall term to refer to judges' discretion, often used to justify departures from local practice or Islamic norms. In combination with the processes of codification and textualization, the British use of *siyasa* began to result in a rigidification and flattening of the shari'a:

> Not until the British took over the mantle of siyasa from the Mughals could they enforce systematic taqlid through a centralizing state, bureaucracy, translation and printing. The British did not create the term "taqlid," but their presence in India did give the term a legal reality which it did not enjoy in any period prior. British dislocation and remodeling of Islamic law erased all presence or potential for ijtihad: once again, their assumption slowly became a coercive reality.[46]

The use of *siyasa* as a basis for the discretion of the ruler in matters of law as well as public policy had the effect, in India, of erasing an earlier meaning of *siyasa* as a balancing, ordering principle for the pluralism of Islamic legal practice. [47] The idiom of *siyasa* allowed the British to take on the discretionary leeway the Mughals had reserved for themselves, but it also carried its own limitations and logic. The power of the ruler was conditioned upon his upholding of the shari'a, and the duty of Muslim subjects, the *ulama* (religious scholars) most particularly, was to tread the difficult line between obedience to the ruler and holding the ruler accountable to Islamic standards of just rule.[48] Time and time again, colonial claims to legitimacy articulated in mixed idioms of universal justice and local custom, administrative order and legal right, proved also to provide the vocabulary by which counterclaims against the colonial project were advanced.

The suppression of local elites and the replacement of local institutions by the British did not silence opposition, nor did attempts at "jural colonization" (Hallaq 2009, 21) entirely succeed. In India, Malaya, and Egypt, British officials saw the powers which preceded them—the Mughals, the Malay sultanates, the Ottomans—as an important source of legitimacy, and also of scholarship on Islamic law.

Legal scholarship thrived under these circumstances; the imperial court patronised the 'ulama, or legal scholars, and Aurangzeb commissioned the influential fatwa Alamgiri, a collection of legal opinions in the fiqh tradition. On the administrative side, the sharia was supplemented with a comprehensive set of imperial regulations as well as a cadre of officially sponsored qadis drawn primarily from the 'ulama.[49]

The presence of British officers in local governments in India and the requirements of colonial government gave rise to a proliferation of texts which worked to define Islam, Islamic law, Muslim society, and local practice for both local and colonial elites: codes of law; sociological, historical, and theological studies; manuals of judging; translations of Qur'an; and local myths, so that "(p)aradoxically, the decline of the Mughal Empire appears to have stimulated a moral and cultural competition among successor powers that fuelled an increase in Islamic legal scholarship."[50]

Muslim legal officials, interpreters, jurists, advisors, and other functionaries of the courts and the colonial government continued to play an important role in the everyday articulation and delivery of Islamic law. However, their growing association with the British caused a contradictory situation: they now had the means to enforce and regularize Islamic law across their jurisdictions, but were losing the authority and mandate to do so. *Kadis* in Malaya, for example, often appeared in court to perform multiple functions, which could conflict—in the Federated Malay States, *kadis* were called to advise on matters of property and inheritance, or as the tax collector for the state.[51] In the Anglo-Muhammadan system, court-appointed *maulavis* acted as "native law officers" who provided legal opinions (*fatawa*) to British judges, who then applied these as abstract legal principles, against the previous practice of Islamic legal institutions.

These native law officers, drawn from traditional local centers of Islamic law, faced resistance both from the colonial establishment and from the local communities in which they were based, as "collaborat(ors) with colonial rule in the most overt sense."[52] Among British judges, the general opinion was that these local officials could not be trusted to be impartial, their low salaries and local connections left them open to corruption, their inconsistency and diversity of opinions—a central asset in Islamic legal scholarship—a clear sign of their lack of training and professionalism. British policy and the problem of local legitimacy conspired to produce a decline in the presence of local judicial officials in courts, and a rise in the resort to unofficial venues and non-state jurists to adjudicate matters of Islamic law. [53] Even though the position of native law officer was abolished in 1864 in India, qadis still played an important unofficial role, in the registration of marriage and divorce, the provision of notary services, and the adjudication of religious questions, to the extent that pressure grew to appoint official qadis for nonreligious matters—state-appointed qadis were reinstated in 1876. By that time, though, the debate on who might qualify to be an authoritative qadi was well under way, and unofficial jurists continued to adjudicate outside the jurisdiction of the colonial state.

As discussed in chapter 2, the Ottomans had delineated a legal system in which the shari'a presided, as an authorizing force, overall, but in which discrete legal domains were given over to codified laws, *kanun*, authorized by the sultan. These came to dominate the legislative content of the Ottoman state, taking over the domain of public policy, but legitimated and elaborated according to shari'a rules—*siyasa shar'iyyah*, shari'a-guided public policy. Vikor argues that even though these two logics of law appeared quite different, in particular because they were based upon different and often competing authorities, by the eighteenth century Ottoman administrative practice across the empire had united their execution under the same adjudicative power: the qadi, legal officials under the employ of the state.[54] The qadi oversaw justice across the Ottoman state, employing both shari'a and *kanun*:

> Thus we can see a clear change from the classical system where a Shari'a court only operates within the restrictive framework of the Shari'a and where separate Sultan-dominated courts employ siyasa shar'iya. As the Ottoman sultan "unified" the law into a kanun that encompasses the Shari'a, modified by the

> sultan's legislative work and local custom, he could also unify the judiciary into one unified court, administered by a qadi.[55]

These developments in the Ottoman Empire show that it was not European colonialism in and of itself that determined the course the shari'a would take in the colonial period, but convergent strands of political and institutional change, that made jurisdictional politics critical for the development of the Muslim state. In Egypt, these jurisdictional politics began as a way to establish the independence of the khedive from the Ottoman state, and came to a head when the legal chaos precipitated by capitulations to European powers made possible an appeal to the Ottoman sultan to allow the establishment of Mixed Courts in Egypt, thereby opening the door for French civil law to be applied by Egyptian and European judges as Egyptian (distinct from Ottoman) law.

Patterns of legal change in Egypt in the nineteenth and twentieth centuries show a new kind of Islamic elite rising to prominence during this time and playing a unique role in Egyptian legal development, in particular in the fields of Islamic and family law (Asad 2001; Skovgaard-Petersen 1997). This new role was made possible in part through institutional developments in the state: the centralization of state authority, the bureaucratization of religious and social life, the standardization of administration and state rules for the everyday conduct of Egyptian life. Khaled Fahmy argues that the changes in the form of Egyptian legislation did not spell the emptying of their shar'i content, and that institutions and procedures remained in place to examine the correctness of legislation according to Islamic jurisprudential rules. Speaking of the introduction of new methods of forensic science into the criminal justice system of the Egyptian state, Fahmy argues:

> Far from signalling its demise, the introduction of these novel methods of establishing legal proof was meant to bolster the shar'. At no time were any of these new methods . . . considered contrary to the shari'a. Rather, like the old qânûn legislations of the Ottoman sultans, the use of medicine was meant to complement shari'a in areas where the stringent fiqh principles made it difficult to convict the defendant or in defining as illegal acts that had not been criminalized by shari'a.[56]

Egypt prior to the Mixed Courts already exhibited a legal system that had been significantly reformed, and was both flexible and accountable. The system that replaced it was more enduring because of a confluence of factors: European legal forms and categories were incorporated into the state in ways that allowed this state to govern everyday practices. In so doing, this new system reached further into the individual state. By allowing the khedives and sultans disciplinary and control measures that enhanced the output of the state, it also gave these elites who ran and benefited from the governmental state further reason to extend the reach of government into the lives of ordinary Egyptians.

Similarly, the adoption of the Majalah in Johor incorporated Islamic institutions within the administrative order of the state, a state with a new legislative and institutional hierarchy. Within this hierarchy, Islamic elites would be under the employ and the supervision of the state. With this newly unified hierarchy came new modes of unifying interpretation: in Kelantan, a legal "notis" issued by the Sultan in Council in 1917 "provided that no fatwa on any question of fiqh might be given by anyone without the prior approval of the Majlis Agama, and that all fatwas issued to applicants of the Shafi'i school must follow Shafi'i doctrine, save when given by the mufti." *Surat kuasa* that appointed muftis and qadis and defined the scope of their authority charge them with "following the Muhammadan shari'a or administrative regulation [*siasat shariah*], in accordance with the most approved Shafi'i opinions [*qaul yang mu'tamad pada madzhab Shafi'i*], and in the interests of the governance of the state [*yang jadi maslihat bagi perentahan negeri.*]"[57]

For Hallaq, even as they struggled against imperial currents, Muslim elites found themselves in the paradoxical position of leading an overall movement toward the forms and logics of the colonial state. This in turn was part of the further alienation of shari'a content, wherever it remained in the legal systems of these societies, from Islamic modes of reasoning, institutions, and social networks, part of the gradual "jural colonization" of the Muslim world in the late eighteenth and nineteenth centuries. Native elites such as Sir Syed Ahmed Khan and Sultan Abu Bakar among his Malay counterparts, were part of this new cadre of men:

> This condition represented one of the most typical ironies of colonized peoples: what they deemed to the unjust law of occupation was the only available and legitimate means by which they could bargain against their occupiers . . . in their bid for agency they were systematically bound by the colonizer's higher will-to-power and, specifically, by the terms that this power dictated.[58]

By the end of the nineteenth century, the legitimating force of the doctrine of *siyasa* as shari'a-compliant legislation had competition from

European models of law, in particular positivist legal models. New codes of Egyptian law could neither be easily justified according to principles of *siyasa shar'iyya*, nor did Egyptian Muslims referring to these classical principles alone when calling for Islamic law. In fact, the experience of European models of law and legal administration in Egypt was such that the marginalization of Islamic law in favor of European law was, by 1875, a trend with which Egyptian elites were quite familiar. The demand for shari'a content as the major, or the sole, source of Egyptian law developed later, and by this time carried with it the imprint of European legal administration, "calling for the adoption of codes that were Islamic according to new, distinctly unclassical theories of Islamic law."[59]

The relationship between *siyasa* and shari'a was also changing in the thought of Muslim reformists: whereas earlier in the nineteenth century, Muslim reformists in India devoted much of their attention to the relationship between the individual Muslim and his religious practice, by the end of the century these movements had become invested in political leadership beyond the colonial state. Recent detailed scholarship of the writings of Egyptian reformists like Jamal al-din al-Afghani, Muhammad 'Abduh and Rashid Rida from the 1880s to the 1930s trace a progression of their understanding of shari'a and its relationship to the laws of the state and the politics of anticolonial struggle. Whereas in the 1880s, the term "shari'a" tended to refer to an Islamic way of life, rather than positive law or the work of legislation, by the last years of the nineteenth century the focus had shifted to explicit criticism of the encroachment of European law within the Egyptian legal system. By the 1930s, shari'a had become symbolically central to the political platforms of Muslim reformists, anticolonialists, and many Muslims within the state structure, in Egypt, India, and the Malay States. With the establishment of the nation-state in the postindependence period, shari'a had become understood as a necessary part of the law of the state, but shari'a transformed—*siyasa shar'iyya*, as state shari'a politics—as codified law in a limited but symbolically central domain.[60]

Networks and Circulations of Law

Although it has long been understood that Islam depended upon and facilitated mobility and exchange throughout its history, the increasingly global nature of colonialism from the mid-eighteenth century onward presented new challenges and opportunities. During the late colonial period, technologies such as mass print, railways, and mass maritime transport made exchanges among geographically distant places far speedier and more common. As Muslim scholars, writers, and teachers in Deoband, Singapore, and Cairo realized, the widespread availability of new technologies that facilitated markets and colonialism—presses, railroads, public education, and literacy—could also aid in the search for new responses to imperialism and colonialism. For Muslims who wished to advocate for reforming Islam and Muslims to become more "rational," more ethical, and more concerned with questions of development, modernity, and social welfare, the conjunction of these elements of state formation and social life were crucial.[61]

The development of these technologies alone should prompt closer investigation of exchanges among Muslim communities, yet the movement of colonial officers from one site of empire to another, and the travels of Muslims and non-Muslims among crucial nodes of exchange—especially in the Indian Ocean—is a kind of circulation about which current scholarship on Islamic law has had little to say.[62] It was not simply the speed and pluralization of movement that matters, but the specific networks and flows made possible in this period, that accepted some colonial logics in order to challenge others, that allied with state institutions and then found ways to critique them. These networks and flows carried particular orientations of center and periphery—India was the central site for British colonial administrators, from which policy and experience could be extrapolated to Egypt and Malaya; Egypt was central for Muslim movements of reform and modernization in India and Malaya—and these orientations shifted with time and context.[63]

From early on in the colonial encounter, Islamic elites (such as al-Zahir, below) traversed a circuit that included Muslim courts from Constantinople to Aceh, carrying with them a wide range of possible responses to Western imperial pressure. Muslim rulers such as Abu Bakar of Johor often undertook long world tours to both Muslim and European ports of call, seeking recognition and alliance. For colonial officials such as Cromer and Salisbury, India served as a laboratory for governing Muslim society, from which lessons could be derived for Egypt and Malaya. Other circulations centered around legal training: Muslims trained in law in London or Paris and then served in the legal systems of India or Egypt, interpreting local Islamic practices into the idiom of common or civil law, or print media: presses in Cairo, Constantinople, and Singapore, producing papers that then circulated through networks of Islamic reformists traveling between Mecca, Deoband, and Penang.[64]

It is clear that both local and colonial actors in all three sites of this study were fully aware of the world beyond their borders, and borrowed freely from the experiences and strategies of others for their own actions. Both local and colonial elites in the nineteenth and twentieth centuries were products of increasingly interconnected political, economic, cultural and social worlds: the sultans of Johor were well-known in London, as were the nawabs of Indian states; the Ottoman sultans were important references for Malay, Indian and Egyptian elites; British colonial officers often began their careers in Ireland or India, and then were sent to Malaya, Egypt, or Africa. The courts of India and Malaya frequently hosted travelers from farther West, and some of these stayed, served as interpreters, diplomats, teachers, and governors. Muslim diasporas such as the Hadhrami played critical role in these circulations, and of the many Hadhramis who wove together the Indian Ocean world through trade, intermarriage, diplomacy, and religion, ʻAbd al-Rahman bin Muhammad al-Zahir plays a particular role in this narrative because of his service to the new Temenggong of Johor, Abu Bakar, who became Sultan Abu Bakar of Johor. Al-Zahir's biography encapsulates Hadhrami mobility and networks at this time—born in Hadhramaut in 1833, raised in Malabar, educated in the Islamic sciences in Egypt and Mecca, he traded between India and Arabia and traveled widely in Europe.[65] He served rulers in military and administrative capacities from Hyderabad to Calicut to Aceh. Al-Zahir's "masterful command of a whole diasporic repertoire of constituting a persona—routes, relatives, and representations" was likely not to have been lost to the new ruler of Johor whom he served from 1862 to 1864.[66]

When al-Zahir left Johor, it was to play a pivotal role in Aceh, as jurist and administrator, building onto the apparatus of the state by taking charge of the taxation system and spearheading mosque-building and public works and, later, by taking over as regent upon the sultan's death and leading the Acehnese revolt against the Dutch. His leadership involved diplomacy to (and recognition by) the British in the Straits Settlements, the Ottoman Empire, and critical notables in the Muslim world, including the Sharif of Mecca; intermarriage with the ruling families of several key ports and states and their wealth; strategic use of the pan-Islamic press; and the symbols of both Islamic and Western power and authority. Law as it traveled with diasporic groups like the Hadhrami came in many forms—as texts of *fiqh* and commentary, as learned men and women who became teachers, scholars, judges, muftis, and rulers throughout the reach of the diaspora, as institutions and practices that moved with families, property, and businesses.

British officials traveled from India to Egypt and brought with them lessons learned from India, as well as institutions, policies, and understanding, and applied them in the courts, the police, the army, public health, engineering, politics, education, and finance:

> For these reasons there is considerable justification for calling this entire process the Indianization of the Egyptian administration. Or to be more precise, what is meant by the term Indianization as applied to Egypt in this period is the grafting of Indian institutions and methods onto Egyptian institutions which in themselves reflected Ottoman, French, and purely Egyptian influences.[67]

A paradigmatic example of these officials was Evelyn Baring, Lord Cromer, the British consul-general from 1883 to 1907. Cromer had been involved in the financial policies of India from 1880, after which he was sent to Egypt to manage financial matters, with the hopes that he would perform as well there. Cromer was not alone, however; several key actors in the British strategy for Egypt were experienced India hands. Cromer also managed the reform of Egyptian education, attempting to correct the problems of Indian education when it was applied in Egypt. In India, the gap between the educated upper classes and the rest of the country had been too large, and the education of the upper classes too literate and impractical, resulting in discontent and political turmoil for the British.[68] In Egypt, Cromer had determined that the policy on mass education was to be "the three R's in the vernacular language; nothing more." Further, in his experience, he remarked,

> India furnished rather an object lesson in what should be avoided. As to education, we have created a superficially educated upper class . . . and we have done absolutely nothing towards furnishing an antidote in the way of raising the general level of education throughout the country, in order in some degree to balance the influence of the agitator. . . . In the meantime, here I am taking to heart the lesson of India, that is to say without discouraging higher education, I am doing all I can to push forward both elementary and technical education. I want all the next generation of Egypt to be able to read and write. Also, I want to create as many carpenters, bricklayers, plasterers, etc., as I possibly can.[69]

There were limits to Indianization in Egypt: the entrenchment of pre-British institutions, such as French law, the amount of resources available for the implementation of policy, and the support of the British government in these policies.[70] With regard to the Egyptian legal system and the place of Islamic institutions within it, Cromer was similarly invested in the Indian experiment, but this time as a positive model. In an 1896 letter to Lord Salisbury, then prime minister and former secretary of state for India, Cromer argued explicitly for India to be understood as a precedent for British policy on Egypt:

> There is only one effective remedy for the state of things. It is to abolish the Mehkeme Sheraieh as a separate institution altogether, and to transfer their jurisdiction to the ordinary civil courts. This is what was done many years ago in India and I do not altogether despair of securing a similar change ever being made in Egypt.[71]

Processes that had begun well before the impact of colonial interventions were felt continued into the colonial period, and accelerated with the coming of the colonial state. In India, Hanafi scholars who relied upon Abu Yusuf and Al-Shaybani were sponsored by the colonial state to produce texts like the Hidaya. They had competitors, who were more innovative and whose appeal to the general public was strong: Shah Wali Ullah (1703–62) was an early advocate of eclecticism within the Sunni schools of thought, and Shi'a scholars whose approach presented further resources for Muslim thought and action continued to be influential in the absence of a central orthodoxy.

Cairo in particular was a central site for the articulation of Islamic reform in the late nineteenth century, as well as for the dispersal of new and popular ideas about how Muslims should confront the challenges of their time, the pressures of Europe not least among them. The 'Urabi revolt, while it did not figure Islamic themes as its central argument, was widely seen as the struggle of Muslims against a Christian colonizer, combining the language of nationalism with that of Islam, and of anticolonial Muslim sentiment.[72] Singapore became a hub for the printing of newspapers in a number of Muslim vernacular languages, many of which carried reformist ideas about Islam and Muslim societies between Southeast Asia, South Asia, and the Middle East.[73]

Just as periodicals such as al-Afghani and 'Abduh's journal *al-'Urwa al-Wuthqa* (The strongest link, published 1884–1886) and 'Abduh and Rida's *al-Manar* (The beacon, 1898–1935) circulated in the Malay world, Malay periodicals were printed in Istanbul, Cairo, Medina, and Mecca, and *ulama* from Southeast and South Asia contributed to the debates in the pages of all these journals.[74] Many of these periodicals were explicit about the need to counter colonialism with a response that combined "Western" knowledge with a new fidelity to the Qur'an and Hadith. A Malay language paper founded in 1906 in Singapore called *Al-Iman* described its mission "*mengingatkan mana yang lalai dan menjagakan mana yang tidur dan menunjukkan yang sesat dan menyampaikan suara yang menyeru dengan kebajikan* [to remind the forgetful and wake the sleeping and guide the lost and raise our voices with compassion]."[75] Many of these also articulated a diagnosis of contemporary Muslim society that saw colonialism itself as a symptom of Muslim complacency.[76]

These media broadened the terms of debate about Islam, colonialism, and the Muslim state, and its levels of participation, beyond elites to wider circles of literate and engaged Muslims across the world.[77] Facilitated by technological advances and the colonial peace, more and more pilgrims went on the Hajj to Mecca, and there experienced Islam as it was practiced in the "center" of the Muslim world, but also met Muslims from other parts of the world with whom ideas about colonialism, modernity, and the future were debated.[78] Movements that began in Deoband or Cairo spread far beyond their regions of origin, through the efforts of writers, correspondents, merchants, and evangelists. By the beginning of the twentieth century, Islam was part of the repertoire of nationalist and anticolonial movements all over Malaya—in Singapore, in Johor, and all the way up the peninsula.

The rise of the Salafi movement, in which Muhammad Abduh played a critical role, has been tied to the experience of urban and cosmopolitan Muslim intellectuals in the colonized Muslim world seeking a way between what they saw as the secular modernism of reformist elites and the hidebound traditionalism of the *ulama*. In the lives of these rising elites, medium and message were inextricable, in fact, inevitable—"(i)n the Salafi vision, printing is important because it is an instrument of activism, of awakening, of making public. Thus, the dichotomy of *ijtihad* and *taqlid* also comprises two different sets of knowledge and tensions between public and private, *'amma* and *khassa*."[79] The new possibilities for Islam were critically conjoined with the mobility of Muslim intellectuals, the ability to spread ideas through print and mass education, and a way of expressing Islamic ideas in translatable, moveable ways.

Yet the growing mobility and visibility of Islamic ideas, facilitated by the colonial peace and new technologies, and at least in part supported by colonial involvement in Islamic institutions, also raised anxieties about pan-Islamism and "Wahhabism," and encouraged alliances between British colonialism and new groups of Muslim elites, who articulated their utility to the British as interpreters, interlocutors and moderators between the colonial state and Muslim society. Shortly after the 1857 revolt in India, figures such as Sayyid Ahmad Khan (1817–1898) made the case for the utility of "loyal and educated Muslims . . . as brokers between the British and India's Muslims," [80] conjuring for the British the specter of Wahhabism and pan-Islamism, forces that would otherwise occupy and enlarge the distance between rulers and ruled. As Faisal Devji (2014) has recently observed, the utility of this brokering class depended on their enunciation of continued Muslim threat, and British anxieties about this threat could be used to negotiate a better status for Muslims in India. "What the Protestant is to the Catholic, so is the Wahabi to the other Mahomedan creeds," Sayyid Ahmad posited as part of a published debate on the loyalty of India's Muslims; drawing a further connection between the English and the Indian experience, "the civil wars in England saw fathers fighting against sons and brothers against brothers, and no one can tell what the conduct of the whole community would be in any great political convulsion. I have no doubt, but that the Musulmans would do what their political status—favorable or the contrary—would prompt them to do."[81] Men such as Sayyid Ahmad Khan, known as loyalists and apologists for empire, were therefore also careful and strategic mediators between empire and Muslims; their mediation depended not only upon their ability to speak for Muslim communities to the British, but upon their facility in the idiom of imperial anxiety and memory. The utility of this group of Muslim elites—educated, loyal moderates, and moderators—would extend in the next generation into key institutions of imperial governance, the law in particular, and it is to this generation that we now turn.

The Making of the Muslim Subject

> If Anglo-Muhammadan scholarship endorsed a scripturalist version of Islam, that same version was transformed into an oppositional Islam that could be used in the anticolonial struggle. It is one of the ironies of British rule that a jurisprudence which first served to implement colonial rule in the eighteenth century could give form to a part of the independence movement of the twentieth century. Meanwhile, the intimate interaction of legal administration and

indigenous identity formation lent scripturalist Islam an enduring quality that has continued into the postcolonial period.[82]

In all three of the sites with which this book is concerned, the institutionalization of Islamic law within the ambit of state courts, and the increasing reliance on the logics and language of colonial legality meant that Muslim lawyers trained in European law began increasingly to play important intermediary roles in interpreting Islamic law within the legal idioms of the colonial state, and strategizing the use of state courts and legislation for the interests of Muslims. In India, lawyers such as Syed Ameer Ali, Abd ur-Rahim, Faiz Badruddin Tyabji, and Asaf Ali Asghar Fyzee became interlocutors between the colonial state and Indian Muslims into the twentieth century, the 1857 revolt having removed a large number of Muslim elites from positions of influence in British India.[83] Yet these lawyers performed their functions assured of the basic unassailability of English legal logic and largely untrained in matters of *fiqh* and Islamic legal practice. As such, the turn to law as an avenue for the expression of Muslim interests and identity, as articulated by British-trained Muslim lawyers loyal to the colonial state, took on "'the shari'ah' that had been framed by Anglo-Muhammadan court activity as 'Muslim personal law.'"[84]

The British High Court judge Syed Mahmood (1850–1903), son of Sayyid Ahmad Khan, was one such figure, and his legacy within the colonial system of law sheds some light on how Muslim elites—lawyers and civil servants now, rather than aristocrats—navigated colonial institutions of law to bring shar'i content back into the system. These elites actively participated in the new institutions of colonial law, and their presence provided a visible signal of the legitimacy and justice of the colonial state, at the same time that their actions within these institutions continued to negotiate the state's boundaries. In particular, despite their acceptance of the forms of colonial rule, its logics and jurisdiction, they continued to negotiate the boundaries of Islamic law and struggled to retain shari'a content and logics, using the new institutional avenues of the colonial law system. Whereas the earlier replacement of *fiqh* experts with legal texts in colonial law courts served to reify Islamic law into a limited and somewhat static domain, Muslim lawyers and judges working in the colonial law courts in the late nineteenth and early twentieth centuries found ways of turning this reliance on text and precedent to their advantage.[85] Syed Mahmood, who was the first Indian Muslim appointed to a High Court judgeship in British India, used the institution of precedent and the citational practices of British law to bring Islamic legal logic and texts back into the legal system of British India.[86] The India Law Reports, which published High Court judgments that were then binding on all the subordinate courts of British India, published about three hundred of his opinions, which quoted, translated, and interpreted Arabic jurisprudential sources, thereby making them usable throughout British India as sources of law.[87]

One such case was Queen-Empress vs Ramzan & Ors (March 7, 1885), a case heard in the Allahabad High Court.[88] Here, as in other cases, Judge Mahmood was called into the case because he was Muslim and knew the "Muhammadan Ecclesiastical Law." As Alan Guenther (2009) has noted, Mahmood was not a scholar of *fiqh* nor a lawyer trained in Islamic adjudication; rather, he was "an Islamic modernist committed to individual interpretation of sacred texts with limited attention to the historical traditions of commentators."[89] Instead of *fiqh* experts serving as advisors and witnesses, therefore, increasingly, British-trained Muslim judges functioned as knowledgeable arbiters of Islamic legal issues in the courts of British India and generated a significant amount of authoritative law in multiple arena—including who should be considered a Muslim, how worship in a mosque should be conducted, and how to understand the relationship between Muslim practice in India and the authoritative texts of Islamic law. Like Judge Mahmood, they brought with them a new orientation toward the sources and logic of the shari'a and an acceptance of the jurisdictional divisions and some of the assumptions of British law in India.

When the case reached the Allahabad High Court, Mahmood noted, "in view of the peculiarities of the question with regard to the right of worshipping in mosques possessed by Muhammadans, my learned brother referred the case to a Division Bench, of which, at his suggestion, and with the approval of the learned Chief Justice, I was to be a member."[90] Once on the Bench, at several points, Mahmood questioned or steered the process of the trial: from the Division Bench, the case was referred to the Full Bench "to obtain an authoritative ruling on the question"; from the Full Bench, Mahmood reserved his order, refusing to either concur in or dissent from the decision to uphold the conviction. He finally provided a written dissenting opinion to the decision of the Bench, which was printed in the India Law Report of 1885, thus contributing to the sources of law for the determination of future such cases in British India. In the details and reasoning of this case, Judge Mahmood questioned not only the absence of "the authorities of Muhammadan Law," but the general principle upon which this absence was justified, therefore calling into question the understanding of the domain of religion implicit in the law.

The judge argued that the matter of the case, which was "the right of a Muhammadan being able to pray in a mosque according to his tenets," required reference to the "express guarantee given by the Legislature in Section 24 of the Bengal Civil Courts Act (VI of 1871), that the Muhammadan law shall be administered with reference to all questions regarding 'any religious usage or institution.'" Mahmood argued that, in fact, these "rules of civil law" conditioned the justice of the Penal Code in India:

> If it is conceded that the decision of this case depends . . . upon the interpretation of the Muhammadan Ecclesiastical Law, it is to my mind the duty of this Court, and of all Courts subordinate to it, to take judicial notice of such law . . . whenever a question of civil right or the lawfulness of an act arises in a judicial proceeding, even a Criminal Court is bound, ex necessitate, to resort to the Civil branch of the law. . . . That the application of some of the sections of the Indian Penal Code depends almost entirely upon the correct interpretation of the rules of civil law, cannot, in my opinion, be doubted. . . . Indeed, I am prepared to go to the length of saying that, but for this principle, the rules of the Penal Code would in many cases operate as a great injustice.[91]

Further, Judge Mahmood argued that Muhammadan law should not be equated with foreign law in cases like these, providing a potentially expansive rationale for reference to Islamic legal sources more generally:

> I hold therefore that in a case like the present, the provisions of Section 56 of the Evidence Act fully relieve the parties from the necessity of proving the Muhammadan Ecclesiastical Law upon the subject, that that law is not to be placed upon the same footing with reference to this matter as any foreign law of which judicial notice cannot be taken by the Courts in British India; and it follows that I can refer to the Muhammadan Ecclesiastical Law for the purposes of this case, notwithstanding the absence of any specific evidence on the record regarding its rules.[92]

Muslims newly incorporated into the legal hierarchy of British India were called upon not only to judge matters of the law relating to religious usages and institutions, but they were also often pressed to define who a Muslim was, and what the proper conduct of Muslim worship and religious observance should be. The original conflict occurred in a mosque in

Benares in 1884: three men entered the mosque and pronounced the word *amin* during prayer. A heated argument ensued about whether this was permitted during prayers, and the three were expelled from the mosque with the help of police and prohibited from entering again unless they recanted their position on this practice. Abdulla, the person Mahmood refers to as the "prosecutor" of the initial charge, was the brother-in-law of the mosque's founder and declared himself to be the mosque's "superintendent"; the principal accused, Ramzan, was the son-in-law of the mosque's founder and related to Abdulla as well.

Amid what appeared to be disagreements about the mosque's accounts, Abdulla complained to the Magistrate about the incident, and when the Magistrate failed to take action, he filed a petition charging Ramzan and two others with "the offence of insulting the religion of the Hanafia Musalmans" under Sections 297, 298, and 352 of the Indian Penal Code (1860). Abdulla's argument was that the three men were "not the followers of any of the four Imams," that they intended "to set up a new form of worship for themselves" and were therefore "no longer Muhammadans."[93] Abdulla argued that the three men were Wahabis, an allegation that in the context of heightened British concerns about "Wahabi" Muslims in India, following the notorious "Wahabi trials" of the 1860s and 1870s, raised the specter of fanatic and violent Muslim attacks against the empire.[94] Abdulla made the argument that these men were Wahabi and not Hanafi Muslims, and therefore their pronouncement of *amin* loudly during prayers in the mosque was "insulting the religion of the Hanafia Musalmans."[95] The Magistrate tried the case and found the three guilty under Section 296 ("disturbing religious assembly") and sentenced them to a fine or a month's imprisonment, based on the interpretation that saying *amin* loudly during prayers in a mosque constituted causing disturbance to religious worship and was therefore a criminal offence.

Mahmood's arguments as to the interpretation of the act and his method of reasoning the case show a keen awareness of the potential breadth of his audience, and they allow a glimpse into the "intimate interaction of legal administration and indigenous identity formation" that Anderson argues helped inscribe "scripturalist Islam" into the Muslim state.[96] In doing so, they help show that indigenous identity formation was a process in which particular local elites played critical mediating roles, and they reveal the logic by which scripturalist Islam appealed to both Muslims and British actors in the late nineteenth century.[97] The first of these logics of scripturalist Islam was translative, making Islam and the content of Muslim religiosity fully legible in Anglo-Christian terms. Mahmood's arguments about the relationship between authoritative Islamic texts, Muslim practice and orthodoxy were based on an assumption that Islam is comparable to Christianity, Anglicanism in particular, and that his audience would be persuaded to his point of view more readily if they understood this comparability. He referred from the beginning of his judgment to "the Muhammadan Ecclesiastical Law" (1), which in his argument means the "Koran," "Sunna," and the teachings of the four schools of Sunni *fiqh* (jurisprudence); at other points he referred to four "orthodox schools of Muhammadan Ecclesiastical Law," thereby equating Sunni *fiqh* with church law. He referred to mosques as having "congregations" and being "consecrated"; in attempting to determine whether the alleged offences were actually committed during worship, he compared Muslim prayers with the reading of the Nicene creed. The word *amin* itself "has been adopted in prayers by Muhammadans as much as by Christians" (11). The only point of distinction he drew was to comment that unlike "an ordinary Christian church," mosques were also places for "religious and moral teaching and discussion" (17).

The second strand of this scripturalist logic was to demonstrate a methodology for determining the content of Muslim practice, tradition, and orthodoxy, and to make that methodology both usable in the courts and relatable to other sources of colonial law. To this end, having made an argument that the Muhammadan Ecclesiastical Law must be referred to in cases of this type, it remained the task of the judge to determine which texts and practices mattered. Firstly, while Mahmood acknowledged that there were other Muslims besides Sunnis in India, "orthodox" here was understood to refer to Sunnis and the four schools of Sunni jurisprudence. Here, Mahmood cited Hamilton's preface to his "translation of the Hedaya," which Mahmood defines as "the most celebrated textbook of the Hanafi school of law" (13), before discussing the conflicting opinions of commentators found within the Hadith collections of Bukhari and Muslim. Secondly, therefore, he arranged an order of authoritative texts—Mahmood's argument situated Hamilton within the Hedaya corpus, and then placed the Hedaya at the top of the hierarchy of jurisprudential sources to consult.

Thirdly, he acknowledged the prevalence of debate in Islamic jurisprudence and the need for consensus on matters not clearly enunciated in the Qur'an, and went on to list the opinions of jurists in the Hanafi and Shafi'i school, noting that while the Malikis and Hanbalis would concur on this issue, their opinions were not pertinent because "their followers do not exist in British India" (13). Mahmood also referred to the practices of Muslims at the Kaaba ("the greatest mosque in the world") and "all the Muhammadan countries like Turkey, Egypt, and Arabia itself," where the practice of saying *amin* was varied but not controversial. Finally, and with prescience, Mahmood's judgment made clear that determinations as to the proper and lawful conduct of Muslim worship needed to be sensitive to the rights of the minority *within* a religious group. He argued that the Public Prosecutor's opinion that "the mere fact of the disturbance being caused to the religious assembly is sufficient to constitute the offence" (18) placed undue emphasis on Section 296, valuing maintenance of peace above the right of individuals to worship according to their tenets.

Other Muslim judges serving in British courts in this period brought up comparable arguments with regard to the interpretation of Islamic law, to the use of Anglo-Muhammadan texts in deciding cases, and to the appropriate relationship between British and Muslim law. These arguments both reinforced the jurisdiction of the overarching system of British law over previously shari'a domains such as *wakf* (Arabic *waqf*, referring to religious endowments) and marriage, while at the same time arguing for the inclusion of Islamic legal logic and sources, and implicitly for the prioritization of Muslim judges in the interpretation of these sources. The judge Ameer Ali, appointed to the Bengal High Court in 1890 and the first Indian to be appointed to the Privy Council (1909), wrote a dissenting opinion in the 1893 case *Shuk Lal Poddar & Ors v Bikani Mia*, regarding the practice of waqf. In this opinion, Justice Ameer Ali argued *against* an easy equivalence between the Islamic law of waqf and the British law governing trust and charitable giving; when British judges used the Hedaya as an authoritative source of shari'a, "it must be remembered that the English version is a rendering of a Persian translation of the original Arabic Hedaya with many interpolations and omissions."[98] Speaking as a member of the British legal establishment—first in India and then in the United Kingdom—Ameer Ali argued that both Hindu and Muslim law, as delivered by the colonial state, was an integral part of the faith of Hindus and Muslims, and therefore that these laws should be recognized in British India on similar footing as British law:

> In considering the propriety of altering or abrogating the Hindu or Mahomedan Laws . . . it should never be forgotten . . . that they are an integral part of the faith of that people, and that though we may not be bound by absolute treaty,

> we have virtually pledged ourselves to preserve them by repeated proclamations and enactments.[99]

Ameer Ali's opinion did not carry the case, and later judgments by the Privy Council disagreed with his argument, and continued to draw parallels between Islamic and colonial law in ways that disadvantaged wealthy Muslim landowners and angered those who wanted to preserve the domain of wakf for the shari'a domain. "Thus, by the end of the nineteenth century, colonial jurists' responses to demands for Islamic law reform had brought together what had earlier appeared to be an unlikely coalition of forces: landed elites, lawyers and more religious orthodox Muslims."[100]

Rising Muslim Elites and the Redefinition of Islamic Law

Moving from Muslim judges and lawyers to *ulama* and Islamic institutions, I trace the development of ideas of reform and responses to colonialism among state-sponsored Islamic elites, then their interaction with non-state Islamic institutions and actors. For many Islamic legal scholars, the incorporation of Islamic jurisprudential institutions and elites into the administrative and epistemic hierarchy of the modern state constituted the replacement of an entire system of shari'a knowledge and practice.[101] For Hallaq, for example, "the most pervasive problem in the legal history of the modern Muslim world has . . . been the introduction of the nation-state and its encounter with the Shari'a" (2009, 359). Yet the incorporation of traditional Islamic elites within the employ and influence of the state also gave rise to new figures with differing ideas about Islam and whose bases of authority came from outside the state.

The capture of the state by a non-Muslim colonial government required a new role for many of the *ulama*, whose location outside the control of the colonial state gave them a new legitimacy as popular religious leaders, and a new focus on inculcating in individual Muslims a deeper adherence to fundamental Islamic practices.[102] Through a focus on Islamic law as personal status law, we discuss how Muslim elites like Muhammad 'Abduh and the *ulama* of Deoband, who might have been expected to resist the reform of the shari'a into a division of the modern state, found instead reasons to invest in the ongoing codification, reification, and limitation of shari'a content even as they campaigned for its reform and revivification. The institutional incorporation of established Islamic elites and their challenge from outside the state raised the level of debate about Islam, politics, and reform at a time when both Muslim state and society were seeking new solutions to problems of modernity, nationalism, colonialism, and authority. Rather than leading to a deadening of debate on Islamic law, these circumstances precipitated an efflorescence of Islamic legal scholarship, although not all of it came from within the shari'a episteme. Reform and revivification had, by the end of the nineteenth century, found a new locus: the Muslim family.

Islamic Institutions and the Colonial State

In Islamic institutions closely associated to the colonial state, the pressure to rationalize and unify Islamic law was strong; Islamic institutions with more distance from the state responded to and drew from state-based Islamic elites, but had more latitude for critiquing state policies and logics. Even so, both state and non-state Islamic institutions in the late nineteenth century can be seen to have oriented themselves to the fact that Islamic law was now part of the administrative structure of the state. Even when Islamic institutions formulated a strategy based upon institutional autonomy from the state, their philosophical leanings owed much to the colonial encounter. In combination with the British reliance on codification, translation, and text, the rise of Muslim voices from new centers of thought and jurisprudence, and technological and educational change, Islamic reformism became part of the language of popular Islam. However, this popular Islam was itself deeply altered by the beginning of the twentieth century—it was spread by text and took the power of the state for granted, in fact evaluating the legitimacy of the state in terms of its delivery of shari'a goods.[103]

Prominent writers on Islam and modernity in this period reimagined Islamic practice and the history of *fiqh* in similar ways to the British—as static and unresponsive to changing circumstances—but for different ends, arguing that the revivification of Muslim societies and states could only be undertaken if the shari'a were restored.[104] Whereas Egypt's Islamic institutions, al-Azhar preeminent among them, found themselves in the position of needing to accommodate state policies and institutional encroachment on shar'i domains from the Ottoman period, in India powerful non-state institutions of Islam such as the madrasa at Deoband articulated a vision of Islam that minimized state intervention. For differing reasons, in both cases Islamic family law came increasingly to be seen as a key component of the Muslim response to colonialism, and became widely articulated as an essential strategy for limiting European incursions into Muslim social, political, and religious life.

In Egypt, systematic reforms of the shari'a court system introduced the procedural rules of French civil law to the shari'a courts, buttressed this change by allowing lawyers trained in civil law to work in the shari'a courts, and placed judges from the Native Courts on the shari'a bench.[105] Muhammad al-'Abbas al-Mahdi, who was Grand Mufti of Egypt between 1848 and 1897, instituted greater Hanafi control over the content of law and court decisions, imposing the uniformity of Hanafi jurisprudential opinions and institutions on a largely Maliki and Shafi'i populace.[106] Muhammad Qadri Pasha prepared a code of Islamic personal status law in 1893 which codified the majority views of the Hanafi school, an attempt at reform of the Egyptian legal system whose impetus was both the influence of the French and British view of law as a rational rule-based system, and also the desire to continue to have Islamic legal content in a legal system in which European law and judges were increasingly powerful.[107] In this context, shari'a and *fiqh* became cast by Egyptian Islamic elites as positive law that could supplant foreign sources of law.

Both the Ottomans and the French had punished muftis and *ulama* for open dissent—for example, exiling al-Afghani and 'Abduh in the 1870s and 1880s for antigovernment activity. Muhammad 'Abduh (whose actions with regard to the shari'a courts in Egypt will be an important focus later on), when allowed to return to Egypt in the late 1880s, would take great care not to be seen to criticize the system openly. Later in the century, his students placed outside state institutions, most notably the Islamic revivalist Rashid Rida, would build their critiques of Egyptian law upon the intellectual foundations 'Abduh laid, applying these critiques to a more profound restatement of shari'a's role in the state. Rida's base of power was not his position as a state mufti or alim but his leading role in publications such as *al-Manar* ("The lighthouse" or "The beacon," published from 1898 to 1935), founded with 'Abduh. In the early issues of *al-Manar*, Rida expressed a critique of the Europeanization of Egyptian law that emphasized its alienness and its illegitimacy, arguing that "the Muslim only follows man-made law with repudiation and under pressure of force."[108] In contrast, Rida argued (in 1898) for *qanun shar'i wahid* (one single shari'a law).[109]

The "reformist" *ulama* of the *madrasa* (seminary/Islamic school, founded 1866) at Deoband embodied a new kind of Islamic response to colonialism, based largely outside the state. This was a response based on individual knowledge and action, a response that was at once entirely reliant on the central texts and institutions of Islam (the Qur'an, Hadith, and the writings of the *ulama*), and which made use of the new challenges and opportunities afforded by the colonial state. They attracted most of their students from the rural peasantry, expressing a desire to reach a population other than that of elite men, and taking the further step of appealing to women as well. They did not rely on government funding, holding on to an ideal of religion as a realm outside the reach of government, and remaining politically and materially autonomous from the colonial state. They capitalized on the rise in the availability and spread of printed material to reach Muslims not only all over India, but as far away as Singapore and Mecca.[110] Rejecting the long-standing melding of Islam with rural customs and bases of power, they provided a vision of Islam in which saint and tomb veneration, music and dance, as well as "outside" influences from Europe or other Indian communities were denounced. The *ulama* at Deoband maintained that jihad would be a central strategy for the goal of Islamic revival, and saw that revival as an explicit answer to both British colonialism and Muslim weakness in the face of European incursions.[111]

Making the Muslim Family: Conflating Family Law and Personal Status

From differing institutional bases and for different strategic reasons, therefore, in late nineteenth-century India and Egypt, the Muslim family became a focus of concern for Islamic elites articulating the role of the shari'a as a response to colonialism. In India and Malaya, the question of jurisdiction began with a bifurcation of the state into two domains—one to be governed by British colonial officials, rules, and institutions; the other a space of autonomy for local Muslim rulers. These bifurcations were powerful fictions whose foundational legal text was the treaty bringing the British in as colonial rulers. In Egypt, the question of jurisdiction had already received a number of imperial answers by the time of the British: from 1798 to 1812 it was occupied by France, and until 1875 it was at least nominally a part of the Ottoman Empire. Between 1875 and 1882, British and French ministers were inserted into the Egyptian cabinet to monitor the interests of their states after Egypt defaulted on its loans; after 1882 Britain occupied Egypt until 1952. Each of these imperial arrangements had different implications for jurisdictional division; each layer of legality worked upon the ones that came after it. French and Ottoman influence on law and legal reform had at least one major effect on the direction in which Islamic law in Egypt was transformed—both systems lent themselves to the emergence of personal status law *as* codes governing the family. By doing so, they set the scene in Egypt for Islamic family law to become the center of the Islamic legal system of the state, constructing the category of family law itself anew and prioritizing the Muslim family—the Muslim woman at its heart—as the natural safe haven for the shari'a in the modern state.

As theoretical as these divisions may have initially been, they made a new space for politics, a space made powerful by the investment of local elites in their newly constructed authority over the religious sphere. Islamic law as it functions within the Muslim postcolonial state has often been treated as if it were family law or the continuation of "traditional" Islamic practices, and it is often assumed that family law is the last province of Islamic law because of the importance of the family unit in Islam. This importance seems, in the light of historical evidence, to be a backward projection, or is at the very least due almost as much to British imperial interests and Victorian values as it was to the special value of the family in Islam. Even where preservation of Islamic law and local practices was a stated policy objective, the colonial state became involved in the smallest details of Muslim life, legislating and confining these details within codes and administrative regulations. The identification of Islamic law with elite and ethnic customary law, and its containment within the European categories of personal status, are themselves constructions of the colonial period.

We will discuss the creation of the domain of Islamic family law in terms of two central arguments. The first is that the reform of personal status law as family law was essential to the project of producing a secular state (but of a particular kind); and the second, that the politics of this development was driven by local elite participation as well as colonial intervention. In Egypt, Islamic reformers saw the development of laws governing the Muslim family as a way to preserve a domain for shar'i legislation in state administration. In India, the Muslim family and the religiosity of the Muslim individual became central to the preoccupations of Islamic reformers precisely because of their exclusion from the legislative processes of the state.

While the process of jurisdictional division changed the answer to the question, "whose law?," it also had profound effects on the law itself, on the issue, "what law?" The very divisibility of Islamic law into jurisdictions separate from the state indicates a profound departure from earlier notions of Islamic law, where the practices and norms of religion were not easily distinguished from that of the state. By dividing law among different groups, colonial and local elites profoundly altered Islamic law itself, and the yoking of separate domains of law to different ruling groups, institutions, and interests would continue to have dramatic consequences for Islamic law, the Muslim state, and Muslim identity itself, well into the contemporary period. Shari'a content and institutions were marginalized through their reification into codes and their limitation into one domain of law—the family—out of many. However, Islamic family law became a central component of state power and authority, through the growing importance of the family as a target of governance and as a new locus for Islamic morality. It was in Egypt that the civil law concept of personal status; the modern idea of family law; and the growing power of the state over shari'a content, personnel, and institutions combined to form what is today taken to be the core of Islamic law all over the Muslim world: Islamic family law.

Personal Status Law as the Reform of the Family: Egypt, 1896

It was in Egypt that the term "personal status law" seems to have first been used in the 1870s to describe Islamic law, by the jurist Muhammad Qadri Pasha (d. 1886), in the title of a codification of Hanafi laws relating to the family.[112] It was also in Egypt that the project of Muslim personal status law, which came to converge upon the category of Islamic family law, was tied firmly to the idea of modernization and reform. Qadri Pasha's compilation, entitled *Kitab al-ahkam al-shar'iyya fi al-ahwal al-shakhsiyya wa al-mawarith* (The Book of Laws of the Shari'a in Matters of Personal Status and Inheritance), was not promulgated as law—matters of marriage, divorce, and inheritance were adjudicated largely by qadis in the shari'a courts on the basis of the jurisprudence of the appropriate schools of thought (Shafi'i in the Delta and Maliki in Upper Egypt) and on customary local practices (*'urf.*)[113] Instead, the codification was intended for the guidance of judges in the Mixed Courts who were not trained in the shari'a.[114]

In this light, the use of the term *al-ahwal al-shakhsiyya* as the Arabic translation of the French concept of *statut personnel* reflects the realities of divided jurisdiction already in place in Egypt in the 1870s. During the period covered in this study, the French concept of *statut personnel* (personal law), the Ottoman *millet* system (in which religious minorities were permitted to adjudicate accordning to their own rules), and Anglo-American debates on private international law and "personal status," seem to have converged. This convergence and its chronology are clearest in Egypt, subject first to Ottoman law, and the law of the Capitulations, then to French law, and then to British law—the nineteenth-century Arabic formulation of Islamic personal status law, *al-ahkam al-shar'iyya fi al-ahwal al-shakhsiyya*—emerged from this encounter of multiple legal frames, in Qadri Pasha's text. In Egypt from the 1870s to the middle of the twentieth century, an individual's standing before the law depended upon a number of things: nationality, religious identification, gender. Basing jurisdiction on these principles of personality was common to both the French and the Ottomans and adds confusion to the matter of where the concept of personal status might have originated, and over what legal territories it might hold sway. The Ottoman system of *millet* granted some non-Muslim groups (Christians and Jews in particular) a measure of legal autonomy (in cases not involving Muslims), and this concept of personality based upon religion carried on in Egypt well after the Ottoman period. The system of Mixed Courts defined the jurisdiction of the court by the nationality of parties involved, applying codes derived from the civil law (more specifically, Napoleonic) system. The British occupation of Egypt did not involve a significant departure from this civil law outline, and the establishment of the Native Courts in 1883 paralleled that of the Mixed Courts, including in the style and sources of its legislation.

The reform of the shari'a that took place in the second half of the nineteenth century in Egypt took on some of the principles of law reform in this wider system, prioritizing legibility and regularity in the law—hence Qadri Pasha's codification. This text of law, advisory as it may have been, exemplifies a number of other transformations also taking place in the area of shari'a reform at the time—the redefinition of the Muslim family as the nuclear family, itself becoming a central target of reform, the selection of Hanafi jurisprudence rather than local practices or a more flexible interpretive framework for the adjudication of disputes, and the increasing emphasis on the state as the recipient—and enforcer—of the benefits of the reform of family law. Qadri Pasha's code also chose among opinions within the jurisprudence, preferring the more conservative interpretation of law—for example in the case of a woman's right to give herself away in marriage—to interpretations that allowed potentially more leeway to women.[115]

The reform of the Muslim family took center stage in the thinking of Egyptian reformers—al-Afghani and 'Abduh played leading roles in arguing for changes in Islamic legal institutions and family law in particular, in keeping with the needs of a modern state and modern Muslim subjects. They were not the only ones: "modernist" lawyers, journalists, and members of the Egyptian government, many of them trained in the West or influenced by European ideals of legal reform, participated actively in debates about the proper place and content of Islamic law, family law, and relations between the sexes.[116]

> "Legal reform" in Egypt was inspired not only by liberal European ideas but also by a less enlightened aspect of this same "modern" Europe, an aspect that taught the rulers of Egypt how to tighten their grip over their subjects and how to make their rule more efficient and productive.[117]

Whereas Qadri Pasha's semi-official codifications did not carry the force of law, the same cannot be said of Muhammad 'Abduh's efforts at reforming the shari'a courts. Abduh (1849–1905), in his capacity as Grand Mufti of Egypt, submitted a report on shari'a court reform in 1899, entitled "Taqrir Islah al-Mahakim al-Shar'iyya."[118] The report addressed reforms needed in the institutions of the shari'a court: physical infrastructure, personnel standards, the need for more efficient handling of cases, for inspections and records. When he addressed the contents of the shari'a, Abduh was at pains to clarify that the shari'a itself did not need reform, but that its texts did: they required standardization and clarification. Abduh framed the shari'a courts essentially as family courts and therefore critical to the project of saving the Egyptian family and by extension the moral fabric of society itself. The courts must therefore balance the work of administration with the social function of maintaining individual privacy and dignity, as part of the modern state, and as part of the modern state, the shari'a, as family law, also has a role in upholding the political order.[119] For Talal Asad,

> these interwoven concepts and sensibilities put in place a particular contradiction: on the one hand, religion is placed in a private domain, ostensibly to

> be protected *from* state intervention, but on the other, family is placed in this same domain, but to be protected *by* state intervention as part of its sovereign responsibility to sustain and defend the public order.[120]

Asad's reading of the report aims to "look for the ways it adapts itself to the new spaces of the modernising state," and argues that it is in 'Abduh's treatment of the family in law that this adaptation can most clearly be seen.[121] Asad sees the division of jurisdiction in Egypt between religious and secular courts—first with the separation of the mixed courts in 1875 and then with the *ahliyyah* courts in 1883—as a crucial moment in the process of Egyptian secularization, of the growth of the scope of the state to encompass ever-larger areas of life. What European historians have labeled "religious courts" became so out of a process of secularization, where the state took on the task of dividing jurisdictions—and the social realities they described—as "religious" (meaning family and *awqaf*, religious endowments) separate from criminal, commercial, and public law, which came to be defined as "secular."[122] This process was not simply the encroachment of one realm of state over another, it was a transformation of Islamic law—defined as the law of personal status—into an arm of the state:

> It is in this context that . . . one may place the reform that eventually translates the shari'a as "family law," for the family is not merely a conservative political symbol or a site of gender control. By virtue of being a legal category, it is an object of administrative intervention . . . that is part of the re-arrangement of the modern nation-state . . . the legal formation of the family gives the concept of individual morality it own "private" locus, and the shari'a can now be spoken of as the law of personal status—*qanun al ahwal al shakhsiyya*—the product of a secular formula, a defined place in which "religion" makes its public appearance through state law.[123]

For Asad, "when the shari'a is structured essentially as defining personal status in the law, it is radically transformed . . . what happens to the sharia is not curtailment but transmutation. It is rendered into a subdivision of law that is authorised by the centralizing state . . . it is secularised in distinctive ways."[124] This process of secularization does not revolve around the separation of church and state or the removal of religion to the private sphere but around the right and ability of the state to assign religion its role and to define that role as a subsidiary of the state.

Asad argues that the point is "not to speculate about an old motive (resistance) but about new spaces (institutional and discursive models) that make different kinds of knowledge, action and desire possible," and for this reason he argues against reading the actions of Muslim elite groups during the colonial period either as resistance or a failure to modernize.[125] However, placing Abduh's report solely within the context of the realignment of shari'a along the power grids of the modern secular state may serve precisely to obscure the new spaces Asad seeks out. The close affinity between Islamic family law and the policies of the modern nation-state need not lead us to assume that the state—in Egypt at the end of the nineteenth century or elsewhere—had won a unilateral victory; at the very least we need not assume that a victory won by the secular modern state could be secure for long.

It is amid a worldwide concern for the redefinition of Islamic law and its relationship to the ascendancy of the modern state that 'Abduh's report might be read, and the influence of 'Abduh himself might be understood. In India, in Malaya, and in Egypt, the jurisdiction of Muslim family law came to include matters of marriage and divorce, child custody, inheritance, and religious endowments (*awqaf*). The 1880s saw a proliferation of laws regulating the family in Egypt, in Malaya and the Straits Settlements, and in India: marriages and divorces were required to be registered with the state and came for the first time under state Islamic bureaucracies; laws relating to the abolition of practices like slavery (in Malaya) and sati (in India), to the promulgation of education for girls (in Malaya and Egypt) and the "protection" of women (often anti-vice laws), were passed; rules were introduced regarding what kinds of property could be classified as religious endowments and therefore be exempt from state control. All these were made in the name of Islamic law and promulgated under the authority of Muslim rulers and Islamic religious elites, but they came into being amid a range of other changes in the state: the growing incorporation of Islamic institutions into the colonial state, the unification of laws and practices with regard to matters of religion and culture, the consolidation of religious authority under one set of ruling elites, and the growing identification of Islam with the interests and worldviews of those elites. In this period, the British understanding of "personal status," marking religious divisions between communities, became intertwined with the civil law understanding of *statut personnel* and the colonial manner in which this was applied, to the family as a target of modern state reform.

The Family as Target of Reform in India: Deoband, 1905

The late nineteenth century was a productive period for the diversification of ideas about Islam and Muslim life. Islam had become the solution to whatever was understood to ail both the Muslim state and the Muslim person. Many of these varieties of Islamic thought sidelined the state and concentrated on the miraculous, the esoteric and the local, finding "success from being located in (the) sphere of religion rendered distinct from 'politics.'"[126] Others found ways to engage the state and capitalize upon its new capacity to extend their appeal to Muslim audiences. Whereas the trajectory Asad identifies above in the case of late nineteenth-century Egypt involved elites closely associated with the state, whose range of strategies depended upon state institutions, in India at the turn of the century we see different permutations of thought and action that, even as they underline the importance of Asad's key insights, might serve to elaborate diverse pathways to the privatization of religion and the making of contemporary Islamic law.

Asad locates state power, in which law plays a critical role, at the center of the "process of governance," by which

> the individual acquires his or her rights mediated by various domains of social life—including the public domain of politics and the private domain of the family—as articulated by the law. The state embodies, sanctions, and administers the law in the interests of its self-governing citizens . . . it is in this context that "the family" emerges as a category in law, in welfare administration, and in public moralising discourse.[127]

Asad goes on to argue that, while the common assumption has been that colonial governments left the domain of the family alone because it was "the heart of religious doctrine and practice . . . on the contrary . . . the *shari'a* thus defined is precisely a secular formula for privatising 'religion' and preparing the ground for the self-governing subject." On the one hand, the evidence from Malaya and India on the ways that Muslim elites, in and out of the colonial state, sought to make themselves and their experiences legible, translatable, and transportable in the late nineteenth century further underscore the power of the "secular formula" Asad describes. On the other, the diversity of these representations, their unique and strategic positions with regard to state power and local institutions, and the multiple visions they presented of the Muslim subject, might perhaps invite deeper exploration of the variety and depth of Muslim representations of Islam as the modern state inserted itself deeper and deeper into their lives. During this period, the self-governing subject to whom the modern state, in Asad's view, would inevitably tend, was nested in multiple hierarchies of gender, patriarchy, knowledge, and class. The following brief exploration of one of the most egalitarian of these visions of Islam serves to illustrate the complexities of Muslim representations of the individual, emergent from the colonial logic of Islam as a private domain.

This reorientation toward Islam in the private domain adapted to the contours of the growing colonial state, but it also drew on deeper roots in the institutional retreat of earlier Muslim states, which had already led to a more prominent role for the *ulama* of India. With the rise of a non-Muslim colonial state, many Indian *ulama* developed their leadership roles further, relying upon new resources made salient by colonialism: political debate, popular preaching, and mass printing of religious material in Urdu. Each of these resources were trained upon the reformation of the Muslim as an individual, whose relationship with Islam would be refined through attention to "the fundamentals of personal Islamic practice."[128]

In India, the appeal of the Deobandi movement in the last decades of the nineteenth century lay in part in its refusal to cast either the colonizing West or the colonized Indian as the problem. The Deobandi movement was a central source of ideas about a new kind of Islam, whose motive force would be the "education of religious leaders, preaching and teaching, public debate and . . . a flood of pamphlets and books."[129] Its core institution, the *Dar al-Ulum* (Realm of knowledge/sciences), was founded in 1867; its leaders were jurisprudents and religious scholars who were deeply influenced by Sufi teachings. Recognizing that the institutions of the state were no longer within the reach of Muslim control, the target of Deobandi activism became Muslim private life.

Representative of the second generation of *ulama* at Deoband, Maulana Ashraf 'Ali Thanawi (1864–1943) had great influence among middle-class and elite Indians, who flocked to Deoband on the new railway, read widely available books and pamphlets, and were increasingly aware of the spread of colonial government into their daily lives. Thanawi's popular text, the *Bihishti Zewar* (The heavenly ornaments), illustrates that the language of modernity and reform was central to Islamic discourses during the colonial period, and that this language of reform saw as its unit of change the individual Muslim believer: "The movements epitomized by

Thanawi and people like him helped to spread an ethical Islam of individual responsibility, which was suitable to a more integrated and more mobile population; it also fostered self-esteem among a subject population. This religious style contributed . . . to a heightened sense of religious affiliation as the primary focus of social identity in a pluralistic society."[130]

The *Bihishti Zewar* had the same target as many European reformers of law, society and Indian life—women and the family. If women were given the tools with which to understand the shari'a, Islamic law and norms, Thanawi reasoned, both their worship and their social roles could be reformed. Custom, according to Thanawi, was the major factor preventing women from fulfilling the shari'a: it was superstitious, backward, and not only did it contradict Islam, it competed with proper Islamic practices and led Muslims astray even in their homes. The task of texts like the *Bihishti Zewar* was to correct mistaken adherence to custom, that was usually enshrined within the home by women, and argue for a more rational, educated, socially constructive way, the way of the shari'a. Texts like the *Bihishti Zewar* were aimed at elites: landowners, government servants, business families. They promoted an orderly vision of society, in which proper hierarchy was all-important—elite men over elite women over lower-class men over lower-class women. The texts would govern Muslim behavior, and the *ulama* would interpret and convey the texts. Elites and nobles were placed and confirmed in their status at the head of Muslim life and authority, and the cultural and religious production of their society supported their vision of Islam.[131] In India and later on in Malaya as well, the reformulation of the role of Islam in society, motivated partly by colonialism and partly by ongoing processes within Muslim societies, had become an increasingly elite activity.

These elite visions of Islam had much in common with that of the British reformers, although some of the commonalties we now tend to see between Muslim patriarchy and Victorian values arose later (for example, the idea that men and women were essentially different, and that women were the embodiment of tradition).[132] Unlike his counterparts at Aligarh (the Madrasat al-Uloom Musalman-e-Hind, also known as the Muhammadan Anglo-Oriental College, established in 1875 by Syed Ahmed Khan to train Muslims for Indian government service), Thanawi saw women as entirely in possession of the ability to reform their beliefs and behavior through education and reading. Unlike later scholars like Maududi (1903–1979), Thanawi did not preach reform as an anticolonial action, and neither did he see women as the last line of defense against the encroachment of Western values. It was perhaps the very commitment of the *ulama* of Deoband to the core traditions of Islam that made their vision of women in Muslim society far more egalitarian, in fact, than that of modernizers like Maududi and the Aligarh school.[133]

Conclusion

By the end of the nineteenth century, the Muslim state was two things—one, an administrative state that upheld Islamic law in matters of personal status; and two, an individual condition of being tied to the observance of an Islam that was marked increasingly by adherence to a textualized shari'a organized around the marital family. The relationship between the two was forged through the delivery of Islamic law by the state, and Islamic law itself had become defined largely as the law of the Muslim family. The British colonial period offered both opportunity and hazard for Muslim elites, and that elites responded to these new circumstances in ways that attempted to push back against the encroachment of colonial power but often ended up taking on the language and logic of imperial institutions of law.

The making of the Muslim state in the late eighteenth and nineteenth centuries featured a careful balancing between multiple sources of power, and authority, as evidenced by our discussion of the shifting definition of *siyasa shar'iyyah* during this period. Figures like the Sultan of Johor rose in prominence and power, making use economic and strategic advantage to secure his own position and that of his dynasty, gaining proficiency in both the vernaculars of local authority and the narratives of British legitimacy. Institutional innovations taken from the Ottomans as well as from other states facing imperial pressure had long-range consequences, limiting sovereign autonomy at the same time that they stabilized the character of government. Other elites, drawing from new centers of power such as that at Deoband, took advantage of British technologies of extraction and administration—railroads, mass education, printing—to present alternatives to British power and the local elites who facilitated colonial rule. In order to do this, though, many of these elites had to operate on a scale, and in a language, that accepted the fundamentals of the colonial state—one in which the category of "Muslim" referred to a unified interest and social group, and whose access to the rights and privileges due from the state required a provisional acceptance of that state.

The categories by which Islamic law are most often defined today—personal status or family law—emerged in the context of this struggle. Even when nationalists disagreed over the direction and content of reform, differing vehemently on issues such as women's rights, education, veiling and the character of the nation, "state elites and Islamic activists shared similar conceptions of 'religion' as circumscribed domains of interpretation and efficacy, which were in many ways comparable to the reformist ideas of the first part of the twentieth century."[134] Rather than ascribing the relegation of Islamic law to the law of the family to any purported lack of interest on the part of the colonial state, or to any a priori importance of the family unit within shari'a or *fiqh*, I have argued that the equation of Islamic law with personal status or the law of the family occurred in the mid- to late nineteenth century as a result of the confluence of British legal logic and local elite strategy. Responding to the challenges and the opportunities of colonial intervention, Muslim elites such as those at Deoband saw in the domain of the family a space to defend *as private* from the incursions of the British colonial state, envisioning the family as a site for the social reproduction of a new kind of Islam. In Egypt, reformers within the state hierarchy such as Muhammad Abduh saw in the domain of personal status law an opportunity for the continued relevance of the shari'a system within the logic of an expansionist state. The privacy of the family and the particularity of Islamic law had other effects as well, among the most critical the use of Islamic law to articulate a Muslim interest and identity both contingent upon state recognition and in opposition to state hegemony.

The colonial imperative to define its subjects led to a new fixity of identity categories in India, to the extent that actors in court cases had to present themselves as Hindu or Muslim, regardless of whether they themselves identified as either. "Courts repeatedly faced the problem of accommodating the diversity of social groups within these two categories." [135] A share of the resources of the state required being visible to the state, and this increasingly meant appealing to the state in terms of community identity. New coalitions based upon religious identity emerged that drew groups together who would otherwise be delineated by class, ethnicity, or language: "The administration of Muslim law by a non-Muslim colonial power transformed personal law into a ground for organised political struggle."[136] In this new contest, the definition of Islamic law as a fixed text with divine precedents, that needed to be defended against the encroachment of a Christian, alien ruler, played an important role for a number of Muslim groups.[137] The fundamental irony of this political and religious choice is an irony that dogs Muslim activists to this day: the defense of a codified, authoritarian and essentialist Islamic law as authentically "Islamic," when its history shows it to be a colonial construct, used initially to define and control a subject population.[138]

The increasing encapsulation of shari'a within the ambit of state law, and its redefinition as family law, did not just benefit the power of the colonial state. Certainly, just as land was an important resource upon which to build state power and control, the family gave the colonial state access to regimes of property and labor, and so the British commitment to preserving "Islamic family law" was more than a sensitivity to local family values. However, local elites benefited from the reorganization of law as well, and those elements of local organization that supported the colonial state were often strengthened rather than done away with. Seen in this vein, the codification, textualization, and limitation of Islamic law within a personal law system "served to consolidate the authority of certain community groups, and thus incorporate(d) community-based forms of surplus extraction into the colonial state."[139]

Group representation as a principle of Indian nationalism emerged in the 1880s and the combination of these new definitions of identity based upon a pan-Indian ("national" rather than regional) state continued into the twentieth century, expressed in the Morley-Minto reforms of 1909 and the Montagu-Chelmsford reforms of 1919.[140] British constitutional strategies attempted to maintain imperial control based upon local elite cooperation: "Far from paving the way for full dominion status, the Government of India Acts of 1919 and 1935 sharpened the dualities in Indian political society, making the goal of freedom with unity so elusive that the price of independence could only be partition."[141] The idea of a unified interest that could be represented by a single identity—"Muslim," as expressed through the 1937 Shariat Act that effaced any remaining diversity of Muslim customary practice under the law—was not unique to India.

In Malaya, Islam became more and more identified with the Malay elites and the rural Malay peasants they claimed to protect. British officials did not dissuade this perception, and it became a large part of political and anticolonial discourse as Malaya entered the twentieth century. The controversy that erupted after British attempts to evade the language of group representation in the Malayan Union, after World War II, served to further entrench elite Malay investments in the identification of Malayness with the importance of Islam for the Federation of Malaya. This ethnicization of Islam saw its fullest legal expression in the Federal Constitution of Malaysia, that equates Malay ethnic identity with Malay language and culture and with Islam. The power of the sultans as guardians of Malay privilege and culture was generally enhanced by this association with Islam, and many took on the role of protectors of Islam and heads of religion during the colonial period. However, when Islamic discourses of rulership, reform, and modernism changed in the nineteenth century, Malay rulers found themselves confronted by a new kind of Islamic elite who saw their institutions, symbols, and legitimacy as essentially Hindu accretions.[142] Then, their claims to Islamic legitimacy became problematic political issues. These issues continue to pose problems for sultans in Malaysia, as they attempt to maintain their status in the face of challenges from a nationalist government and Islamic opposition parties.

PART III

The Paradox of Islamic Law

CHAPTER SIX

The Colonial Politics of Islamic Law

The political, legal, and cultural struggles of today's Muslims stem from a certain measure of dissonance between their moral and cultural aspirations . . . and the moral realities of the modern world . . . realities with which they must live but that were not of their own making. —Wael Hallaq, 2013[1]

When we look at the closing years of the nineteenth century and the opening years of the twentieth, we are struck by names applied to what they do not mean. —Tariq al-Bishri, 1996[2]

The Paradox of Islamic Law

In *The Impossible State*, Wael Hallaq puts forward a trenchant and far-reaching critique of the concept of an Islamic state, the driving argument behind which is that the impossibility of the Islamic state is a symptom of the impossibility of the modern project.[3] For Hallaq, Islamic governance and the modern state both arose out of particular historical and institutional trajectories, and any effort to build a compromise form between the modern nation-state and the principles of Islamic governance is doomed to fail. This failure would stem not only from the inability of the "Islamic state" form to function within the existing capitalist and international global order, but from deep contradictions within the modern state itself. "For Muslims today to seek the adoption of the modern state system . . . is to bargain for a deal inferior to the one they secured for themselves over the centuries of *their* history,"[4] Hallaq argues, drawing what seems at times to be an impermeable line between Muslim history and the history of the modern nation-state. There are many ways in which this important work draws Islamic legal studies into ongoing debates on the place of law in politics, and extends a broader analysis of power and hegemony into fields of scholarly inquiry usually content to leave these aside. Yet Hallaq's placement of Muslims and Islamic governance outside the processes and politics of modern state making serves at times to downplay the ways in which it is precisely the entanglement between Muslim politics, ideals of Islamic governance, and the modern Muslim state that produce an ongoing politics of paradox today. The experience of paradox was a familiar thing to Muslim elites in colonial Egypt, Malaya, and India, as they reformed law in the model of European states in order to avoid being overtaken by them, as they appealed to the authority of the colonial state to be left outside of its jurisdiction, as they made claims for the application of Islamic law before judges who questioned its utility. This was paradox in the sense that Joan Scott deploys the term—the political foundations upon which the Muslim subject stood before the colonial state were built upon assumptions that denied the logic of their demands.[5] At the level of legal and political discourse, the ability to make claims on behalf of a Muslim interest required an acceptance of the space within which Islam had been assigned, thereby often undermining the logic and power of the claim itself.

The Egyptian jurist and constitutional scholar Tariq al-Bishri, commenting on Egyptian legal transformations at the turn of the last century, saw the adoption of European codes and institutions as taking place not only through political and military might, but through transformations of language and meaning. In his 1996 book, *The Islamic-Secular Dialogue* [*Al-Hiwar al-Islami al-'almani*], al-Bishri characterized the transformation as involving an inversion of language and value, in which "reform" (*al-islah*), previously meaning "continuity with improvement," was valorized by being synonymous with taking on Western law, even though this was more a case of "change and substitution" (*al-taghyir wa al-istibdal*).[6] Reliance on "the old" (*al-qadim*) came to be denigrated as "imitation" (*taqlid*) and taking from the West "renewal" (*tajdidan wa 'ibda'an*), "despite the fact that it was taking from the West that was imitation, that is, mimicry. For when a person mimics he does not mimic himself, but mimics another."[7] The dissonance that Hallaq diagnoses as underlying the "struggles of today's Muslims" with "the moral realities of the modern world . . . realities with which they must live but that were not of their own making," al-Bishri sees as having been authored and enacted at least in part by Muslims themselves, in a process where old and new, Western and Islamic, Egyptian and European, came to evoke each other, "names applied to what they do not mean." Al-Bishri, who served as a judge in the Council of State (Egypt's highest administrative court) for several decades, has long been acquainted with the ironies and paradoxes attendant in Muslim struggles with law. After the 2011 revolution, he was appointed by the Supreme Committee of the Armed Forces to chair the committee tasked with revising the Egyptian constitution; the constitution of 2012 was suspended by the coup of 2013, undertaken by the Armed Forces.[8] Al-Bishri's observations of nineteenth-century Egyptian legal and political change, and his own career in the judiciary and legal system, indicate that paradox is multi-generational, passed through language and institutions such that Muslims who seek legal and political change today find themselves caught in multiple institutional and historical double binds.[9]

This book has steered a theoretical path between one in which modern state power assumes control over all areas of Muslim life and meaning, and one in which Islamic institutions and ideas remain a refuge from both history and considerations of power. This path combines a view of Muslim agency and politics with a particular analytic strategy, tracing the development of the category of Islamic law as an institutional and political paradox that condition both our readings of the past, and our understanding of possible futures. David Scott, building on Talal Asad's work on religion, politics, and the secular, has argued that postcolonial history in particular, precisely because it carries a permanent legacy of paradox, requires a "tragic sensibility":[10]

> The tragic sensibility is more cognizant of the historical disruption in the temporalities that gave the longing for emancipation its philosophical as well as its political drive, that generated the end at the beginning. . . . A tragic sensibility is more attuned to . . . the myriad ways in which we carry our pasts within ourselves as the not-always-legible scripts of our habitus. In contrast to the constructivist (indeed too . . . the genealogical) emphasis on the self as little more than a series of invented—and therefore chooseable, replaceable—masks behind which lies an echoless metaphysical vacancy, the tragic sensiblity is poignantly aware of the ineradicable metaphysical traces that connect us to what we leave behind.[11]

This tragic sensibility offers a way to reintegrate Muslim societies and the study of Islam into history and, further, to see the Muslim state and subject as part of the process by which the modern state itself was made, and through which the contemporary paradox of Islamic law was formed. Scott's use of the concept of "problem-space" resonates with the concern in this project to understand how the formation of Islamic law as a new space for the modern state—a space that was limited in its institutional scope but magnified in its symbolic politics—conditioned the modern Muslim state as an institutional entity and a condition of being.[12] The struggle between local elites and colonial officials over the scope, content, and meaning of Islamic law radically transformed it, and gave rise to a new "ensemble of questions and answers around which a horizon of identifiable stakes . . . hangs . . . what defines this discursive context are not only the particular problems that get posed as problems as such . . . but the particular questions that seem worth asking and the kinds of answers that seem worth having" (2004, 4), a new problem-space of Islamic law. As al-Bishri's comments illustrate, this problem-space has been constructed through inversions of language and value, "names applied to what they do not mean." The horizon of identifiable stakes in the problem-space of Islamic law contained an interlinked hierarchy of values, often defined through their opposites: Western/Islamic, reform/imitation, secular/religious, public/private, foreign/indigenous, law/custom. These oppositional stakes were constructed, negotiated, and reiterated in multiple arena and registers: treaties, trials, and texts of Muslim representation, across the nineteenth-century Muslim world. It should not be surprising that Muslims, both in the colonial period and in various types of contemporary Muslim states, have been aware that Islamic law was not fully the shari'a as imagined by the early generations of Muslims, nor that the states they live in do not fully live up to the ideals of Islamic governance; yet the symbolic appeal and institutional logic of Islamic law remains powerful.[13]

I have sought to trace the transformation of Islamic law *both* as a way of thinking about state power and Muslim authority, *and* as a series of interlocking institutions, and to detail how these institutional arrangements removed some local actors and replaced them with others, provided resources to some visions of legitimate authority and not others, rewarded some kinds of political acts, and savagely punished others. The violence and despotism of colonial projects was part of the colonial repertoire, but so was the enticement and opportunity for some local elites to take on new roles, new authority. At times, the discursive and the institutional elements of Islamic law reinforced each other, and at others they clashed, and the role of local elites in engineering, magnifying, and capitalizing upon both resonance and dissonance should not be underestimated. The *ulama* of Deoband saw the exclusion of *fiqh* from the domain of British colonial law in India as an opportunity to argue for Islamic law as private law, outside the purview of the state, and to aim their reforms at the domain of the family, constructed increasingly as a private domain. The sultans of Malaya, having rejected outright resistance to British intervention, relied upon the initial limitation of their domain to "Muslim religion and Malay custom" to construct for themselves an unassailable role as guardians of a bastion of Malay privilege and Islamic authority. Muhammad 'Abduh, working to reform the shari'a court system within a state that valorized code and statute, reimagined a role for Islamic law as personal status law, and the Muslim family as the core of Islamic law.

New scholarship in comparative politics and historical institutionalism has invited more study of the dynamics of long-term institutional change. Thelen and Mahoney, for example, have pointed to the need to think not only about institutional change, but institutional stability, as "dynamic outcomes" (2010, 9): the determinants of long-term institutional change include ambiguous compromises between actors with varied motivations, interests, and understandings (Schickler 2001; Palier 2005), the combined effects of institutions and processes (Skocpol and Pierson 2002), and the ambiguity of rules themselves. The cases of legal transformation presented here indicate that long-term institutional change often hinges critically upon "names applied to what they do not mean," and that processes by which institutions are reconstructed and given new scope and power while continuing to retain their claims to authenticity are part of the story historical institutionalism has to tell, particularly about the colonial state, but also about the modern state. In order to explore this further, I have paid particular attention to the institutional components of the paradox of Islamic law, in which colonial efforts to contain Islamic law to one marginal domain of state administration became a condition of possibility for the centralization of Islamic law as a critical and increasingly prominent component of the modern state. Even when particular individuals sought to escape the dominant logic of Islamic law, durable institutional elements—in the texts of the law, in precedents and administrative regulation, in the training of judges and lawyers, in the relationship between state and local Muslim institutions—continued to drive the politics of paradox. Institutions such as Islamic law coordinate the interests of multiple groups; hold the potential to distribute significant resources, material, and discursive; and embody a set of rules about the conduct of state and politics that are themselves open for capture. Islamic law is a critical institution for the study of the modern Muslim state, but in order to understand its role in current political configurations, it will be important to see not only the interplay between the stable and the changeable within the institution, but also the ways in which the modern state's concepts, its aspirations, and its capacity have been conditioned by its growth alongside, and in competition with, Islamic legal institutions, logics, and actors. In addition, the picture this book paints of colonialism itself is one in which the project of the colonial state was by no means secure, the extension of colonial law by no measure complete, and the possibility for retrenchment and reversal ever-present. Comparative politics itself as tragedy, perhaps.

Picking up the threads first spun out at the beginning of this book, I draw together debates on Islamic law and the modern state, legal pluralism, secularism, and the valorization of law. We proceed by discussing what comparison between India, Malaya, and Egypt has yielded in the way of comparative findings: that in all three cases, Islamic law represented a major transformation of Islam and Muslim life, with the ascendance of the state at its center, but the relocation of local elite authority mattered a great deal for the scope, content, and meaning of Islamic law. As we consider the future of Islamic law and the modern Muslim state in the Middle East, South and Southeast Asia, and increasingly in Europe, Africa, and North America, the way that Islamic law functions within plural legal systems will continue to be a matter of analytic and policy concern. Drawing on legal pluralist and postcolonial analyses of law, I present an account of legal pluralism that pays particular attention to questions of power, of the logic that orders multiple sources of law, and for the implications of legal plurality for the future of state authority. I conclude by engaging debates on secularism, modernity, and religion to make the case for continued attention to the diverse pathways by which Islamic institutions and actors came to occupy their contemporary places, in order to more rigorously question the assumption that modernity *happened* to the Muslim state, and that it rang the death knell for the shari'a system. The institutional conditions of the formation of Islamic law in each context, even though they marginalized shari'a content and subjugated or eliminated Islamic legal elites, also constructed Islamic law as an entrenched and highly resonant resource for claims against the power of the state.

India, Malaya, Egypt: The Implications of Continuity and Change

The transformation of Islamic law into a domain of state administration—legislated by rulers, codified and interpreted by state employees, bankrolled by state funds, a department of governance among others—has arguably been the single most significant change in Muslim life in the last two hundred years. Surprisingly, we still have little detail about how this change was effected: how did changes at the level of legislation and code affect everyday life? How did judges and bureaucrats untrained in the shari'a apply and interpret it? How did the independent scholars, jurists, and teachers who had previously been the backbone of the shari'a episteme respond to its takeover by a system entirely different in structure, discourse, and organization? Pointed questions such as these have tended to be answered by Islamic legal scholars (a formidably precise collective) in generalities: colonization, modernization, replacement, secularization. In part, this is because what Islamic legal scholars worked with in the periods before the coming of the colonial state, in terms of shar'i jurisprudence—theological complexity, juristic debate, jurisprudential reasoning referencing the depth and breadth of the tradition—was, by the nineteenth century, very thin indeed if compared to earlier periods. In part, however, this is a "history of the present" problem—the transformations about which we ask have become so much a part of what a state is, what a Muslim is, that it is difficult to see the developments of the last two centuries as anything but inevitable. The spread of these transformations, far from raising questions, quells them—if Islamic law was transformed in India as well as Egypt as well as Malaya and in all points between, then the answer lies in a larger force: colonization, modernization, secularization. The state, in particular, is credited as the motive force in this change, and "modern scholarship proceeds with extraordinary innocence, unaware of the culpable dependency of its project on the ideology of the state."[14]

When continuity is the only story, local variations are taken to be irrelevant details, and when they take on larger dimensions, these are attributed to exogenous shocks. The first task before us, then, is to draw out what a networked comparison between India, Malaya, and Egypt allows us to clarify in the way of continuity and change. There was considerable variation among India, Malaya, and Egypt in the content of Islamic legislation, in which elites took on the institutions of the shari'a, and in what direction transformations in Islamic law took. These differences point to the need to question, with far more precision than we have thus far, what changes occurred in the content of Islamic law during the period of European colonization, and in what order. Reading between India, Malaya, and Egypt, we see continuities and discontinuities that derive from deep interconnection—in the administrative and occupational organization of British colonialism, in the assumption of comparability between sites of empire, in the growing interests among Muslims to make themselves visible and legible to the colonial state, translatable, and transferable beyond their local contexts. Yet this interconnection did not tend uniformly toward convergence, and different trajectories for the institutionalization of Islamic law and Muslim identity in the state have led to continued variations in the contemporary politics of Islam in India, Malaysia, and Egypt.

In British India, where the chronology of this narrative begins, colonial officials governed based upon a claim to the legitimacy of the *law*—understood as a binary division between the laws of the Qur'an for Muslims, of the Shasters for Hindus. The strategy of colonial administration of religion in India was driven by the need to replace people—elite interpreters of juristic tradition and local usage—with texts, first with Anglo-Muhammadan law, and then in the late nineteenth century with colonial codes that defined Islamic law within the confines of marriage, divorce, and inheritance. It was these codes that then became the basis for Muslim efforts to wrest political power from the British; as the institutional expression of the line between Hindu and Muslim, these codes were then deployed as proofs of the incommensurability of Hindu and Muslim law within a single state.

The picture from Malaya a century after the Indian case begins is quite different: in accordance with changes in the ideology and capacity of the colonial project, indirect rule was the mode of colonial governance. Here, the initial compact with Malay ruling elites fenced off matters of Muslim religion and Malay custom and constructed these matters as the basis for the sovereignty of Malay sultans. The definition of religion and custom was determined, by violence and by legal force, early on in the history of the relationship between the sultans and the British. As such, the institutional development of Islam in the Federated and Unfederated Malay States proceeded largely without colonial intervention as long as it remained within the newly defined bounds of Islam—marriage, divorce, inheritance, religious endowments (*awqaf*) and ritual observances. The application of Islamic law was largely left uncodified, at times untranslated from Arabic sources, to the discretion of Islamic elites formally under the aegis of the state but not under its interpretive control. Having made these matters the sultans' *raison d'etre*, it became in the interests of the sultans to emphasize Islam and Malay custom as *raisons d'état.*

In Egypt at roughly the same time as in Malaya, the British inherited a system already heavily influenced by the Ottomans and by the reforms of Muhammad Ali and his successors, and these provided much of the legitimation for the codification and the limitation of Islamic law as personal status law. Here, the impact of colonialism was twofold: it was both in the ongoing system of indirect rule in Egypt after the British occupation in 1882, but the more significant changes occurred through Ottoman and Egyptian efforts to stave off European intervention. The reform of Islamic law was constructed as a choice by Islamic and Egyptian legal elites to forestall colonial intervention, to reform instead of being reformed. Because the colonial power to be forestalled was British, the reform of law took on the French model, with profound consequences: statutes took the place of independent juristic reasoning, Islamic legal elites were appointed to positions of responsibility within a highly hierarchical state bureaucracy, and law became the central focus of Islamic intellectual activity.[15] The reform of Islamic institutions of learning and teaching, as well as the structural reorganization of the courts and judiciary, deprived Islamic legal elites of their authoritative connection to Qur'an and *fiqh*; "with their introduction, the codes become the primary source."[16] In the struggle against colonialism, Egyptians—those who articulated their resistance explicitly in Islamic terms and those who did so in language more recognizable as nationalist—had by the end of the nineteenth century taken as a given the concept of Islamic law as a codified and limited department of the state.

What do these variations indicate about the politics of Islamic law under colonialism? I address this question by exploring debates on the concept of Islamic law as a repository for culture and tradition, on legal pluralism and the problem of power, and on the way that comparative politics has approached networked institutions such as law and religion.

Islamic Law: Tradition and Culture against the State?

Both "rule of law" and "shariah" advocates have tended to see Islamic law as the repository of tradition and culture in Muslim states. This view is a-historical, since tradition and culture themselves were redefined repeatedly and therefore must be understood not as primordial categories but as historical constructions;[17] politically loaded, since the casting of Islamic law as "traditional law" has been part of the logic of Western self-definition and a rationale for the dominance of West over East;[18] and fundamentally problematic, since it allows the equation of family law and Islamic law to go unquestioned. The colonial period has shaped our understandings of what Islam is, what its proper place in the state should be, and what local practices were in the precolonial period by providing both the sources upon which much scholarship on Islam and Muslims is based, and the frame within which they are studied. The colonial relationship shaped Europeans' understandings of themselves, casting the colonized as slaves, oppressed, irrational, retrograde and/or bound by tradition, while nineteenth-century Europe was seen as enlightened, humane, progressive, and modern.[19] This relationship between Western societies and an imagined Muslim "other" continues into the present moment, and has far-reaching implications for scholarship and politics on a global scale. Writing in 1994, Jane Collier commented:

> If, as seems possible, Islamic "fundamentalism" comes to replace communism as the principal perceived threat to Western reason and democracy, sociolegal scholars may incur a special obligation to analyze the historical processes that constructed the cultural opposition between "our" supposed rule of law and "their" imagined religious fanaticism. Law, particularly criminal law but also family law, occupies a central place in the developing opposition between "us" and "them," in contrast to the focus on economic issues that dominated the cultural opposition between "communism" and the "free world."[20]

The developing opposition about which Collier wrote has taken on new and more troubling proportions since then, as has the role of law as both a way of maintaining the opposition—the analysis of differences in law as a signifier of fundamental and intractable differences between civilizations and worldviews—and as a way of justifying intervention—the rule of law as a supposedly objective and culture-neutral good of Western neocolonialism. The view of Islamic law as traditional, as a repository of culture, therefore, potentially carries a double implication: not only does it mark the fundamental difference of the Muslim state (as a condition of being as well as nation), it demarcates a broad target for modernization, for reform and for correction.

For Weber, and those influenced by his model of law and society, culture resided in "traditional" law, and was a powerful factor in the behavior of groups reacting to processes of modernity. His central motif of Islamic law was that of the qadi under the tree, dispensing "qadi justice." Whereas Western justice was based upon rules applied objectively and uniformly,

Islamic justice revolved around the subjective and arbitrary judgments of one judge who applied his reasoning to each case which came before him.[21] And whereas the assumption of a historical progression between "traditional" societies and "modern," Western states is one many contemporary scholars are less willing to make, the opposition between Islam and modernity, Islamic law and "rule of law," continues to be a theme in comparative legal studies.[22] Scholars routinely use the term "rule of law" to mean rule of laws based upon European or US systems, or imported by international organizations, and see this as a precondition to democracy. Western-style laws are seen as progressive, in contrast to Islamic laws, which are "traditional" or "conservative."

In a valuable study which compares Tunisia, Morocco, and Algeria in order to understand how the political circumstances of state development affect the postcolonial position of women, Mounira Charrad (2001) lays out "three paths to nation-state and family law." The Moroccan path involved the preservation of Islamic law through alliance between "palace" and "tribe"; the Algerian path saw a stalemate in law caused by elite competition; the Tunisian path featured the autonomy of the state from tribal power. Charrad argues that women benefited most in the Tunisian case because a strong state independent from "traditional" elites made family law reform. She applies this powerful analytic argument to conclude that women's rights are best served by this kind of state, and her evidence from Morocco and Algeria indicates that Tunisian women have more state-given rights. Charrad's study parallels some of my own findings: fragmented elites tend to be more conservative, and the target of their conservatism tends to be Islam and the family—women, in particular. We also agree that Islamic law is diverse and articulates with state hierarchies differently in each case, and that Muslim-majority states are not all similar in their approaches to Islam—on the contrary, even states as geographically, culturally, and historically proximate as those in North Africa differ to a large extent on this issue. The historical development of state, elite relations, and law are critical components of any discussion on Islamic law.

However, Charrad's basic assumptions are problematic when applied to other cases, such as the ones in this project, and the problem with some of these assumptions stem from the equation of "family law reform" with women's rights, the equation of "Islamic law" with women's oppression, and the association of tribal elite interests with Islamic interests based on a shared patriarchal attitude to law and society. Patriarchy during the colonial and postcolonial periods came in the guise of state as well as tribal and Islamic law, and a strong state can just as well suppress women's rights through family law reform as maintain them. Further, Islamic law is not "traditional," nor can it be equated with elite interests—some elites benefited from the association of Islam with their power, and some groups used Islamic law to resist the power of elites they claimed were not Islamic or progressive enough. The postcolonial Muslim state is not locked into a zero-sum battle for women's rights against a traditional, patriarchal Islam: as movements like Sisters in Islam in Malaysia argue, Islamic law can and has been used as a resource for women's rights, and family law reforms can and have been used to buttress the power of the state and its elites, any benefit to the women they claim to serve incidental and therefore dispensable.

For Geertz (1983), Islamic law represents a unique cultural system. Culture provides and expresses meaning and is a powerful component of law as a system of meaning, as well as giving us reason to study legal systems as unique and justice as locally defined and narrated, and therefore particularly amenable to ethnographic and anthropological research methods. In his study of Islamic law in Morocco and Indonesia, law represents different sensibilities, law is "a species of social imagination" and comparisons should be drawn in those terms, "law is about meaning not about machinery."[23] Lawrence Rosen has argued that comparative law has made assumptions about Islamic law that can be falsified through the empirical study of Muslim courts: Rosen is concerned to show that, despite its lack of precedent and records, the courts do not make arbitrary decisions, and do *not* simply dispense qadi justice, even though the judge has a great deal of discretion.[24] "The regularity lies . . . in the fit between the decisions of the Muslim judge and the cultural concepts and social relations to which they are inextricably tied."[25]

Thinking about Islamic law as a venue for culture may not sufficiently capture conflict and power inequalities within the law. The discussion of culture in the colonial context, especially, brings up the question of power and domination. For Moore, "culture has lost its political innocence. Today, when cultural difference is offered as a legitimation for and explanation of legal difference, cultural context often comes up as an aspect of a consciously mobilized collective identity in the midst of a political struggle."[26] This does not mean, however, that law was simply a tool of domination—it was also an arena of dispute. According to Collier and Starr, conflict is the central reality of law, not order or consensus, and law creates conflict, while "legislation always bears the traces of continually renegotiated disputes and compromises."[27] Even where power was not equal between disputants, law was rarely merely the legislated interests of a ruling class. Although elites had disproportionate influence on forms and content of legal relationships, there a wide range of actors used law, and these were at times actors who had very little power in society, such as women or rural peasants.

At the same time, even those who vehemently resisted the state's definitions of Islamic law and opposed its treatment of Muslim subjects found that the very act of challenging the state took place on state terms and involved its own dynamics of incorporation into state realities and power, and that this situation of state hegemony became more prevalent with time.[28] Ayesha Jalal, for example, argues that the formation of the category of "Indian Muslim" as a self-identifier (rather than a colonial census category) emerged in part out of the need for actors to identify according to state categories in order to be recognized as challenging its policies. In this case, in order to be seen and heard by the state as opposing a particular vision of Islamic law and identity, actors had to first identify with an "Indian Muslim" community, and by doing so brought it into being as a political and public reality.[29] These moments, in treaties, in legislation and codification, at trial, in claims to represent a Muslim community, contributed to an evolving state hegemony over the terms by which Islam would be articulated.[30]

The construction of tradition and custom played an important role during the colonial period, helping to persuade local subjects of the legitimacy of colonial rule, and provide local rulers with the support of precolonial practices, symbols and institutions.[31] Oral traditions and local practices tended to be neglected in favor of written texts, and formalization and regularization became priorities in the implementation of law in novel ways. And even then, "colonial administrators may never have changed Islamic legal arrangements quite so profoundly as when they were trying to preserve them," since their reliance on ancient texts and written rules reduced the fluidity and adaptability of Islamic legal practices to a rigid and archaic formalism which then served as proof of the unchangeability of Islamic law and its unsuitability for a modern legal system.[32] However,

> the appropriation of a past by conquest carries with it the risk of rebounding upon the conquerors. It can end up by sacralizing the past for the subject people and encouraging them to use it in their effort to define and affirm their

> own identity . . . the appropriated past came to serve as the sign of the Other not only for the colonizers but, ironically, for the colonized as well. The colonized, in their turn, reconstructed their past for purposes opposed to those of their rulers and made it into the ground for marking out their differences in cultural and political terms. History became thus a game for two to play.[33]

Perhaps even more importantly, discussing colonialism and state building as separate but complementary processes sheds light on both, in new ways. One example of the analytic implications of this approach is in the debate over the "authoritative" and the "authoritarian" in Islamic discourse. [34] The legal scholar Khaled Abou el Fadl locates the distinction as such: whereas *authoritarian* Muslim discourse insists that there is one Islamic law, and one correct version of Islamic legal interpretation, Islamic history indicates that the heuristic of diversity among legal opinions is what is *authoritative*. The politics of Islamic law in the formative periods of the modern Muslim state indicate that the transformation of Islamic law from authoritative to authoritarian arose from the conjunction of the rise of formalist visions of Islamic law (made necessary and possible by the intervention of the colonial state through treaties, trials and texts) with the growing sense among Muslim elites of the need to protect the shrinking jurisdiction allowed to Islamic law. In the colonial state it was often colonial officials themselves who appealed to this authoritarian voice, who in fact brought it into the discourse on Islamic law (not, of course, without the complicity of local elites). The rise of authoritarian variants of Islamic law is modern, rather than traditional, but this authoritarianism is anchored in the institutional legacy of elite politics in the Muslim world, in which state-enforced, state-interpreted law has come to be seen as the proper preserve of Islam.

Legal Formalism, Legal Realism, Legal Pluralism

In the current language of global geopolitics and imperium, law has a particularly strong resonance. In the rebuilding of Iraq and Afghanistan, the debate ranges between those who argue for a stronger shari'a presence in government, and those—the United States government among them—who argue for rule of law based on the separation of religion and state.[35] Both of these understandings of law are, at their core, equivalent: both the advocates of "rule of law" on the Western model and "shari'a" on the Islamic model see law as a tangible deliverable of policy, and see law as the solution to problems of political order and social instability. These are formalist and realist visions of law which ignore the politics of legal development and legal systems. In refusing to see Islamic law and rule of law as having political content and negotiable meaning, they strongly resemble the British administrators of this study, whose commitment to finding and fixing "the law" of Islam in order to placate, control and reform Muslims had so many unintended and lasting consequences.

Legal formalism views the law as legitimate objective rules for the preservation of justice and social order, which could be applied neutrally by judges (who merely delivered the law, and did not interpret it), and once applied would solve the particular problem it addressed. According to Alan Hunt (1993), this Enlightenment vision of law dominated scholarship on law, state, and society until the 1960s, and it was against this vision of the law that legal realists reacted. Legal realists assumed not only that there was one real law to unmask, but that once the problems of the law were diagnosed, they could be solved, and that law could once again work for the benefit of society and state. To this end, they applied behavioral and functional analysis of courts, judges' decisions and institutions of the law associated with the state. Political scientists who study the law undertake realist analysis of legal systems still: studies which look at the writing of constitutions as experiments in social engineering, looking for the constitutional solution to the problem of intransigent government or elusive democracy, assuming that law has the capacity to deliver an Enlightenment promise of justice, democracy, and progress. Galanter (1974) to a certain extent assumes that the right combination of players in the courts can deliver the justice the law promises. Shapiro (1986) applies neo-functionalist analysis to a comparison of court systems, seeing courts as the place of law, and justice itself as a universal concept. Stone Sweet (2000) applies political science empirical methods to the question of whether, and how, judges make policy in the European Union. Ginsburg (2003) compares new Asian democracies, asking where judicial power comes from, and what impact it has on democratic growth. The focus of these studies, as is the focus of legal realism, is law as an instrument of the state, as an institutional component of politics, as enacted by legal professionals, bureaucracies, and social elites.

The functionalism of legal realism implies that culture is vestigial, and that justice is a universal concept, and universally achievable through procedural and institutional mechanisms. The problem of power remains unresolved: where does the power of law come from? For what ends is it applied? Realists assume that the problem with the law is a technical one, and that adjustments will allow the law to deliver justice, when the experience of both colonized and subjugated peoples would point to the agenda of state law as expropriating and dominating its subjects to serve the ends of the powerful. Realism ignores the violence of law, as it ignores the narratives and elisions of law: neither the project of legitimation in which the law is always involved, nor the threat of violence behind that project, is important in realist analyses, whereas it has been a central part of my own concerns.

As a contrast to the legal realist vision, legal pluralists have been particularly concerned with questions of culture, domination, and power in the law. Legal pluralism has made major contributions to the study of law, society and the state: first, it has decentered the state, as have state-in-society studies done, allowing a view of the state as itself plural, acting within a field of relationships, both creator and subject of law. Second, it highlighted the importance of language, of performance, of discourse and audience, in the modern state. Third, it viewed the law not as a univocal tool of the state, or a product of political action, but as a source of meaning, a system of rules, acting upon many different levels simultaneously, deeply embedded in the state but also radically outside it. Fourth, legal pluralism has made the project of comparison highly appropriate not only between states, but between domains within the state itself. Fifth: it has taken postcolonialism and modernity as critical objects of inquiry, which opens up new analytic and methodological possibilities in the study of Islamic law, a subject that has until recently been studied in formalist and realist terms.[36]

However, for the task of exploring the relationship between Islamic law, colonialism, and the growth of the modern state, legal pluralism as an analytic approach continues to require theoretical distancing from legal pluralism as a strategy of state power. An analysis of the politics of a mixed legal system must ask: Can legal codes which function within a context starkly different than that where they originated coexist within a single national system without distortion of their intent, function, and meaning? When principles of the shari'a are taken to govern women and children, families, and property, and placed alongside commercial codes taken from Western legal systems and administrative law created to serve a new nation, plurality may not be the most accurate representation of the relationship between these legal codes. Pluralism implies that Islamic law functions within the personal status law of the postcolonial nation as an autonomous domain within the national legal system.[37] But the function and meaning of Islamic law as contained within a personal status or family law is contingent upon the workings of the entire system of which it is a part. The circumstances within which this "plurality" was arrived at were rife with power inequalities, and the particular type of plurality which was achieved looks less like the coexistence of separate but equal elements of different legal systems within one structure than it resembles a peculiar legal Frankenstein creature—different functional elements pieced together to achieve a singular and unique purpose, the other parts of each system discarded by design. Islamic law is often discussed separately from the context of the modern state processes within which it functions, and the encapsulation of shari'a concepts and *fiqh* logics into European colonial legal structures is usually seen through the lens of legal pluralism. For an exploration of these multiple orders of law and the ways in which actors chose among them, or were confined between them, legal pluralism has ultimately been insufficient. The codification, organization, and implementation of Muslim personal status required the translation of local and British values and processes, creating a product quite different from the sum of its parts—a hybrid law, not a plural law.

This study has emphasized both the moment of intersection and the process of transition, to explore the anatomy of that hybridity and its consequences, to escape the formalism of both "shariah law" and "rule of law" advocates. For an analysis of legal pluralism to capture the multiplicity, the hierarchy and the interaction of legalities which most Muslim states now face, it must understand the circumstances of their construction and reveal the logics upon which they were founded. The expansionist character and aspirations of the modern state have become a fundamental and crucial component of law, whatever its origin. Networks of people, ideas, and institutions make national borders porous and draw patterns of legal change into a global circulation. The layering of multiple systems of law constitutes the creation of an entirely new legal system, rather than an aggregation of separate strands.[38]

Boaventura de Sousa Santos has argued that legal pluralist analysis is crucial to the postmodern view of law, but law itself needs to be read as "a map of misreading," "a system of signs which distort and represent reality through different mechanisms of scale, projection and symbolism."[39] These distortions are patterned, not random: *scale* requires decisions about detail, *projection* requires the positioning of a center and a logic of legibility, *symbolization* requires a language through which reality might be presented. Santos argues along with this for "a new theory of subjectivity . . . to account for the fact that we are an increasingly complex network of subjectivities."[40] This book has sought to delineate the patterned ways in which Islamic law distorted and represented reality, and by doing so provided new ways to navigate that reality going forward. The scalar politics of Islamic law meant that was precisely the limitations imposed upon Islamic law during the colonial period that facilitated its new centrality among elites in India, Egypt, and Malaya. The rearrangement of local elite hierarchies and the new reach of the state made possible by colonial power gave local elites a vested interest in this twinning of the centrality of Islamic legitimacy and the marginalization of its legal content. The colonial process shaped local legal traditions in the service of state power and a particular vision of justice and order. Not least within this new system is the shift it marked in ideological content, a shift made invisible by the overarching ideology of the modern state, of personal law as private law: liberal legal conceptions of the subject were replaced with a view of communities defined by traditions, internally homogenous and deliverable through the religious law of the state, limited to the law of the family.[41]

Global Circulations of Law: Thinking Differently about Comparison

Thinking about Islamic law in cartographic terms highlights not only its scalar and symbolic distortions, but its propensity to travel: both Islamic law and rule of law are concepts in global circulation, with their own networks of actors, institutions and resources. Comparativists have tended to compartmentalize the internal and external causes of institutional change and continuity, and this study has explored ways of thinking of comparison in the context of networks, far more prevalent and wide-ranging than independent case studies would suggest. Rather than parallel cases analyzed independently, this analysis takes interconnections between colonial and local systems seriously, and emphasizes the fact that borders are porous, that ideas and actors are mobile, and because of that, laws and institutions travel. This study is not a comparison of parallel cases, but of sites of colonization, of state building and the development of Muslim identities whose local conditions are intertwined with global flows of colonial agents and travelers, Muslim traders and teachers, of commodities, ideas, and interests. Looking back and forth between India, Malaya, Egypt, and Britain makes it possible to see that texts, ideas, institutional models, and political interests traveled with judges, pilgrims, missionaries, bureaucrats, and soldiers across the Indian Ocean.

In 1798, for example, when Napoleon invaded Egypt, Muslim rulers in India saw the possibility that they would have to Westernize in order to block further Western encroachment into their domains, and Malay rulers were soon to follow. In 1874, economic interests whose lifeline was the new Suez Canal led British officials to leave India for Egypt and Malaya, bringing their ideas of Islam and how to govern a Muslim polity with them (their treaties, trials, and texts.) The codification of some laws governing Muslims in India in the 1870s arrived in Malaya in the 1880s, and native religious courts in Egypt in 1892. Robert Tignor refers to the "Indianization" of Egyptian administration under British rule, pointing to "the grafting of Indian institutions and methods onto Egyptian institutions which in themselves reflected Ottoman, French, and purely Egyptian influences."[42] Not only this, but British officials trained in India traveled to Egypt and Malaya, carrying their experiences of government and their knowledge of Islam and local practices with them. Muslim teachers, traders, and pilgrims also traveled, corresponded, and actively engaged other Muslims, and as chapter 5 discusses, technological developments in printing, maritime travel, and communications accelerated the proliferation of modernist, reformist Muslim movements all over the Muslim world in the nineteenth and twentieth centuries.

Just as British networks carried Indian experiences and institutions with them to other outposts of empire, they also carried a vision of Islam, Muslim society and Islamic law. And just as Indians adapted to, challenged, and took advantage of opportunities presented by the colonial encounter, they traveled, corresponded, and discussed these new approaches with other Muslims. There was a rich and multidirectional exchange of ideas, texts, opinions, and legal actors across the Indian Ocean.[43] If Egypt and Malaya's administration was Indianized, further empirical study may substantiate that their personal status law was similarly shaped by the Indian experience. Rather than an Arab export, then, "Islamic law" in many postcolonial Muslim states may in fact be significantly more South Asian in content, structure, and interpretation than previously assumed.[44] Further, what scholars of the Indian Ocean arena and Southeast Asian Islam have long argued may provide a way of continuing to think about currents of Islamic legal change today—the ways in which Islamic law exists not in state silos but in a context where institutional trajectories, elite interests, and patterns of Muslim learning, legal training, judicial influence, and policy all interact across multiple networks of exchange.

The view of law, society, and the state that emerges from this meeting of comparative politics and legal pluralism lends itself to a tragic sensibility: causality is unlikely to be an achievement of theory derived in this manner; power is a complex and contradictory force; rationality is a thin assumption of strategic motivations. That said, political scientists have something to offer here: a deeper engagement with political economy, with wider systems of power and domination beyond the nation-state, with methodologies of comparison and theories of strategic action and bargaining. Instead of a linear path to an idealized point of progress and development, the tandem development of law, society, and the state may be viewed as part of a dynamic and not entirely successful project of control sponsored by the modern state, implicated in flows of international economic and strategic power, where the subject itself is reformed. As chapter 5 detailed, toward the end of the nineteenth century, in particular, efforts at imperial consolidation and Muslim strategies of countering imperial control came together to create a dynamic by which Islamic law came to be conflated with personal status and private law. Networks of colonial, Muslim, and Asian exchange helped these conflations become operative categories for the articulation of Islam beyond the boundaries of British colonialism, across the majority of the Muslim world, by the first decades of the twentieth century.

Islamic Law: Paradox Institutionalized

Some of the most compelling treatments of the transformation of Islamic law in the modern period have been tales of its demise: among them, Wael Hallaq has famously argued that the institutional takeover of the shari'a system during the rise of the colonial and then the nation-state, by detaching the delivery of legal judgment from the institutions of debate, discourse, and scholarship that sustained the dynamism and internal coherence of Islamic law, constituted the "structural death" of the shari'a episteme (2009, 15). Thomas Bauer, making a wider point about language, discourse, and culture, argues that a "culture of ambiguity" was an intrinsic part of the relationship between classical Islamic culture and text, and that efforts to fix notions of the "Islamic" have, in the modern period, led to the loss of this culture.[45] For Asad, the transformation of Islamic law, family law in particular, into a province of state power amounts to the secularization of Islamic law.[46]

This book began from a different premise and aims at a different target: the Muslim women I met in Malaysia, the Egyptian reformers of the turn of the nineteenth century, the litigants of inheritance cases in eighteenth-century India, all knew something called "Islamic law" existed. In their discourse and their strategies, they all found it somewhere in the spaces between the shari'a, the state, and the pressing concerns of their lives, and made of the incongruity between their belief in the shari'a and the claims of the state, new opportunities for making claims, building identities, pressing advantages. Similarly, neither the chiefs of Malaya confronted by a belligerent Birch, claiming "the Pangkor Treaty is just like the Qur'an," nor the Indian qadis, muftis, and *ulama* to whom Hastings justified his Plan as *siyasa shar'iyya*, nor the *ulama* of Deoband and Cairo, working to redefine Islamic law as family law, were likely to have been persuaded that the Islamic law being offered to them was the shari'a. The historical record shows that, despite this incongruity, Muslim elites found reasons to invest in the marginalization of Islam and its transformation into a domain of state law focused on the family and the private. The bulk of this book has been focused on why and how this investment occurred, and how, despite its institutional marginalization, Islamic law served as a platform from which these elites, and other nonelite Muslims, articulated challenges to state authority and made for Islam a central place in the language of state legitimacy.

The Secularization of Islamic Law: Jural Colonization, Privatization

Hallaq's strikingly original *Shari'a: Theory, Practice, Transformation* (2009) analyzes the state as a field of power, and the conflicts introduced by the encounter between two fundamentally different systems: the modern state ("imported" by European colonialism) and Islamic law.[47] Hallaq asserts that the colonial production of "legal hybridity"—elements of shari'a translated, codified, and rigidified for the purposes of colonial extraction and control—constructed a trap from which local Muslim elites could not escape: "What they deemed to be the unjust law of occupation was the only available and legitimate means by which they could bargain against their occupiers" (379). For Hallaq, the central symbolic value of "Islamic family law" owed its place in Muslim self-identity "not only because it was built into Muslim knowledge as an area about which they should display sensitivity, but also because it represented . . . the last fortress of the Shari'a to survive the ravages of modernisation" (446).

However, a closer examination of these changes in India, Malaya, and Egypt shows that local elites played critical rather than supporting roles in the redefinition of Islamic law during the colonial period; modernity was not a uniform wave that swept through the Muslim world, but consisted of a series of moments in which local elites—hemmed in as they most certainly were by the resources, the administrative machinery and the violence of the colonial state—participated in the construction of family law as Islamic law, and Islamic law as the institutionalization of shari'a, and made of their new situation new meanings and new discourses about what Islamic law could and should be. Hallaq's central point is that the transformation destroyed an epistemic system, that the shari'a could not function as such without a living dynamic between Islamic institutions, courts, texts, judges, and *ulama*. Without detracting from the much-needed energy this strong claim has already lent to scholarship on shari'a and the state, I suggest that the shari'a episteme has long involved a struggle to balance the dictates of mundane power and daily administration with the disciplinary rigor of Islamic legal scholarship and the ethical demands of ordinary Muslims. The challenge for those of us interested in the aftermath of colonialism and modernity for the Muslim state is to understand how this struggle continues, and continues to be productive of durable structures of authority as well as deep resources for strategic challenges to state power.

Following on Foucault, Talal Asad has taken up the role of law as the transformative link between the family and the disciplinary regimes of the state in his discussion of shari'a and secularization in Egypt: "The family is the unit of "society" in which the individual is physically and morally reproduced, and has his or her primary experience as a "private" being. The secular formula of privatizing "religion" is adhered to by confining the shari'a to the family" (2001, 8). As Asad illustrates in the case of Egypt, liberalism, law, and the family became more closely linked in this new discourse: "The law separates and secures public and private domains of life, and the state embodies and administers law in the interests of its self-governing citizens." In this self-governance, the family played an important role, predicated upon its new duality as a private space, but also a space upon which public good was founded and in which the individual was formed. According to Asad, "by being identified with the family, the sharia becomes at once functionally central to political order and theoretically the guarantor of individual privacy and of individual self-government in what is increasingly becoming a secular society."[48] For Asad, the equation of shari'a with "family law" or personal status law—in Egypt, "qanun al ahwal al shakhsiyya"—is directly related to the development of the secular state. The categories of "public" and "private," "religious" and "secularist," "family" and "state," therefore, are dyads, interdependent and co-constitutive. In the modern state, the religious has no meaning separate from the secular, the private cannot be understood except through reference to the public:

> A secular society . . . is a modern construct based on the legal distinction between public and private, on a political arrangement requiring "religion" to be subjected by law to the private domain, on an ideology of moral individualism and a downgrading of the knowing subject, on a celebration of the physical body as well as on a range of personal sensibilities, that all emerged in Western Europe together with the formation of the modern state.[49]

This study owes a great analytic and substantive debt to the questions Asad asks and the pathways he has indicated for answering them. In his study of nineteenth-century Egyptian legal reform, Asad makes clear a rich and compelling agenda for the study of Islam, modernism, and reform: "How the reordering of social life . . . presented certain priorities to Islamic discursive tradition."[50] Perhaps most importantly, then, as David Scott suggests, Asad's major contribution to these issues has been to reorient the discussion to ask "not whether the colonized accommodated or resisted but how colonial power transformed the ground on which accommodation or resistance was possible in the first place, how colonial power reshaped or reorganised the conceptual and institutional conditions of possibility of social action and its understanding."[51] Yet for Asad, the emergence of the shari'a in nineteenth-century Egypt as "a secular formula" should be understood as "preparing the ground for the self-governing subject."[52] This study has attempted, by tracing the relationship between changes in concepts and changes in practice in the area of Islam and law, to seek out the multiple pathways by which Muslims navigated the challenges and opportunities of colonialism. As some of our cases have suggested, these pathways did not uniformly lead through the construction of a self-governing subject, but more often than not involved the creation of a domain of local autonomy characterized by multiple nested hierarchies of class, gender, ethnicity, learning, and community. These domains of partial autonomy, and the hierarchies and authority structures they helped sustain, became important sites for the articulation of challenges against state visions of law, state power and of Islam itself, into the contemporary period.

British intervention in India, Malaya, and Egypt introduced the state as a prize to be captured at the same time that it dictated the conditions under which power taken from the state would be exercised. Through treaties, trials, and texts, the colonial state raised some issues to prominence (like the need to protect "matters of religion and culture" in realms of personal law) while making other issues disappear (like the presence of religion and culture in areas of revenue and trade). In doing so, the colonial state made opportunities for struggle over resources, power, and legitimacy at the same time as it ordered the manner and realms in which those struggles would be conducted. In Malaya, for example, Malay elites were allowed autonomy over matters of religion and culture, and because of this became guardians solely of religion and culture, at the expense of the multiple roles they had previously played. Changing what Malay elites represented ultimately changed who these elites were in relation to state and to society, and focused their interests on preserving this domain of religion and culture. This is a somewhat different picture of subject formation than Asad posits in the case of Egypt, and subject formation is particularly important in this case because of its relationship to law.:"It is because the ideology of self-government seems also to call for the 'civilizing' of entire subject populations through the law that the authority of the law and its reconstructive power come to be taken as supremely important."[53] The treaties, trials, and texts presented in this study provide a a closer look at the relationship between the making of the Muslim subject, the Muslim state and the rise of law as an instrument of state power, in which law is undoubtedly ascendant, but in which law's functions depend upon uncertainty, conflict, struggle, and contingency. Law, too, then, might be read not as a high modernist romantic genre but, going back to Scott, as "a broken series of paradoxes and reversals in which human action is ever open to unaccountable contingencies"—as a tragic genre.[54]

Secularization, in Asad's account, seems in its ineluctability also to be a force for homogeneity, the triumph of the modern state a matter of time; however, it is not at this moment clear that the modern state has triumphed, nor that secular power will continue to dominate either the Muslim or any other state. Perhaps by presenting secularism in language that lacks agents—the "secular formula is adhered to," "the individual is . . . reproduced," "the sharia becomes"—Asad's analysis also, rather surprisingly, adds to the overall picture of colonialism as something that happened to Muslims. As part of a larger theoretical tack toward the political formation of the Muslim state and its logics, this forecloses important questions about the relationship between Islam, colonialism, and modernity, if what it does is shift attention squarely to the logic, structures, and self-presentation of the modern state.

Keeping our analytic focus firmly on local elites makes it possible to see that what happens next offers a variation on the analytic of secularization that Asad provides, shedding light on diverse Muslim strategies in the face of secular power that both accepted its terms and found bases from which to contest it. Some Muslims benefited from the opportunities of the colonial project, and some were silenced; some institutions were transformed and elevated, and others starved of resources; some ways of engaging the state formalized and other avenues shut off. In 1930s India, Muslim elites demanded the codification of Islamic law, even though earlier codifications of Islamic law were recognized as tools of colonial administration, contrary to Islamic legal practices. Islamic law then became an expression of a new "Indian Muslim" identity, irreconciliable with Hindu law, itself an ascendant feature of Hindu identity. Malay Muslim elites in colonial Malaya entrenched their interests within an expression of the law that made ethnicity a key component of Islam, and an inextricable but consistently problematic component of the contemporary Malaysian state. Chapter 7 discusses the contemporary implications of the conflation of Islam and Malayness in Malaysia.

Islamic Law as Sacred Law: Ethnicity, Family, and the Rise of the Legal

At the start of this book, the first British Resident in Malaya's claim that the Pangkor Treaty should be understood to be "just like the Qur'an" was evidence brought by the Malay chiefs to prove their case that the British had stepped well beyond their rightful place. Today, state law is where the law of Islam resides, and delivery of Islamic law is a key criteria by which the state's Islamic credentials are judged. The rise of law as a mode of state power has been detailed in this book through the work of trials that articulated law as a panacea to colonial ills, Islamic law as the core value of Muslim civilization, religion as the central preoccupation of Muslim individuals—from the middle of the eighteenth century to the end of the nineteenth, and from India to Malaya and Egypt, the arc of law was ascendant. This ascendance was reinforced by the incorporation of Islamic law into the law of the state—whatever its reality, the fact that Islamic law would be delivered through the law of the state sacralized state law as well.

Even when litigants came to attack the sanctity of Islamic law as presented by the state, they had first to accept its jurisdiction, the qualifications of its judges, the texts of its laws. John Comaroff has observed that "faith and the law, arguably, are the twin fixations of this-worldly being all over the place nowadays";[55] this book has traced one long process by which faith *in* the law arose, comprised both in the assumption that the law can and should contain all things necessary to solving the problems of both state and individual, and in the conviction that the law should also contain all things necessary to salvation. For Hussein Agrama, even *lack* of conviction in the law contributes to its ascendance, especially so, in fact: "Suspicion and legal entrenchment go hand in hand in a kind of looping effect . . . the rule of law, as part of the liberal regulatory state, constantly produces spaces of exceptions wherein it constantly expands."[56] Agrama offers a revised way of thinking about secularism as a problem-space: "It is perhaps those religious practices that have been deeply configured through modern liberal reform, (that) are by and large apolitical and do not in any particular way oppose liberal secular tenets, that evade secular power in significant ways and offer possibilities for rethinking it."[57]

The family, having been constructed as the space most worthy of protection from the state and at the same time a key target of state intervention, also emerges as a key site for the making of ethnicity in the Muslim state. Here, too, faith in the law continues, part of the arsenal of both the individual Muslim and the Muslim state itself. John Comaroff attributes this "rise of legal theology" to two factors:

> The first is the fetishism of the law itself: the ever deeper inscription of personhood, sociality and identity within it; the almost occult faith in its capacity . . . to enable the transaction of value across lines of difference; the reduction of the social to the contractual; the judicialisation of politics. The second is the asso-

> ciation of ethnicity with "naturally" owned property and, by extension, its sedimentation into a jural status: a right-bearing, commodifiable species of collective being-and-consciousness.[58]

The matter of this book has worked to illustrate the deep roots of this fetishism, a contemporary legatee of investments in the political theology of law as a counter to other political theologies, a long ascendance alongside the political theology of the colonial state.[59] The centrality of the case of Malaya also serves to emphasize the ways in which ethnicity, rather than sedimenting from customary to jural status, has in some places and times also been a category ascendant with modern law. In chapter 7, we examine the contemporary consequences of this ascendance, through two court cases in Malaysia over the issue of apostasy. These cases indicate the ways in which constitutional law, the institutionalization of colonial-era understandings of "religion and custom," the sovereignty of Malay rulers, and the matter of individual Muslim belief intertwine with the reproduction of Malay and Muslim identity. They point to the continued utility of the analytic of paradox for the study of Muslim politics and Islamic law, through an emphasis on jurisdictional politics, applications of Islam in and out of Islamic courts, and representations of the Muslim state at multiple levels of state and society.

CHAPTER SEVEN

The Contemporary Politics of Islamic Law

The space that religion may properly occupy in society has to be continually redefined by the law because the reproduction of secular life within and beyond the nation-state continually affects the discursive clarity of that space.[1]

Here, at the conclusion of this work, we return to the central paradox with which we began: Islamic law was marginalized during the colonial period and, at the same time, Islam and Islamic law became central components of the power of both state and social actors. Through a discussion of recent cases on apostasy in Malaysia, the only state in the world where ethnicity is legally tied to Islam, this chapter demonstrates how colonial-era remakings of Islamic law matter for current Muslim politics, and grapples further with the analytic implications of paradox for comparative studies of states, religion, and secularism.[2] These cases indicate that the paradox of Islamic law is neither an analytic puzzle to be explained away nor a political problem to be solved, but an *institutionalized* historical outcome of the last two centuries, that itself is now productive of a troubled politics, in which the Muslim and the Muslim state is now enmeshed.

The paradox of Islamic law endures firstly because it is produced by the tension between these durable forms—in law, language, and institutional configurations—and the shifting opportunities and resources of the daily political life of the state. This has been the preoccupation of the early chapters of this book. The second reason for the endurance of the paradox of Islamic law is that it continues to be productive of resources, both tangible and symbolic, that groups use in order to attempt to capture a dominant share of the state and its power. This is the central focus here, in which jurisdictional politics, the application of Islamic law both in and out of shari'a courts, and the politics of representation are turned from the colonial frame, to exploring the continuing production of paradox in the contemporary politics of Islamic law in Malaysia.

In the wake of political upheaval and change across the Middle East and the Muslim world, the question of what constitutes an Islamic state has been reopened in critical ways. If the question is to be answered in any meaningfully new way, its key assumptions, its central concepts, and its boundaries need to be understood with more clarity. If a Muslim state is to be measured by the religious identity of its majority, what does the Muslim state do about conversion out of Islam, since in this case the confessional identity of each citizen has an impact on the religious identity of the state? If a Muslim state is defined by its application of *some* Islamic law, in its constitution or its family law, for example, but not its administrative or commercial law, what might the relationship be between the shari'a and the non-shari'a legal system, and what happens when the logic, jurisdiction, or authority of these systems conflict? If there is disagreement within the state about what kind of Muslim state to be—as there certainly has been in the contemporary legatees of our colonial cases, Egypt, Malaysia, Pakistan, and Bangladesh, but also in Turkey and Indonesia, Saudi Arabia and Iran, Tunisia and Afghanistan, Syria and Iraq, among many others—upon what principles might this conflict be decided, and by whom?

Despite the treatment of September 2001 as a point of historical rupture for Muslim politics, I seek to underscore the deep institutional and political continuities that run through the politics of Islamic law for most Muslims today, even as the geopolitical and national order has pushed violence, securitization, and order to the fore. As advocates for "shari'a" or for "Islamic law" speak out for governmental imposition of Islamic law, for codification, for the law of the Qur'an, it will continue to be important to see the ways in which they are in fact upholding a vision of Islam and Muslims forged during the colonial period. As Muslim parties speak of upholding Islamic law but mean only within the province of family, gender, and religious observance, a limit originally imposed by the colonial state, it will continue to be important to remember the historical pathways along which Islamic law as it is understood today has traveled, and to note the durability of its institutional, symbolic, and political-economic formations. And as these struggles make their way through the waiting rooms of government buildings, into the offices of bureaucrats and judges, through courts and into legislatures, carrying with them increasing demand for the state to define, order, and maintain Islamic law, it will be crucial to note how this demand is generated, how these paradoxes underwrite the ongoing work of law and the state. As Hussein Agrama has noted, drawing on the case of Egypt, the question of "where to draw a line between religion and politics . . . is historically connected with modern state sovereignty and its constitutive indeterminacies," and the question itself is continually generated by the processes of secular doctrine.[3] As Malika Zeghal has argued in the case of Tunisia after the Arab uprisings, these politics of paradox have taken center stage: "Indeed, it seems that Islam as a political concept was simultaneously repressed by a desire to marginalize its political significance and persistently brought up as an object of public interest."[4]

Islam and Ethnicity in Malaysia: Paradox Institutionalized

The matter of this book has shown that dynamics of jurisdictional division, redefinitions of Islamic law and Muslims, and state making at the both the individual and the governmental level had far-reaching implications for colonial negotiations of Islamic law. Legal cases in postcolonial Malaysia here serve to illustrate the extent to which these dynamics still matter for Islamic law today, and their reasoning reveals a set of assumptions about what it means to be Malay and Muslim in Malaysia, institutionalized and reproduced through jurisdictional politics. Lazarus-Black and Hirsh advocate "reading for paradox": for methodologies which approach law both as a force for institutional order and an arena to which actors bring their own resistance, strategies, and interests.[5] As discussed in chapter 6, reading for paradox in the context of Muslim legal systems involves an understanding of contemporary Islamic law as twofold: carrying the colonial conditions of its institutionalization, at the same time as it signals the rise of a particular vision of Islam and Muslims, a vision that relies upon increasing state intervention in Muslim life.

Clearly, however, colonial legacies cannot provide a full explanation for the contemporary state of politics in Malaysia. Recent studies of the issue of apostasy in Malaysia, for example, have concentrated on the controversy surrounding these court cases as symptoms of growing anxiety among Malay-Muslims about their position in Malaysian politics and society, as part of electoral competition between the ruling government and Islamic parties (Hamayotsu 2010 and 2012), as a sign of the encroachment of Islam and authoritarianism within the Malaysian legal system (Thio 2006), in terms of its violation of international human rights law (Barry 2009; Sani and Shah 2011), and as an outcome of binary logics in law and Malaysian postcolonial politics (Moustafa 2013). In these studies, the issue of apostasy stands for a wider constellation of Malaysian troubles, locating the politics of Islam, ethnicity, and democracy, in Malaysian politics after Mahathir. The analytic tools presented in this book offer a way to make legible the actions and logic of courts in Malaysia on the thorny issue of religion and ethnicity, that otherwise seem incongruent or biased, or read the law as a simple mirror of national politics. In fact these logics and their outcomes are deeply embedded in the history of the postcolonial state and the politics of Islamic law, inherited from elite power dynamics in colonial Malaya. As Tamir Moustafa has recently argued, binary tensions within the Malaysian state "were all constructed and contingent on particular institutional and political circumstances. Yet, the power of this construction . . . is that its own starting point is obfuscated. The construct diverts attention away from its institutional source and, to the extent that it becomes enmeshed in wider political struggles, it becomes further rooted in popular legal consciousness."[6]

Contemporary entanglements between ethnicity and religion in Malaysia also underscore the importance of understanding the specific historical pathways of Islamic law in its local context. Islamic law in Malaysia shares many commonalties with that of Egypt, India, Pakistan, and Bangladesh, having a shared legacy of British colonialism and common law, and having inherited much of its institutional logic and placement from colonial India. However, in Malaya, the early definition of the sultans' authority over matters of Malay custom and Muslim tradition, as exemplified in the Pangkor Engagement of 1874, made possible the conjoining of Malay ethnicity and Muslim identity in ways quite distinct from that in India and Egypt. In British colonial Malaya, British and Malay elites negotiated the scope, content and meaning of "Islamic law" in such a way that Malay elite identity and Islam were entwined, and that the nationalist elites of the postindependence period further consolidated the inextricability of Malayness and its attendant privileges with Islamic legitimacy and institutions. The close relationship between Islamic religious and Malay ethnic identity in Malaysia has multiple roots, among them negotiations between local Malay elites and British colonial officials in the Federated Malay States between 1874 and 1914, which constructed a domain of relative autonomy over "matters of religion and culture" for Malay sultans in the Malay States.[7] This domain of autonomy gave the sultans and other elites in Malay society reasons to invest in ongoing colonial classifications ordered by race and religion, such that by the immediate pre-independence period, race was understood within the struggle for Malaya as a key social and political category.[8] Malay privilege, in particular, and the relationship of the sultans to this privilege, became a critical point in negotiations over the shape and content of the Malayan Union, the grouping of Malay States that succeeded British Malaya. The potential loss of this privilege in the final composition of the state—the reduction of sultans' powers, automatic grants of equal citizenship to residents of British Malaya and Singapore—galvanized opposition to the Union. This opposition was led by aristocratic Malay elites, and these elites were instrumental in the formation of the United Malay National Organisation in 1946.

During independence negotiations, the Reid Commission (1956), tasked with drafting the Federal Constitution, put into place not only constitutional monarchy and federalism, but protected the special rights of Malays and made Islam the religion of the federation (Art. 11), while at the same time guaranteeing freedom of worship (Art. 11) and equal protection under the law (Art. 8). Matters of Islam were left to the states, in part because the sultans of each state wished their positions as heads of Islam in each state not to come under the overarching power of the federation. The Yang di-Pertuan Agong was tasked with the protection of special Bumiputra and Malay rights (Art 153). Article 160 defines a Malay as a person who professes the religion of Islam, habitually speaks the Malay language, and conforms to Malay custom. States were given the right to adjudicate matters of Islamic law independently of the federal government, which had legislative oversight over the rest of Malaysian law, establishing the states and their rulers as the locus of Islam. These matters have continued to follow the broad contours outlined during the colonial period.[9] Article 121 (1A) (1988) states that the federal courts have no jurisdiction over state Syariah Court matters, preventing matters that come under the jurisdiction of state syariah courts to be appealed to the federal civil courts. In recent years, as royal privilege and the authority of the state sultans to speak for Islam has come under question, in part due to the efforts of the federal government and UMNO to weaken the role of the monarchy, some royal figures have asserted their Islamic credentials, and others have underscored the importance of the sultans in safeguarding the rights of Malays.

Colonial and the postcolonial governments in Malaya oversaw the extension of territorial sovereignty across the various states of the Malay Peninsula, but the federal structure of Malaysia continues to allow local rulers—the sultans of each state and the chief ministers of state governments (and other elites—Muslim religious leaders, political parties, state courts)—significant power over matters of religion and administration. Territorial sovereignty, tied to notions of indigeneity, has particular implications for ethnic identity in Malaysia because the constitutional definition of "a Malay" has, since the Independence period and especially since the beginning of Mahathir's New Economic Plan, been tied to economic privileges based upon *bumiputra* status ("sons of the soil," i.e., "indigenous people"). As in the colonial period, control over land tenure means far more than the economic benefit of ownership of land: it stands for a larger system of local powerholders, for networks of influence based upon relationship to land, for a claim on the resources of the state, for belonging and citizenship. Overlaid against the backdrop of ethnic privilege and anxiety, three conditions—the colonial bifurcation of jurisdiction into "religious" and nonreligious domains, the dependence of Malay sultans' authority upon the religious domain, and postindependence efforts by UMNO and the federal government to gather authority over Islam to itself—have positioned Islamic law as a critical arena for the production and maintenance of political and institutional power in contemporary Malaysia.

Many scholars of postindependence Malaysia have discussed the question of "Islamic resurgence" beginning in the 1980s, placing it within the context of global pan-Islamism after the Iranian Revolution, Prime Minister Mahathir's program to revitalize the Malay core of support for his government, and increasing economic anxiety among the Malay middle class.[10] Others have seen the growing resort to Islamic appeals by "secular" parties in Malaysia, the United Malay National Organisation (UMNO) foremost among them, as shrewd electoral strategy or, as in the case of the "Islam Hadhari" ("civilizational Islam," combining Islamic ideals with an economic and social "developmentalist" plan) campaign of PM Abdullah Badawi, part of a program to "discipline Malays."[11] As the strength of the sultans waxes and wanes, and as English rises to replace Malay as the language of upward mobility, Islam has become an increasingly critical component of Malaysian politics and governance. Especially among Malaysia's ethnic minorities and those committed to a more secular vision of the Malaysian nation, the appearance of an upward Islamizing trend in government discourse and political debate, in policy and in public space, has been cause for concern.

However, the trend is neither linear nor univalent, and since independence the issue of Islam has repeatedly been invoked to bolster state authority as well as to question it.[12] Whereas in the 1980s and 1990s, the issue of "the Malay" was at the center of Malaysian political discourse, since the 2000s Muslim identity has moved to the forefront of public debate, and the locus of controversy has moved to the legal and bureaucratic arena. Institutionally, "Islamization" in Malaysia has meant, broadly speaking, the incursion of the federal government into areas previously reserved for state Islamic bureaucracies, the takeover of Islamic judicial appointments, mosque committees and Islamic legislation by the ruling party. The competition between state rulers and the central federal government has largely been won by the central government, in part because of its Islamizing policies. However, the effect of these policies have been an increase in anxiety among the other constituents of the ruling coalition—non Muslim Chinese and Indians and urban "secular" elites—as well as a growing assertiveness on the part of Islamic actors to press further Islamization of law. These Islamic actors are not uniformly part of the opposition; they are increasingly "salaried Islamic bureaucrats, Sharia legal practitioners and intellectuals."[13] Among these Malay Muslims, "Islam Hadhari," often translated as "civilizational Islam," carries the aspiration for a wider cultural and ethical influence for Islamic values in Malaysia, partly a response to perceptions that Islamic parties such as PAS seem too dogmatic and narrow to be accepted across Malaysian society. Civilizational Islam is articulated as a moderate cultural vision for an Islamic society that could contain ethnic and religious minorities, and that could be recognized as a moderate exemplar in global society as well.[14] Institutionally, however, the moment of Islam Hadhari has featured extensive legislation and litigation of the scope, meaning, and content of Islamic law in Malaysia.

So far, these discussions of jurisdiction and definition have focused upon the actions of state officials—judges, bureaucrats, and politicians. However, as was the case during the colonial period, relatively less powerful groups have also made strategic use of divided jurisdictions and definitional struggles. Groups such as Sisters in Islam have found that arguments for women's rights may in fact have better traction when allied to Islamic values than to secular principles, but that Islamic authority can be far more difficult to challenge than secular patriarchy. The Malaysian courts have increasingly become an arena to which the issue of jurisdiction over Islam and its role in Malaysian society have been brought, and litigants's strategies have shown a keen understanding of the jurisdictional struggle between state shari'a courts and federal courts. Non-Muslim litigants have employed syariah lawyers to represent them in the Syariah Court, presenting their evidence in ways that were instrumental to achieving the verdict they desired.[15] Choosing the jurisdiction in which one is heard can be a highly significant strategy—in a highly debated and prominent case on the issue of apostasy, the plaintiff, Lina Joy, repeatedly refused the jurisdiction of the syariah courts in Malaysia, arguing that since she was baptized, she was no longer Muslim and therefore the syariah courts had no jurisdiction over her.[16] Citizens like Lina Joy have found that, to contest the control of the state and its laws, they had first to accept its terms and authority in the courts, but still citizens continue to make full use of the opportunities afforded by layered legality to press their cases in Malaysia.

In particular, they have begun to invoke another layer of legality, that of human rights and religious freedom as a constitutional guarantee and human rights as defined by Malaysia's status as a signatory to various international human rights agreements, to press their claims both at home and abroad. Joy's legal claims have emphasized her rights as a citizen: to religious freedom under the Federal Constitution, to procedural justice from the federal bureaucracy, to equal treatment under the law. In doing so, her case has pushed the debate on religion in Malaysia, both legal and popular, further in the direction of rights-claiming and equal citizenship, and the international profile of this case has polarized the debate in Malaysia further, portraying the case as one of religious freedom and casting the conflict in international human rights terms. In the 2006 appeal she submitted against the 2001 High Court decision, Joy had in fact limited her case to arguing only the administrative law aspects, but by then nongovernmental groups had taken the language of rights and citizenship into the public debate on the case. Both the plaintiff's arguments and the judicial reasoning of the cases bear clear traces of the internationalization, and the Americanization, of legal language pertaining to constitutional law, with both the plaintiff and the judges arguing for the sanctity of the Federal Constitution in terms reminiscent of US Bill of Rights legal activism. Although the Federal Civil Court of Appeals refused Joy's appeal, one of the judges, Judge Richard Malanjum, submitted a dissenting opinion that asserted many of these rights arguments within the framework of constitutional guarantees.[17] While the importance of the Federal Constitution in Malaysia has long been to enshrine deeply held values as well as established political compacts, ironically, the liberal language of constitutional sanctity has entered Malaysian politics through cases whose focus has been the centrality of Islam to the Malaysian state.

The issue of apostasy—the ability of Malays to detach Islam from their identity—carries with it a profound challenge not only to Malaysia's religious politics but also to crucial matters of economy, society, gender, federalism, and authority. It has also been an arena for the articulation of new visions of the Malaysian state and its citizens, new meanings of Islam and Muslim identity, and new struggles for control over the future of these developments. These cases are part of a mutually productive relationship between law and the popular mobilization of Malaysian Muslim identity politics, as they are also part of a longer continuum of legal decision making about the rules and logics that apply to the question of Islam, religion, and ethnicity in Malaysia more broadly. They also chart a particular trajectory of change in the Malaysian politics of religion and law—the *Nyonya Tahir* case properly began in the 1980s, when state religious officials took notice of her living as a Chinese Buddhist but took no action; the *Lina Joy* case began in 2001 and incited public debate, administrative changes, and a demand for clarification from the state and federal courts on the status of non-Muslim Malays, ending finally in 2007. By 2009 and into the 2010s, the courts were defining the religious rights of non-Muslim non-Malays, framing their free exercise of religion in national security terms, and seeking to uphold the sanctity of Islam as the state religion. While the fears of proponents of a secular Malaysia may be well-founded, the paradoxes of law and institutionalization work even in the spaces where Islamization is being performed, in both civil and syariah courts, bringing forth the language of citizens' rights, the standing and testimony of non-Muslims, and the reluctance of even the most "Muslim" of Malaysian states to declare apostasy, into direct conversation with discourses of Malay/Muslim dominance over Malaysian law and politics.

Lina Joy and Nyonya Tahir

Two court cases will serve here to illustrate the paradox of postcolonial state approaches to Islam and Muslim identity, its implications for Malaysian law and society, and the utility of the analytic framework this project offers: one, *Lina Joy v. Majlis Agama Islam Wilayah Persekutuan & Anor* (2001), tried in the civil Federal High Court of Malaya; the other, *Nyonya binte Tahir, Ex P Majlis Agama Islam Negri Sembilan & Anor* (2006), tried in the Syariah High Court of Seremban in the state of Negri Sembilan.[18] Both these cases had, at their center, the question of whether, and under what circumstances, a Malay/Muslim in Malaysia could leave the religion of Islam, and hence were widely understood to be cases of apostasy (*murtad*) and freedom of religion.[19] In the case of *Lina Joy*, the federal court ruled against the ability of a Muslim to leave the religion of Islam; in the case of *Nyonya Tahir*, the syariah court ruled that Nyonya Tahir had indeed left the religion and chose to recognize that departure officially. On the face of it, these cases together present a puzzle of outcomes: why was it the civil federal court that ruled against a Malaysian Muslim leaving Islam? Why was it a syariah state court that ruled in favor of a Malaysian Muslim's apostasy?

On April 18, 2001, the High Court of Malaya ruled on *Lina Joy v the Islamic Religious Council of the Federal Territories & Anor*.[20] Lina Joy had been born into a Malay/Muslim family and had originally been named Azlina Jailani; she had chosen to be baptized into Christianity as an adult and wished to marry her Christian fiancé. Malaysian law does not permit Muslim women to marry non-Muslim men, and so Joy applied to the National Registration Department (NRD) for a change in the name and religious status recorded on her national identity card. The NRD allowed the change of name, but required certification from the Syariah court of her conversion from Islam, and in the meantime recorded her religion as "Islam." Joy applied to the federal courts in a series of cases, arguing that she no longer came under the Syariah Courts' jurisdiction since she was not Muslim, and further that the Malaysian Constitution allowed for freedom of religion.

In 2001, a judge dismissed Joy's applications for declaratory orders that asserted her right to religious freedom based upon the Federal Constitution; the nullification of Section 2 of the Administration of Islamic Law (Federal Territories) Enactment 1993 and other state enactments due to their inconsistency with Federal Constitution Article 11(1); the inapplicability of Syariah Criminal Offenses Act (Federal Territories) 1997 and other state enactments to Lina Joy because she was no longer Muslim; and the recording of Joy's conversion by the National Registry Department. These rulings were based, the judge argued, not on any matters under Syariah Court jurisdiction, but simply upon constitutional grounds:

"A person as long as he/she is a Malay and by definition under Article 160 cl. (2) is a Malay, the said person cannot renounce his/her religion at all. A Malay under Article 160(2) remains in the Islamic faith until his or her dying days."[21] In other words, the judge rejected Lina Joy's assertion—that the jurisdiction of the syariah courts did not apply to her because she considered herself to be Christian, and to have exercised her constitutional right as a Malaysian citizen to religious freedom—on the basis of her ethnicity.

It was against the backdrop of high-profile cases like *Lina Joy* that the case of Nyonya binti Tahir (*Nyonya Tahir*) came before the Syariah High Court of Negri Sembilan. On January 23, 2006, the Syariah High Court of Negri Sembilan heard an application by the Islamic Religious Council of Negri Sembilan for a ruling on the religious status of Nyonya binti Tahir. This is a case that took up, in substance, the argument of Judge Faiza Tamby Chik in *Lina Joy* (2001) that a Malay under Art 160 (2) remains in the Islamic faith until her dying days. Coming from a syariah court, this decision took on exactly the issues the civil court judge in *Lina Joy* (2001) would not: the matter of the belief or unbelief of a Muslim person. The manner in which it did so, however, reveals a number of important elements of Malaysian state administration of Islam, the circumstances under which a Muslim was able to renounce her faith, the leeway provided the syariah court judge in matters of evidence, and the concerns of the judge in this matter to provide additional commentary on the wider issue of apostasy.

Tahir had passed away five days earlier, and her family wished to bury her next to her husband's grave in a Buddhist cemetery. Tahir's identity card showed her to be Malay and Muslim, so in order for the burial to take place as planned, a ruling as to her religious status had to be obtained from the Syariah High Court. The court found, based upon documentary evidence and testimony from her family, that she had long lived as a Chinese Buddhist, and based upon reports by the Islamic Religious Affairs Department in Tampin as to her manner of life and community associations, concluded that Tahir was indeed *murtad* (apostate) and ordered the release of her body to her family for burial as a Chinese Buddhist.

The Federal Constitution of Malaysia ties the race and religion of Malays together in a knot that so far the courts have not been able or willing to untie. The political, cultural, and legal entanglements between race and religion continue to proliferate in Malaysia, and it will be continue to be important to track where race and religion coincide in Malaysia, and where they diverge. Official figures, for example, indicate that there were 863 applications to the Syariah courts by Muslims to change their religious status; 168 were approved. The reason for this approval, according to the Islamic Affairs Minister (2010), was that the court "had determined that the 168 applicants were not Muslims to begin with," referring to the fact that most of these applicants were neither Malays nor Muslims at birth.[22] As the *Nyonya Tahir* case indicates, the judicial and cultural criteria for determining Malayness are ambiguous and contingent. As the permutations of the *Lina Joy* case illustrate, religious freedom as a legal issue shifts registers and venues, and moves from administrative regulation to constitutional law, state to federal jurisdictions, civil to religious courts, with rapidity. Each of these shifts and movements has an impact on matters of evidence and witnessing, standing and jurisdiction. For the plaintiffs, legal actors, politicians, citizens, and external observers involved in the issues, these shifts have differing meaning and import.

Since these cases emerged, the issue of religious identity, and its impact on race relations in Malaysia, has become much more visible and heated. What has now been constructed as a problem of apostasy, arising from cases such as these above, also plays into debates about interfaith relations; proselytization and evangelism; the ownership of religious language and symbols; the relationship between internal security and extremism; and the rights of non-Muslim, non-Malay Malaysians. The issue of apostasy, by being cast in terms of the legal status of Malays in Malaysia, produces a demand for further regulation of these shifts and ambiguities, and further requires the definition of Islam and Malayness by the state. Moving from a focus upon the dynamics of definition, jurisdiction, and state making during the colonial period, I seek here to delineate the ongoing productivity of these dynamics in contemporary Malaysia. These are the ongoing politics of Islamic law in many Muslim states today, in which the institutional placement of Islam into specialized domains of law continually requires maintenance and clarification, and in which contestation over the definition of Islam and Muslim continually requires resort to the language, institutions, and authority of law.

Jurisdictional Politics: Demanding State Islam

Both the civil and the syariah courts agreed that the matter of apostasy came under the jurisdiction of the syariah courts. Having done so, the judge in the civil court case of *Lina Joy* established other grounds by which the decision could be arrived at, arguing instead on constitutional grounds, and at the same time making a veiled claim about her competence to judge the case on syariah grounds. Chapter 3 delineated how struggles over jurisdiction constructed a separate domain of law for religion and custom, and how jurisdictional division had to be built and maintained along a number of fronts: administrative, territorial, and authoritative. In contemporary Malaysia, the law is quite clear on the matter: the Federal Constitution (121 1(A)) carved out a space for the syariah courts of each state to adjudicate matters of Islamic law, narrowly conceived. Where the syariah courts have jurisdiction, the federal civil courts do not. Yet in these trials of apostasy, the issue of jurisdiction, the blurring of boundaries between a question of Islamic law and a question of the interests of the state, continued to require boundary maintenance. As chapter 3 illustrated, and as scholars like Benton (2002), Cormack (2008), Richland (2012), and Agrama (2012) have argued, jurisdictional crises gave rise to new opportunities for the centralizing state to assert its authority, its interpretive frames, and its hierarchy of administration.[23]

The federal court, having asserted its *lack* of jurisdiction, then proceeded to dictate the terms within which the issue of apostasy would be framed in Malaysia, as a matter of the constitutional position of Islam and Muslims within the state. As recent scholarship on jurisdictional discourse has also argued, moments of jurisdictional conflict are particularly jurisgenerative:

> The law at once assumes its power to decide generally (that is, that the law has some power, over some thing), asks after the particular limts of that power as it may apply to the case at hand, and then elides the fact that in asking it is announcing that power anew. The net effect of this juris-diction is to convert difficult questions regarding the ultimate sources of legal power and authority into much easier questions of its practical scope and distribution.[24]

In the case of *Nyonya Tahir*, the judge addressed the issue of jurisdiction by determining through official records the race of the deceased and her place of domicile. If the deceased were found to be Muslim and resident in Negri Sembilan, the law required that she fall under the jurisdiction of the state syariah court in Negri Sembilan. In a far less ambiguous manner than the federal judge in the *Lina Joy* case, the syariah judge pointed out that, in the case at hand, jurisdiction fell to the Syariah High

Court not only because the deceased had been found to be Muslim, but because Article 121(1A) List 1 of the Federal Constitution bars the civil courts from having jurisdiction "over any matter within the jurisdiction of the Syariah Court. In other words, the Federation has itself clarified the separation of jurisdiction between the two systems of courts and it must be obeyed."[25] This assertiveness has arisen out of the need to clarify the boundary between state and civil courts in struggles over jurisdiction between syariah and civil courts, and the desire of the syariah courts in each Malaysian state to assert their jurisdictional domain. These two cases from contemporary Malaysia illustrate the productive terrain of jurisdiction, and the complexity of jurisdictional struggle. In the arena of apostasy, both civil and syariah courts were acutely aware of public ambivalence on the issue, and both sought to defer determinations of apostasy, while at the same time using the debate itself to establish their Islamic credentials. In addition, the civil court established further that the definition of "Malay" under the Federal Constitution included a religious component—Islam—and that the two were considered to be inseparable, for reasons of public order, constitutional harmony, and legislative intent.

In the case of *Lina Joy*, the two defendants, the Islamic Religious Council of the Federal Territories and the National Registration Department, asked that the suit be denied largely on grounds of jurisdiction: since the plaintiff was a Muslim, the issue of her conversion was within the sole jurisdiction of the Syariah courts. The plaintiff argued that, since she was no longer Muslim, but Christian, she was no longer subject to the jurisdiction of the Islamic Religious Council or syariah law. The judge, in his final decision, argued that "the issue of apostasy is an issue coming under the category of religious affairs . . . and therefore it ought to be determined by eminent jurists who are properly qualified in the field of Islamic jurisprudence and definitely not by the civil court" (257). The constitutional test applied by Judge Faiza Tamby Chik in the *Lina Joy* case was one of "Malayness," and emphatically excluded criteria of religion: "I am going to decide this case as a civil matter in accordance with the Federal Constitution"(271).

Chapter 3 showed that the general trend in jurisdictional change was toward greater state influence in public and private life: I would argue that both these cases illustrate that the trend in postcolonial Malaysia has continued to bolster the power of the central state. However, the institutional features of the contemporary Malaysian state—a federation of states in which most Islamic law matters are determined at the state level—mean that, in addition to overall state encroachment into public and private life, there has also been a struggle for jurisdiction between the states and the federal government. Both cases began as problems of *administration*—the everyday execution of policy at the local level—in these cases, within bureaucratic offices governing identity cards, marriage and death certifications. While the administrative dimension of jurisdiction may seem the most innocuous, this is the level at which most Muslims and most citizens encounter the law, and the gateway through which apostasy de facto became apostasy de jure. By becoming a matter of constitutional law, implicating questions of racial and religious definition, of privileged citizenship in the Malaysian state, and of the proper domain of states versus the federal government, and of civil court judges versus shari'a judges, jurisdictional politics also broadcast the issue of apostasy—theoretically a shari'a matter—across multiple levels of political and social life, and brought all these levels under the jurisdiction of the law. Once within the domain of the law of the state, the meaning of the cases, and the reasoning applied to them, reveal complex dynamics of interconnection, mutual definition, and competition between civil and syariah courts.

Shari'a in and out of Islamic Courts: Trying Islamic Law

In chapter 4, the application of Islamic law was shown to be a matter not only of determining a verdict using the applicable *fiqh* rules, but also a question of determining where to draw the line between the domain of Islamic law and the domain of the state. State courts in the British period continually overtook areas of Islamic law, state bureaucracies imposed the logics of civil law on Islamic adjudication, and the application of Islamic law by judges untrained in its methods and sources often resulted in unexpected outcomes. The questions we asked in chapter 4 might be productively deployed in the case of contemporary Malaysia as well: how do judges both in and out of the syariah courts apply Islamic law? In the syariah courts in Malaysia, the question of apostasy is handled with a combination of doctrinal severity and the avoidance of judgment—in the case of *Nyonya Tahir*, the courts knew of her apostasy decades before they ruled on the matter, and only ruled her an apostate when the matter of punishment had become moot. In the case of *Lina Joy*, the judge explicitly denied any jurisdiction over matters of Islamic law, but then quoted Qur'an extensively, the text of the decision working to re-Islamize an explicitly secular legal decision. As in chapter 4, reading both trials *in* and *of* Islamic law helps clarify not only the ways in which Islamic law is applied, but placed and given meaning within the wider context of the legal and political system in which it functions.

The judge in the case of *Lina Joy*, having denied the jurisdiction of the federal court to adjudicate the matter of apostasy, then proceeded to deliver a series of arguments on the case. Despite the assertion that this was a case to be decided on its constitutional merits, other matters being the sole jurisdiction of the syariah courts, the decision devoted a large amount of attention to discussion of Muslimness and of *hukum syarak* (Islamic law in Malaysia). For example, the judge noted that the plaintiff's parents were Muslim: "The plaintiff was born a Muslim, she was brought up as a Muslim or her upbringing was conducted on the basis that she was a Muslim, she lived as a Muslim with her family and is commonly reputed to be a Muslim. All of this is strong evidence of her being a person who professes the religion of Islam. Therefore the plaintiff is a Muslim" (263). Being Muslim, and having not applied to the Syariah courts on the matter of her conversion out of Islam, the plaintiff did not have, in this judge's opinion, recourse to the federal courts.

The constitutional arguments in this decision were followed by a number of nonconstitutional law sections, foremost among them a list of Qur'anic quotations (259–261). The judge used quotations from the Qur'an first to assert that freedom of religion is a "fundamental teaching of Islam": 2:256, stating "let there be no compulsion in religion"; 109:1–6, that recommends the proper response to nonbelievers be "to you be your Way, and to me mine"; 29:46, that exhorts to Muslims, "dispute ye not with the People of the Book"; and 2:62, that goes even further to assert that "those who follow the Jewish (scriptures), and the Christian and the Sabians,—any who believe in God and the Last Day, and work righteousness, shall have their reward with their Lord."

Without accompanying commentary, the next quotations carried a somewhat different message. The judge quoted 4:137, warning against ambivalence in matters of belief: "Those who believe, then reject faith, then believe (again) and (again) reject faith, and go on increasing in unbelief,—God will not forgive them nor guide them on the way." Also, 18:29, which, while it recommends that matters of belief be freely chosen, also makes clear the spiritual penalties for those who choose wrongly: "For the wrongdoers We have prepared a fire whose (smoke and flames), like the walls and roof of a tent, will hem them in: if they implore relief they will be granted water like melted brass, that will scald their faces, how dreadful the drink! How uncomfortable a couch to recline on!" The last two quotations in this argument seem to point to a less punitive, but no less condemnatory, view of unbelief. 10:99 makes the case that compulsion in matters of belief is not the duty of Muslims: "If it had been thy Lord's Will, they would all have believed,—all who are on earth! wilt thou then compel mankind against their will, to believe!" Finally, 9:6, *Surah al-Tawbah* (Repentance), counsels mercy for those who act in ignorance: "If one amongst the Pagans ask thee for asylum, grant it to him, so that he may hear the Word of God, and then escort him to where he can be secure. That is because they are men without knowledge."

The legal function of these quotations are questionable, but their discursive impact was to firmly underscore the judge's earlier comments on Islam's position as the main and dominant religion of the federation, and to emphasize his subsequent argument, that such weighty matters of faith could only be properly managed by qualified Islamic jurisprudents in a syariah court. Further, the judge argued that a judge's competence to decide the matter hinged not upon jurisdiction but upon qualifications:

> If the civil judge is simultaneously also appointed by the Ruler of a State to be an Appeal Judge in the Syariah Appeal Court in that State or has obtained a syariah qualification recognised by the State Syariah Court I am of the view that he is competent to hear and decide the said matter . . . although I am qualified to hear the matter at hand . . . I am not going to decide this case based on my syariah qualification because I am more comfortable to leave it to the Syariah Court to make a decision on the matter of faith or belief of a Muslim person (270–271).

Whereas Art 121(1A) of the Constitution, limiting the jurisdiction over Islamic matters to the Syariah courts, seems to have been intended to reduce confusion between branches of the judiciary over jurisdictional issues, their discussion in this decision indicates that the matter is far from clear. The judge's discussion of the doctrine of harmonious construction, and of the general jurisdiction of the civil courts—as opposed to the particular mandate of the syariah branch—could leave open the question as to whether civil courts can handle matters relating to Islam. Further, the "principle of harmonious construction" (Jain, Indian Constitutional Law) lead the judge "to read Art. 11(1) together with Art. 3(1), 12(2), 74, 121(1A) and 160 so as to give effect to the intention of the framers of our constitution. When read together Art. 11(1) must necessarily be qualified by provisions of Islamic law on apostasy" (252). The judge's interpretation of harmonious construction, as a device to reconcile otherwise problematic elements of constitutional law, brought together the legacy of British colonial rule, the deliberations of the Reid Commission, the "intent" of the "founding fathers" of the Constitution, the precedent of Malaysian cases (some of which invoked *fatawa*, shari'a opinions issued by the state Islamic authorities) and legal scholarship in a continuous stream of legal development. The end result of this development was to constitute Malaysia as a "hybrid" state, somewhere between a secular system and a theocracy, in which Islam is "the main and dominant religion" (254).

The shari'a courts, on the other hand, seem to have gone somewhat out of their way to avoid applying Islamic law in the case of *Nyonya Tahir* and others: while it could be said that the judge merely found Nyonya Tahir apostate and cannot be said to have honored her wishes, the fact remains that the state of Negri Sembilan was aware of her manner of life and beliefs a full twenty years before this case, and did not enforce any punishment upon her. In fact, no Malaysian state has thus far applied the death penalty for the crime of apostasy, nor would any state currently be permitted to apply such a penalty without approval at the national level. In the states where apostasy is punishable by law, the maximum penalty is caning, a fine and/or a jail term not exceeding three years. In Negri Sembilan, where apostasy is not illegal, those who do go to the syariah courts seeking to leave Islam face a mandatory waiting period and voluntary counseling. [26] The list of states that have criminalized apostasy do not correspond neatly along party lines—not all states governed by the Malaysian Islamic Party (PAS) have criminalized apostasy, and some solidly ruling-party (UMNO) states have done so.[27]

The *Nyonya Tahir* decision made a number of departures, in content and reasoning, from the pattern of past syariah court decisions. Firstly, the manner in which the judgment was laid out, its reference to case law and constitutional issues, and its quotation of previous civil court judgments on issues of religious identity, placed it firmly within the Malaysian legal discourse on apostasy, rather than a separate domain of Islamic law insulated from developments in civil law. Secondly, the judge used terminology, at times in English, to underscore his familiarity with civil law procedure and norms, for example, "take cognizance." Thirdly, the decision to allow the testimony of non-Muslims—when other judges in similar jurisdictions had not, was unique, and controversial, not least because it came only one month after a high-profile case involving a man who had been buried as a Muslim despite his family's contention that he was a Hindu.[28] These departures indicate that, despite the judge's findings that apostasy was a crime punishable by death, the actual impact of this syariah case was in favor of a more accommodationist approach to civil law and procedure and the inclusion of non-Muslim witnesses. Based upon the Department of Islamic Religious Affairs report of 1986, the testimony of her children, the deceased's own Letter of Declaration (1986), and the determination that Nyonya Tahir was of sound mind and undertook these actions voluntarily, the judge ruled that the deceased "was not a Muslim at the time of her death." In consequence, the heirs were allowed to collect her body and bury it in accordance with Buddhist practices alongside her late husband.

Yet, despite the procedural pluralism of the case, when it came to discussing the evidence before him and the actual ruling of apostasy, the judge sought to achieve outcomes somewhat removed from the adjudication before him. Having found Nyonya Tahir apostate, the penalty could not be applied to her, since she was deceased: yet the discussion of penalties covered a third of his ruling. The judge turned to examine the major issue in the case—was Nyonya Tahir a Muslim at the time of her death? To do this, he defined the sin of "riddah" (apostasy) as a "return from Islam to a state of *kuffar* (kekufuran), whether by intention or by actions that show kufr or by words that ridicule, obduracy or *i'tiqad* (belief)," citing the popular Syrian jurisprudent Wahbah al Zuhaily.[29] He defined the penalty for apostasy to be death, taking as his sources "the sayings of the Messenger s.a.w. Riwayat al Jamaah except for Muslim, the Riwayat ibn Abi Shaybah and Abdul Razzaq from Akramah from Ibn Abbas's [46], "Riwayat al Bukhari and Muslim from Ibn Masud r.a., Subul al Salam" (47). Further, he laid out the consequences for apostasy, from Qur'an 2:217 ("Whosoever is apostate among you from his religion, and he dies in a state of rejection [kekafiran], then it is they who have done good works in vain, on earth and in the hereafter, and it is they who are denizens of hellfire they who abide in it [forever]") and 4:48 ("Verily Allah does not forgive the sin of *shirk* and Allah forgives all else besides shirk, for whomever He wishes. Whomever associates partners with Allah, he has committed a grave sin."). He concluded this theoretical reference to *fiqh* sources, covering a third of his decision, with the finding that "a large proportion of the ulama" consider apostasy to be a *hadd* offense, "on which the sentence is death (killing)" (50). Unlike the Qur'anic references used in the civil court case of *Lina Joy*, here, no mention was made of religious freedom, nor was mention made of the applicable penalties under the law of the state, which were far lighter than death.

Both judges incorporated discussions of *fiqh* and shari'a into their arguments, but in neither the civil nor the shari'a courts was the large body of Qur'anic and Islamic legal argument arranged in order to arrive at a verdict. In other words, the majority of references to Islamic law in both courts did not perform adjudicative functions. Qur'anic quotations in *Lina Joy*, for example, occupied a narrative place quite separate from the constitutional decision, while the *fiqh* discussions in *Nyonya Tahir* on penalties for apostasy could not apply to the deceased. Within the Malaysian courts, the apostasy debate is less a barometer of religious tolerance within the law of the state, as it is a theater for the performance of Islamic legitimacy and Malay supremacy on the part of state and federal courts. To call this theater is not to cast this arena of politics into the genre of performance alone; the discursive and logical leeway the courts allowed themselves, all the while protesting their limitations, presented powerful public visions for what kind of state Malaysia could be, and provided critical framing for social and political mobilization around this question.

Making the Muslim State: Reinforcing Malayness in the Muslim State

Crucial to the politics of Malaysian emancipation from colonial rule was the continued image of the Malay sultans as protectors of Islam and the special position of Malays in each state of the new federation. Processes of state making affected both individual Muslims as well as evolving conceptions of the Muslim state, helping construct what it meant to be Muslim, as well as what was necessary to be a Muslim state. Both the persona of Muslim elites as well as the content of state policies were critical components of colonial policy, and state policies that defined "Muslim" and "Islam" in particular ways had, because of their ability to secure and divert resources, also the ability to affect Muslim self-definition, even in opposition to these categories.

The two contemporary cases we discuss here, while they have implications for elite privilege, did not revolve around elite persons; in postcolonial Malaysia, the issue of Muslim identity has become a mass issue. Therefore, a question that seems somewhat trivial at first—exactly *when* does a person stop being a Muslim?—turns out to have important legal implications. Cast in another way, how does the change in someone's religious affiliation *de facto* become apostasy *de jure*? Clearly, in the eyes of the Malaysian state, it is not sufficient simply to alter one's manner of life or confessional identity; in fact, the state has placed significant obstacles in the way of changing religious status. Nyonya Tahir's conduct of life for the decades she lived as a Chinese Buddhist was not sufficient for the state to determine that she was, de jure, no longer Muslim, as the testimony of her family made clear. Her apostasy may have been made more socially and politically possible when she was deceased: therefore any discussion of penalty could serve an instructional and theoretical purpose.

This question also lays bare the importance of bureaucracy and administrative law in the everyday lives of contemporary Muslims, and makes visible the previously unremarked gender dimensions of the two cases in Malaysia. Here, as in colonial debates on personal status and the state, religion, ethnicity, and governmental power center on the family and on women. Lina Joy's need to have her name and religion changed on her identity card arose out of her desire to marry her Christian fiancé, something that would not be permitted if she were still Muslim. Nyonya Tahir wished to be buried next to her Buddhist husband in the Chinese Buddhist manner, something that would not be permitted if the state still recorded her religion as Islam. Some advocacy groups argue that these cases illustrate a problem of unequal citizenship under the law, not just of non-Malay Muslim Malaysians, but of Muslim women. The burden of ethnic and religious identity may weigh more heavily on women than men in Malaysia, and on Muslim women more than others, and thus the assumption of the ethnic primacy of Malays in Malaysia needs further qualification and investigation.

The larger body of the decision treated first the matter of the plaintiff's constitutional claims, and is revealing perhaps more for the manner in which it treated the matter of state jurisdiction over Islam and ethnicity, than for the judgment to which it led. One issue the judge treated with some detail was the relation between the constitutional provision for freedom of religion (Art 11(1) Fed. Const.) and the place of Islam in the Malaysian state: "The plaintiff is so obsessed with the first part of Art. 11(1) of the Federal Constitution and had given it an interpretation to the effect that the said first part of Art. 11(1) gives her the right to profess and practise the religion of her choice"(247). The judge's argument was that Art. 11(1)'s statement that "every person has the right to profess and practise his religion" cannot be read independently of the clauses that follow it, in which every religious community has the right to administer its own affairs (11(3)) and the propagation of religious doctrine among Muslims may be regulated (11(4)). Further, 11(5) states that "this article does not authorise any act contrary to any general law relating to public order, public health or morality."

The argument made by the judge in refuting Lina Joy's claims was that freedom of religion is provided to all Malaysians by the Constitution, but that Muslims are subject to the additional requirements of syariah law: "The freedom to convert out of Islam in respect of a Muslim is subject to qualifications, namely the syariah laws on these matters. Only such construction would support the 'smooth workings of the system'" (257). The combination with Article 160(2) means that "a person as long as he/she is a Malay and by definition under Article 160 cl. (2) is a Malay, the said person cannot renounce his/her religion at all. A Malay under Article 160(2) remains in the Islamic faith until his or her dying days" (271). The plaintiff argued that, since she was no longer Muslim, but Christian, she was no longer subject to the jurisdiction of the Islamic Religious Council or syariah law. The judge disagreed, based upon arguments of public and administrative order, but more crucially, based upon "a special position and status" accorded to Islam in the Constitution. Article 3 (1) states: "Islam is the religion of the Federation; but other religions may be practised in peace and harmony in any part of the Federation." He quoted articles by both legal and political actors as well as judgments in the civil courts to support this argument (251). The constitutional provision for freedom of religion, therefore, does not take precedence over that obligation.

For the judge, the rights of the Malay as a citizen had, at least in discourse if not in law, to be balanced against the interests of the state. Allowing a Muslim to unilaterally leave Islam "will create chaos and confusion with the administrative authority which manages the affairs of Islam and the Muslim community and consequently the non-Muslim community as a whole. I am of the opinion that this would threaten public order and this cannot have been the intention of the Legislature when drafting the Federal Constitution and the Act" (249). The right of a community to manage its own affairs required that the plaintiff's conversion out of Islam be registered with the Islamic Religious Council, and that failure to do so had implications not only for the plaintiff but for state administration and public order.

The argument here is that freedom of religion is provided to all Malaysians by the Constitution, but that Muslims are subject to the additional requirements of "syariah law." "When [the above provisions are] construed harmoniously, the inevitable conclusion is that the freedom to convert out of Islam in respect of a Muslim is subject to qualifications, namely the syariah laws on these matters" (257). However, these qualifications are, according to the judge, fundamentally ethnic: "A Malay under Art. 160(2) remains in the Islamic faith until his or her dying days."[30] Having asserted that the legal basis for denying Lina Joy's claims were constitutional rather than religious, the judge then underlined the basic logic of the constitutional issue to be the inextricability of the religion of Islam from the ethnic category of Malay. It was the civil court, not the Islamic, that argued for the inextricability of ethnicity and religion, because of the need to maintain a particular vision of the Malaysian state, a state whose identity hinges upon the tension between privileged Malay/Muslim identity, a particular variety of non-liberal secularity, and a divided sovereignty increasingly formalized by the courts.

In the case of the *Nyonya Tahir* decision, the individual Muslim state was tied to matters of ethnicity and social belonging. The decision of the judge in the syariah court began with race, continued with issues of family and gender, and ended with a determination of religion. First, the judge determined: "The race (bangsa) is recorded as Malay . . . these documents clearly provide primary proof that Nyonya binti Tahir is someone of the Malay race, domiciled and resident in Tampin, Negri Sembilan" (9). Here too, as in *Lina Joy* (2001) the judge pointed out the definition of "Melayu" (Malay) under the Constitution: "Someone who adheres to the religion of Islam, habitually speaks the Malay language, follows Malay custom (adat *istiadat*)" (10). Section 5 of the Islamic Family Law Enactment (Negri Sembilan) 2003 requires that the determination of the religious status of a person be decided "following criteria of public reputation, without making any attempt to question faith, beliefs, manner, behavior, character, actions, or suspicions of such person"(11). Based on these findings, the judge determined that Nyonya binti Tahir was "an adherent of the religion of Islam" (12), and that her case came properly under the jurisdiction of the Negri Sembilan Syariah High Court.

The second set of questions revolved around the religious status of the deceased at the time of her death, that is, was she apostate, and how did she apostatize? The evidence reveals the mechanisms of the Department of Islamic Affairs of Negri Sembilan and the manner in which the state handled matters of apostasy in the decade prior to the rise of high-profile apostasy cases. In 1986, the Department of Islamic Affairs and the Kadi Court in Alor Gajah, Melaka, conducted an investigation into religious status of Nyonya binti Tahir, entitled "Cohabitation with Chinese Man, Nyonya Bt Tahir/Chiang Meng." The report detailed Nyonya Tahir's history, her marriage to Chiang Meng, and other matters that indicated her departure not only from Islam but from *Malayness*: "Since marriage to the Chinese man she has lived as a Chinese, venerating idols and eating pork . . . separated from Malay community . . . All her children married Chinese people" (18–19). By criteria of family ties—she was raised by her "convert Chinese grandfather," of marriage, of the results of that marriage—children who identified as Chinese and married Chinese, by the manner and location of her household, and in fact by her name—Nyonya indicates a woman positioned culturally between Malays and Chinese—Nyonya Tahir was not Malay, neither was she contributing to the social reproduction of Malay society.

The final line quoted from the report was the only one that explicitly addressed the matter of belief: "In her house there is a Chinese idol and she admits that she venerates it" (19). Tahir "made a declaration that she will continue to live as a Chinese and if she dies wishes to be buried as a Chinese" (18). The report appeared neither to discuss the issue of *murtad* explicitly, nor did there seem to have been any action taken against Nyonya Tahir at that time, twenty years before her death. Its conclusions as to the possibility of her return to Islam were cast in terms that further emphasis the conflation of ethnicity and religion: "From outside appearances Nyonya bt Tahir will not return to Islam because she has long lived as a Chinese person and since she was a child she was raised by her convert Chinese grandfather in the way of Chinese people and was separated from Malay community" (19).

These statements from Nyonya Tahir's children all corroborated the 1986 report, presenting a picture of her life conducted as religiously Buddhist and culturally Chinese. Evidence was presented and recorded as *qarinah* to corroborate their testimony, including photographs of the family, "on the drinking table were two bottles (believed to be alcohol)" (24), the house altar at her residence, and a photograph of a grave dug beside the deceased husband's burial plot, reserved for the deceased. Further, the witness testified that his mother had left a declaration stating that "I do not intend to return to Islam and here I make a declaration that I have left the religion of Islam and I will continue to live as a Chinese and if I die wish to be buried in the traditions of the Chinese." For *Nyonya Tahir* as well as for the judge in the case, race and religion had become intertwined to such an extent that they were indistinguishable, and Tahir's entry into a Chinese family and community were taken as definitive proof of her exit from Islam, and, therefore, from being Malay.

The definition of "Malay" in the Constitution of Malaysia has tied the individual Muslim state to the governmental in unique and unprecedented ways: to the relationship between sultans and the federal government, to the balance between upholding Malay privilege and the rights of non-Malay citizens, to the distribution of state resources, to the place of Islam as the religion of the federation. The federal court's comments on the question of constitutional conflicts underline rather than dispel the intractability of the matter: while the Constitution upholds the principle of freedom of religion for Malaysians, this right does not extend to Malays. Ironically, therefore, in a state privileging the rights of Malays over others, in matters of Islamic law and confessional identity, Malays have fewer rights than other Malaysian citizens, a fact that points to the need to rethink the relationship between ethnic primacy in law and the overarching effects of state racial logic on the lives of its citizens. Ethnic and religious primacy in law, whether it is of Jews in Israel, Hindus in India, or Muslims in Malaysia, seems in fact first to curtail the autonomy of those it proritizes.[31]

Not only this, but the effort to define religion, whether it is ostensibly done by a state seeking to provide religious freedom or by a state seeking to curtail it, seems to have the same effect, which is to prioritize some experts and texts over others, to extend the control of some interpretations over most, and, above all else, place religion firmly within the ambit of state control.[32] In other cases on the religious freedom of non-Muslims since the *Lina Joy* judgment, the balance between Islam as the religion of the federation and the the right of other religions to be practiced has been tested, and further attempts made by the courts to define not only the language of constitutional rights but the content of religions other than Islam. A 2009 case on the use of the word "allah" to refer to God by non-Muslims—in Christian publications in the Malay language, in particular—was first decided in favor of the Catholic Church, and then overturned by the court of appeal.[33] The judgment of the court of appeal rested upon the rights of the government to protect Islam and public order, but, as in the *Lina Joy* case, also made arguments as to the content of sacred text—in this case, however, those of Roman Catholicism.

> For completeness, I note that from a quick research on the history of the language of the Bible, it is clear that the word "allah" does not appear even once

> as the name of God . . . in the Hebrew scriptures. The name "allah" does not appear, even once in either the Old or New Testament. There is no such word at all in the Greek New Testament. In the Bible world, God has always been known as Yahweh. . . . That being the historical fact it can be concluded that the word or name Allah is not an integral part of the faith and practice of Christianity, in particular that of the Roman Catholic Church. I do not intend to make this judgement to be a study of comparative religions. . . . However, I must state that to refuse to acknowledge the essential differences between religions will be an affront to world religions. To begin with, due recognition must be given to their respective Gods in their respective Holy Books; such as "Yahweh" the God of the Holy Bible; "allah" the God of the Holy Qur'an and "Vishnu" the God of the Holy Vedas.[34]

The comparative and sociological content of this comment, given special force as part of a judicial ruling, seems very much in keeping with the style of British colonial judges, attempting to ascertain the content of religions with which they were unfamiliar, but over which increasingly they had to rule. Its intellectual stance is colonial, its appearance a symptom of the expansionism of the state over religion, not just over Islam but in this case, Christianity and Hinduism as well. This line of reasoning concluded with reference to the relationship between the Malay language and Islam—since the word "Allah" is not integral to Catholicism, the Catholic Church could not argue for its use on religious freedom grounds, in particular in the Malay language, given a special constitutional status in Article 160 in relation to Malay ethnicity and the religion of Islam.

Reasoning on constitutional grounds, the court of appeal judged that freedom of religion was in fact to be interpreted as conditioned by the need for "peace and harmony," and to protect the position of Islam as the religion of the federation. [35] The government couched its appeal of the High Court decision partly in terms of the protection of "public safety and public order" (21), and the presiding judge in the case argued that Article 3(1) "was a by-product of the social contract entered into by our founding fathers" (28), who inserted the words "in peace and harmony . . . to protect the sanctity of Islam as the religion of the country and also to insulate against any threat . . . to the religion of Islam" (29). The rights to freedom of expression and religion could and should be limited if these were understood to hold "potentiality to disrupt the even tempo of the community" (33), the judge argued, tracing the emergence of this principle to India.[36]

In this case and others, the legal concern for public order and the primacy of Islam as the religion of the federation has been articulated against the backdrop of increasing violence and threat against non-Muslim communities and places of worship, and heightened anxiety regarding proselytization to Muslims. The judgment's emphasis not on actual but potential threats to public order, and its reservation of discretion in matters of "national security" to the executive, with "no particular standard of proof to show that the decision was based on national security" (35), preserved extensive latitude for the government in matters relating to the preservation of order.[37] The potential for disorder was located in the actions of non-Muslim religious groups and the "confusion" it might cause Muslim Malays; according to the judge, "the most possible and probable threat to Islam, in the context of this country, is the propagation of other religion (sic) to the followers of Islam."[38] While relations between ethnic and religious groups have long been understood in Malaysia as matters of national security, the language and logic of the "allah" case indicates that debates over religion, in particular that of non-Muslims, are increasingly being articulated as threats to the nation, and as such law enforcement and government agencies are granted the same broad powers over these as they might be over issues of terrorism.[39]

Recent work on Muslim states has opened up multiple avenues for inquiry into the entanglement of state sovereignty and the secular with sources of Islamic authority and the spaces of Muslim politics. Hussein Agrama's discussion of *hisba* (the Islamic principle of commanding the good and forbidding evil) in Egypt "shows how secularism itself tends to make religion into an object of politics," a process I have explored in contemporary Malaysia. Further, Agrama points to the possibility that secular power brings together two things typically thought to be opposed: "a growing space of normative critique and contestation, and the increasing assertion of state sovereignty within social life."[40] In his work on contemporary Malaysia, Tamir Moustafa shows that the assumed opposition of "secular" and "Islamic" not only fails to capture important ways in which Islamization has "subverted" the Islamic jurisprudential tradition—something that scholars of Islamic law such as Wael Hallaq have also argued about modern state capture of Islamic law more generally—but that the dichotomy between secular and Islamic, liberal rights and Islamic law, is powerfully evocative in states such as Malaysia.[41] Jeremy Menchik's work on "godly nationalism" in Indonesia suggests that "intolerance and nation building are part of a mutually constitutive process."[42]

Jurisdictional and definitional struggles are profoundly juris-generative, and these contemporary cases have shown that jurisdictional ambiguity, definitional struggle, and the entanglement of ethnicity and religion, continue to produce new domains for the extension of law into religion, and religion in law, and above all, the intervention of the many organs of the state in larger realms of life. In seeking to understand the proliferation of conflict over religion not only in the Muslim world, but in North America and Europe, Latin America and Africa, it may be important to see efforts to clarify, define, and interpret religion through law less in terms of legal solutions to societal problems, but in terms of mutually reinforcing relationships between the religious and the legal. Faith in the law, and the law in faith, in a mutual spiral.[43]

Conclusion: Muslim States and the Politics of Paradox

The politics of defining and controlling Muslim societies through the establishment of strong states and hard facts has, if anything, only become more relevant today, and the basic problem of colonial control has become a fundamental matter for the contemporary state. In this, debates about what Islamic law is, and its incorporation into the state, take on the character of "protosociology" as well as governing device: then, as now, "the rule of law was a common piece of ideological baggage that linked law to public sentiments as well as public order."[44] What began as a legitimating conceit on the part of the colonial state—the making of a limited but sovereign space for Islam—became a central component of local elite power. The contemporary Muslim state thus finds itself in a double bind, in that it governs through many of the durable legacies of colonial statehood, including the institutional marginalization of Islam, but relies for its authority upon Islam's symbolic centrality.

In the long life of the law, jurisdiction is a two-edged sword, not only in Malaysia but in many states with Islamic bureaucracies and judiciaries. While this bureaucratized, state-administered, and state-enforced Islamic law that is prevalent in much of the postcolonial Muslim world now authorizes the state's jurisdiction over private life, the family, the domain of worship and ritual, the definition of a Muslim, and like matters, it also makes the state answerable to the judgment of that law and dependent upon its continued maintenance. Having incorporated Islamic law into the domain of the state, the state cannot avoid being shaped by continued struggles over the definition of Islam and Muslims.[45] The quotidian maintenance of the law that juris-diction—law's speech, speaking the law—makes visible, therefore, in many Muslim states requires boundary maintenance on multiple fronts: to sustain a claim to represent Islam and Muslims, to shore up the authority and capacity of state administration and legislation, to maintain facility in the working languages of state modernity and legitimacy. Yet the discursive underpinnings of each of these juris-dictions operate in tension with each other, and so the relationship between Islam and the state in law routinely reveals its fractures and weaknesses, at the same time that it asserts its indispensability and unassailability.

In the workings of Islamic law today, therefore—not simply in its fidelity to *fiqh* or its codification of Islamic rules—we see the contours of the terrain of contestation on which this book began, onto which new borders and states of being have been mapped. The ascendance of law and the state seem assured within these new borders and states, but in the wake of revolutionary activity and the collapse of states throughout the Middle East and North Africa, new questions and concerns have arisen. In Malaysia, as in India, Bangladesh, and Pakistan—and in Egypt, Turkey, Tunisia, and increasingly in states beyond the usual ambit of the concept of "Muslim world"—the relationship between individual Muslim identity and the character of the state continues to be a matter of contest. "Islamic law" in these states is more than one department of state among many, more than a symbol to be used for political advantage: it is a contentious and dynamic process with social, economic, moral, and political implications. In this process, the question—"whose law?"—is as important, if not more so, than the question "which law?" Some of these questions add to a growing agenda for the study of the politics of Islamic law: in what domains of Muslim life is Islamic law being raised once again, and by whom? In what domains of Muslim life is Islamic law silent or absent? What political compacts and struggles underwrite these claims for presence or absence, and upon what institutional and social foundations do they rely? To what version of the past do they refer, and to which vision of the future? Over what kind of human subject do they lay claim, and how might this subject speak to the law and speak the law?

Seeking to understand Islamic law as a problem space extends the analytic possibilities of this agenda, to investigate the bases of "the particular questions that seem worth asking and the kinds of answers that seem worth having,"[46] for Muslims who are not only legatees but have been coauthors of the modern state from its inception. The tragic sensibility that David Scott diagnoses as integral to the postcolonial condition is neither one that pulls Muslims between the binaries of Islamic authenticity and modernity, nor one that presupposes the end of shari'a thought and the articulation of *fiqh*. The conditions of doubt, of tension, and of deep historical investment that characterize much Muslim debate and struggle today represent not a series of failures to be overcome, but legacies in need of continued evaluation.[47] Insofar as there may be such a thing as a Muslim modernity that might serve as a condition of possibility for constituting new futures, it is, it turns out, something that has been with us all along: ongoing investments in intertextuality, facility in reading between the lines, fluency in multiple languages of authority and authenticity, that have often served as counters against the authoritarianism of codification and reification.

The institutionalized politics of paradox, borne out of the colonial encounter, produced through ongoing jurisdictional politics, and maintained through continuing local investments in the Muslim state as an individual and collective good, guarantee the continuity of the politics of Islamic law. Further, the hybrid nature of this law, and these states, indicates a trajectory for the future in which paradox will continue to play a productive political role—an Islamic legal politics that is a matter of elite negotiation locally, but tightly interwoven into religious, economic, and political networks worldwide; an Islamic legal politics that is highly ambivalent, taking on the language and power of the state in order to contest its values, its conduct, and its actors; an Islamic legal politics active at multiple levels—in the education and culture of its professionals, in the language and institutions of the state, in the strategies of activists and opponents, as well as never limited to, the text of the law.

There is a politics of Islamic law. It is contentious, based upon local elite networks and global flows of ideas, resources, and people. It is path-dependent, tied to the circumstances of its making and to nostalgia for an ideal Islamic polity and an Enlightened modern state. It is dynamic, fueled by changing interests, strategies, and opportunities, and shifting alliances among Muslim and non-Muslim groups in the state and beyond. It is continuous, driven by deep individual beliefs in the law that, even as it frustrates desires for a simple justice, holds out the promise of a divinely inspired good.

Notes

Chapter One

1. CO 273/87, 282–295 (5.6.1876): Testimony of Pangulu Mat Akib.

2. John Comaroff, "Reflections on the Rise of Legal Theology: Law and Religion in the Twenty-First Century," *Social Analysis* 53, no. 1 (Spring 2009): 193–216 (24).

3. Perhaps the translation that gives the best sense of the sentiment is "I got Islamic law-ed yesterday."

4. For detailed discussion of the differences between shari'a, *fiqh*, and the law of the modern Muslim state, see Hallaq 2005, 2009; Vikor 2005.

5. Vikor 2008.

6. Thelen and Mahoney 2010, 4.

7. Ibid., 18.

8. Cf. Mamdani's concept of "politics as the changing of preferences" (1999, 864).

9. Asad 2003, 25.

10. Mamdani 1996, Comaroff and Comaroff 1991, Burke 2014.

11. Messick 1993.

12. My thanks to the anonymous University of Chicago Press reviewer for this phrasing.

13. Barzilai 2008, Benton 2010, Darian-Smith 2013.

14. Hallaq 1997.

15. Kandiyoti 1991.

16. The genealogy of the concept of personal status law, and how it has come to refer to family law that generally derives from religion, is complicated and deserving of further study. See chap. 5. Also see G. Tedeschi, "Personal Status and Statut Personnel." *McGill Law Journal* 15, no. 3 (1969), 452–65.

17. Migdal 2001.

18. Merry 1998, McCann and March 1996.

19. Foundational studies on legal pluralism (e.g., Hooker 1975) tend to be built upon the model of colonial legal pluralism imposed from above; more recent legal

pluralist analysis has paid close attention to issues of power and hierarchy, but largely continues to accept the frame of a unitary system within which plurality might function.

20. Merry 2000; Hirsch and Lazarus-Black 1994; Roff 1967.

21. "What are the guiding cultural and political principles behind organization and process in the state that promote the existence of some kinds of institutions and not others? Are these guidelines and principles cohesive and unifying, or are they . . . fragmented, tending to gather around opposing symbols of legitimacy like metal particles around the poles of a magnet?" Lev 1972, 3.

22. Lazarus-Black and Hirsh 1994.

23. Comaroff and Comaroff 1991.

24. Hussin 2007.

25. "Insights and Pitfalls: Selection Bias in Qualitative Research," with James Mahoney, *World Politics* 49, no. 1 (1996): 56–91. Also, Skocpol and Somers 1980, Lijphart 1971 and 1975; Skocpol and Somers 1980; Gerring 2007, "The Case Study: What It Is and What It Does," in *Oxford Handbook of Comparative Politics*, ed. Carles Boix and Susan Stokes (New York: Oxford University Press), 90–122.

26. Thomas Metcalf, for example, has referred to the "sub-imperial role of India" in the Indian Ocean during this period, although not with detailed reference to Islam. *Imperial Connections: India in the Indian Ocean Arena, 1860–1920* (Berkeley: University of California Press, 2007).

27. Metcalf 2007, 8; Bose 2006; Risso 1995; Voll 1994, 2005; Eickelman and Piscatori 1990.

28. Mallampali 2004; Sharafi 2010; Dubois 2009.

29. Hefner and Zaman 2006.

30. Hallaq (2010) provides a general overview of transformations during the colonial period across Muslim states, with a particular emphasis on codification of Islamic legal content and the separation of shar'i content from shari'a institutions. Chapter 6 discusses further how these patterns and analytic approaches might be applied to other contexts.

31. Motadel 2014.

32. Burke 2014, 4; Devji (in Motadel 2014), 257–58.

33. Messick 1989, 26–27.

34. The Malaya material presented in this project is most often the result of original research in archives in Malaysia, Singapore, and the United Kingdom, whereas the bulk of material on India and Egypt relies upon secondary sources.

35. Not all, however: there is extensive intertextuality even in colonial records, with marginalia containing pencilled-in comments from a series of colonial officials up the chain of hierarchy, inserts and appendices in multiple languages, all purporting to be identical but in effect meaning somewhat different things; translations of treaties and laws that differ in significant ways from the English version upon which most scholarship relies. Hussin, "Textual Trajectories," 2013

36. Hefner 2011, 20.

37. Feldman 2008; Agrama 2012.

38. Kristen Stilt, "Islamic Law and the Making and Remaking of the Iraqi Legal System," *George Washington International Law Review* 36 (2004): 695–756.

39. Brown 2002 and 2005; "Symposium: Constitutional Transitions in the Middle East," http://icon.oxfordjournals.org/content/11/3?etoc#SymposiumConstitutionalTransitionsintheMiddleEast, *International Journal of Comparative* Law 11, no. 3 (July 2013).

40. Hallaq 2009.

41. Representing the common use of "secularist" and "Islamist" does not constitute agreement with the division or the terminology.

42. Kristen Stilt, " 'Islam Is the Solution': Constitutional Visions of the Egyptian Muslim Brotherhood," *Texas International Law Journal* 46 (2010): 73.

43. Griffiths 1986, 1.

44. Hooker 1975.

45. Galanter 1981; Hirsch and Black 1994; Merry 2000. The role of law and conceptions of legality is prominent in this literature: Guha (1997) and Cohn (1996) tie the making of law to colonial knowledge of the subject (law as "protosociology"); Mitchell (1998) and Sousa Santos (1987) both see law as part of colonial techniques of ordering, legibility, and projection.

46. Moore 1978; Merry 1988; Galanter 1974.

47. Migdal 2001.

48. Benveniste 1973; Hussin 2014; Richland 2011; Cormack 2008.

49. Cormack 2008, 1.

50. Messick 1998, 29–30.

51. Justin Richland, "Perpetuity as (and against) Rule: Law, Tradition, Jurisdiction," unpublished paper presented to the American Bar Foundation, October 17, 2012, p. 8.

52. Iza Hussin, "Revelation and Redemption: Colonial Precedents for the Politics of Islam in India and Malaysia," in *The Everyday Life of the State: A State-in-Society Approach*, ed. Adam White (Seattle: University of Washington Press, 2012), 142–59.

53. Migdal 2001; Comaroff and Comaroff 1991.

54. Key exceptions include Abdullahi an-Naim (2008) and Khaled Abou el Fadl (1997).

55. Much of Islamic legal scholarship does the same, something for which Wael Hallaq has taken them to task: Hallaq's recent work turns a Saidian critique upon Islamic legal studies scholarship itself, arguing that the "extraordinary innocence" of modern scholarship on Islamic law and society "proceeds . . . unaware of (its) culpable dependency . . . on the ideology of the state" (2009, 5).

56. Constitution of Egypt, Article 2 (1971), "*Mabadi' al-shari'a al-islamiya al-masdar al-ra'isi lil-tashri'*." Vogel, "Conformity with Islamic Shari'a and Constitu-

tionality under Article 2: Some Issues of Theory, Practice, and Comparison," in Cotran and Sherif, eds., *Democracy, the Rule of Law, and Islam* (1999); Stilt 2004, 723.

57. This is the phrase that emerged at the end of the drafting process for the Iraqi constitution in August 2005; Article 2.1 uses the phrase "*masdar asas lil-tashri'*." Brown, N. 2005. Carnegie Endowment for International Peace. Available at http://carnegieendowment.org/files/FinalDraftSept16.pdf, last accessed June 2, 2015.

58. About this, more in chapter 7.

59. Ayesha Jalal discusses this process in *Self and Sovereignty* (2000), arguing that the political conditions under which local elites articulated their interests gave rise to a new and particular "communal" awareness, which eventually fed into the forces driving partition between India (characterized as a "Hindu" national entity) and Pakistan (characterized as "Muslim").

60. W. Hallaq, *Shari'a: Theory, Practice, Transformations* (Cambridge: Cambridge University Press, 2009).

61. S. Zubaida, *Law and Power in the Islamic World* (London: I. B. Tauris, 2005), 130–58.

62. "The Command of Language and the Language of Command," in *Subaltern Studies* 4 (1985).

63. T. Bauer, *Die Kultur der Ambiguität: Eine andere Geschichte des Islams* (Berlin: Verlag der Weltreligionen, 2011). Bauer's argument is that Islamic history has generally featured a large degree of tolerance for ambiguity and plurality, and that contemporary Islam's reputation for intolerance of plurality and ambiguity is in fact because of the encounter with the West (far less tolerant of ambiguity) in the late modern period: "The collision of Islam with a culture that hardly knew such a tolerance of ambiguity and tended to reject it had to lead to a reformulation of the fundamentals of Islam in the form of ideologies that were more in conformance with modernity, which in both their pro-Western liberal form as well as in their Islamist variation, are equally characterized by the rejection of their own cultural traditions." (Bauer, http://www.uni-muenster.de/imperia/md/content/wwu/exini/extracts_religion_and_politics_final.pdf, p.53. Accessed February 8, 2012.) My thanks to Ahmed el-Shamsy for this reference.

64. Hallaq 2009, 360. Hallaq points to the late nineteenth and twentieth centuries as a period of "structural death" (15) of the shari'a episteme resultant from transformations brought about by state building and jural colonization.

65. Hallaq 2012.

66. Even my divergence with Scott (1985) relies upon the bedrock of his earlier work, in which power is not decisive when it comes to resistance; even the relatively powerless have surprisingly effective strategies for countering the agenda of the state. In our case, relatively weak local elites found a domain within the colonial state in which they could build a powerful base of authority.

67. In *Weapons of the Weak* (1985), James Scott argued that Malay peasants, usually seen as compliant subjects of government policy, "resisted" in subtle but

powerful ways. Some of these can be seen in the ways elites in Malaya, India, and Egypt reacted to colonial policy as well: evasion, stalling, misdirection, and other indirect methods.

68. For Foucault, the phenomena of which we have been speaking are a common part of the psychodynamics (or "microphysics") of the state. *Psychiatric Power: Lectures at the College de France, 1973–74*. 28 Nov 1973, English 82–83; French 84. My thanks to Bernard Harcourt for his thoughtful advice on the subject.

69. Asad 2001, 7.

70. Asad 2003, 201.

71. Comaroff and Comaroff 1991.

Chapter Two

1. Voll 1994 and 2005; Hallaq 2005; Azra 2004; Tagliacozzo 2009.

2. Gerber 1994, 26.

3. This also helps explain why the movement petered out in the 1910s, once the stage was set for World War I. Edward E. Morris, "Imperial Federation: A Lecture for the Victorian Branch of the Imperial Federation League," *Melbourne: Victorian Review*, August 28, 1885, http://www.slv.vic.gov.au/vicpamphlets/0/1/4/pdf/vp0144.pdf.

4. Michael Burgess, *The British Tradition of Federalism* (Madison, NJ: Fairleigh Dickinson University Press, 1995), 57.

5. J. E. Nourse, The maritime canal of Suez, from its inauguration, November 17, 1869, to the year 1884, Washington, DC: G.P.O., 1884, 23.

6. *Queen Victoria's Journals*, vol. 64 (January 1, 1875–February 29, 1876), 300–301. http://www.queenvictoriasjournals.org/search/displayItemFromId.do?FormatType=fulltextimgsrc&QueryType=articles&ItemID=qvj15633&volumeType=PSBEA#zoomHolder), last accessed July 25, 2012.

7. *Indian Society and the Making of the British Empire* (Cambridge: Cambridge University Press 1988), 11.

8. Anderson 1996.

9. *Queen Victoria's Journals*, vol. 64 (January 1, 1875–February 29, 1876), 300–301. http://www.queenvictoriasjournals.org/search/displayItemFromId.do?FormatType=fulltextimgsrc&QueryType=articles&ItemID=qvj15633&volumeType=PSBEA#zoomHolder, last accessed July 25, 2012.

10. Fahmy 1997; F. Robert Hunter 1984, 9–33; P. J. Cain 2006, 181–82; Cole 1993.

11. Empire of Difference: The Ottomans in Comparative Perspective (Cambridge University Press 2008), 8.

12. Ibid, 5.

13. With thanks to Robert Hefner for this important point. Cf Vikor 2005, 207; Gerber 1994.

14. Gerber 1994, 50–55.

15. For Mantena (2010), these differences are arranged temporally rather than spatially—the result of changes in British imperial ideology and capacity.

16. Ann Stoler, "Imperial Formations and the Opacities of Rule," in Calhoun et al., *Lessons of Empire: Imperial Histories and American Power* (New York: New Press 2006), 48–60, at pp. 55–56.

17. Gerber 1994, 16; Hallaq 2009; Vikor 2005; Johansen 1998.

18. J. Schacht, *An Introduction to Islamic Law* (Oxford: Oxford University Press, 1964); Gerber 1999; Zubaida 2003, 79.

19. Hooker 1984; Milner 1982; Peletz 2002.

20. Roff 2003, 181–83.

21. Moore 2015, 174; Hefner and Zaman 2006.

22. Roff 2009, 12. Roff also points out that Dutch understandings of Islam and adat were further elaborated, in Indonesia, within the logic of *adatrecht*, customary law, understood as legally applicable customary practices in place within the local context, in contradistinction to "any tendency towards more unified systems of law for indigenes, whether engedered by the Dutch colonial system itself or by Islam." 9, cf. Cornelis van Vollenhoven (1921), "Families of Language and Families of Law," *Illinois Law Review* 15: 417–23.

23. See Maxwell (1894) in chapter 3. There are of course many reasons for this effort to reconcile the two bodies of law, not least among them the need to justify British actions in the idiom of local law and with the authorization of Islamic jurisprudence.

24. Muhammad Khalid Masud, "Anglo-Muhammadan Law," *Encyclopaedia of Islam*, vol. 3 (Brill Online, 2012). Reference. University of Chicago Libraries. July 28, 2012, http://referenceworks.brillonline.com.proxy.uchicago.edu/entries/encyclopaedia-of-islam-3/anglo-muhammadan-law-COM_22716.

25. Hegel, Lectures on The Philosophy of World History: Introduction, trans. H. B. Nisbet (Cambridge, 1975), 103.

26. Mantena 2010, 7.

27. David Washbrook notes, "In the terms through which they viewed the world, Bentinck and Macauley were preaching sermons on Westernization and progress to an Indian society which was actually becoming more 'Oriental' and 'backward'" (1999), 397.

28. Asad 2001.

29. Hallaq 1984; Gerber 1994; Roff 2009.

30. Zubaida 2003, 107

31. Zubaida 2003, 107–20.

32. Roff 2009, 5; Eickelman 1976, 10; Kessler 1978, 19–20.

33. Messick 1993, 252–53.

34. Brown 1995, 106.

35. Washbrook 1999, 414.

36. Jalal 2000, Tignor 1963.

37. Gullick 1992, 333.
38. Ziadeh 1968; Cannon 1988.

Chapter Three

1. Cover 1983, 8 at footnote 23.

2. June Starr, *Law as Metaphor: From Islamic Courts to the Palace of Justice* (Albany: State University of New York Press, 1992), xviii.

3. Chapter 7 discusses contemporary struggles over Islamic law in Malaysia, in which one consequence of colonial-era jurisdictional divisions has been the pairing of Islam and ethnic Malay identity in constitutional law.

4. British Library: BL/Mss_Eur_D620.

5. Parkinson 1960, 323–25.

6. Cf. Bernard Cohn 1983, in Hobsbawm and Ranger, *The Invention of Tradition*, 165–209.

7. On "juris-diction," see Hussin 2014, Richland 2012, Cormack 2008.

8. The *Oxford English Dictionary*'s entry for "jurisdiction" highlights four major categories of meaning for the concept, which carry within their definitions the history of the development of English law:

> [orig. a. OF. *jure-*, *juri-*, *jurdiction*, *-dicion* (F. *juridiction*), ad. L. *jrisdictin-em*, f. *jris*, gen. of *js* law + *dictio*, n. of action f. *dcere* to say, declare.]
>
> 1. Administration of justice; exercise of judicial authority, or of the functions of a judge or legal tribunal; power of declaring and administering law or justice; legal authority or power.
> 2. Power or authority in general; administration, rule, control.
> 3. The extent or range of judicial or administrative power; the territory over which such power extends.
> 4. A judicial organization; a judicature; a court, or series of courts, of justice.
>
> "Jurisdiction," Oxford English Dictionary Online. Reference. University of Chicago Libraries. February 18, 2012, http://oed.com/view/Entry/102156?redirectedFrom=jurisdiction#eid.

9. British India is part of the OED definition of jurisdiction, which cites the development of the term through British India: "1844 H. H. WILSON *Brit. India* II. 129 The districts . . . were not intended to be exempted from the jurisdiction of the Company's officers (Horace H. Wilson, *Works*, 1860 (1861–71); *Essays on the Religion of the Hindus*, 1860 (1862); *A Glossary of Judicial and Revenue Terms*, from the Arabic, Persian, Hindustani, etc. 1855; J. Mill's *History of British India* ed. with continuation (1840–46)."

10. Mamdani 1996. I am particularly grateful to Mahmood Mamdani for his comments on this chapter in October 2012.

11. Mamdani 1996; Comaroff and Comaroff 1991.

12. "Well before "indirect rule" was articulated as a political strategy, colonial administrators understood and expressed the need to sustain indigenous legal forums as a means of promoting order." Benton 2002, 127.

13. Dirks 2001, 64.

14. Ibid.

15. East India Company courts would administer Hindu laws for Hindus and Muslim law for Muslims, based upon Sanskrit, Persian, and Arabic texts. "Muslim law" was defined in the Hastings Plan as "indigenous norms" to be derived from the Qur'an "in all suits regarding inheritance, marriage, caste, and other religious usages or institutions." (Letter from Governor-General and Council to Court of Directors, Fort William, November 3, 1772, printed in Great Britain: Parliament, *Reports from Committees of the House of Commons*, vol. 4, (East Indies, 1772–73; reprinted London 1804), at pp. 345–46 cited in Bernard S. Cohn (1985), "The Command of Language and the Language of Command," in *Subaltern Studies* 4 (1985): 289.

16. Rudolph and Rudolph 2001, 39.

17. Letter from Governor-General and Council to Court of Directors, Fort William, November 3, 1772, printed in Great Britain: Parliament, *Reports from Committees of the House of Commons*, vol. 4, (East Indies, 1772–73; reprinted London 1804), at pp. 345–46 cited in Bernard S. Cohn (1985).

18. We will discuss the textualization of Islamic law in more detail in chapter 5, but it is important to note here that the Hastings Plan supported a particular kind of text from the classical tradition of Islamic *fiqh*, which further emphasized its elite and theoretical character. Messick (2003) has made a case for looking at the multi-layered textuality of an Islamic law system in function, and in this schema labels *fiqh* texts as the highest level of text, the exclusive province of jurists. "Property and the private in a Sharia System," *Social Research* (Fall 2003) 70, no. 3: 711–36.

19. Michael Anderson, "Islamic Law and the Colonial Encounter in British India," in *Institutions and Ideologies: A SOAS South Asia Reader*, eds. David and Peter Robb Arnold (London: Curzon, 1993), 165–85, at p. 170.

20. Letter from Governor-General and Council to Court of Directors, Fort William, November 3, 1772, printed in Great Britain: Parliament, *Reports from Committees of the House of Commons*, vol. 4 (East Indies, 1772–73; reprinted London 1804), at pp. 345–46 cited in Bernard S. Cohn (1985). "The Command of Language and the Language of Command," in *Subaltern Studies* 4 (1985), at p. 289.

21. Ramkrishna Mukherjee, *The Rise and Fall of the East India Company* (New York: Monthly Review Press, 1974), 314–23.

22. M. Anderson 1993, 11.

23. Shahnaz Huda paper, "Anglo-Mohammedan and Anglo-Hindu Law: Revisiting Colonial Codification"; "The Command of Language and the Language of

Command," in *Subaltern Studies* 4 (1985), at p. 289. Also, G. C. Rankin, "Civil Law in British India before the Codes," in *Law Quarterly Review* 58 (1942), at p. 469.

24. Rankin 1942, 469.

25. Bernard S. Cohn, "The Command of Language and the Language of Command," in *Subaltern Studies* 4 (1985), at p. 290.

26. M. Anderson 1993, 6.

27. M. Anderson 1993, 5.

28. Cohn 1980.

29. Mantena 2010.

30. Otherwise known as the Sepoy Mutiny/Rebellion, the Indian Mutiny, the First War of Indian Independence.

31. Alavi 1995, 5; Hibbert 1978, 51–54.

32. Fisher 1990, 423.

33. British Library: BL/Mss_Eur_D620.

34. November 1, 1858. British Library: BL/Mss_Eur_D620.

35. Fisher 1990, 424.

36. M. Anderson 1993, 5.

37. Cowan 1961; Gullick 1992; Parkinson 1960. The Straits Settlements were Penang, Melaka and Singapore, procured by the East India Company between 1786 and 1826 and ruled through the governor general.

38. Portions of this discussion appear in Hussin 2007.

39. "Malaya" here refers to peninsular Malaya, today corresponding with West Malaysia. The four federated states of Malaya were Perak (1874), Selangor (1874), Pahang (1888), and Negri Sembilan (1895). These federated states were protectorates, technically independent states each with its own British Resident, and by 1896 a Resident General who was also the Governor of the Straits Settlements (comprised of Singapore, Penang and Malacca; procured by the East India Company between 1786 and 1826). Four northern states were signed over by Siam to be British Protectorates in 1909 as unfederated states: Perlis, Kedah, Kelantan, and Trengganu. A fifth, Johor, accepted a British advisor in 1914. What was referred to as "British Malaya" was comprised of the Straits Settlements, the four Federated States and the five unfederated states. The settlements were ruled as a crown colony directly from London after 1867, whereas the Malay states were protectorates, governed by the doctrine of "indirect rule," i.e., a British "advisor" whose realm of control covered the domain except for "matters of religion and custom" (Parkinson 1960, 323–25).

40. The English version provided here appears to be the official version of the Engagement, whose language provided the understanding held by colonial officials of the agreement reached between the Perak chiefs and Sir Andrew Clarke. As we will discuss below, other versions of this document indicate a range of possible meanings. Vetch 1905, 329–33. cf. Arkib Negara Malaysia: Jawi document, bearing chops of Malay chiefs; English document, including agreement signed with the Chinese societies of Perak, in Proceedings of the S. S. Legislative Council for

1874. Enclosure F. in Clarke to Earl Kimberley, no. 43, Singapore, February 24, 1874.

41. Cowan 1961.

42. Perjanjian Pangkor, Arkib Negara Malaysia. 2001/0025944.

43. Vetch 1905, 329–33.

44. Gullick 1992, op. cit. 31.

45. H.S. Barlow's (1995) biography of Swettenham (1850–1946). This episode occurred early in Swettenham's career as a colonial administrator, which later included arranging the Federation of the Malay States.

46. CO 273/88: Birch to Colonial Office: Report on Perak, April 2, 1875.

47. Skeat's reports (1953) from his travels in Malaya in 1899: sources from the period show that royal regalia were treated with extreme reverence throughout the region.

48. Skeat 1953, 27.

49. Hussin 2007.

50. For an account of the Pangkor proceedings, at which the agreement of Malay rulers was elicited on a British ship, see Barlow 1960, 47. For evidence provided by some Malays present at the plenary session, see CO 273/87:392.

51. See chapter 4.

52. Laws of Perak 1899.

53. M. Anderson 1987, 68.

54. M. Anderson 1993, 7.

55. Al-Hidaya, the Hanafi jurisprudential text (translated into English in 1791), al-Sirajiyyah, on inheritance (translated in 1792), the Fatawa Alamgiri and a Shi'a (Ithna-'ashari) text (compiled in English in 1865.)

56. Hallaq 2009; c.f. Anderson 1993; Kolff 1992.

57. Hallaq 2009, 376–77.

58. The Melaka laws (Hukum Kanun Melaka), which represent a major source of Malay customary law, are a good example of this hybridity: separated into general and maritime law, its forty-four sections dealt with law in various ways: its Islamic law provisions were based on the Fath al-Qarib of Ibn Qasim al-Ghazzi and Abu Shuja's al-Taqrib; its customary laws were based on adat temenggong and a quarter of its provisions allowed for Islamic alternatives to adat laws. As this corpus of law spread over the other states of Malaya, some local customs and interpretations of Islamic law were substituted for others in varying degrees (Jusoh 1991, 5).

59. Hooker (1984) writes:

> The vagueness of the term "Islam" is undoubtedly one of its religious and political strengths, but it is a scholar's nightmare . . . the term tends to cloak more complexities than it reveals; it refers simultaneously, but on a series of levels, to a cultural heritage and a political inheritance, to a social identity or ontology, to an epis-

> temology, and to a simple faith. Not to recognise these multiple references is to compound confusion, not least in respect of the legal elements of Islamic culture (3).

60. British officials commented in the early 1800s on finding in "almost every state . . . (a) constant struggle between the adherents of the Old Malay usages and the Hajis, and other religious persons, who are desirous of introducing the laws of the Arabs" (Milner 1991, 114.). The growth of European influence in Southeast Asia coincided with the reign of the Ottoman Sultan Abdulhamid (1876–1908), whose dwindling power in the European sphere and support from the Muslim world led some to believe that he "hoped to make up in Asia for the influence he could not retain in Europe" (Reid 1967, 279).

61. For example, Leila Ahmed 1992.

62. M. Anderson 1993, 6.

63. Mamdani (1996, 1999), for example, has made a compelling case for understanding the postcolonial African state in terms of the complex of relationships between local elites and colonial powers in the colonial state.

> Customary justice was administratively driven. . . . This is clear if we return to our discussion of how custom was defined with regard to two spheres of social life: the family and the economy (development). When it came to regulating relations between men and women, as between generations, customary law privileged one of several points of views—a view both male and senior—as traditional and enforced it as law. But when it came to "development" measures—such as compulsory crops, terracing, culling cattle—the only "tradition" it could highlight was that of obeying the chief. In case of failure to do so, the response was force, claimed to be equally "traditional." In this case, "custom" masked the will of a colonizing power (1999, 859–87).

64. See Kuala Selangor correspondence, f. 87.

65. Royal records from Kedah, for example, indicate that the sultan's religious teachers were close advisors, that they had prominent influence over the sultans and were even buried next to their royal pupils in the family burial grounds in Alor Setar. See Undang-Undang Kedah, 109; Abdul Aziz b Mohd Ariff, *Undang-undang Islam di Kedah Sebelum Penjajahan Inggeris—Satu Penilaian Sejarah*. UKM Bangi 1996–97. (Kedah State Archive TS096)

66. The appointment of a qadi in Selangor arose in British Residency and State Council correspondence in June 1884, indicating that the process had become part of state business by then. (Malaysian National Archives, KL1142/84: electronic record no. s0003341, 0092914) Also, 0004035: (17.03.1885) Submitting the draft of qadi's *kuasa* "for the Resident's inspection and approval." And Misc 678/85—0004152—from Kadi Haji Jaafar bin Haji Abdul Samad—"Memaklumkan mengenai perlantikan dan pemberhentian Naib Kadi dan Imam" (Explanations of

the appointment and dismissal of deputy qadi and imam.) The interdependence between sultan and Islamic religious elites in the Malay States continued regardless of this, however, and the extent of the sultan's expansion into Islamic elite jurisdiction varied from state to state.

67. State Council minutes, Durbar, 1896.

68. W. R. Roff, "Whence Cometh the Law? Dog Saliva in Kelantan, 1937," *Comparative Studies in Society and History* 25, no. 2 (1983): 323–38. Roff argues that Kelantan was unique among the Malay States in its adoption of Majlis Agama Islam (established 1915, after a rural rebellion against British rule, and at the insistence of local aristocratic and religious elites) and a *meshuarat ulama* (1917) to adjudicate Islamic matters.

69. C.f. Rafiuddin Ahmed on late nineteenth-century Bengal, in *Contributions to South Asian Studies*, ed. Gopal Krishna (Delhi: Oxford University Press, 1979), 1, 92–94. In the context of modernist disputation in Egypt: Abduh and Rida in Hourani, *Arabic thought in the Liberal Age* (London: Oxford University Press, 1962), 152–53, 236–37; Rifa'a al-Tahtawi and Abd al-Rahman al-Kawakebi in Khaldun S. al-Husry, *Three Reformers: A Study in Modern Arab Political Thought* (Beirut: Khayats, 1966) 26, 62. Also see Aram A. Yengoyan, "Cultural Forms and a Theory of Constraints," in *The Imagination of Reality: Essays in South East Asian Coherence systems*, ed. A. Becker and Aram Yengoyan (Norwood, NJ: Ablex Publishing Co., 1981), 326–27.

70. Ibid., 337.

71. It seems to have been Colonial and India Office practice to have the most junior officials who were appointed to adjudicate matters between locals, another reason perhaps for the Malay elites to prefer their own administration of personal status law (Keith 1922, 114–55).

72. Hamayotsu 2003 and 2008; Peletz 2002.

73. Roff 1987.

74. Dirks 2001, 110.

75. Maxwell 1894.

76. Introduced in South Australia in 1858, the Torrens title system established a state registry of land titles and indisputable land ownership rights to those registered: "The result was a system of tenure which provided the cultivator with the right of perpetual occupancy and power of alienation, subject to the reassessment of land at regular intervals. This was an ingenious and practical marriage of Malay land tenure to modern land principles" (Lim 1976, 16).

77. Maxwell 1894.

78. Scholars of Islamic institutions have shown the critical linkages among land and ownership regimes, educational institutions, and legal institutions—for example, Hefner and Zaman 2006; Sikand 2005.

79. The connection between jurisdiction and territory continues to matter in postcolonial states, where ethnicity and religion are still linked to land and resource ownership. Chapter 7 discusses the issue of conversion from Islam in con-

temporary Malaysia, where Malay ethnic identity is tied to preferential rights to land ownership and economic benefits of the state. If a Malay converts out of Islam, does she also lose special land rights? Is this a matter for civil or shari'a courts to handle?

80. Anderson 1996, 15.

81. "From Little King to Landlord," 1986. Also J. B. Norton, *The Administration of Justice in South India* (Madras, 1953).

82. E. Stokes, *The Peasant and the Raj* (Cambridge: Cambridge University Press, 1978), 84. Also, Galanter 1974.

83. Gullick 1992, 196.

84. "The British were concerned about property partly because they perceived it as the fundamental means for ordering Indian agrarian society and also because they wanted to establish an ideologically coherent and functionally systematic basis for revenue collection" (309), Dirks 1986, "From Little King to Landlord: Property, Law, and the Gift under the Madras Permanent Settlement," *Comparative Studies in Society and History* 28, no. 2. (Apr. 1986), pp. 307–33.

85. Dirks 2001, 111.

86. Cornwallis, Governor-General of India 1786–1793, appealed to a different sense of tradition when he suggested that the Permanent Settlement would create in India the landed gentry of England. We will discuss the construction of tradition and culture with regard to Islamic law at greater length in chapter 4, which deals with the redefinition of Islamic laws and institutions.

87. Freitag 1991, 229: "By definition, the very creation of this social order marginalized certain groups . . . [whose] responses . . . particularly in the way they chose which elements of their own cultural subsystems to alter and which to protect against the encroachments of an alien state, also formed an important component of the resulting social order." Also, Metcalf 1979; Dirks 1988.

88. Guha (1963) traces the idea of permanent settlement through the debates among British colonial officials—Phillip Francis and Warren Hastings among them (see chapter 4 for further clashes between the two at the time of Hastings's trial)—on the best revenue policy for India. Cornwallis's Permanent Settlement, Guha claims, relied initially upon the physiocratic and mercantilist logic of Francis's argument, which was that wealth derived from private property in land, but failed in part because of the pressure of English trading interests and in part because of the abiding differences between Indian and English social systems (Guha 1963).

89. Guha 1996; Bernard S. Cohn, "The Initial British Impact on India: A Case Study of the Benares Region," *Journal of Asian Studies* 19, no 4. 1960: 418–31.

90. Jalal 1990: "The kingpin of an imperial system based on the collaboration of rural intermediaries, the Act became a magna carta for all those whom the colonial mind deemed politic to classify as 'agricultural tribes'"(2). The Act encouraged their proliferation, and helped create the Islamic gentry despite the fact that imperial policy was against distributing land to religious institutions: "By the early twentieth century pirs and sajjada nashins had become part and parcel of the

landed 'tribally' based leaders who were the mainstay of British administration in the Punjab." Also, D. Gilmartin 1988.

91. Merry 2000, 114.

92. Mamdani 1996, 24.

93. Skovgard-Petersen 1997, 56–59; Ziadeh 1968, 8–13.

94. Cited in Rudolph Peters 2003, "From Jurists' Law to Statute Law"; Gulhane from *Dustur* 1865–66: 2–3.

95. Fahmy 1999, 225.

96. Brown 1995, 115; Asad 2003, 214.

97. Wood 2011, 59; Vikor 2005, 236–37.

98. Skovgaard-Petersen 1997, 59–61; Agrama 2012, 112–13.

99. Brown 1995, 105: "Since imperialism often worked through, around, or in spite of local elites, we must consider the possibility that those elites may have played an independent role in constructing and maintaining an extensive role in erecting new legal systems. In fact, such a role has been noted for rulers and regimes that felt foreign pressure without coming under direct imperial control." He cites David Engel (1978)—studying Japan, Ethiopia, Turkey and Thailand, where direct colonization did not occur: "While the end result of judicial centralization . . . was comparable in many ways to the process that took place in her colonised neighbours, a greater flexibility and adaptability in the Thai legal system probably resulted from the fact that it was administered for the most part by the Thais themselves."

Chapter Four

1. Letter from Governor-General and Council to Court of Directors, Fort William, November 3, 1772, printed in *Great Britain: Parliament, Reports from Committees of the House of Commons*, vol. 4, (East Indies, 1772–73; reprinted London 1804), at 345–46, cited in Cohn, Bernard S. (1985). "The Command of Language and the Language of Command," in *Subaltern Studies* 4 (1985), at p. 289.

2. Hastings's Regulation II of 1772, Section 27 states: "In all suits regarding inheritance, succession, marriage, and caste, and other religious usages and institutions, the laws of the Koran with respect to Mohammedans and those of the Shastras with respect to the Gentoos, shall be invariably adhered to" (R. K. Wilson 1930, 24).

3. India Office Archives, "Bengal Law Council Proceedings." Fort William: 25 November—16 July 1777, 135–45; cf. pp. 566–70 in Lauren Benton, "Colonial Law and Cultural Difference: Jurisdictional Politics and the Formation of the Colonial State," *Comparative Studies in Society and History* 41, no. 3. (July 1999), 563–88. Also, B. Misra, *The Judicial Administration of the East India Company in Bengal, 1765–1782* (Delhi: Montilal Banarsidass, 1961), 236–41.

4. As scholars like Scott Kugle have argued, this shift from fatwa as used in classical jurisprudence to fatwa as court ruling was a critical feature of the transformation of law under British rule in India: "Through the instrument of a fatwa, the qazi was expected to issue his decision on which litigant was justified by 'Islamic law'. This use of the fatwa constituted a major departure from the fatwa in classical fiqh or Mughal jurisprudence. The Anglo-Muhammadan fatwa determines guilt or innocence in a specific case according to a fixed standard codified in legal hand-books. The Muhammadan law was to be regulated by the Fatwa of the law officers, which was directed to be given according to the doctrine of [Abu] Yusuf and [Imam] Muhammad . . . the Judges were enjoined to refer to the translation of the Hedaya by Hamilton . . . as likewise to a tract entitled 'Observations' which then constituted a part of the criminal Code. The fatwa does not affect the body of law itself-its impact is limited to a singular case presented to the qazi by an English magistrate" (Kugle 1996, 285).

5. Benton 1999.

6. Hallaq 2009, 15–21.

7. Hastings, who posted bail for the arrested qadi and muftis, still critiqued their conduct, commenting that local adjudication was often "in some degree defective in point of form and precision." India Office, Bengal Law Council Proceedings, November 25, 1776–July 16, 1777, p. 135.

8. Fisher 1990, 420. Trials and other civil rituals had "many private authors, public actors, and audiences . . . the symbols employed in these formal meetings, even when mutually agreed upon, at least in part held divergent meanings for each audience." Also see Joan Vincent, "On Law and Hegemonic Moments: Looking Behind the Law in Early Modern Uganda," in *Contested States: Law, Hegemony and Resistance*, ed. Mindie Lazarus-Black and Susan Hirsh (New York: Routledge, 1994).

9. May 28, 1784. Edmund Burke, *The Complete Works of the Right Honourable Edmund Burke*, rev. ed. (Boston: Little, Brown & Company, 1866), 2: 219.

10. "Speech on Mr Fox's East India Bill," December 1, 1783, *Works of Edmund Burke Vol II* (London: Bell, 1894), 182. Also Jeremy Bernstein, *Dawning of the Raj: The Life and Trials of Warren Hastings* (Chicago: Ivan R. Dee, 2000); Carl B. Cone, *Burke and the Nature of Politics: The Age of the French Revolution* (Lexington: University of Kentucky Press, 1964); C. Colin Davis, *Warren Hastings and Oude* (Oxford: Oxford University Press, 1939); Keith Feiling, *Warren Hastings* (Hamden, CT: Archon Books, 1967); P. J. Marshall, *The Impeachment of Warren Hastings* (London: Oxford University Press, 1965); Penderel Moon, *Warren Hastings and British India* (1947, reprinted, New York: Collier Books, 1962); Patrick Turnbull, *Warren Hastings* (London: New English Library, 1975); Sophia Weitzman, *Warren Hastings and Philip Francis* (Manchester: Manchester University Press, 1929); Frederick G. Whelan, *Edmund Burke and India: Political Morality and Empire* (Pittsburgh: University of Pittsburgh Press, 1996).

11. Stephen Browne, *Edmund Burke and the Discourse of Virtue* (Tuscaloosa: University of Alabama Press, 1993), 93–98; Marouf Hasian, Jr., "Nostalgic Longings and Imaginary Indias: Postcolonial Analysis, Collective Memories, and the Impeachment Trial of Warren Hastings." *Western Journal of Communication* 66, no. 2 (Spring 2002): 229(27).

12. Burke's Speech in Reply, June 16, 1794, in Marshall 2000, 653–55.

13. Horace Walpole (quoted in July 1773), in Lawrence James, *Raj: The Making and Unmaking of British India* (New York: St. Martin's Press, 1998).

14. P. J. Marshall has commented that "it was axiomatic that British rule in India became increasingly benevolent in intention and in its effects." P. J. Marshall, ed., *The Writings and Speeches of Edmund Burke, Volume VII: India: The Hastings Trial, 1789–1794* (Oxford: Clarendon, 2000), 20.

15. Dirks 2001, 64.

16. Hasian 2002.

17. Edmund Burke, Final Speech at the Trial of Warren Hastings, May 28, 1794 in *The Works of the Rt. Hon. Edmund Burke, vol. 8* (5th ed., 1877), 51.

18. See Cohn 1977: "The British and the Mughal court in the 17th Century," in Guha 1996.

19. Fisher 1990: "Indeed, the British were themselves redefining the royal rituals of their own monarch during the nineteenth century and discovering the power such ceremonies held over the British public" (423). Perhaps even more than the British public, however, the British colonial officials who had left England as middle-class career servants and arrived to acquire positions of nobility and honor in India, "revised upward their perception of their own social class. Few of the Company's career servants were themselves from the hereditary British nobility yet, in India, the Residents in particular took a place of honour and power among noble and titled Indians" (431–32).

20. Fisher 1990, 454. Fisher points out that even when at the height of British mastery of, and hostility to, Indian rulers, British officials used the language of Islamic/Mughal ceremony, holding Christian services in Bahadur Shah's audience hall and quartering cavalry in the Imperial Mosque (456).

21. Warren Hastings, *Mr. Hastings' Review of the State of Bengal* (London: G. Kersey, 1796). Hastings set out his defense, arguing this doctrine of "necessity."

22. Dirks 2001, 125.

23. P. J. Marshall, ed., *The Writings and Speeches of Edmund Burke*, Volume 7, *India: The Hastings Trial 1789–1794* (New York: Oxford University Press, 2000), 23. Hasian (2002) argues that Burke succeeded in pushing for a public debate on the "Indian question on its own merits," that his moral justifications of empire would allow other governors of India, like Cornwallis, to make reforms and policy changes in India, and that "these commentaries on British imperial responsibilities would resonate with many future generations that took pride in the maintenance of the empire."

24. Dirks 2001, 125.

25. Mantena 2010, 2.

26. The British "acquisition" of an Egypt interest through the purchase of Khedive Ismail's Suez Canal shares in 1875 was a matter of heated debate between liberals—who wished to avoid annexation at all costs—and imperialists—who saw control of Egypt as a logical step from India. R. C. Mowat, "From Liberalism to Imperialism: The Case of Egypt 1875–1887," *The Historical Journal* 16, no. 1. (March 1973), 109–24. The language of liberalism is evident in correspondence between colonial officials in Malaya and the Straits Settlements (who, because of the need to implement British policy and protect British mercantile interests, tended to favor more interventionist positions) and their superiors in London (who tended to be very cautious about annexation or any approach toward direct rule in Malaya).

27. Ronald Robinson and John Gallagher with Alice Denny, *Africa and the Victorians* (London, 1970); Alexander Schölch, "The "Men on the Spot" and the English Occupation of Egypt in 1882," *The Historical Journal* 19, no. 3. (September 1976): 773–85.

28. *The Trial of Muhammed Bahadur Shah* (Lahore: Punjab Government Record Office Publications, 1932). January 27—March 9, 1858. The Punjab Government Record Office published a series of monographs of trials involving Indian elite figures accused of crimes against the state. It reveals that the making of treaties, a rebellion against the state, a war of retaliation, and a trial of prominent local elites was part of a pattern during the British period in India, and not confined to Muslim elites. E. g. H. L. O. Garrett, ed., *Trial of Diwan Mul Raj* (Punjab: Punjab Government Record Office Publications, 1932), which covers the trial of the Governor of Multan in northern India in the 1840s, the revolt against the British which led to the Second Sikh War, and the subsequent absorption of the Sikh Kingdom into British India. Earlier, the Lahore minister, Raja Lal Singh, had been tried in the aftermath of the First Sikh War, which was sparked off by violations of the Lahore Treaty. Garrett, ed., *Trial of Raja Lal Singh* (Punjab: Punjab Government Record Office Publications, 1933). Also A. G. Noorani, *Indian Political Trials 1775–1947* (Oxford: Oxford University Press, 2005).

29. Metcalf 1965, 301. "Much of this discrimination doubtless arose naturally and inevitably from the reluctance of the Muslim community to take up English education" (302). Metcalf argues that English education played an important part in the definition of communities in India—the Hindus were comparatively eager to take up English education, whereas the Muslims continued to prefer Urdu and Persian.

30. Metcalf 1965, 255.

31. Reformers such as Canning had pushed for one Indian judge to sit on the Bengal High Court in order, as J. P. Grant put it, "to show that the provision in the Act is not intended to be inoperative, and to withstand that growing spirit of

contempt with which Europeans now treat all native officials"(275–76). Whatever their own feelings in the matter, Company officials "doubted that Indian judges or district officers would be able to hold their own when confronted with insolent European planters, and the Government had no desire to antagonize the settler community by attempting such an experiment" (Metcalf 1965, 277).

32. Metcalf 1965, 298–301.

33. William Dalrymple cites 20,000 Persian and Urdu documents called "The Mutiny Papers" in the National Archives of India, Bahadur Shah Zafar's prison records in Rangoon, and the pre-Mutiny records of the British residency in Delhi—which were believed to have been destroyed—in Lahore's Punjab Archives. Dalrymple says that he discovered there were "two parallel streams of historiography" about 1857. One, in English, where even postindependence Indian writers used only English language sources and "padded" in the gaps. The other, by contemporary Urdu writers in India and Pakistan, which relied on a rich seam of Urdu and Persian texts (DS478 Dal 2006).

34. Charles Allen, "The Hidden Roots of Wahhabism in British India," *World Policy Journal* 22, no. 2 (Summer 2005): 87(7). Allen sees a continuity among several Muslim movements in India which he attempts to explain through an allegiance to Wahhabism. "One curious feature of these trials was that those convicted, besides being shackled in irons, were dressed in orange overalls (a color code replicated at the U.S. base at Guantanamo)."

35. Mahdi Husain, *Bahadur Shah II and the War of 1857 in Delhi with its Unforgettable Scenes*, (Delhi: Atma Ram & Sons, 1958). "Amherst's successor Bentinck proceeded to put an end even to the legend of Mughal rule, by introducing a new phrase—Hukm Company Bahadur—in all public announcements. Furthermore, responsible British officers began to treat the Mughal Emperor with studied disrespect" (86–87).

36. Husain 1958, 89–90.

37. Hashmi, 1999, 5–7. "On 12 May 1857, Bahadur Shah took out the ceremonial Silver Throne (placed in the vault by the British, in 1842) and held a *durbar* in the *Diwan-i Khas* for the fist time for fifteen years. . . . After this, the troops presented him with the customary *nazr* and a twenty-one gun salute was fired to publicly proclaim the King's authority and assumption of the reins of Government over Hindustan" (5).

38. Dalrymple 2006, 406–7.

39. Shakila Tabassum Hashmi, "The Trial of Bahadur Shah: Representation and Reality in Mughal India," BA thesis, Department of History, National University of Singapore, 1999.

40. Thomas S. Metcalf, *The Aftermath of Revolt: India, 1857–1870* (Princeton, NJ: Princeton University Press, 1965), 323–24.

41. Ibid.

42. Metcalf 1965, 253, paraphrasing Raikes. "The Mutiny vastly enhanced the prestige of the Punjab system [where both executive and judicial power were con-

trolled by a single deputy commissioner]. . . . In the minds of many Englishmen, the hostility shown by the people toward the courts seemed clearly to indicate that they preferred a simple unitary form of government." Metcalf 1965, 250.

43. Shahnaz Huda, "Anglo-Mohammedan and Anglo-Hindu Law: Revisiting Colonial Codification," 7:1&2 (2003), *Bangladesh Journal of Law*. Metcalf 1965, 255.

44. British Library: BL/Mss_Eur_D620.

45. Fowler 1988, 150, quoted in Rudolph and Rudolph 2001, 42.

46. Rudolph and Rudolph 2001, 43; Mantena 2010.

47. CO 273/87, pp. 282–95: 5.6.1876 Testimony of Pangulu Mat Akib (in service with Birch since Nov 1874).

48. Straits Settlements Secret No. 95 (5.11.1875)—No. 101 (24.11.1875): Correspondence between the Colonial Office (Lord Carnarvon) and the Straits Settlements (Governor Jervois) indicates anxiety on the part of the Colonial Office that officers in Malaya will use the opportunity provided by the Birch assassination to "annexe" Malaya ("I hope that this may be capable of being treated as an individual outrage, and not lead to military operations which would jeopardise our whole policy in the Malay Peninsula" (95 Secret, Carnarvon to Jervois 5.11.1875); Jervois was cautioned in no uncertain terms against unnecessary troop requisition and reprimanded for not consulting the CO sufficiently ("I have no means of judging for what purpose you desire a military force apparently so much in excess of what would be required in the infliction of punishment in what you originally described as an isolated outrage"). Jervois had asked the secretary of state for India for 1,500 men with artillery and a million cartridges, which Carnarvon called "a force nearly as large as was sent against Ashantee." "Ashantee" refers to the Anglo-Ashanti war which stretched throughout most of the 19th century (97 Secret, Carnarvon to Jervois 12.11.1875).

49. National Archives, Supplementary Correspondence Straits Settlements, 1873–1884, Secret 176B: Governor, Straits Settlements to Lord Carnarvon: September 6, 1876, Singapore:

Have discussed in Executive Council mode of proceeding in Sultan Abdulla's case. The Supreme Court has no jurisdiction; and Council consider the Executive Government, in absence of special authority from Her Majesty's Government, has no power to deal with case either politically or criminally. Think best plan that Governor and the Executive Council should deal with case as a political one, giving Abdulla a statement of the charges and the option of appearing before Council to clear himself.

50. Barlow 1995, 171.

51. The sultan said, "Mr. Birch was doing what he chose with regard to the collection of taxes, and was in fact acting as if he had superior authority to him instead of being under him," CO 273/87: 229: 4.7.1876: Long Mahnoom testimony: "They [the chiefs] spoke as if they thought that the white men had no right to collect taxes in the country. On another day I heard Abdullah say that unless the

white people were turned out of Bandar Bahru they (the Sultan and chiefs) could not get the taxes" (ibid.). The sultan's assessment of Birch's attitude was borne out by reports sent by Birch himself to the Colonial Office: "It really concerns us little what were the old customs of the country, nor do I consider they are worthy of any consideration in dealing with the present taxation of the country." CO 273/88:518–549, 14.12.1874.

52. "Historicizing Power and Responses to Power: Indirect Rule and Its Reform," *Social Research* 66, no. 3 (Fall 1999): 859–87.

53. William Roff 1967, 12.

54. CO 273/87, p282–295: 5.6.1876 Testimony of Pangulu Mat Akib (in service with Birch since November 1874).

55. A number of judgments in the British courts, in cases involving the governments and rulers of the states of Kelantan, Pahang, and Johor, all underlined the sovereignty of these states, and the inapplicability of English law. E.g., Duff Development v. The Government of Kelantan & Anor, 47; Mighell c Sultan of Johore 1894 1 QB 149; Pahang Consolidated Co Ltd v State of Pahang (Privy Council) 50–1.

56. CO 882/3/7: Further Correspondence relating to the Affairs of Certain Native States in the Malay Peninsula in the Neighborhood of the SS CO June 1876, No 64. Jervois to Carnarvon, 24.4.1876: Rajah Dris, appointed judge by Sultan Abdullah, tried the men "in open court at Bandar Bahru Perak, Mar 3 1876." Davidson and Swettenham were the British assessors. (Trial of Se Gondah, Ngah Ahmat and Seputum. Evidence: 347–350.)

57. Ibid.

58. The evidence and testimonies gathered by the commission are extensively documented, covering hundreds of pages of Colonial Office records: CO 273/70, 273/86, 273/87, 273/88, 273/203, 882/4/3 among the most central. Plunket's precis of the evidence is at Co273/86, 122–169.

59. Co 273/87: 19.7.1876: pp1–559.

60. Supplementary Correspondence Straits Settlements 1873–1884: 128 Secret. 21.2.1876, Jervois to Carnarvon: "Prisoners charged with Birch's murder will be tried by Malayan court aided by two British assessors. Abdulla appoints Rajah Dris head of Malayan Court."

61. Maharaja Lela was a powerful chief who was later charged with conspiracy to murder Birch and executed. CO 273/87, Testimony of Mohamed Essaack (scribe and translator for the sultan and chiefs), 108–17.

62. Co273/86: Enclosure 5 in no. 46: Abridgement of Evidence submitted by Mr Plunket: Appendix 1, no 40, p. 152.

63. CO 273/87, Testimony of Mohamed Essaack (scribe and translator for the sultan and chiefs), 108–117: The sultan kept asking, "what was the use of his being Sultan, if he was to be under the control of the Resident, saying that according to the Pangkor Treaty, the Resident was to be under him." Birch sent communication saying the Government did not want the country for the Queen, "only that the Sul-

tan should authorise his Excellency to administer the government of the country." The sultan commented, "I will take all good advice, but to give up my country to the Queen, I will never do, because if I did so I would be disgraced before all the chiefs and most likely I should be continually annoyed by the people of my country." Birch asked the sultan to sign a letter asking the governor to authorize Birch to govern the country as the representative of the queen, and the sultan said he would think about it, "and that he would be guided by the Pangkor Treaty." Birch's response was heavy-handed: he came and showed the sultan a letter from the Governor stating that if the Sultan did not take the advice of Mr Birch, and give him full power to govern the country His Excellency would not acknowledge him as Sultan of Perak. When Mr Birch had gone the Sultan consulted with the chiefs who were present . . . the letter was written but the Sultan did not put his Chop to it; he seemed very down hearted, he did not sleep all night, but kept smoking opium. The next morning before day break, the Shah Bandar pressed him to put his chop to the latter, and the Sultan threw his chop to Hadji Hussein without turning round his face, and Hadji Hussein stamped the letter with it.

64. CO 273/87, Testimony of Indoot, one of the sultan's boatmen, 6.7.1876., pp. 217–18: Sultan Abdullah gathered the chiefs and said, "He wished to get rid of Mr Birch, because of his relations with him regarding the government of the country, because it had been agreed that Mr Birch should be under him, and that now "our positions are reversed—slaves run away to him and he will not give them up, he puts people in gaol without consulting me (one of whom was a relation of one of his concubines) and sent notices to the chiefs." Also, G.A. de C. De Moubray, "A Sketch of Malayan Administration against Its Background of Race and History," transcript of talk given by author on July 14, 1943, in the Singapore prisoner of war camp (Rhodes House Library).

65. CO 273/88:518–549, 14.12.1874.

66. CO 273/88, Testimony of Soodrin, 4.12.76, p. 20.

67. CO 273/88, 1: Last statement of Se Putum, 19.5.76, Bandar Bahru.

68. National Archives: CO 882/4/3: Further Correspondence Relating to the Affairs of Certain Native States in the Malay Peninsula in the Neighborhood of the SS; Period November 10, 1876–March 31, 1877. no. 46, pp. 28–30: Jervois to Carnarvon, January 13, 1877:

> The object of the investigation was, not to ascertain by legal procedure whether or not Sultan Abdullah was guilty of a criminal offense, but by careful inquiry to satisfy Her Majesty's Government whether he had or had not disqualified himself for being retained in the high position to which he had been advanced by the Straits Government, by instigating or conniving at the conspiracy against Mr Birch, or by such other treacherous conduct as would make it inexpedient to retain him as Sultan. It was argued that although his statements as to not being confronted with his accusers

> might be of great importance if he were being tried before a quasi-judicial tribunal, yet that it is not always desirable or expedient, in a political point of view, to have such an investigation in the case of a person in the position of a Sultan of an independent state.

69. Co273/86, 38.

70. For an account of the Pangkor proceedings, at which the agreement of Malay rulers was elicited on a British ship, see Barlow 1960, 47. For evidence provided by some Malays present at the plenary session, see CO 273/87:392.

71. Swettenham 1906, 246.

72. Barbara Harlow, "Sappers in the Stacks: Colonial Archives, Land Mines, and Truth Commissions," *boundary2* 25, no. 2 (1998): 179–204, at p. 187.

73. Blunt, Cromer and 'Urabi's paths all took them to India: at the time of the revolt, Cromer had come to Egypt from a career in India. Blunt and 'Urabi met again in India after 'Urabi's exile to Ceylon, on the occasion of the campaign to establish an institution of Muslim higher education.

74. Cole 1999.

75. Cole 1999, 210.

76. A. M. Broadley, "How We Defended Arabi Pasha and His Friends," London 1884, 193–94. Letter to the Times dated November 8, 1882. "Arabi" was a common transliteration of 'Urabi at the time.

77. Ibrahim Abu-Lughod, "The Transformation of the Egyptian Elite: Prelude to the Urabi Revolt," *Middle East Journal* 21, no. 3 (Summer 1967): 325–44, footnote 55.

78. Ibid, 184–85.

79. Cromer, *Modern Egypt*, 2: 202.

80. Ibid, 351. Letter to *The Times*, December 4, 1882.

81. Lombardi 2006, 70–71; Nathan Brown, *The Rule of Law in the Arab World: Courts in Egypt and the Gulf* (Cambridge: Cambridge University Press 1997), 38–39; Ziadeh 1968, 34–35. Also Jakob Skovgaard-Petersen, *Defining Islam for the Egyptian State: Muftis and Fatwas of the Dar Al-Ifta* (Leiden, Netherlands: Brill, 1997).

82. Ibid, 72.

83. Lombardi characterizes this shift in Egypt as "the emergence of Islamic modernism." 2006, 73.

84. Mitchell (1991) also raises the example of the 'Urabi trial in his chapter entitled "The Machinery of Truth," as part of a change in the ways authority and language were conceived in Egypt and in the colonial relationship (137–41).

85. Allen 2005.

86. W. Blunt, *The Future of Islam* (London: Kegan Paul, Trench and Co., 1882).

87. In India: widow immolation was banned in 1829, widow remarriage became legal in 1856, female infanticide was prohibited in 1870, the age of consent for consummation of marriage was raised from eight to twelve years in 1892.

88. Sinha (1997), Meera Kosambi, "Gender Reform and Competing State Controls over Women: The Rukhmabai Case (1884–1888)," in *Social Reform, Sexuality, and the State*, ed. Patricia Uberoi (New Delhi: Sage, 1996), 239–90.

89. Skovgaard-Petersen 1997.

90. 1867 Leic. 462: "Kaedah umum undang-undang England tidak boleh dipakai kepada para penduduk tempatan yang mempunyai institusi sosial dan agama mereka sendiri yang berlainan. Memakai kaedah demikian akan mengakibatkan ketidakadilan dan penganiayaan." E. N. Taylor, "Malay Family Law," *JMBRAS* 15, pt. 1, 41–42.

91. "It has repeatedly been decided as a legal doctrine that our principles cannot be applied to this community whenever untoward injustice and cruelty might result from such an application." [Telah berulang kali diputuskan sebagai doktrin undang-undang kita bah kaedah kita tidak boleh dipakai kepada kaum tersebut apabila ketidakadilan dan penganiayaan yang tidak tertanggung terjadi akibat daripada pemakaian itu.] Ibid.

92. Sinha 1997, 154; Ahmed 1992: Cromer joined the Men's Committee for Opposing Suffrage in 1908 and became president of its successor, the Men's League, in 1909.

93. Benton 1999, 574.

94. Benton 1999, 571.

95. Bengal Law Council Proceedings. November to July 16, 1977, p. 141.

96. Mrinalini Sinha, *Colonial Masculinity: The "Manly Englishman" and the "Effeminate Bengali" in the Late Nineteenth Century* (New Delhi: Kali for Women, 1997); Ashwini Tambe, "Colluding Patriarchies: The Colonial Reform of Sexual Relations in India," *Feminist Studies* 26, no. 3 (Fall 2000): 587.

97. Janaki Nair, *Women and Law in Colonial India: A Social History* (New Delhi: Kali for Women, 1996).

98. Uma Chakravarti, *Rewriting History: The Life and Times of Pandita Ramabai* (New Delhi: Kali for Women, 1998).

99. Janaki Nair posits a correlation between legislation on women and the needs of the labor market in India. From 1850 to 1900, there was a need for women and children in the workforce, and consequently no legislative action concerning their welfare. Single women workers became an issue of morality, as did the model of a working-class family, and married women could no longer be recruited for work, once this need was met. *Women and Law in Colonial India: A Social History* (New Delhi: Kali for Women, 1996).

100. Tambe 2000.

101. Fisher 1990, 426.

102. Fisher 1990, 427.

103. Fisher 1990, 421–22. Rulers used Residents to display their favor with the EIC to competing elites, as well as to advertise to the Company the proper place of the ruler in India. Ritual obligations were used also to delay unwanted negotiations and demands by the British, in order to gain time and bargaining advantage

(435), and complaints about the failure of Company officials to respect ceremonial obligations often occurred just when political disagreement was at its highest pitch (450). But Residents also used their own symbolic importance to good effect, knowing that their presence in the ruler's court was a comparative asset which the rulers could not afford to lose: "So long as he had a Resident separately deputed to his court, he felt he was still considered as one of the Princes of India—by his [Resident's] removal he would be lowered to the level of a poligar [landholder]." (Resident of Mysore correspondence, December 12, 1842, no. 118, letter about the Maharaja of Mysore.)

104. "Goods of Abdullah," 1835 2 Ky Ec 8 (Ky=Kyshe's Reports), in Salleh Buang, *Sejarah Undang-Undang Malaysia: Kes dan Material* [The History of Malaysian Law: Cases and Material] (Kuala Lumpur: Dewan Bahasa dan Pustaka, 1996).

105. Laws of Perak, 1899.

106. 36 Fatimah & Ors v Logan & Ors 1871 1 Ky 255, in Buang 1996.

107. Secretary of State for the Colonies, 1875, in Barlow 1995, 127.

108. Waghela v Sheikh Masludin 1887, 14 IA 89 at 96.

109. Ridzuan Awang 1994. *Undang-undang Tanah Islam: Pendekatan Perbandingan* [The Land Law of Islam: A Comparative Approach] (Dewan Bahasa dan Pustaka, 1994), 7.

110. Anderson 1993.

111. 1868, the Privy Council argued that custom could outweigh Hindu law. Anglo-Muhammadan law tended to circumvent custom; A. Gledhill, "The Compilation of Customary Laws in the Punjab in the Nineteenth Century," in *La Rédaction des Coutumes dans le Passé et dans le Présent*, ed. J. Glissen (Brussels 1962).

112. Anderson 1993, 15. Also, N. Bhattacharya, "Custom and Rights: A Conflict of Interpretations," presented at Oxford University Centre for Indian Studies, November 13, 1987.

113. Anderson 1993, 15.

114. Customary prostitution conducted as a family business, for example, was judged immoral and contrary to Islam. Ghasiti v Umrao, January 1893 20 IA, 193.

115. Anderson 1993, 16. Also, D. Gilmartin 1988, for an account of the political contestation of the codification of custom.

116. Minute Perak State Council—18.1.1907—Adat "sebahagian daripada undang-undang umum negeri"; "Bahawa adat orang Melayu Perak dalam hal membahagikan harta selepas bercerai, apabila harta tersebut telah diperoleh kedua-dua pihak atau seorang daripadanya semasa perkahwinan, adalah untuk menerima pembahagian dua bahagian kepada lelaki dan satu bahagian kepada wanita dan bahawa pemberian antara orang yang berkahwin tidak boleh ditarik balik mahupun selepas bercerai."

117. "Law and Imperialism: Egypt in Comparative Perspective," *Law and Society Review* 29, no. 1 (1995): 104–50, at p. 115.

118. This may help explain why the Indian Princely States were at times more progressive than those under direct British rule; it may also explain the progressivism of Malay states such as Johor, which resisted British intervention far longer than most Malay states, and provide some of the impetus for Ottoman and Egyptian reform movements in law.

119. Selangor Secretariat papers, British Resident Office:

> 1957/ 0004363: (16.07.1885.) *Enquiring whether the kadi has power to imprison the Mahomedans, and if the gaol is to be opened for their execution etc.*
>
> 16.7.85, From Kuala Selangor district collector to his superior the Selangor Resident (J. P. Rodger):
>
> Sir, I have the honour to report that a man named Rantow was divorced from his wife by Hadji Abdul Rhamen, some twenty days ago. He then left for Perak but returned here unexpectedly on the night of the 11th and straightaway proceeded to the house of his former wife whom he found sleeping with a man named Dowd upon whom he at once committed an assault. The Kathi called Dowd and the divorced woman before him and sentenced them to three months imprisonment and requested Rajah Mahmud to send them to the Gaol here but on Rajah Mahmud representing that I was away and he could not himself do so the Kathi has sentenced both of the offenders to forty blows of the stick (battan cromar) because he says by Mahometan law the woman cannot marry again until the three months and ten days have expired since she was divorced.
>
> I shall be obliged if you will instruct me as to whether the Kathi has power to pass sentences of this description and if the Gaol here is to be open for the execution of the same."

120. 16.7.85, From Kuala Selangor district collector to his superior the Selangor Resident (J. P. Rodger), continued: "Since writing the above the Kathi has called upon me and requested that I will help him to carry his sentences into effect by which I understand him to meant that the police force is to be put at his disposal and I am to imprison anyone whom he thinks well to name and supervise the flogging of other individuals which I have told him distinctly that I cannot do or in any way mix myself up with religious matters."

121. 21.7.85: Resident to district collector:

> "Collector K Selangor, The accompanying 'Kuasa' will show you what are the Kadi's powers, and on what occasion he can invoke the aid of the district collector.
>
> 2. It is quite true that by Mahomedan law a divorced woman cannot remarry until after the period of her Edda and you had

better have the pair called before you, with the Kadi, and in default of payment of a fine, the man might be imprisoned for three months but we have no Gaol accommodation for women."

24.7.85: Kuala Selangor district collector to Selangor Resident: "In your last visit here I understood you to say that I had acted improperly by informing the Kadi that I had nothing whatever to do with Mahometan law and if I remember rightly you added that that was the kadi's business. But now I understand you to say that I am expected to pass judgement against people who have committed no offense, as far as I am aware, against any law except that of Mahomet and Malay religious persuasions. By so doing I should take upon my own shoulders . . . the justice of any argument the kadi chooses to enunciate but from this I trust it will be possible for you to exempt . . . (refers to his last letter) by which you will see that the kadi reads the power granted to him, to call on the magistrates for help, in it's [Author: unclear: *worst?*] intended sense and I shall therefore be obliged if you will define what it is and the punishments he has authority to inflict."

28.7.85, Resident to district collector: "Collector, K Selangor,

1. I told you that cases connected with the Mahomedan religion will be decided by the Kadi, and that in cases tried by you, you will be guided by the provisions of the Penal Code in criminal, and the English law in civil cases.

2. You are however an official in a native Mahometan state, and consequently your strictures on the actions of Mahometan law are entirely uncalled for and improper. Instead of ignoring Mahometan law and customs, you should endeavor to become conversant with them, and obtain such a knowledge as is required from any collector and Magistrate in India. The relations between the Collector's court and that of the Kadi, are very similar to those which formerly existed between the common law and ecclesiastical courts in England—until recently, the latter courts had jurisdiction over all probate, matrimonial, and religious questions, but they frequently required to invoke the aid of the ordinary law courts to enforce their decrees."

122. 28.7.85, Resident to district collector, continued:

"3. If the Kadi imposes a sentence which either because of recalcitrance on the part of the person sentenced, or otherwise, he requires your assistance to enforce, you must satisfy yourself on these points before assisting him (1) that an offense against Mahomedan law has been committed (2) that the person sentenced is guilty, (3) that the sentence is just—

The Mahometan 'Edda,' or period before remarriage after divorce is analogous to the period of six months which elapses between a decree nisi and a decree absolute, in a divorce suit in England, but a reference to sections 497 and 498 of the Penal Code will show you that matrimonial offences are much more seriously treated by the Code than by the English criminal law.

4. If you agree with the Kadi's sentence, having regard to the nature of the offense, the position of the offender, you can enforce it to the extent of a fine of $50, or, in default, for a period of not exceeding three months. Should you disagree with the sentence, or should the Kadi wish to impose a sentence exceeding the above mentioned limits, let the case be adjourned (ordering the defendant to find bail necessary for his appearance, if necessary, when called upon for judgement) and send me a special report on the subject."

123. 11.8.85: Kuala Selangor district collector to Selangor Resident: "As you consider that what I said in my former minute as to Mahometan law was 'uncalled for and improper' I have to apologise for having done the same. The man shall be fined or imprisoned and the woman allowed to go at large, according to the instructions contained in your minute of the 21.7.85 but I do not think that I should be acting rightly to myself if I did not state that have respectfully to differ entirely from you on this subject."

124. Benton 1999, 575–76; c.f. Mantena 2010.

125. Benton 1999, 588.

Chapter Five

1. Mahmood Mamdani, "Historicizing Power and Responses to Power: Indirect Rule and Its Reform," *Social Research* 66, no. 3 (1999): 864.

2. Portions of this chapter relating to the state of Johor have been discussed in greater detail in Hussin 2013 and 2014.

3. Mamdani 1999, 2001.

4. Mamdani 1999, 863.

5. Mamdani 1999, 864.

6. This approach has been used under different names by a number of scholars of colonialism, religion, and law to great effect: Mitchell (1988) interpreted the colonial process in Egypt through the concept of "representation" and "exhibition"; de Sousa Santos uses the understanding of law as a "map of misreading" (1992); Scott (1998) argues that the modern state sees both the nation and the space it occupies as terrain for reshaping; Cohn (1996) and Comaroff and Comaroff (1991) detail the ways in which colonial states re-visioned and then refashioned their subjects.

7. Comaroff 1991.

8. Thomas Metcalf 1994, 38; Kolsky 2005.

9. Muhammad Qadri Pasha, "Kitab al-Ahkam al-Shar'iyya fi al-Ahwal al-Shakhsiyya ala Madhhab Imam Abi Hanifa al-Nu'man," in Rushdi al-Sarraj, Kitab Majmu'at al-Qawanin al-Shar'iyya, Jaffa 1944, 80–182. "The book of Shari'a-compliant laws in personal matters of the school of Imam Hanifa al-Nu'man" may be the most literal parsing; the usual formulation is along the lines of "Laws of the Shari'a in Matters of Personal Status," a phrasing that carries traces of its passage through French. Cf. Qadri Pacha, "Muhammad: Code du statut personnel et des successions d'apres le rite Hanafite," in *Codes Egyptiens et lois usuelles en vigueur en Egypte* (Cairo 1939). Hussein Agrama (2012) relates the formulation of personal status to the problem of public order in Egypt (pp. 98–100), describing the 1897 reform of the shari'a courts as having "brought into affinity a new set of concepts and affects—family, intimacy, publicity, secrecy, and public order—through which the domains of public and private could be mutually entailed and authorized by the state" (100).

10. Mitchell 1991, ix.

11. Mitchell 1991, 156–60. Also, Collier, Intertwined Histories, 1994.

12. Hussin 2014.

13. Cf. Nathan Brown 1993.

14. Temenggong (Andaya 1975 and Nadarajah 2000). The Maharaja of Johor was formerly known as Dato' Temenggong Abu Bakar, the son of Dato' Temenggong Daing Ibrahim, to whom the control of Johor was ceded under the terms of a treaty signed in 1855 between the British in Singapore and Sultan Ali of Johor.

15. The Johor Royal Museum shows portraits of him in white and black tie, and posed with his wives, one of whom was English, and the other of Acehnese-Dutch descent. The sultan died in 1895 in London.

16. Weeks (1998), 46. "About Face: Sir David Wilkie's portraits of Mehmet Ali, Pasha of Egypt." In *Orientalism Transposed: The Impact of the Colonies on British* Culture, ed. Julie Codell and D. S. Macleod (Vermont: Ashgate). Codell and Macleod argue that the colonial relationship, while not an equal one, involved a certain amount of cultural exchange, and that Orientalist discourse had "Easternizing" effects in England. The dynamic of Easternization is worth exploring in greater depth in the area of Islamic law and contemporary discussions of Islamic legal discourse, especially in light of scholarly discussion of Westernization as a local strategy against imperialism (e.g., Curtin 1984, 251; Freitag 2003).

17. Heather Streets, "Orientalism Transposed: The Impact of the Colonies on British Culture (review)," *Victorian Studies* 43, no. 1 (2000): 144–46.

18. Cf. Codell (1998), on the biographies of one of Abu Bakar's contemporaries, the Maharaja of Baroda, in Codell and Mcleod. Also, Julie Codell, ed. *Power and Resistance: The Delhi Coronation Durbars* (Ahmedabad: Mapin, 2012).

19. Homi Bhabha 1994, 85–92.

20. David Cannadine, *Ornamentalism: How the British Saw Their Empire* (Oxford: Oxford University Press, 2002); Cannadine, "The Context, Meaning and Performance of Ritual: The British Monarchy and the Invention of Tradition," in *The Invention of Tradition*, ed. Hobsbawm and Ranger (Cambridge: Cambridge University Press, 1983), 101–64; also Cohn in Hobsbawm and Ranger 1983, 165–210.

21. Harper 2013, 13.

22. Gullick 1987, 192, quoting a newspaper report about Penang Malays in the 1850s.

23. Annabel Gallop, personal correspondence Spring 2012.

24. Cowan 1961, 38–39.

25. Andaya 1975; Nadarajah 2000.

26. CO 882/4/22, 1885.

27. Muhammad Kamil Awang, *The Sultan and the Constitution* (Kuala Lumpur: Dewan Bahasa dan Pustaka, 1998), 29. Awang cites: CO 273/445, Nov 30 1894; CO 273/281, Sept 11 1902, CO 273/189, August 2, 1893.

28. 57, Sahari Jantan, Mesyuarat Kerajaan Johor 1895–1914 (The Johor State Council 1895–1914). Thesis: Jabatan Sejarah UKM Bangi 1975.

Part 1.1 "Raja yang memerintah dan memiliki kerajaan Johor ini dan segala daerah takloknya serta pula dengan syor persekutuan dan persetujuan sekalian ahli2 jemaah menteri dan mesyuarat kerajaan kita."

29. "Jelas bahawa beginda melihat perlembagaan itu sebagai alat bagi memperkukohkan kedudukannya melalui penggunaan dan kerjasama pembesar-pembesar negeri dalam pemerintahan. Apabila tidak ada ancaman dari dalam negeri maka difikirkan dapat memelihara kemerdekaan Negeri Johor. Perasmian hak Sultan atas Johor dan pengesahan kerajaan yang ada dikirakan penting pada masa itu oleh sebab perkembangan pengaruh British di Negeri Melayu." 57, ibid.

30. Borham, ed. *Majalah Ahkam Johor: Kod Undang-Undang Sivil Islam Kerajaan Negeri Johor 1331H/1913M* [Majalah Ahkam Johor: The Islamic Civil Code of the State of Johor, 1331H/1913AD] (Johor: UTM Skudai, 2002). Borham traces the Majalla from its compilation by a body chaired by the Ottoman Minister of Justice Ahmed Jewdet Pasha and overseen by the Shaikh al-Islam, its adoption by the Ottoman sultan in 1885, then by the Johor Sultan Abu Bakar in 1893, and its translation into Malay by his son Sultan Ibrahim in 1913, making it the formal guide for *hukum syara* ("shari'a law") in Johor.

31. Divisions of the Johor Majalah were: 1. Buying and selling; 2. Rent, wages and pay for labor; 3. "Kifalah"; 4. "Hiwalah"; 5. "Rahn" (Pawning); 6. "amanah" (Trusts); 7. "Hibah" (Gifts); 8. Seizure and Damages; 9. "Hajr, Ikrah, Syuf'ah"; 10. "Syarikah" (Incorporation); 11. "Wakalah" (Agency); 12. "Sulh, Ibrar"; 13. "Ikrar"; 14. "Dakwa"; 15. "Baiyyinah, Tahaluf"; 16. "Qada'."

32. Collier 1994.

33. Art. 14, 26, Terengganu Constitution 1911.

34. Laffan traces the rise of Arabic printed sources in the region in the late nineteenth century as a signal of movement toward new globalized forms of Islam and away from older vernacular modes of Islamic discourse (2008, 115).

35. Hugh Clifford, "An Expedition to Kelantan and Trengganu: 1895," *MBRAS* 34, no. 1 (1961), reprint 1992; Buyong Adil, *Sejarah Terengganu* (Kuala Lumpur: Dewan Bahasa dan Pustaka, 2002); Muhammad Yusuf Hashim (1991), 107; Hashim Musa, "The Terengganu State Legal Text of 1911 Analysis of Islamic Influence in Statecraft and the Authority of the Ruler in a Malay State," *Pertanika J Soc Sci and Humanities* 20, no. 3 (2012): 683–94.

36. The English translation provided is the official English translation of the 1913 printing.

37. Hisham Musa 2012, 690.

38. "Kebenaran ini menurut kecualian yang dinyatakan dalam Undang-Undang Kerajaan Johor fasal yang ke-49." Borham 2002, vi; Correspondence between Sultan Ibrahim, the Mufti of Johor (Abdul Qadir bin Mohsin al-Attas) and Dato Pemangku Setiausaha Kerajaan Johor (Bil. 998/13, 29.11.1913.)

39. "Berkenaan dengan Undang-Undang Tubuh Kerajaan Johor Fasal 49 dan 57, Sultan Ibrahim dengan persetujuan ahli-ahli jawatan keadilan dan beragama berkenan dan membenarkan Kitab Majalah Ahkam Johor supaya digunakan oleh sekelian pegawai-pegawai, majistret-majistret dan hakim-hakim di Negeri Johor dalam perkara yang berkenaan dengan hukum Islam. [In relation to Sections 49 and 57 of the Johor Constitution, Sultan Ibrahim with the agreement of judicial and religious personnel approves the Majalah Ahkam Johor for use by all officers, magistrates and judges in the state of Johor in matters relating to the law of Islam.]" al-Mansor Adabi, *Malayan Law Journal*.

40. Printed by Matba' Khairiyyah in Muar in 1913: "Kitab ini mengandungi perbicaraan hukum-hukum fiqh yang diterbitkan daripada syari'at al-Islam yang telah digunapakai oleh kerajaan Johor selama-lamanya dengan bahasa Arab."

41. "Siyāsa." *Encyclopaedia of Islam*, 2nd ed. (2012). Reference. University of Chicago Libraries, February 18, 2012, http://referenceworks.brillonline.com.proxy.uchicago.edu/entries/encyclopaedia-of-islam-2/siyasa-COM_1096.

42. Kugle 2001.

43. Masud, 2001. "The Doctrine of Siyasa in Islamic Law," *Recht van de Islam* 18 (2001), 1–29, at p. 4.

44. Masud 2001, 8–13.

45. G. C. Kozlowski, *Muslim Endowments and Society in British India* (Cambridge: Cambridge University Press, 1985), 97.

46. Kugle 2001, 299.

47. Kugle 2001, 264 at ft 20. Cf: Kugle 2001, 280–81.

48. The scholarship on *siyasa* is too extensive to cover with justice here; key texts include Ibn al-Mukaffa (d. 757), *Risalah fi al-sahaba*, which elucidates the concept of the extra-shar'i prerogatives of the ruler; Bernard Lewis, "Siyāsa," in *In Quest of an Islamic Humanism. Arabic and Islamic Studies in Memory of Mo-*

hamed al-Nowaihi, ed. A. H. Green (Cairo, 1984), 3–14; Miriam Galston, *Politics and Excellence: The Political Philosophy of Alfarabi* (Princeton, NJ: Princeton University Press, 1990); Aziz al-Azmeh, *Islams and Modernisms* (New York: Verso, 1993), 91.

49. Anderson 1993, 170.

50. Anderson 1993, 170.

51. "Kadi telah dipanggil sebagai penasihat tentang dasar apabila tuntutan terhadap harta tersebut dibicarakan oleh mahkamah atau pemungut hasil tanah dalam kes tanah yang didaftarkan dalam daftar mukim." Awang 1994, 57.

52. Anderson 1993, 173. Also, A. Hussain, *Muslim Law as Administered in British India* (Calcutta, 1935).

53. Both Hindu and Muslim native law officers were replaced by a growing reliance on case law and British judicial experience, and in 1864, the position of court *maulavi* was abolished (Act XI 1864). Also, U. Yaduvansh, "The Decline of the Role of the Qadis in India, 1793–1876," *Studies in Islam* 6 (1969); T. Mahmood, *Muslim Personal Law: Role of the State in the Sub-Continent* (Delhi, 1977), 60–69.

54. Vikor 2008, 209–210.

55. Ibid., 212.

56. Khaled Fahmy, "Law, Medicine and Society in Nineteenth-Century Egypt," *Égypte/Monde arabe*, Première série 34 |1998, mis en ligne le 07 juillet 2008, consulté le 03 juin 2015. URL: http://ema.revues.org/1488 Quote is at 60, last accessed June 3, 2015.

57. Roff 1983. Italicized words in square brackets show the original Malay/Arabic terms used.

58. Hallaq 2009, 379.

59. Wood 2011, 63; Lombardi 2006, 62.

60. Vikor notes that this postcolonial version of *siyasa shar'iyya* is, in "Islamist" states, "in principle identical to the system inherited from *kanun* that the same forces attack with such vigour . . . when they try to apply *siyasa*, these "Islamist" states pick out the rules that have the greatest symbolic power, the *hudud* rules, which are those which were *least* practices in actual Shari'a-based system before, and thus those that have been least refined and adapted to social reality throughout Muslim history." Vikor 2008, 279.

61. Asad 2001. Also, Jakob Skovgaard-Petersen, *Defining Islam for the Egyptian State: Muftis and Fatwas of the Dar al-Ifta* (Leiden: Brill, 1997). Skovgaard-Petersen points out that the market for mass printing in Egypt between 1863 and 1897 was dominated by books on "secular" topics, and that this itself also framed the discourse on reform (55–56).

62. Nile Green (2011), Eric Tagliacozzo (2009), Michael Laffan (2003), and Azyumardi Azra (2004) have all made important contributions to our understanding of Muslim networks in this period, but Islamic legal scholarship has not made full use of this body of scholarship.

63. Moosa 2009, 159.

64. cf. Ronit 2011; Francis Bradley 2013; Hussin 2013.

65. Also Freitag 2003, 195; Ho 2004, 220; Reid 1967; Azra 2000.

66. Ho 2004, 220–21. Also Hussin 2014.

67. Robert L. Tignor, "The "Indianization" of the Egyptian Administration under British Rule," *The American Historical Review* 68, no. 3. (April 1963): 636–61.

68. Tignor 1963, 658.

69. Cromer Papers, PRO, FO 633/VIII. 6E Cromer to Strachey, April 3, 1906.

70. Tignor 1963, 661.

71. Cromer to Salisbury 8.11.1896 FO 371/14620, no. 30, cited in Brown 1997.

72. Karpat speculates that the Ottoman sultan may have been reluctant to interfere against 'Urabi precisely because of support, among Arabs and Anatolian Turks, of 'Urabi as a Muslim hero. He eventually conferred upon 'Urabi the title of Pasha, in part to maintain his own position as caliph and "chief spokesman for Muslim causes." Kemal Karpat, *The Politicization of Islam: Reconstructing Identity, State, Faith and Community in the Late Ottoman State* (New York: Oxford University Press, 2001), 269.

73. Roff, "The Malayo-Muslim World of Singapore at the Close of the Nineteenth Century," *Journal of Asian Studies* 24, no. 1 (November 1964): 75–90. Also, Roff, *Bibliography of Malay and Arabic Periodicals Published in the Straits Settlements and Peninsular Malay States 1876–1941; With an Annotated Union List of Holdings in Malaysia, Singapore and the United Kingdom*, 1972.

74. Roff 1972 and 1967; Azra 2006, "The Transmission of al-Manar's Reformism," in Dudoignon et al. 2006, 144.

75. Roff 1975, 71.

76. In a Penang paper called *al-Ikhwan* (The Brothers/Brotherhood), Sheikh Tahir Jalaluddin wrote that the weakness of Islam in administration caused British officers to interfere in the administration of the state. Islam di Kedah Darul Aman. Konvensyen Sejarah N KDA, 29–30.9.1996, Alor Setar KDA. Majlis Kebudayaan Negeri. Arkib Negara Kedah.

77. Anderson 1983; Messick 1993.

78. Peters, *The Hajj: The Muslim Pilgrimage to Mecca and the Holy Places* (Princeton, NJ: Princeton University Press 1995), 206–66.

79. Skovgaard-Petersen 1997, 67.

80. Devji 2014, 264–65.

81. Sayyid Ahmad Khan, Review on Dr Hunter's Indian Musalmans: Are They Bound in Conscience to Rebel Against the Queen?" (Lahore n.d., 5–6). Quoted in Devji 2014, 264–65.

82. Anderson 1993, 24.

83. Fyzee, *Outlines of Muhammadan Law* (Delhi: Oxford, 1974), 51.

84. Kugle 2001, 301–2.

85. Alan Guenther argues convincingly that the Law Reports Act of 1875 had the unintended consequence of creating a new source of Muslim law. The Act re-

quired that all High Court judgments that were printed in the India Law Reports would be binding on all subordinate courts in British India; these judgments often included the fatwa issued by court officers to 1864. Guenther, "A Colonial Court Defines a Muslim," in Metcalf 2009, 293–304, at p. 294.

86. Ibid.

87. Ibid., 295.

88. (1885) ILR AII 461. I discuss this case in further detail in "Colonial Conflations and the Making of the Muslim State," in *The Many Hands of the State: Theorizing Political Authority and Social Control*, edited by Kimberly Morgan and Ann Orloff. Cambridge University Press, forthcoming 2016.

89. Guenther 2009, 294.

90. (1885) ILR AII 461 at 1.

91. (1885) ILR AII 461 at 7.

92. Ibid.

93. (1885) ILR AII 461 at 13.

94. Stephens 2013, "The Phantom Wahhabi: Liberalism and the Muslim Fanatic in Mid-Victorian India," *Modern Asian Studies* 47, no. 1 (January 2013): 22–52.

95. (1885) ILR AII 461 at 13.

96. Anderson 1993, 24.

97. Cf. Ebrahim Moosa in *Islam and Modernity: Key Issues and Debates*, ed. Masud, Salvatore, and van Bruinessen (2009), 166.

98. 1893 ILR 20 Calcutta 132–5, cited in Newbigin 2013, 49.

99. [1893] ILR 20 Calcutta 138–39.

100. Newbigin 2013, 51.

101. Hallaq 2009, 15–21.

102. Metcalf 1982, 198–234; Gilmartin 1988, 52–56.

103. "A scripturalist approach to the sharia spread from urban to rural areas, and from elite classes to middle classes. Adherence to the sharia became more widespread and was increasingly perceived to be central to the maintenance of Muslim identity." Anderson 1993, 181. Also Geertz 1967; B. Metcalfe, *Islamic Revival in British India: Deoband 1860–1900* (Princeton, NJ: Princeton University Press, 1982); Aziz Ahmad, *Islamic Modernism in India and Pakistan 1857–1964* (London, 1967); Rafiuddin Ahmed, *The Bengal Muslims 1871–1906* (Delhi, 1988); B. Metcalf, *Perfecting Women: Maulana Ashraf 'Ali Thanawi's Bihishti Zewar* [Heavenly Ornaments] (Berkeley: University of California Press, 1990); K. M. Yusuf, "The Judiciary in India under the Sultans of Delhi and the Mughal Emperors," *Indo-Iranica* 18 (1965); W. Hallaq, "Was the Gate of Ijtihad Closed?," *International Journal of Middle Eastern Studies* 16 (1984); Mohammad Daud Rahbar, "Shah Wali Ullah and Ijtihad," *Muslim World* 45 (1955). P. J. Marshall, *Bengal: The British Bridgehead* (Cambridge: Cambridge University Press, 1988).

104. Johansen 1999.

105. Wood 2011, 89–92.

106. Rudolph Peters, "Muhammad al-'abbas al-Mahdi (D. 1897), Grand Mufti of Egypt, and His 'al-Fatawa al-Mahdiyya,'" *Islamic Law and Society* 1, no. 1. (1994): 66–82.

107. The 1870s and 1880s were especially eventful times in Egyptian legal history. Egypt gained administrative independence from the Ottoman Empire in 1874. The Mixed Courts (*Al-Mahākim al-Mukhṭaliṭah, Tribunaux Mixtes d'Egypte*) were established in 1875 as part of a new reform-oriented regime (see later comments from Nathan Brown, "Law and Imperialism: Egypt in Comparative Perspective," *Law and Society Review* 29, no. 1 (1995): 115: "Contrary to the repeated claim that the mixed courts were imposed because of the capitulations . . . the Mixed Courts were a means by which the Egyptian government sought to limit the capitulations. This motivation . . . should be attributed to the entire movement of legal reform along European lines because the latter can be seen as a tool for resisting direct European penetration."). The native (*ahliyyah*) courts were formed in 1883, a year after formal British rule began. Qadri Pasha's Qanun Ahwal al-Shakhsiyyah was published in 1893. Lama Abu-Odeh, "Modernizing Muslim Family Law: The Case of Egypt" *Oxford U Comparative L Forum* 3 (2004).

108. Wood 2011, 77.

109. Rida, *Al-Manar* 1898 (2), 764–71; Abduh, 'Alquwwah wa al-Qanun" [Power and the Law], *al-Manar* 1899 (2), 174. Cf. Wood 2011.

110. Allen 2005.

111. Yet, as Kugle notes, these *ulama* largely worked in response to problems raised by their constituents: "After the initial enthusiasm passed, their requests were limited to ritual affairs, doctrinal points and family relations" (2001, 47).

112. Abu-Odeh points out that Qadri's use of Hanafi law privileged a more patriarchal family law than that of the Shafi'i school, to which most Egyptians belonged. Lama Abu-Odeh, "Modernizing Muslim Family Law: The Case of Egypt," *Vanderbilt Journal of Transnational Law* 37, no. 4 (October 2004): 1043(104); also Jamal J. Nasir, *The Islamic Law of Personal Status* (Leiden: Brill, 2002), 12–13.

113. Abu Odeh 2004; Shaham 1994; Sonbol 1996.

114. Hans-Georg Ebert, "Personal Status Laws in the Arab States: Traditions and Innovations," in *Islamica: Studies in Memory of Holger Preissler (1943–2006)*, ed. Andreas Christmann and Jan-Peter Hartung, *Journal of Semitic Studies*, Suppl. 26, Oxford University Press (2010): 151–69.

115. Peters 2003, 90.

116. Ron Shaham, "Judicial Divorce at the Wife's Initiative: The Shari'a Courts of Egypt, 1920–1955," *Islamic Law and Society* 1, no. 2. (1994): 217–57, at p. 217. Shaham includes in this latter category of "modernizers" men like: Qasim Amin, Sa'd Zaghlul, Ahmad Lutfi al-Sayyid, 'Abd al-Razzaq al-Sanhuri, 'Aziz Khanki, Mustafa Sabri, 'Abd al-Hamid 'Abd al-Haqq, Muhammad 'Ali 'Aluba, Mahmud 'Azmi, 'Abd al-Fattah al-Sayyid, and Ahmad Safwat.

117. Fahmy 1999, 226.

118. Muhd Imara, *Al-A'mal al-kamila lil-imam Muhammad Abduh* [The complete works of Imam Muhammad 'Abduh], vol. 2 (Beirut 1980), 217–97.

119. Asad 2001, 9.

120. Agrama 2012, 158.

121. Asad 2001, 1.

122. Asad 2001, 3–7.

123. Asad 2001, 10. The use of the word *qanun* instead of *hukm* is itself telling—while both might be translated as law, *qanun* refers to laws pronounced by the secular ruler, neither derived from the shari'a nor reliant upon its authority.

124. Asad 2001, 7.

125. Asad 2001, 4.

126. Green 2009,7.

127. Asad 2003, 227.

128. Gilmartin 1988, 54.

129. Metcalf 1990, 3.

130. Metcalf, 1990, 5.

131. Metcalf 1990, 26.

132. Metcalf 1990, 9.

133. Metcalf 1990, 13.

134. Zeghal 2013b.

135. Anderson 1993, 21. In Abraham v. Abraham (1863, 9 M.I.A., 195) the Privy Council held, "The profession of Christianity releases the convert from the trammels of Hindu Law, but it does not of necessity involve any change in the rights or relations of the convert in matters with which Christianity has no concern, such as his rights and interests in, and powers over, property."

136. Anderson 1993, 20–21.

137. Both Muhammad Iqbal and Abul Ala Maududi, for example, offering quite different political programs for the future of India and Islam, rested their arguments upon the assumption that a centralized state would deliver both the procedural and substantive content of Islamic law. Kugle 2001, 308–10.

138. The irony goes further: colonial and later Western attempts to "reform" Islamic law attack this very same vision of the law: rigid, formalist, patriarchal, and unchanging, as "Islamic," when a strong argument can be made that it reflected Victorian values and colonial power strategies more than Muslim practice or values of the time. "In the late nineteenth century, various groups adopted a new approach to Islam, mobilising around Muslim identity in opposition to colonial rule. In this process, a particular version of Islamic law came to be juxtaposed with colonial attacks upon it." Anderson 1993, 22.

139. M. Anderson 1993, 6. Also, Bayly, Rulers Townsmen and Bazaars 129–30; G. C. Kozlowski, Muslim Endowments and Society in British India (Cambridge: Cambridge University Press, 1985), 351.

140. Rudolph and Rudolph 2001, 52.

141. Ayesha Jalal, "Review: R. J. Moore (1988) Endgames of Empire: Studies of Britain's Indian Problem," *Journal of Asian Studies* 49, no. 2 (May 1990): 427–28.

142. Roff 1967; Milner 1982 and 1991; Hirschman 1986.

Chapter Six

1. Hallaq 2013, 3.

2. "Asma' atlaqat 'Ala ghair musammiyyatiha," [names applied to what they do not mean.] Tariq al-Bishri, *Al-Hiwar al-Islami al-'almani* [The Islamic-Secular Dialogue] (Cairo: Dar al- Sharuq, 1996), 9. Asad translation, 2003, 213.

3. Hussin, "A Discussion of Wael Hallaq, The Impossible State: Islam, Politics, and Modernity's Moral Predicament," *Perspectives on Politics* 12, no. 2 (June 2014).

4. Hallaq 2013, 72.

5. Joan Scott's characterization of this paradox in the case of French feminists resonates strongly with the paradoxes that face the modern Muslim subject: "The history of feminism is the history of women who have had only paradoxes to offer not because—as misogynist critics would have it—women's reasoning capacities are deficient or their natures fundamentally contrary, not because feminism somehow hasn't been able to get its theory and practice right but because historically, modern Western feminism is constituted by the discursive practices of democratic politics that have equated individuality with masculinity." Scott 1997, 5.

6. Al-Bishri 1996, 9.

7. Al-Bishri 1996, 9; cited in Asad 2003, 213.

8. Speaking against the coup in July 2013, al-Bishri continued to use the language of paradox: "The (Armed Forces) leadership took advantage of popular opposition against the Muslim Brotherhood, and drove them to support it in the battle of extinguishing the spirit of the January 25 2011 revolution, along with constitutional democracy, and to take us back to the brutal totalitarian regime. . . . The people must realise that their present quest does not concern the restoration of the Muslim Brotherhood's rule, but the defence of the constitution and the democratic system . . . we are facing a dilemma, which is the fact that it is almost impossible for those who resort to a military coup to abandon it because their personal fate has become linked to the fate of the coup. On the other side, those who may wish to compromise on certain constitutional democratic matters to avoid the material wrath of the coup, any such compromise would create a dangerous constitutional precedent that would always continue to threaten the democratic system." Al-Bishri, "The Current Conflict is Between Democracy, Governance and the Military Coup, not the Brotherhood and the Opposition," *Shorouk*, July 10, 2013; *Middle East Monitor*, July 11, 2013.

9. Ellis Goldberg, "Tariq al-Bishri and Constitutional Revision," February 15, 2011, *Nisr al-Nasr: Occasional Thoughts on Middle Eastern and US Politics*, http://

nisralnasr.blogspot.co.uk/2011/02/tariq-al-bishri-and-constitutional.html, last accessed December 5, 2014.

10. "Tragedy . . . is about the *paradox* of enlightenment. . . . The tragedy of colonial enlightenment . . . is not to be perceived in terms of a flaw to be erased or overcome, but rather in terms of a permanent legacy that has set the conditions in which we make of ourselves what we make and which therefore demands constant renegotiation and readjustment." D. Scott 2004, 20–21.

11. David Scott, "The Tragic Sensibility of Talal Asad," 134–53, at pp. 152–53, in Scott and Hirschkind 2006.

12. Scott 2004, 4.

13. Scott points to the figure of the tragic hero of enlightenment, "a conscript of a larger and more profound condition that simultaneously enables and disables him, that is at once the source of his strength and his weakness, a condition whose script is barely legible to him because it is written in a language whose familiarity is both recent and coerced, and which, in consequence, he cannot clearly recognise, much less fully command and master." Scott 2004, 171.

14. Hallaq 2009, 5.

15. Skovgaard-Petersen 1997; Hefner and Zaman 2004.

16. Skovgaard-Petersen 1992, 64.

17. Comaroff 1991; Cohn 1996; Rudolph 1967.

18. Said 1993.

19. Peter Fitzpatrick (1992 and 1999).

20. Jane Collier, "Intertwined Histories: Islamic Law and Western Imperialism," *Law & Society Review* 28, no. 2. (1994): 395–408, at p. 395. Collier uses Said's argument of "intertwined histories" to reason: "The legal ideas and practices of very different peoples developed in similar ways because all groups were interacting over the past two centuries. The appearance of evolutionary progress is not coincidental. Western imperial powers had, and continue to have, the control over communication technologies and the military might to define our legal system as the goal of human development" (397).

21. Turner 1974, 107–21.

22. Charrad 2001; c.f. Ann Mayer, "The Internationalization of Religiously Based Resistance to International Human Rights Law," in *Global Justice and the Bulwarks of Localism: Human Rights in Context*, eds. Christopher L. Eisgruber and Andras Sajo (Leiden: Martinus Nijhoff, 2005); Parvez Manzoor, "Legal Rationality vs. Arbitrary Judgement: Re-examining the Tradition of Islamic Law," *Muslim World Book Review* 21, no. 1 (October–December 2000): 3–12.

23. Geertz 1983, 232.

24. Rosen 1980.

25. Rosen 1989, 18.

26. Moore (2001) summarized three strands of anthropological analysis of law: law as domination, law as culture and law as problem solver.

27. Starr and Collier 1989, 16.

28. "Hegemony" used here builds on Ranajit Guha's analysis of colonialism, to characterize a dynamic of dominance and subordination in the state, where the element of persuasion had effects and impact beyond that of coercion. Guha, *Dominance without Hegemony: History and Power in Colonial India.* (Cambridge, MA: Harvard University Press, 1997), 23.

29. Jalal 2000. Also, D. Gilmartin, *Empire and Islam: Punjab and the Making of Pakistan* (Berkeley: University of California Press, 1988): Dealing with a later period of Indian history, Gilmartin discusses the Shariat Act of 1937, which mobilized Muslims for and against it. While Jinnah and the Muslim League supported it as a confluence of local political interests and Islamic ideals, the reformist *ulama* opposed the Shariat Act as "the achievement of Muslim unity at the expense of the religious content of Muslim identity" (173).

30. Joan Vincent (1994, 119) uses the concept of the "hegemonic moment" to come closer to the processes through which ideology becomes hegemony, how choices are made between particular legal orders, elements and meanings, and what mechanisms of language, theater, violence, and governance are employed in the transition. Vincent's approach takes seriously the agency of both local and colonial actors, and while she makes clear that history is shaped by the exercise of power, she is also clear that its outcomes are not predetermined.

31. Comaroff 1991; Rudolph 1976.

32. Anderson 1993, 8.

33. Guha 1997, 3.

34. Abou El Fadl 1997. Also see Abdullahi an-Naim 2002.

35. Stilt 2004; Brown 2005.

36. Merry 1988.

37. I argue that a distinction must be made between legal pluralism as a descriptive concept, as Hooker (1975) uses it—the attempt by colonial and state governments to combine elements of various legal systems within one framework—and legal pluralism as an analytic concept (Merry 1988).

38. Ugo Mattei, "A Theory of Imperial Law: A Study on US Hegemony and the Latin Resistance," *Ind. J. Global Legal Stud.* 10 (2003): 389. "Legal Transplant? Comparative Law? Mattei Criticizes the "naively anthropomorphic nature of most traditional analyses. Legal transplants cannot be seen as happening as a result of the choice of one model that freely or coactively receives the produced model. Both in the phase of production and in the phase of reception, legal transplants are a lively dialectic between consent and dissent, between hegemonic and counter-hegemonic forces, between mainstream and critical approaches. In other words, dominant and dominated positions have to be considered in the picture because they allow an understanding of the high complexity of the picture." Also William Twining, "Social Science and Diffusion of Law," *J.L. & Soc'y* 32 (2005): 203–40.

39. De Sousa Santos 1987, 358.

40. Austin Sarat and Thomas Kearns, eds. *The Fate of Law* (Ann Arbor: University of Michigan Press, 1991), 105.

41. Susanne and Lloyd Rudolph have argued for a more detailed exploration of the contemporary consequences of the post-1857 transition from legal universalism to legal pluralism in India, for example, in Rudolph and Rudolph 2001. Also see Mehta 1999; Mantena 2010.

42. Robert L. Tignor, "The 'Indianization' of the Egyptian Administration under British Rule," *American Historical Review* 68, no. 3. (April 1963): 636–61, at p. 637.

43. Tagliacozzo 2009, Ho 2004, Green 2011, Azra 2004, Risso 1995; Metcalf 2008.

44. Devji 2014, 257–58.

45. *Die Kultur der Ambiguität: Eine andere Geschichte des Islams* [The culture of ambiguity: A different history of Islam] (Berlin: Verlag der Weltreligionen, 2011).

46. Asad 2001, 7.

47. Hallaq 2009, 360.

48. Asad 2001, 8–9.

49. Asad 2001, 1; 2003, 201.

50. Asad 2003, 226.

51. Scott 2004, 119. Cf. Asad, "Afterword: From the History of Colonial Anthropology to the Anthropology of Western Hegemony," in George W. Stocking Jr, ed., *Colonial Situations: Essays on the Contextualization of Ethnographic Knowledge* (Madison: University of Wisconsin Press, 1991), 314–24.

52. Asad 2003, 227–28.

53. Asad 2003, 252.

54. Scott 2004, 13.

55. Comaroff 2009, 194. Comaroff associates "theo-legality," "the rising salience of the law—at once as ideology, as species of practice, as utopic-cure-all, as landscape of political struggle, as landscape of governmentality—with changes in the global order of things," 194–95.

56. Agrama 2012, 35.

57. Agrama 2012, 25.

58. Comaroff and Comaroff 2009, 58.

59. Schmitt 2006, 36; Strong 2012, 240.

Chapter Seven

1. Asad 2003, 201.

2. Federal Constitution of Malaysia Art. 160, cl. 2., defines a "Malay" as "a person who professes the religion of Islam, habitually speaks the Malay language . . . (and) conforms to Malay custom."

3. Agrama 2012, 29–30.

4. Zeghal 2013a, 258.

5. Lazarus-Black and Hirsh 1994.

6. Moustafa 2013a, 799–800.

7. G. Brown 2010, Hirschman 1987.

8. Mandal 2004; Brown 2010.

9. Federal Constitution of Malaysia 1957, Art. 74, Sched. 9, List I (State List), Item 1.

10. Milne and Mauzy 1980; Mutalib 1990; Peletz 2002.

11. G. Brown 2010. Further, "The Ninth Malaysia Plan, the first of the country's 5-year development programmes to be designed and implemented by the Abdullah administration . . . gave Abdullah's conception of Islam Hadhari a central place in the government's development vision, stating that all development initiatives would "be guided by the universal principles of Islam Hadhari" as a "comprehensive and universal development the universal principles of Islam Hadhari" as a "comprehensive and universal development framework for the nation" (Malaysia, 2006). Second, the Plan returned the practice of setting specific targets for the reduction of ethnic inequalities across multiple dimensions, a practice that had largely been dropped by the Mahathir administration.

12. Michael Peletz, for example, argues that even at the height of the "resurgence," "most Malays live in rural areas and conceptualise and enact their religiosities and cultural identities in terms that are distinct from—and in some cases mutually incompatible with—those of the resurgents." "Ordinary Muslims and Muslim Resurgents in Contemporary Malaysia: Notes on an Ambivalent Relationship," in Hefner and Horvatich 1997, 264–65.

13. M. Mohamed, "Making Majority, Undoing Family: Law, Religion and the Islamization of the State in Malaysia," *Economy and Society* 39, no. 3 (August 2010): 360–84. Also, Hamayotsu, 2003; Martinez, 2001; Nik Noriani, 2009.

14. Islam Hadhari is associated strongly with the public platform of UMNO leaders such as Abdullah Badawi, who succeeded Mahathir Mohamed as prime minister in 2003 and served in that capacity till 2009. His successor, Najib Tun Razak, continued this platform, extending its appeal to the international stage, calling for a "global movement of the moderates" at the United Nations General Assembly in 2010. Even though Islam Hadhari is widely defended in Malaysia as a moderate vision of Islam, it continues to attract criticism for its expansionist view of the role of Islam in Malaysian political and national life.

15. Nyonya binte Tahir, Ex P Majlis Agama Islam Negri Sembilan & Anor (2006).

16. Lina Joy v. Majlis Agama Islam Wilayah Persekutuan & Anor (2001).

17. Dato' Richard Malanjum (Chief Judge of Sabah and Sarawak), 30.5.2007. Dalam Mahkamah Perseketuan Malaysia (Bidang Kuasa Rayuan), Mahkamah Persekutuan Rayuan Sivil No.: 01–2-2006 (w), Antara Lina Joy dan Majlis Agama

Islam Wilayah Persekutuan dan Kerajaan Malaysia dan Ketua Pengarah Pendaftaran Negara, 1–58.

18. The official Malaysian spelling of shari'a is *syariah*.

19. *Lina Joy* as discussed in this chapter is one in a series of Lina Joy cases between 1999 and 2007. For detailed analysis of the texts of each of these cases, see Hussin 2010.

20. Current Law Journal Malaysia 6 (2004): 242–72.

21. *CLJ* 6 (2004): 271.

22. US State Department Report on Religious Freedom in Malaysia, 2011. These figures, and their reporting, continue to be a matter of dispute in Malaysia.

23. Agrama 2012, 35.

24. Richland 2012, 8; Cormack 2008.

25. "*Dalam Perkara Nyonya binti Tahir, Ex P Majlis Agama Islam Negeri Sembilan dan Yang Lain; Syariah High Court Seremban Negeri Sembilan; Judge Mohamad Shukor Sabudin. 23 January 2006.*" *Current Law Journal* (Syariah Reports) 1 (2006):335–54, 15. Author's translation; unless otherwise indicated, numbers in square brackets [] refer to the numbered sections of the Malay-language decision.

26. Administration of Islamic Law Enactment 2003.

27. Pahang, Perak, Sabah, Malacca, Kelantan, and Terengganu have instituted criminal penalties for apostasy; these last two states have made apostasy a capital offense but have not prosecuted any cases. Kedah, the Federal Territories, and a number of other states have no syariah provisions for apostasy, although these have at times been interpreted by state religious authorities to provide wide latitude for detention and attempted rehabilitation. Other states, like Sarawak and Negeri Sembilan, allow a Muslim to leave Islam after meeting certain conditions, applying to the syariah courts, a mandatory waiting period and counseling included. Mohamed Adil, Mohamed Azam (2007) "Law of Apostasy and Freedom of Religion in Malaysia," *Asian Journal of Comparative Law* 2, no. 1, Art. 6.

28. The M. Moorthy case was a high-profile and controversial case whose central figure had been part of the first Malaysian team to climb Everest; based upon reports that he had converted to Islam before his death, he was buried as a Muslim despite the objections of his Hindu family. The case was heard before the Kuala Lumpur Syariah High Court, but Moorthy's Hindu wife was not named as a party to the suit. K. Shanmuga, "A Summary of the Case and Related Events of *Kaliammal Sinnasamy v Islamic Religious Affairs Council of the Federal Territory, Director Kuala Lumpur General Hospital & Government of Malaysia.*(Decided December 28, 2005, K. L. High Court Originating Summons No. R1–24–102–2005.) Malaysian Bar Council Website: www.malaysianbar.org.my/bar_news/berita_badan_peguam/re_everest_moorthy_.html, accessed September 14, 2009.

29. '*Al Fiqh al Islami wa Adillatuhu*, Juz 6 (Damascus, Syria: Dar al Fikr, 1989), 173.

30. *CLJ* 6 (2004): 271.

31. Barzilai 2003 makes a similar point with regard to the legislation of Judaism in Israel, for example.

32. Winnifred Sullivan, *The Impossibility of Religious Freedom* (Princeton, NJ: Princeton University Press, 2005).

33. "Titular Roman Catholic Archbishop of Kuala Lumpur v. Menteri Dalam Negeri and Kerajaan Malaysia," 31 December 2009, R1–25–28–2009, [2010] 2 MLJ 122. The judge in the case was Justice Lau Bee Lan. The appeal case, "Menteri Dalam Negeri & Ors v. Titular Roman Catholic Archbishop of Kuala Lumpur," [2013] 6 MLJ 468, was brought before the Federal Court of Malaysia appellate jurisdiction, and decided 4–3 in favor of the government in 2014 (*Titular Roman Catholic Archbishop of Kuala Lumpur v. Menteri Dalam Negeri & Ors* 08–690–11/2013).

34. "Menteri Dalam Negeri & Ors v Titular Roman Catholic Archbishop of Kuala Lumpur," Civil Appeal No. W-01–1-2010, 38–39.

35. Judge Hj Mohamed Apandi b Hj Ali, Court of Appeal Malaysia, "Summary of Decision," October 14, 2013.

36. Cited Kishori Mohan Bera v The State of West Bengal [1972 (3) SCC845].

37. In this section, the judgment cited recent cases from the United Kingdom with regard to national security: *A, X and Y v Secretary of State for the Home Department* [2004] QB 335, and *R. v. Secretary of State for the Home Department, ex parte Hosenball* [1977] 3 AII E.R. 452. Both citations emphasized the need for faith in the Home Secretary to determine the necessary balance between national security and the rights of the individual; however, these were not religious freedom cases. The former involved foreign nationals detained under suspicion of terrorism; the latter also involved a foreign national deported under suspicion of illegal espionage.

38. "Menteri Dalam Negeri & Ors v Titular Roman Catholic Archbishop of Kuala Lumpur," Civil Appeal No. W-01–1-2010.

39. See note 571, above. Both UK case citations in this judgment emphasized the need for faith in the Home Secretary to determine the necessary balance between national security and the rights of the individual; however, these were not religious freedom cases. [2004] QB 335 involved foreign nationals detained under suspicion of terrorism; *Hosenball* also involved a foreign national deported under suspicion of illegal espionage.

40. Agrama 2012, 30–31.

41. Moustafa 2013b, 16; 2013c, 798–99.

42. Menchik 2014, 595, 611. "Productive Intolerance: Godly Nationalism in Indonesia," *Comparative Studies in Society and History* 56, no. 3 (2014): 591–621. Menchik argues that "conflicts over blasphemy reflect Muslim civil society's effort to delinate an incipient model of nationalism and tolerance while avoiding the templates of liberal secularism or theocracy" (595).

43. Comaroff 2009, 194.

44. Anderson 1993, 10.

45. Talal Asad, "Trying to Understand French Secularism," in *Political Theologies*, ed. Hent deVries (New York: Fordham University Press, forthcoming).

46. David Scott 2004, 4.

47. Scott 2004, 20–21.

References

Abou el Fadl, Khaled. 1997. *The Authoritative and Authoritarian in Islamic Discourses: A Contemporary Case Study*. Austin, TX: Dar Taiba.

———. 2003. "Islam and the Challenge of Democracy." *Boston Review* (April/May).

Abu-Lughod, Lila. 1998. *Remaking Women*. Princeton NJ: Princeton University Press.

Abu-Odeh, Lama. 2004a. "Egyptian Feminism: Trapped in the Identity Debate." *Yale Journal of Law and Feminism* 16:2: 145–91.

———. 2004b. "Modernizing Muslim Family Law: The Case of Egypt." *Vanderbilt Journal of Transnational Law* 37: 1043–146.

———. 2004c. "The Politics of (Mis)Recognition." *American Journal of Comparative Law* 52: 789–824.

Agrama, Hussein. 2012. *Questioning Secularism: Islam, Sovereignty and the Rule of Law in Modern Egypt*. Chicago: University of Chicago Press.

Ahmad, Ibrahim, and Alijah Gordon. 1965. *Islamic Law in Malaya*. Singapore: Malaysian Sociological Research Institute.

Ahmed, Leila. 1992. *Women and Gender in Islam: Historical Roots of a Modern Debate*. New Haven, CT: Yale University Press.

Ahmed, Rafiuddin. 1979. *In Contributions to South Asian Studies*. Edited by Gopal Krishna. Delhi: Oxford University Press.

Alavi, Seema. 1995. *The Sepoys and the Company: Tradition and Transition in Northern India, 1770–1830*. Delhi: Oxford University Press.

Al-Azmeh, Aziz. 1988. *Islamic Law: Social and Historical Contexts*. New York: Routledge.

Al-Hibri, Azizah Yahia. 2000–2001. "Muslim Women's Rights in the Global Village: Challenges and Opportunities." *Journal of Law and Religion* 15, no. 1/2: 37–66.

Al-Husry, Khaldun. 1966. *Three Reformers: A Study in Modern Arab Political Thought*. Beirut: Khayats.

Al-Muhairi, Butti Sultan Butti Ali. 1996. "Islamisation and Modernisation within the UAE Penal Law: Shari'a in the Modern Era." *Arab Law Quarterly* 11, no. 1: 34–49.

Andaya, Barbara Watson, and Leonard Y. Andaya. 1982. *A History of Malaysia*. New York: St. Martin's.

Andaya, Leonard. 1975. *The Kingdom of Johor, 1641–1728*. Kuala Lumpur: Oxford University Press.

Anderson, B. 1983. *Imagined Communities: Reflections on the Origins and Spread of Nationalism*. London: Verso.

Anderson, J. N. D. 1957. "Law as a Social Force in Islamic Culture and History." *Bulletin of the School of Oriental and African Studies*, University of London, vol. 20, no. 1/3: 13–40.

———. 1959. *Islamic Law in the Modern World*. New York: New York University Press.

———. 1963. *Changing Law in Developing Countries*. Studies on Modern Asia and Africa. London: Allen & Unwin.

———. 1968. *Family Law in Asia and Africa*. Studies in Modern Asia and Africa. New York: Praeger.

———. 1976. *Law Reform in the Muslim World*. London: Athlone.

Anderson, J. N. D., Norman J. Coulson, and M. Farani. 1979. *Islamic Law in Contemporary Cultural Change*. Lahore: Lahore Law Times Publications.

Anderson, Michael. 1993. "Islamic Law and the Colonial Encounter in British India." In *Institutions and Ideologies: A SOAS South Asia Reader*, edited by David and Peter Robb Arnold, 165–85. London: Curzon.

———. 1999. "Legal Scholarship and the Politics of Islam in British India." In *Perspectives on Islamic Law, Justice and Society*, edited by R. S. Khare, 65–91. Lanham, MD: Rowman and Littlefield.

An-Naim, Abdullahi. 2002. *Islamic Family Law in a Changing World: A Global Resource Book*. London: Zed.

———. 2008. *Islam and the Secular State: Negotiating the Future of Shari'a*. Cambridge, MA: Harvard University Press.

Antlöv, Hans, and Stein Tønnesson. 1995. *Imperial Policy and Southeast Asian Nationalism, 1930–1957*. Richmond, Surrey, UK: Curzon.

Appadurai, Arjun. 1981. *Worship and Conflict Under Colonial Rule: A South Indian Case*. Cambridge: Cambridge University Press.

Arkib Negara Malaysia., and Frank Athelstane Swettenham. 1970. *Suratan Swettenham* (Swettenham papers). Kuala Lumpur.

Asad, Talal. 1993. *Genealogies of Religion: Discipline and Reasons of Power in Christianity and Islam*. Baltimore: Johns Hopkins University Press.

———. 2001. *Thinking About Secularism and Law in Egypt*. Vol. 2, *ISIM Occasional Paper*. Leiden: ISIM.

———. 2003. *Formations of the Secular: Christianity, Islam, Modernity*. Redwood City, CA: Stanford University Press.

Awang, Muhammad Kamil. 1998. *The Sultan and the Constitution*. Kuala Lumpur: Dewan Bahasa dan Pustaka.

Awang, Ridzuan. 1994. *Undang-Undang Tanah Islam: Pendekatan Perbandingan* [The Land Law of Islam: A Comparative Approach]. Kuala Lumpur: Dewan Bahasa dan Pustaka.

Azra, Azyumardi. 2004. *The Origins of Islamic Reformism in Southeast Asia: Networks of Malay-Indonesian and Middle Eastern 'Ulamā' in the Seventeenth and Eighteenth Centuries*. Honolulu: University of Hawaii Press.

Badie, Bertrand. 2000. *The Imported State: The Westernization of the Political Order*. Redwood City, CA: Stanford University Press.

Badlishah, and Saleh Ismail bin Haji. 1989. *The Sultan Was Not Alone: A Collection of Letters Written by Sultan Badlishah of Kedah in His Effort to Repeal the Malayan Union Policy Imposed by the British Government on Malaya in 1946, and Other Supporting Letters and Documents Written by Others*. Alor Setar, Kedah Darulaman, West Malaysia: State Museum, Kedah Darulaman.

Barlow, H. S. *Swettenham*. 1995. Kuala Lumpur: Southdene.

Barzilai, Gad. 2003. *Communities and Law: Politics and Cultures of Legal Identities, Law, Meaning, and Violence*. Ann Arbor: University of Michigan Press.

Bassiouni, M. Cherif, and Gamal M. Badr. 2002. "The Shari'ah: Sources, Interpretation and Rule-Making." *UCLA Journal of Islamic and Near Eastern Law* (Spring/Summer): 135–81.

Bayly, C. A. 1975. *The Local Roots of Indian Politics: Allahabad, 1880–1920*. Oxford: Clarendon.

———. 1987. *Indian Society and the Making of the British Empire*. New York: Cambridge University Press.

———. 1989. *Imperial Meridian: The British Empire and the World, 1780–1830*. London: Longman.

———. 1996. *Empire and Information: Intelligence Gathering and Social Communication in India, 1780–1870*. Cambridge Studies in Indian History and Society. New York: Cambridge University Press.

———. 1998. *Origins of Nationality in South Asia: Patriotism and Ethical Government in the Making of Modern India*. Delhi: Oxford University Press.

———. 1992. *Rulers, Townsmen and Bazaars: North Indian Society in the Age of British Expansion, 1770–1870*. Delhi: Oxford University Press.

———. 2004. *The Birth of the Modern World, 1780–1914: Global Connections and Comparisons*. Malden, MA: Blackwell.

———. 2007. "Distorted Development: The Ottoman Empire and British India, circa 1780–1916." *Comp Stud of S Asia, Africa and the MidE* 27 no. 2.

Bayly, C. A., Brian Allen, and National Portrait Gallery (Great Britain). 1990. *The Raj: India and the British, 1600–1947*. London: National Portrait Gallery Publications.

Bayly, C. A., and Alan Atkinson. 1989. *Atlas of the British Empire*. New York: Facts on File.

Bayly, C. A., and T. N. Harper. 2005. *Forgotten Armies: The Fall of British Asia, 1941–1945*. Cambridge, MA: Belknap Press of Harvard University Press.

Bayly, C. A., and D. H. A. Kolff. 1986. *Two Colonial Empires, Comparative Studies in Overseas History*. Kluwer Academic Pub.

Bayly, S. 1988. "Islam and State Power in Pre-Colonial South India." *Itinerario* 12, no. 1: 143–64.

Beinin, Joel, and Zachary Lockman. 1987. *Workers on the Nile: Nationalism, Communism, Islam, and the Egyptian Working Class, 1882–1954*. Princeton, NJ: Princeton University Press.

Benton, Lauren. 1999. "Colonial Law and Cultural Difference: Jurisdictional Politics and the Formation of the Colonial State." *Comparative Studies in Society and History* 41, no. 3: 563–88.

———. 2002. *Law and Colonial Cultures: Legal Regimes in World History, 1400–1900*. Studies in Comparative World History. New York: Cambridge University Press.

Berger, Maurits S. 2002. "Conflicts Law and Public Policy in Egyptian Family Law: Islamic Law through the Backdoor." *American Journal of Comparative Law* 50, no. 3: 555–94.

Blunt, Wilfred Owen. 1882. *The Future of Islam*. London: Kegan Paul, Trench and Co.

Borhan, Abdul Jalil. 2002. *Majalah Ahkam Johor: Kod Undang-Undang Sivil Islam Kerajaan Negeri Johor 1331h/1913m* [Majalah Ahkam Johor: The Islamic Civil Code of the State of Johor, 1331H/1913AD]. Johor: Universiti Teknologi Malaysia Skudai.

Bose, Sugata. 2006. *A Hundred Horizons: The Indian Ocean in the Age of Global Empire*. Cambridge, MA: Harvard University Press.

Bose, Sugata, and Ayesha Jalal. 2004. *Modern South Asia: History, Culture, Political Economy*. 2nd ed. New York: Routledge.

Boullata, Issa J., Kamal Abdel-Malek, and Wael B. Hallaq. 2000. *Tradition, Modernity, and Postmodernity in Arabic Literature: Essays in Honor of Professor Issa J. Boullata*. Leiden: Brill.

Bowen, John Eliot. 1886. "The Conflict of East and West in Egypt." *Political Science Quarterly* 1, no. 2: 295–335.

Bowen, John Richard. 2003. *Islam, Law, and Equality in Indonesia: An Anthropology of Public Reasoning*. New York: Cambridge University Press.

———. 2007. *Why the French Don't Like Headscarves: Islam, the State, and Public Space*. Princeton, NJ: Princeton University Press.

———. 2010. "Secularism: Conceptual Genealogy or Political Dilemma?" *Comparative Studies in Society and History* 52, no. 3:680–94.

Bowen, John Richard, and Roger Dale Petersen. 1999. *Critical Comparisons in Politics and Culture*. Cambridge, UK: Cambridge University Press.

Bradley, F. 2013. "Sheikh Da'ud Al-Fatani's Munyat al-Musalli and the Place of

Prayer in 19th-Century Patani Communities." *Indonesia & the Malay World* 41, no. 120 (July): 198–214.

Brinton, Jasper. 1930. *The Mixed Courts of Egypt*. New Haven, CT: Yale University Press.

Brodkin, E. I. 1969. "Proprietary Mutations and the Mutiny." *Journal of Asian Studies* 28, no. 4: 667–83.

———. 1972. "The Struggle for Succession: Rebels and Loyalists in the Indian Mutiny of 1857." *Modern Asian Studies* 6, no. 3: 277–90.

Brown, Graham. 2010. "Legible Pluralism: The Politics of Ethnic and Religious Identification in Malaysia." *Ethnopolitics* 9, no. 1 (March): 31–52.

Brown, Nathan. 1993. "The Precarious Life and Slow Death of the Mixed Courts of Egypt." *International Journal of Middle East Studies* 25: 33–52.

———. 1995. "Retrospective: Law and Imperialism: Egypt in Comparative Perspective." *Law & Society Review* 29, no. 1: 103–26.

———. 1997. "Sharia and State in the Modern Muslim Middle East." *International Journal of Middle East Studies* 29, no. 3: 359–76.

———. 2002. *Constitutions in a Nonconstitutional World: Arab Basic Laws and the Prospects for Accountable Government*. SUNY Series in Middle Eastern Studies. Albany, NY: State University of New York Press.

———. 2005. *The Final Draft of the Iraqi Constitution: Analysis and Commentary*. Carnegie Endowment for International Peace [cited January 3, 2008].

Buang, Salleh. 1996. *Sejarah Undang-Undang Malaysia: Kes Dan Material* [The History of Malaysian Law: Cases and Material]. Kuala Lumpur: Dewan Bahasa dan Pustaka.

Buckler, F. W. 1922. "The Political Theory of the Indian Mutiny." *Transactions of the Royal Historical Society* 5, no. 4: 71–100.

Burke, Edmund. 1866. *The Complete Works of the Right Honourable Edmund Burke*. Boston: Little, Brown and Co.

Burke III, Edmund, ed. 1993. *Rethinking World History: Essays on Europe, Islam, and World History*. Cambridge: Cambridge University Press.

———. 2014. *The Ethnographic State: France and the Invention of Moroccan Islam*. Berkeley: University of California Press.

Burns, Peter L., and R. J. Wilkinson. 1971. *Papers on Malay Subjects*. Oxford in Asia Historical Reprints. Kuala Lumpur: Oxford University Press.

Buxbaum, David C. 1966. "Chinese Family Law in a Common Law Setting: A Note on the Institutional Environment and the Substantive Family Law of the Chinese in Singapore and Malaysia." *Journal of Asian Studies* 25, no. 4: 621–44.

Cain, P. J. 2006. "Character and Imperialism: The British Financial Administration of Egypt, 1878–1914." *Journal of Imperial & Commonwealth History* 34, no. 2 (June): 177–200.

Calhoun, Craig J., Frederick Cooper, Kevin W. Moore, and Social Science Research

Council (U.S.). 2006. *Lessons of Empire: Imperial Histories and American Power*. New York: New Press.

Cannon, Byron. 1975. "Social Tensions and the Teaching of European Law in Egypt before 1900." *History of Education Quarterly* 15, no. 3: 299–315.

———. 1988. *Politics of Law and the Courts in Nineteenth Century Egypt*. Salt Lake City: University of Utah Press.

Chakrabarty, Dipesh. 1989. *Rethinking Working-Class History: Bengal, 1890–1940*. Princeton, NJ: Princeton University Press.

———. 2000. *Provincializing Europe: Postcolonial Thought and Historical Difference*. Princeton Studies in Culture/Power/History. Princeton, NJ: Princeton University Press.

———. 2002. *Habitations of Modernity: Essays in the Wake of Subaltern Studies*. Chicago: University of Chicago Press.

Chakravarti, Uma. 1998. *Rewriting History: The Life and Times of Pandita Ramabai*. New Delhi: Kali for Women.

Charrad, Mounira. 2001. *States and Women's Rights: The Making of Postcolonial Tunisia, Algeria, and Morocco*. Berkeley: University of California Press.

Chatterjee, Partha. 1986. *Nationalist Thought and the Colonial World: A Derivative Discourse?* Totawa, NJ: Zed Books Ltd. for the United Nations University.

———. 1993. *The Nation and Its Fragments: Colonial and Postcolonial Histories*. Princeton Studies in Culture/Power/History. Princeton, NJ: Princeton University Press.

Chatterjee, Partha, and Centre for Studies in Social Sciences. 1995. *Texts of Power: Emerging Disciplines in Colonial Bengal*. Minneapolis: University of Minnesota Press.

Christelow, Allan. 1985. *Muslim Law Courts and the French Colonial State in Algeria*. Princeton, NJ: Princeton University Press.

Clifford, Hugh Charles. 1898. *Studies in Brown Humanity, Being Scrawls and Smudges in Sepia, White, and Yellow, by Hugh Clifford*. London: G. Richards.

———. 1904. *Further India; Being the Story of Exploration from the Earliest Times in Burma, Malaya, Siam and Indo-China*. New York: Frederick A. Stokes Company.

———. 1989. *In Court and Kampung*. Rev. ed. Singapore: Gr. Brash.

Codell, Julie, ed. 2012. *Power and Resistance: The Delhi Coronation Durbars*. Ahmedabad: Mapin.

Cohn, Bernard. 1961. *The Development and Impact of British Administration in India: A Bibliographic Essay*. New Delhi: Indian Institute of Public Administration.

———. 1971. *India: The Social Anthropology of a Civilization*. Anthropology of Modern Societies Series. Englewood Cliffs, NJ: Prentice-Hall.

———. 1977. "The British and the Mughal Court in the 17th Century." Chicago: Special Collections Research Center, University of Chicago Library.

———. 1980. "History and Anthropology: The State of Play." *Comparative Studies in Society and History* 22: 198–221.

———. 1985. "The Command of Language and the Language of Command." In *Subaltern Studies IV: Writings on South Asian Studies and Society*, ed. Ranajit Guha, 276–329.

———. 1987. *An Anthropologist among the Historians and Other Essays*. Delhi: Oxford University Press.

———. 1996. *Colonialism and Its Forms of Knowledge: The British in India*. Princeton Studies in Culture/Power/History. Princeton, NJ: Princeton University Press.

Cole, Juan I. 1999. *Colonialism and Revolution in the Middle East: Social and Cultural Origins of Egypt's Urabi Movement*. Cairo: American University in Cairo.

Collier, Jane. 1994. "Intertwined Histories: Islamic Law and Western Imperialism." *Law & Society Review* 28, no. 2: 395–408.

Comaroff, Jean. 1985. *Body of Power, Spirit of Resistance: The Culture and History of a South African People*. Chicago: University of Chicago Press.

Comaroff, John. 2009. "Reflections on the Rise of Legal Theology: Law and Religion in the 21st Century." *Social Analysis* 53, no. 1 (Spring): 193–216.

Comaroff, Jean, and John L. Comaroff. 1991. *Of Revelation and Revolution: Christianity, Colonialism, and Consciousness in South Africa*. Chicago: University of Chicago Press.

———. 1993. *Modernity and Its Malcontents: Ritual and Power in Postcolonial Africa*. Chicago: University of Chicago Press.

———. 2009. *Ethnicity, Inc.* Chicago: University of Chicago Press.

Comaroff, John L., and Simon Roberts. 1981. *Rules and Processes: The Cultural Logic of Dispute in an African Context*. Chicago: University of Chicago Press.

Cooper, Frederick, Ann Laura Stoler, and History E-Book Project. 1997. *Tensions of Empire: Colonial Cultures in a Bourgeois World*. Berkeley: University of California Press.

Cormack, Bradin. 2008. *A Power to Do Justice. Jurisdiction, English Literature, and the Rise of Common Law, 1509–1625*. Chicago: University of Chicago Press.

Coulson, Noel J. 1969. *Conflicts and Tensions in Islamic Jurisprudence*. Publications of the Center for Middle Eastern Studies. Chicago: University of Chicago Press.

———. 1979. *A History of Islamic Law*. Pakistan ed. Lahore: Lahore Law Times Publications.

Cover, R. 1983. "The Supreme Court 1982 Term—Foreword: Nomos and Narrative." 97 *Harv. L. Rev.* 4: 4–68.

Cowan, C. D. 1961. *Nineteenth-Century Malaya: The Origins of British Political Control*. London Oriental Series. London: Oxford University Press.

Curtin, Philip. 1984. *Cross-Cultural Trade in World History*. Cambridge: Cambridge University Press.

Dalrymple, William. 2006. *The Last Mughal: The Fall of a Dynasty*. Delhi, 1857. London: Bloomsbury.

Darian-Smith, Eve and Peter Fitzpatrick. 1999. *Laws of the Postcolonial: Law, Meaning, and Violence*. Ann Arbor: University of Michigan Press.

David, Kenneth H. 1977. *The New Wind: Changing Identities in South Asia*. Chicago: Aldine.

de Sousa Santos, Boaventura. 1987. "Law: A Map of Misreading: Toward a Postmodern Conception of Law." *Journal of Law and Society* 14: 279–302.

Dewar, Douglas, H. L. Garrett, and F. W. Buckler. 1924. "The Political Theory of the Indian Mutiny: A Reply and with a Rejoinder." *Transactions of the Royal Historical Society* 7, no. 4: 131–65.

Dirks, Nicholas. 1986. "From Little King to Landlord: Property, Law, and the Gift under the Madras Permanent Settlement." *Comparative Studies in Society and History* 28, no. 2: 307–33.

———. 1988. *The Hollow Crown: Ethnohistory of an Indian Kingdom*. Cambridge: Cambridge University Press.

———. 2001. *Castes of Mind: Colonialism and the Making of Modern India*. Princeton, NJ: Princeton University Press.

Diwan, Paras. 1987. *Muslim Law in Modern India*. 4th ed. Allahabad: Allahabad Law Agency.

DuBois, Thomas David, ed. 2009. *Casting Faiths: Imperialism and the Transformation of Religion in East and Southeast Asia*. New York: Palgrave Macmillan.

Dupret, Baudouin. 2004. *Standing Trial: Law and the Person in the Modern Middle East*. London: I. B. Tauris.

Dupret, Baudouin, Maurits Berger, and Laila Al-Zwaini. 1999. *Legal Pluralism in the Arab World*. The Hague: Kluwer Law International.

Eickelman, Dale and James Piscatori. 1990. *Muslim Travellers: Pilgrimage, Migration, and the Religious Imagination*. Berkeley: University of California Press.

Eisenstadt, S. N. 1966. *Modernization: Protest and Change*. Modernization of Traditional Societies Series. Englewood Cliffs, NJ: Prentice-Hall.

El Fadl, Khaled Abou. 2002. "Review: Islamic Law and Ambivalent Scholarship." Review of *The Justice of Islam: Comparative Perspectives on Islamic Law and Society* by Lawrence Rosen. *Michigan Law Review* 100, no. 6: 1421–43.

Epstein, Lee, J. Knight and O. Shvetsova. 2001. "The Role of Constitutional Courts in the Establishment and Maintenance of Democratic Systems of Government." *Law & Society Review* 35, no. 1: 117–64.

Esmeir, Samera. 2012. *Juridical Humanity: A Colonial History*. Redwood City, CA: Stanford University Press.

Ewing, Katherine Pratt, and Joint Committee on South Asia. 1988. *Shar'iat and Ambiguity in South Asian Islam*. Berkeley: University of California Press.

Fahmy, Khaled. 1999. "The Anatomy of Justice: Forensic Medicine and Criminal Law in Nineteenth-Century Egypt." *Islamic Law and Society* 6, no. 2: 224–71.

Fawaz, Leila Tarazi, C. A. Bayly, and Robert Ilbert. 2002. *Modernity and Culture: From the Mediterranean to the Indian Ocean*. New York: Columbia University Press.

Feldman, Noah. 2008. *Fall and Rise of the Islamic State*. Princeton, NJ: Princeton University Press.

Fisch, Jörg. 1983. *Cheap Lives and Dear Limbs: The British Transformation of the Bengal Criminal Law, 1769–1817*. Wiesbaden: F. Steiner.

Fisher, Michael. 1990. "The Resident in Court Ritual, 1764–1858." *Modern Asian Studies* 24, no. 3: 419–58.

Fitzpatrick, Peter. 1992. *The Mythology of Modern Law*. London: Routledge.

———. 2001. *Modernism and the Grounds of Law*. Cambridge Studies in Law and Society. Cambridge: Cambridge University Press.

Foucault, Michel. 2006. *Psychiatric Power: Lectures at the Collège de France, 1973–74*. Edited by Jacques Lagrange and translated by Graham Burchell. New York: Palgrave Macmillan.

Freitag, U., and W. G. Clarence-Smith. 1997. *Hadhrami Traders, Scholars and Statesmen in the Indian Ocean, 1750s–1960s*. Leiden: Brill.

Fyzee, Asaf Ali Asghar. 1955. *Outlines of Muhammadan Law*. 2nd ed. London: Oxford University Press.

———. 1965. *Cases in the Muhammadan Law of India and Pakistan*. Oxford: Clarendon.

Fyzee, Asaf Ali Asghar, and Arifin Bey. 1965. *Pokok-Pokok Hukum Islam*. Jakarta: Tintamas.

Fyzee, Asaf Ali Asghar, and Syed Tahir Mahmood. 1975. *Family Law and Social Change: A Festschrift for Asaf A. A. Fyzee*. Bombay: N. M. Tripathi.

Galanter, Marc. 1974. "Why the "Haves" Come Out Ahead: Speculations on the Limits of Legal Change." *Law & Society Review* 9: 95–160.

Gallop, Annabel Teh, Bernard Arps, and British Library. 1991. *Golden Letters: Writing Traditions of Indonesia* (Surat Emas: Budaya Tulis Di Indonesia). London: British Library, Yayasan Lontar.

Gallop, Annabel Teh, Ernst Ulrich Kratz, British Library., and Arkib Negara Malaysia. 1994. *The Legacy of the Malay Letter* (Warisan Warkah Melayu). London: British Library for the National Archives of Malaysia.

Geertz, Clifford. 1971. *Islam Observed: Religious Development in Morocco and Indonesia*. Chicago: University of Chicago Press.

———. 1983. *Local Knowledge: Further Essays in Interpretive Anthropology*. New York: Basic Books.

Geertz, Clifford, Hildred Geertz, and Lawrence Rosen. 1979. *Meaning and Order in Moroccan Society: Three Essays in Cultural Analysis*. Cambridge: Cambridge University Press.

Gerber, Haim. 1999. *Islamic Law and Culture, 1600–1840*. Studies in Islamic Law and Society. Boston: Brill.

Gilmartin, David. 1988. *Empire and Islam: Punjab and the Making of Pakistan*. Comparative Studies on Muslim Societies. Berkeley: University of California Press.

Ginsburg, Thomas. 2003. *Judicial Review in New Democracies: Constitutional Courts in East Asia*. Cambridge: Cambridge University Press.

Gledhill, A. 1962. "The Compilation of Customary Laws in the Punjab in the Nineteenth Century." In *La Rédaction des Coutumes dans le Passé et dans le Présent*, edited by J. Glissen. Brussels: Université libre de Bruxelles.

Göçek, Fatma Müge, and Shiva Balaghi. 1994. *Reconstructing Gender in the Middle East: Tradition, Identity, and Power*. New York: Columbia University Press.

Goldberg, Ellis. 1986. *Tinker, Tailor, and Textile Worker: Class and Politics in Egypt, 1930–1952*. Berkeley: University of California Press.

———. 1996. *The Social History of Labor in the Middle East*. Boulder, CO: Westview.

Goldberg, Ellis, Resat Kasaba, and Joel S. Migdal. 1993. *Rules and Rights in the Middle East: Democracy, Law, and Society*. Jackson School Publications in International Studies. Seattle: University of Washington.

Green, Nile. 2011. *Bombay Islam: The Religious Economy of the West Indian Ocean, 1840–1915*. Cambridge: Cambridge University Press.

Griffiths, John. 1986. "What Is Legal Pluralism?" *Journal of Legal Pluralism* 4: 1–55.

Guha, Ranajit. 1963. *A Rule of Property for Bengal: An Essay on the Idea of Permanent Settlement*. Paris: Mouton.

———. 1982. "Subaltern Studies: Writings on South Asian History and Society." Delhi: Oxford University Press.

———. 1988. *An Indian Historiography of India: A Nineteenth-Century Agenda and Its Implications, Sakharam Ganesh Deuskar Lectures on Indian History*. Calcutta: Centre for Studies in Social Sciences, Calcutta, by K.P. Bagchi & Co.

———. 1997a. *A Subaltern Studies Reader, 1986–1995*. Minneapolis: University of Minnesota Press.

———. 1997b. *Dominance without Hegemony: History and Power in Colonial India*. Cambridge, MA: Harvard University Press.

Gullick, J. M. 1958. "Indigenous Political Systems of Western Malaya." London: Athlone.

———. 1960. *A History of Selangor, 1742–1957*. Malayan Historical Series. Singapore: D. Moore for Eastern Universities Press.

———. 1963. *Malaya*. Nations of the Modern World. New York: Praeger.

———. 1987. *Malay Society in the Late Nineteenth Century: The Beginnings of Change*. East Asian Historical Monographs. Singapore: Oxford University Press.

———. 1992. *Rulers and Residents: Influence and Power in the Malay States, 1870–1920*. South-East Asian Historical Monographs. Singapore: Oxford University Press.

———. 1995a. *Adventures and Encounters: Europeans in South-East Asia*. Oxford in Asia Paperbacks. Kuala Lumpur: Oxford University Press.

———. 1995b. *Adventurous Women in South-East Asia: Six Lives*. Oxford in Asia Paperbacks. Kuala Lumpur: Oxford University Press.

———. 1998. *A History of Selangor, 1766–1939*. Petaling Jaya, Selangor Darul Ehsan, Malaysia: Falcon Press.

Gullick, J. M., and Royal Asiatic Society of Great Britain and Ireland–Malaysian Branch. 1993. *Glimpses of Selangor, 1860–1898*. Kuala Lumpur: Malaysian Branch of the Royal Asiatic Society.

Haddad, Yvonne Yazbeck, and Barbara Freyer Stowasser. 2004. *Islamic Law and the Challenges of Modernity*. Walnut Creek, CA: AltaMira.

Hallaq, Wael. 1984. "Was the Gate of Ijtihad Closed?" *International Journal of Middle Eastern Studies* 16.

———. 1983. "The Gate of Ijtihad: A Study in Islamic Legal History." PhD diss., University of Washington.

———. 1994. *Law and Legal Theory in Classical and Medieval Islam*. Aldershot, UK: Variorum.

———. 1997. *A History of Islamic Legal Theories: An Introduction to Sunni Usul Al-Fiqh*. Cambridge: Cambridge University Press.

———. 2001. *Authority, Continuity, and Change in Islamic Law*. Cambridge: Cambridge University Press.

———. 2004. *The Formation of Islamic Law*. Aldershot, UK: Ashgate/Variorum.

———. 2005. *The Origins and Evolution of Islamic Law*. Themes in Islamic Law. Cambridge: Cambridge University Press.

———. 2009. *Shari'a: Theory, Practice, Transformations*. New York: Cambridge University Press.

———. 2013. *The Impossible State: Islam, Politics, and Modernity's Moral Predicament*. New York: Columbia University Press.

Haltom, William, and Michael J. McCann. 2004. *Distorting the Law: Politics, Media, and the Litigation Crisis*. Chicago: University of Chicago Press.

Hamayotsu, Kikue. 2003. "Politics of Syariah Reform: The Making of the State Religio-Legal Apparatus." In *Malaysia: Islam, Society and Politics*, edited by Virginia Hooker and Norani Othman. Singapore: Institute of Southeast Asian Studies.

———. 2008. "Beyond Doctrine and Dogma: Religion and Politics in Southeast Asia." In *Southeast Asia in Political Science: Theory, Region, and Qualitative Analysis*, edited by Erik Kuhonta, Dan Slater, and Tuong Vu. Redwood City, CA: Stanford University Press.

———. 2010. "Crises of Identity in PAS and Beyond: Islam and Politics in Post 8 March Malaysia." *Round Table* 99, no. 407 (April): 163–75.

Harlow, Barbara. 1998. "Sappers in the Stacks: Colonial Archives, Land Mines, and Truth Commissions." *boundary 2*, vol. 25 no. 2: 179–204.

Hasan, Mushirul. 1985. *Communal and Pan-Islamic Trends in Colonial India*. Rev. and enl. ed. New Delhi: Manohar.

Hashmi, Shakila Tabassum. 1999. "The Trial of Bahadur Shah: Representation and Reality in Mughal India." Singapore: National University of Singapore.

Hasian, Marouf, Jr. 2002. "Nostalgic Longings and Imaginary Indias: Postcolonial Analysis, Collective Memories, and the Impeachment Trial of Warren Hastings." *Western Journal of Communication* 66, no. 2 (Spring).

Hastings, Warren. 1796. *Mr. Hastings' Review of the State of Bengal*. London: G. Kersey.

Heer, Nicholas, and Farhat Jacob Ziadeh. 1990. *Islamic Law and Jurisprudence*. Seattle: University of Washington Press.

Hefner, Robert W. 2011. *Shari'a Politics: Islamic Law and Society in the Modern World*. Bloomington: Indiana University Press.

Hefner, Robert W., and Patricia Horvatich, eds. 1997. *Islam in an Era of Nation-States: Politics and Religious Renewal in Southeast Asia*. Honolulu: University of Hawaii Press.

Hefner, Robert W., and Muhammad Qasim Zaman, eds. 2006. *Schooling Islam: The Culture and Politics of Modern Muslim Education*. Princeton, NJ: Princeton University Press.

Hibbert, Christopher. 1978. *The Great Mutiny: India, 1857*. London: Allen Lane.

Hill, Enid. 1988. "Al-Sanhuri and Islamic Law: The Place and Significance of Islamic Law in the Life and Work of 'Abd Al-Razzaq Ahmad Al-Sanhuri, Egyptian Jurist and Scholar, 1895–1971 [Part 1]." *Arab Law Quarterly* 3, no. 1: 33–64.

Hirschman, Charles. 1986. "The Making of Race in Colonial Malaya: Political Economy and Racial Ideology." *Sociological Forum* 1, no. 2 (Spring).

Hobsbawm, Eric, and Terence Ranger, eds. 1983. *The Invention of Tradition*. Cambridge: Cambridge University Press.

Hooker, M. B. 1970. *Readings in Malay Adat Laws*. Singapore: Singapore University Press.

———. 1973. "The Challenge of Malay Adat Law in the Realm of Comparative Law." *International and Comparative Law Quarterly* 22, no. 3: 492–514.

———. 1975. *Legal Pluralism: An Introduction to Colonial and Neo-Colonial Laws*. Oxford: Clarendon.

———. 1976. *The Personal Laws of Malaysia: An Introduction*. East Asian Historical Monographs. Kuala Lumpur: Oxford University Press.

———. 1983. *Islam in South-East Asia*. Leiden: Brill.

———. 1984. *Islamic Law in South-East Asia*. Singapore: Oxford University Press.

———. 1986. *Laws of South-East Asia*. 2 vols. London: Butterworth Legal.

Hopkins, A. G. 2002. *Globalization in World History*. London: Pimlico.

Horowitz, Donald L. 1994. "The Qur'an and the Common Law: Islamic Law Reform and the Theory of Legal Change." *American Journal of Comparative Law* 42, no. 3: 543–80.

Houben, Vincent J. H. 2003. "Southeast Asia and Islam." *Annals of the American Academy of Political and Social Science* 588: 149–70.

Hourani, Albert. 1962. *Arabic Thought in the Liberal Age*. London: Oxford University Press.

Hoyle, Mark. 1986a. "The Mixed Courts of Egypt, 1875–1885." *Arab Law Quarterly* 1, no. 1986: 436–51.

———. 1986b. "The Origins of the Mixed Courts of Egypt." *Arab Law Quarterly* 1, no. 2: 220–30.

Huda, Shahnaz. 2003. "Anglo-Mohammedan and Anglo-Hindu Law: Revisiting Colonial Codification." *Bangladesh Journal of Law* 7, no. 1.

Hunt, Alan. 1993. *Explorations in Law and Society: Toward a Constitutive Theory of Law*. New York: Routledge.

Husain, Iqbal. 1998. "The Rebel Administration of Delhi." *Social Scientist* 26, no. 1/4: 25–38.

Husain, Mahdi. 1958. *Bahadur Shah Ii and the War of 1857 in Delhi with Its Unforgettable Scenes*. Delhi: Atma Ram and Sons.

Hussin, Iza. 2007. "The Pursuit of the Perak Regalia: Law and the Making of the Colonial State." *Law and Social Inquiry* 32, no. 3.

———. 2010. "Islam, Ethnicity and the Problem of Mixed Legality: Two Malaysian Cases." *Yearbook of Islamic and Middle Eastern Law*.

———. 2012. "Revelation and Redemption: Colonial Precedents for the Politics of Islam in India and Malaysia." In *The Everyday Life of the State: A State-in-Society Approach*, edited by Adam White, 142–59. Seattle: University of Washington Press.

———. 2013. "Textual Trajectories: Re-reading the Majalah and Constitution in 1890s Johor." *Indonesia and the Malay World* 41, no. 120: 1–19.

———. 2014. "Misreading and Mobility in Constitutional Texts: A Nineteenth Century Case." *Indiana Journal of Global Legal Studies*, Symposium: Regulatory Translations: Expertise, Uncertainty and Affect in Transnational Legal Fields, vol. 21, no. 1: 145–58.

———. 2014. "Circulations of Law: Cosmopolitan Elites, Global Repertoires, Local Vernaculars." *Law and History Review* 32, no. 4: 773–95.

Ismail, Abdul Rahman Haji, Boon Kheng Cheah, Richard Olof Winstedt, and Royal Asiatic Society of Great Britain and Ireland–Malaysian Branch. 1998. *Sejarah Melayu*. Edited by Rumi baru. Kuala Lumpur: Malaysian Branch of the Royal Asiatic Society.

Iqbal, Muhammad. 1934. "The Principle of Movement in the Structure of Islam." In *The Reconstruction in Islam*. London: Oxford University Press.

Jackson, Sherman A. 1996. *Islamic Law and the State: The Constitutional Jurisprudence of Shihab Al-Din Al-Qarafi*. Studies in Islamic Law and Society. Leiden: Brill.

Jalal, Ayesha. 1990a. "Post-Orientalist Blues: Cultural Fusions and Confusions." *Indian Economic and Social History Review* 27, no. 1.

———. 1990b. Review of *Endgames of Empire: Studies of Britain's Indian Problem* by R. J. Moore (1988). *Journal of Asian Studies* 49, no. 2: 427–28.

James, Lawrence. 1998. "Raj: The Making and Unmaking of British India." New York: St Martin's.

Jantan, Sahari. 1975. "Mesyuarat Kerajaan Johor 1895–1914 [the Johor State Council 1895–1914]." Kuala Lumpur: Universiti Kebangsaan Malaysia.

Jeppie, Shamil. 1996. "Leadership and Loyalties: The Imams of Nineteenth Century Colonial Cape Town, South Africa." *Journal of Religion in Africa* 26, no. 2: 139–62.

Johansen, Baber. 1999. *Contingency in a Sacred Law: Legal and Ethical Norms in the Muslim Fiqh*. Leiden: Brill.

Jusoh, Hamid. 1991. *The Position of Islamic Law in the Malaysian Constitution*. Kuala Lumpur: Dewan Bahasa dan Pustaka.

Kader, S. A. 1998. *Muslim Law of Marriage & Succession in India: A Critique with a Plea for Optional Civil Code*. Calcutta: Eastern Law House.

Kamali, Mohammad Hashim. 1998. "Punishment in Islamic Law: A Critique of the Hudud Bill of Kelantan, Malaysia." *Arab Law Quarterly* 13, no. 3: 203–34.

———. 2000. *Islamic Law in Malaysia: Issues and Developments*. Kuala Lumpur: Ilmiah.

Kandiyoti, Deniz. 1991. *Women, Islam and the State*. Philadelphia: Temple University Press.

Keith, A. Berriedale, ed. 1922. *Speeches and Documents on Indian Policy, 1750–1921*. London: Oxford University Press.

Khan, Iqtidar Alam. 2001. "State in the Mughal India: Re-Examining the Myths of a Counter-Vision." *Social Scientist* 29, no. 1/2: 16–45.

Koh, K. L. 1966. "Attorney-General of Ceylon V. Reid. The Malayan Experience." *Modern Law Review* 29, no. 1: 88–94.

Kolff, D. H. A. 1992. "The Indian and the British Law Machines: Some Remarks on Law and Society in British India." In *European Expansion and Law: The Encounter of European and Indigenous Law in Nineteeth and Twentieth Century Africa and Asia*, edited by W. A. Mommsen and J. A. DeMoor, 201–35. Oxford: Berg.

Kosambi, Meera. 1996. "Gender Reform and Competing State Controls over Women: The Rukhmabai Case (1884–1888)." In *Social Reform, Sexuality, and the State*, 239–90. New Delhi: Sage.

Kozlowski, Gregory C. 1985. *Muslim Endowments and Society in British India*. Cambridge South Asian Studies. Cambridge: Cambridge University Press.

Kugle, Scott Alan. 2001. "Framed, Blamed and Renamed: The Recasting of Islamic Jurisprudence in Colonial South Asia." *Modern Asian Studies* 35, no. 2 (May): 257–313.

Laffan, Michael Francis. 2003. *Islamic Nationhood and Colonial Indonesia: The Umma Below the Winds*. Soas/Routledgecurzon Studies on the Middle East. New York: RoutledgeCurzon.

———. 2008. "The New Turn to Mecca: Snapshots of Arabic Printing and Sufi Networks in Late-Nineteenth Century Java." *Revue des Mondes Musulmans et de la Mediterranee*, edited by Catherine Miller and Niloofar Haeri. Aix-en-Provence, France: IREMAM.

Lahiri, Nayanjot. 2003. "Commemorating and Remembering 1857: The Revolt in Delhi and Its Afterlife." *World Archaeology* 35, no. 1: 35–60.

Lariviere, Richard W. 1989. "Justices and Panditas: Some Ironies in Contemporary Readings of the Hindu Legal." *Journal of Asian Studies* 48, no. 4: 757–69.

Lazarus-Black, Mindie. 1994. *Legitimate Acts and Illegal Encounters: Law and Society in Antigua and Barbuda*. Smithsonian Series in Ethnographic Inquiry. Washington, DC: Smithsonian Institution Press.

Lazarus-Black, Mindie, and Susan F. Hirsch. 1994. *Contested States: Law, Hegemony, and Resistance, After the Law*. New York: Routledge.

Lev, Daniel S. 1972. *Islamic Courts in Indonesia: A Study in the Political Bases of Legal Institutions*. Berkeley: University of California Press.

Lev, Daniel S., and Ruth Thomas McVey. 1996. *Making Indonesia*. Studies on Southeast Asia. Ithaca, NY: Southeast Asia Program, Cornell University.

Lijphart, Arend. 1971. "Comparative Politics and Comparative Method." *American Political Science Review* 65, no. 3: 682–93.

———. 1975. "The Comparable-Cases Strategy in Comparative Research." *Comparative Political Studies* 8: 158–77.

Lim, Teck Ghee. 1976. *Origins of a Colonial Economy*. Penang, Malaysia: Universiti Sains Malaya.

Lombardi, Clark. 2006. *Islamic Law as State Law in Modern Egypt: The Incorporation of the Sharia into Egyptian Constitutional Law*. Leiden: Brill.

Mahmood, Saba. 2005. *Politics of Piety: The Islamic Revival and the Feminist Subject*. Princeton, NJ: Princeton University Press.

———. 2009. *Is Critique Secular? Blasphemy, Injury, and Free Speech*. With Talal Asad, Wendy Brown, and Judith Butler. Berkeley: University of California Press.

Mahmood, Syed Tahir. 1980. *The Muslim Law of India*. Allahabad: Law Book Co.

———. 1983. *Muslim Personal Law: Role of the State in the Indian Subcontinent*. 2nd ed. Nagpur, India: All India Reporter.

Mahmood, Syed Tahir, and Institute of Objective Studies (New Delhi). 1997. *Islamic Law in Indian Courts since Independence: Fifty Years of Judicial Interpretation*. New Delhi: Institute of Objective Studies: Qazi.

Malik, Vijay, and Anwar Ahmad Qadri. 1988. *Muslim Law of Marriage, Divorce, and Maintenance: Being a Revised and Enlarged Version of A. A. Qadri's Commentary on the Dissolution of Muslim Marriage Act, 1939*. 2nd ed. Lucknow, India: Eastern Book Co.

Mallampali, Chandra. 2004. *Christians and Public Life in Colonial South India, 1863–1937: Contending with Marginality*. London: RoutledgeCurzon.

Mamdani, Mahmood. 1996. *Citizen and Subject: Contemporary Africa and the Leg-*

acy of Late Colonialism. Princeton Studies in Culture/Power/History. Princeton, NJ: Princeton University Press.

———. 1999. "Historicizing Power and Responses to Power: Indirect Rule and Its Reform." *Social Research* 66, no. 3: 859–87.

———. 2001. *When Victims Become Killers: Colonialism, Nativism, and the Genocide in Rwanda*. Princeton, NJ: Princeton University Press.

———. 2004. *Keywords: Identity*. New York: Other Press.

Mandal, Sumit. 2004. "Trans-Ethnic Solidarities, Racialization and Social Equality." In *The State of Malaysia: Ethnicity, Equity and Reform*, edited by Edmund Gomez. London: Routledge.

Mantena, Karuna. 2010. *Alibis of Empire: Henry Maine and the Ends of Liberal Imperialism*. Princeton, NJ: Princeton University Press.

Manzoor, Parvez. 2000. "Legal Rationality Vs. Arbitrary Judgement: Re-Examining the Tradition of Islamic Law." *Muslim World Book Review* 21, no. 1: 3–12.

Markhani, Mohammado. 1987. *Muslim Law Digest, 1820–1984*. Colombo, Sri Lanka: Mohammado Markhani.

Markovits, Claude. 2002. *A History of Modern India, 1480–1950*. Anthem South Asian Studies. London: Anthem.

Marshall, P. J. 1988. *Bengal: The British Bridgehead: Eastern India, 1740–1828*. New Cambridge History of India. Cambridge: Cambridge University Press.

———. 2000. *The Writings and Speeches of Edmund Burke*. Volume 7: *India: The Hastings Trial, 1789–1794*. Oxford: Clarendon.

Masud, Muhammad Khalid, Brinkley Morris Messick, and David Stephan Powers. 1996. *Islamic Legal Interpretation: Muftis and Their Fatwas*. Harvard Studies in Islamic Law. Cambridge, MA: Harvard University Press.

Matson, J. N. 1957. "The Conflict of Legal Systems in the Federation of Malaya and Singapore." *International and Comparative Law Quarterly* 6, no. 2: 243–62.

Maxwell, W. E. 1894. *Memorandum on the Introduction of a Land Code in the Native States in the Malay Peninsula*. Singapore: Government Printers.

Mayer, Ann. 2005. "The Internationalization of Religiously Based Resistance to International Human Rights Law." In *Global Justice and the Bulwarks of Localism: Human Rights in Context*, edited by Christopher L. Eisgruber and Andras Sajo. Leiden: Martinus Nijhoff.

McCann, Michael W. 1994. *Rights at Work: Pay Equity Reform and the Politics of Legal Mobilization, Language and Legal Discourse*. Chicago: University of Chicago Press.

———. 1996. "Legal Tactics and Everyday Resistance: A Political Science Assessment." *Studies in Law, Politics, and Society* 15 (Winter): 207–36.

Means, Gordon P. 1969. "The Role of Islam in the Political Development of Malaysia." *Comparative Politics* 1, no. 2: 264–84.

———. 1978. "Public Policy toward Religion in Malaysia." *Pacific Affairs* 51, no. 3: 384–405.

Mehta, Uday Singh. 1999. *Liberalism and Empire: Nineteenth Century British Liberal Thought*. Chicago: University of Chicago Press.

Merry, Sally Engle. 1988. "Legal Pluralism." *Law & Society Review* 22, no. 5: 869–96.

———. 1990. *Getting Justice and Getting Even: Legal Consciousness among Working-Class Americans, Language and Legal Discourse*. Chicago: University of Chicago Press.

———. 1992. "Anthropology, Law, and Transnational Processes." *Annual Review of Anthropology* 21: 357–97.

———. 2000. *Colonizing Hawai'i: The Cultural Power of Law*. Princeton Studies in Culture/Power/History. Princeton, NJ: Princeton University Press.

———. 2006. *Human Rights and Gender Violence: Translating International Law into Local Justice*. Chicago Series in Law and Society. Chicago: University of Chicago Press.

Merry, Sally Engle, and Donald Lawrence Brenneis. 2004. *Law & Empire in the Pacific: Fiji and Hawaii*. 1st ed. Santa Fe, NM: School of American Research Press.

Messick, Brinckley. 1989. "Just Writing: Paradox and Political Economy in Yemeni Legal Documents." *Cultural Anthropology* 4, no. 1: 26–50.

———. 1993. *The Calligraphic State: Textual Domination and History in a Muslim Society*. Comparative Studies on Muslim Societies. Berkeley: University of California Press.

———. 2003. "Property and the Private in a Sharia System." *Social Research* 70, no. 3: 711–35.

Metcalf, Barbara. 1982. *Islamic Revival in British India: Deoband, 1860–1900*. Princeton, NJ: Princeton University Press.

———. 1990. *Perfecting Women: Maulana Ashraf 'Ali Thanawi's Bihishti Zewar, a Partial Translation with Commentary*. Berkeley: University of California Press.

———. 2009. *Islam in South Asia in Practice*. Princeton, NJ: Princeton University Press.

Metcalf, Thomas. 1965. *The Aftermath of Revolt: India, 1857–1870*. Princeton, NJ: Princeton University Press.

———. 1979. *Land, Landlords, and the British Raj: Northern India in the Nineteenth Century*. Berkeley: University of California Press.

———. 1994. *Ideologies of the Raj*. Cambridge: Cambridge University Press.

———. 2008. *Imperial Connections: India in the Indian Ocean Arena, 1860–1920*. Berkeley: University of California Press.

Migdal, Joel S. 1975. *Peasants, Politics, and Revolution: Pressures toward Political and Social Change in the Third World*. Princeton, NJ: Princeton University Press.

———. 2001. *State in Society: Studying How States and Societies Transform and Constitute One Another*. Cambridge Studies in Comparative Politics. Cambridge: Cambridge University Press.

———. 2004. *Boundaries and Belonging: States and Societies in the Struggle to Shape Identities and Local Practices*. Cambridge: Cambridge University Press.

Migdal, Joel S., Atul Kohli, and Vivienne Shue. 1994. *State Power and Social Forces: Domination and Transformation in the Third World*. Cambridge Studies in Comparative Politics. Cambridge: Cambridge University Press.

Milne, R. S. and Diane K. Mauzy. 1980. *Politics and Government in Malaysia*. Vancouver: University of British Columbia Press.

Milner, A. C. 1982. *Kerajaan: Malay Political Culture on the Eve of Colonial Rule*. Tucson: Association for Asian Studies by the University of Arizona Press.

Milner, Anthony. 1991. "Inventing Politics: The Case of Malaysia." *Past and Present* 132: 104–29.

Mir Hosseini, Ziba. 1993. *Marriage on Trial: A Study of Islamic Family Law*. London: I. B. Tauris.

Mitchell, Timothy. 1988. *Colonising Egypt*. Cambridge Middle East Library. Cambridge: Cambridge University Press.

———. 2002. *Rule of Experts: Egypt, Techno-Politics, Modernity*. Berkeley: University of California Press.

Mitchell, Timothy, and California Digital Library. eScholarship. 1991. *Colonising Egypt*. Berkeley: University of California Press.

Mohamad Ariff, Abdul Aziz bin. 1996–97. "Undang-Undang Islam Di Kedah Sebelum Penjajahan Inggeris: Satu Penilaian Sejarah." Thesis: Universiti Kebangsaan Malaysia.

Moore, Erin. 1998. *Gender, Law, and Resistance in India*. Tucson: University of Arizona Press.

Moore, Erin, and University of California (System). 1998. *Keep Her Under Control: Law's Patriarchy in India*. Berkeley, CA: University of California Extension Center for Media and Independent Learning.

Moore, R. J. 1979. *Tradition and Politics in South Asia*. New Delhi: Vikas.

———. 2015. "South-East Asian Islam in the Nineteenth Century." In *The Cambridge History of Islam*, edited by M. Holt, Ann Lambton and Bernard Lewis, 155–81. Cambridge: Cambridge University Press.

Moore, Sally Falk. 1978. *Law as Process: An Anthropological Approach*. London: Routledge & Kegan Paul.

———. 2001. "Certainties Undone: Fifty Turbulent Years of Legal Anthropology, 1949–1999." *Journal of the Royal Anthropological Institute* 7, no. 1: 95–116.

Moosa, Ebrahim. 2009. "Colonialism and Islamic Law." In *Islam and Modernit: Key Issues and Debates*, edited by Muhammad Khalid Masud, Armando Salvatore, and Martin van Bruinessen. Edinburgh: Edinburgh University Press: 158–81.

Motadel, David. 2014. *Islam and the European Empires*. Oxford: Oxford University Press.

Moustafa, Tamir. 2003. "Law versus the State: The Judicialization of Politics in Egypt." *Law and Social Inquiry* 28: 883–930.

———. 2007. *The Struggle for Constitutional Power: Law, Politics, and Economic Development in Egypt*. Cambridge: Cambridge University Press.

———. 2013a. "Islamic Law, Women's Rights, and Popular Legal Consciousness in Malaysia." *Law and Social Inquiry* 38: 168–88.

———. 2013b. "Judging in God's Name: State Power, Secularism, and the Politics of Islamic Law in Malaysia." *Oxford Journal of Law and Religion* 2.

———. 2013c. "Liberal Rights versus Islamic Law? The Construction of a Binary in Malaysian Politics." *Law & Society Review* 47: 771–802.

Mowat, R. C. 1973. "From Liberalism to Imperialism: The Case of Egypt 1875–1887." *Historical Journal* 16, no. 1: 109–24.

Mukherjee, Ramkrishna. 1974. *The Rise and Fall of the East India Company*. New York: Monthly Review Press.

Mutalib, Hussin. 1990. *Islam and Ethnicity in Malay Politics*. Singapore: Oxford University Press.

Nadarajah, Nesamalar. 2000. *Johore and the Origins of British Control, 1895–1914*. Kuala Lumpur: Arenabuku.

Nair, Janaki. 1996. *Women and Law in Colonial India: A Social History*. New Delhi: Kali for Women.

Najjar, Fauzi M. 2000. "Islamic Fundamentalism and the Intellectuals: The Case of Nasr Hamid Abu Zayd." *British Journal of Middle Eastern Studies* 27, no. 2: 177–200.

Nandy, Ashis. 2003. *The Romance of the State and the Fate of Dissent in the Tropics*. New Delhi: Oxford University Press.

Nasir, Jamal J. 1990. *The Islamic Law of Personal Status*. 2nd ed. Arab and Islamic Laws Series. London: Graham & Trotman.

Nik Noriani Nik Badli Shah. "Legislative Provisions and Judicial Mechanisms for the Enforcement and Termination of the Islamic Marriage Contract in Malaysia." In *The Islamic Marriage Contract*, edited by Asifa Quraishi and Frank Vogel. Cambridge, MA: Harvard University Press, 2009.

———. 2009. *Case Studies in Islamic Family Law*. Cambridge, MA: Harvard University Press.

Ong, Aihwa, and Michael G. Peletz. 1995. *Bewitching Women, Pious Men: Gender and Body Politics in Southeast Asia*. Berkeley: University of California Press.

Palier, Bruno. 2005. "Ambiguous Agreement, Cumulative Change: French Social-Policy in the 1990s." In *Beyond Continuity: Institutional Change in Advanced Political Economies*, edited by Wolfgang Streeck and Kathleen Thelen, 127–44. Oxford: Oxford University Press.

Parkinson, C. Northcote. 1960. *British Intervention in Malaya, 1867–1877*. Singapore: University of Malaya Press.

Peletz, Michael G. 2002. *Islamic Modern: Religious Courts and Cultural Politics in Malaysia*. Princeton Studies in Muslim Politics. Princeton, NJ: Princeton University Press.

Perusek, Darshan. 1992. "Subaltern Consciousness and the Historiography of the Indian Rebellion of 1857." *NOVEL: A Forum on Fiction* 25, no. 3: 286–301.

Peter, Rudolph. 1994. "Muhammad Al-'Abbas Al-Mahdi (D. 1897), Grand Mufti of Egypt, and His 'Al-Fatawa Al-Mahdiyya." *Islamic Law and Society* 1, no. 1: 66–82.

Peters, F. E. 1995. *The Hajj: The Muslim Pilgrimage to Mecca and the Holy Places*. Princeton, NJ: Princeton University Press.

Peters, R. 2002. "From Jurists' Law to Statute Law or What Happens When the Sharia Is Codified." *Mediterranean Politics* 7, no. 3 (special issue on "Shaping the Current Islamic Refomation," edited by B. A. Roberson): 82–95.

Pierson, Paul and Theda Skocpol. 2002. "Historical Institutionalism in Contemporary Political Science." In *Political Science: State of the Discipline*, edited by Ira Katznelson and Helen Milner, 693–721. New York: Norton.

Poleman, Jenny F. 1942. "The Indian Princes' Treaty Rights." *Far Eastern Survey* 11, no. 19: 196–201.

Provencher, Ronald. 1990. Review of *Readings on Islam in Southeast Asia. Journal of the American Oriental Society* 110, no. 1: 164–65.

Qadri, Anwar Ahmad, and Vijay Malik. 1988. *Muslim Law of Marriage, Divorce, and Maintenance: Being a Revised and Enlarged Version of A.A. Qadri's Commentary on the Dissolution of Muslim Marriage Act, 1939*. 2nd ed. Lucknow, India: Eastern Book Co.

Qadri Pasha, Muhammad. 2006. *Kitab al-ahkam al-shar'iyya fi al-ahwal al-shakhsiyya wa al-mawarith*. Cairo/Alexandria.

Qanungo, Bhupen. 1967. "A Study of British Relations with the Native States of India, 1858–62." *Journal of Asian Studies* 26, no. 2: 251–65.

Rankin, G. C. 1942. "Civil Law in British India before the Codes." *Law Quarterly Review* 58: 469–.

Rawlings, H. F. 1986. "The Malaysian Constitutional Crisis of 1983." *International and Comparative Law Quarterly* 35, no. 2: 237–54.

Reid, Anthony. 1967. "Nineteenth Century Pan-Islam in Indonesia and Malaysia." *Journal of Asian Studies* 26, no. 2: 267–83.

———. 1988. *Southeast Asia in the Age of Commerce, 1450–1680*. New Haven, CT: Yale University Press.

———. 1993. *Southeast Asia in the Early Modern Era: Trade, Power, and Belief, Asia, East by South*. Ithaca, NY: Cornell University Press.

Reid, Anthony, and Lance Castles. 1975. *Pre-Colonial State Systems in Southeast Asia: The Malay Peninsula, Sumatra, Bali-Lombok, South Celebes*. Kuala Lumpur: MBRAS.

Ricci, R. 2011. *Islam Translated: Literature, Conversion, and the Arabic Cosmopolis of South and Southeast Asia*. Chicago: University of Chicago Press.

Richards, John F., and Trustees of the "E. J. W. Gibb Memorial." 1986. *Document Forms for Official Orders of Appointment in the Mughal Empire*. 1st ed,

"E. J. W. Gibb Memorial" Series. Cambridge: Trustees of the "E. J. W. Gibb Memorial."

Richland, Justin. 2012. "On Perpetuity: Juris-dictional Chronotopes and the Transcendent Immanence of Law and Tradition." Unpublished paper prepared for American Bar Foundation, Chicago, IL, October 17. With permission from the author.

Risso, Patricia. 1995. *Merchants & Faith: Muslim Culture and Commerce in the Indian Ocean*. Boulder, CO: Westview.

Robinson, Ronald. 1972. "Non-European Foundations of European Imperialism: Sketch for a Theory of Collaboration." In *Studies in the Theory of Imperialism*, edited by B. Sutcliffe Roger Owen, 117–42. New York: Longman.

Roesler, Shannon M. 2006. "Modern Legal Reform in Egypt: Shifting Claims to Legal Authority." *Cardozo Journal of International and Comparative Law* 393–428 (Fall).

Roff, William R. 1964. "The Malayo-Muslim World of Singapore at the Close of the Nineteenth Century." *Journal of Asian Studies* 24, no. 1: 75–90.

———. 1967. *The Origins of Malay Nationalism*. Yale Southeast Asia Studies. New Haven, CT: Yale University Press.

———. 1972. *Bibliography of Malay and Arabic Periodicals Published in the Straits Settlements and Peninsular Malay States 1876–1941*. With an Annotated Union List of Holdings in Malaysia, Singapore and the United Kingdom, London Oriental Bibliographies. London: Oxford University Press.

———. 1974. *Kelantan: Religion, Society, and Politics in a Malay State*. Kuala Lumpur: Oxford University Press.

———. 1983. "Whence Cometh the Law? Dog Saliva in Kelantan, 1937." *Comparative Studies in Society and History* 25, no. 2: 323–38.

———. 1987. *Islam and the Political Economy of Meaning: Comparative Studies of Muslim Discourse*. London: Croom Helm.

Rosen, Lawrence. 1980. "Equity and Discretion in a Modern Islamic Legal System." *Law & Society Review* 15, no. 2: 217–46.

———. 1989. *The Anthropology of Justice: Law as Culture in Islamic Society*. Lewis Henry Morgan Lectures. Cambridge: Cambridge University Press.

———. 2000. *The Justice of Islam: Comparative Perspectives on Islamic Law and Society*. Oxford: Oxford University Press.

———. 2002. *The Culture of Islam: Changing Aspects of Contemporary Muslim Life*. Chicago: University of Chicago Press.

Rudolph, Lloyd I., and Susanne Hoeber Rudolph. 1967. *The Modernity of Tradition: Political Development in India*. Chicago: University of Chicago Press.

———. 2001. "Living with Difference in India: Legal Pluralism and Legal Universalism in Historical Context." In *Religion and Personal Law in Secular India: A Call to Judgement*, edited by Gerald J. Larson, 36–65. Bloomington: Indiana University Press.

Rudolph, Susanne Hoeber, and James P. Piscatori. 1997. *Transnational Religion and Fading States*. Boulder, CO: Westview.

Rudolph, Susanne Hoeber, Lloyd I. Rudolph, and Paul R. Brass. 1972. *Education and Politics in India*. Studies in Organization, Society, and Policy. Cambridge, MA: Harvard University Press.

Said, Edward. 1978. *Orientalism: Western Representations of the Orient*. New York: Pantheon.

———. 1981. *Covering Islam: How the Media and the Experts Determine How We See the Rest of the World*. 1st ed. New York: Pantheon.

———. 1983. *The World, the Text, and the Critic*. Cambridge, MA: Harvard University Press.

———. 1993. *Culture and Imperialism*. 1st ed. New York: Knopf.

Saleh, Nabil. 1993. "Civil Codes of Arab Countries: The Sanhuri Codes." *Arab Law Quarterly* 8, no. 2: 161–67.

Sanhuri, Abd al-Razzaq Ahmad. 1967. *Masadir Al-Haqq Fi Al-Fiqh Al-Islami, Dirasah Muqaranah Bi-Al-Fiqh Al-Gharbi*. al-Qahirah: Jami'at al-Duwal al-Arabiyah, Ma'had al-Buhuth wa-al-Dirasat al-'Arabiyah.

Sarat, Austin and Thomas Kearns, ed. 1991. *The Fate of Law*. Ann Arbor: University of Michigan Press.

Sarkar, Sumit. 1997. *Writing Social History*. Delhi: Oxford University Press.

Schickler, Eric. 2001. *Disjointed Pluralism: Institutional Innovation and the Development of the US Congress*. Princeton, NJ: Princeton University Press.

Schmidhauser, John R. 1992. "Legal Imperialism: Its Enduring Impact on Colonial and Post-Colonial Judicial Systems." *International Political Science Review* 13, no. 3: 321–34.

Schmitt, Carl. 2006. *Political Theology: Four Chapters on the Concept of Sovereignty*. Translated by George Schwab. Chicago: University of Chicago Press.

Scott, David. 2004. *Conscripts of Modernity: The Tragedy of Colonial Enlightenment*. Durham, NC: Duke University Press.

Scott, James C. 1968. *Political Ideology in Malaysia: Reality and the Beliefs of an Elite*. Yale Southeast Asia Studies. New Haven, CT: Yale University Press.

———. 1976. *The Moral Economy of the Peasant: Rebellion and Subsistence in Southeast Asia*. New Haven, CT: Yale University Press.

———. 1985. *Weapons of the Weak: Everyday Forms of Peasant Resistance*. New Haven, CT: Yale University Press.

———. 1990. *Domination and the Arts of Resistance: Hidden Transcripts*. New Haven, CT: Yale University Press.

———. 1998. *Seeing Like a State: How Certain Schemes to Improve the Human Condition Have Failed*. Yale Agrarian Studies. New Haven, CT: Yale University Press.

Shabbir, Mohd. 1988. *Muslim Personal Law and Judiciary*. Allahabad, India: Law Book Co.

Shaham, Ron. 1994. "Judicial Divorce at the Wife's Initiative: The Shari'a Courts of Egypt, 1920–1955." *Islamic Law and Society* 1, no. 2: 217–57.

Shalakany, Amr. 2001. "Between Identity and Redistribution: Sanhuri, Genealogy and the Will to Islamise." *Islamic Law and Society* 8, no. 2: 201–44.

Shapiro, Martin. 1986. *Courts: A Comparative and Political Analysis*. Chicago: University of Chicago.

Sharafi, Mitra. 2010. "The Marital Patchwork of Colonial South Asia: Forum Shopping from Britain to Baroda." *Law and History Review* 28, no. 4: 979–1009.

Shepard, William E. 1996. "Muhammad Said Al-Ashmawi and the Application of the Sharia in Egypt." *International Journal of Middle East Studies* 28, no. 1: 39–58.

Sikand, Yoginder. 2005. *Bastions of the Believers: Madrasas and Islamic Education in India*. New Delhi: Penguin.

Sinha, Mrinalini. 1997. *Colonial Masculinity: The "Manly Englishman" and The "Effeminate Bengali" In the Late Nineteenth Century*. New Delhi: Kali for Women.

Siraj, M. 1968. "Recent Changes in the Administration of Muslim Family Law in Malaysia and Singapore." *International and Comparative Law Quarterly* 17, no. 1: 221–32.

Skocpol, Theda and Margaret Somers. 1980. "The Use of Comparative History in Macrosocial Inquiry." *Studies in Society and History* 22, no. 2: 174–97.

Skovgaard-Petersen, Jakob. 1997. *Defining Islam for the Egyptian State: Muftis and Fatwas of the Dar Al-Ifta*. Leiden: Brill.

Slater, Dan. 2003. "Iron Cage in an Iron Fist: Authoritarian Institutions and the Personalisation of Power in Malaysia." *Comparative Politics* 36, no. 1 (October): 81–101.

Slater, Dan, Erik Kuhonta, and Tuong Vu, eds. 2008. *Southeast Asia in Political Science: Theory, Region and Qualitative Analysis*. Redwood City, CA: Stanford University Press.

Souaiaia, Ahmed E. 2002. *Islamic Law & Government*. San Jose, CA: Writers Press Club.

Starr, June. 1992. *Law as Metaphor: From Islamic Courts to the Palace of Justice*. Albany: State University of New York Press.

Starr, June, and Jane Fishburne Collier. 1989. *History and Power in the Study of Law: New Directions in Legal Anthropology*. Anthropology of Contemporary Issues. Ithaca, NY: Cornell University Press.

Steinmetz, George. 2007. *The Devil's Handwriting: Precoloniality and the German Colonial State in Qingdao, Samoa, and Southwest Africa*. Chicago: University of Chicago Press.

———. 2008. "The Colonial State as a Social Field." *American Sociological Review* 73, no. 4 (August): 589–612.

Stephens, Julia. 2013. "The Phantom Wahhabi: Liberalism and the Muslim fanatic in mid-Victorian India." *Modern Asian Studies* 47, no. 1 (January): 22–52.

Stilt, Kristen A. 2004. "Islamic Law and the Remaking of the Iraqi Legal System." *George Washington International Law Review* 36: 695–756.

Stokes, E. 1978. *The Peasant and the Raj.* Cambridge: Cambridge University Press.

Stone Sweet, Alec. 2000. *Governing with Judges: Constitutional Politics in Europe.* Oxford: Oxford University Press.

Streets, Heather. 2000. "Orientalism Transposed: The Impact of the Colonies on British Culture (Review)." *Victorian Studies* 43, no. 1: 144–46.

Strong. Traci B. 2012. *Politics without Vision: Thinking without a Banister in the Twentieth Century.* Chicago: University of Chicago Press.

Swettenham, Frank Athelstane. 1898. *Unaddressed Letters.* London: J. Lane.

———. 1903. *Malay Sketches.* 3rd ed. London: J. Lane.

———. 1907. *British Malaya; an Account of the Origin and Progress of British Influence in Malaya.* London: J. Lane.

———. 1914. *Vocabulary of the English and Malay Languages: With Notes.* 11th ed. 2 vols. Shanghai: Kelly & Walsh.

———. 1942. *Footprints in Malaya.* London: Hutchinson.

Tageldin, Shaden. 2011. *Disarming Words: Empire and the Seductions of Translation in Egypt.* Berkeley: University of California Press.

Tagliacozzo, Eric. 2009. *Southeast Asia and the Middle East: Islam, Movement, and the Longue Duree.* Redwood City, CA: Stanford University Press.

Tahtawi, Ahmad ibn Muhammad, and Jeanette A. Wakin. 1972. *The Function of Documents in Islamic Law: The Chapters on Sales from Tahtawi's Kitab Al-Shurut Al-Kabir.* 1st ed. Albany: State University of New York Press.

Tambe, Ashwini. 2000. "Colluding Patriarchies: The Colonial Reform of Sexual Relations in India." *Feminist Studies* 26, no. 3.

Taylor, E. N. 1948–49. "Malay Family Law." *Journal of the Malayan Branch of the Royal Asiatic Society* 15, no. 1: 41–.

Thelen, Kathleen, and James Mahoney, eds. 2010. *Explaining Institutional Change: Ambiguity, Agency, and Power.* New York: Cambridge University Press.

Tignor, Robert. 1963. "The 'Indianization' of the Egyptian Administration under British Rule." *American Historical Review* 68, no. 3 (April): 636–61.

———. 1966. *Modernization and British Colonial Rule in Egypt, 1882–1914.* Princeton Studies on the Near East. Princeton, NJ: Princeton University Press.

Tilly, Charles. 1981. *As Sociology Meets History, Studies in Social Discontinuity.* New York: Academic Press.

———. 2002. *Stories, Identities, and Political Change.* Lanham, MD: Rowman & Littlefield.

———. 2005. *Identities, Boundaries, and Social Ties.* Boulder, CO: Paradigm.

———. 2006a. *Regimes and Repertoires.* Chicago: University of Chicago Press.

———. 2006b. *Why?* Princeton, NJ: Princeton University Press.

Tilly, Charles, and Russell Sage Foundation. 1984. *Big Structures, Large Processes, Huge Comparisons.* Russell Sage Foundation 75th Anniversary Series. New York: Russell Sage Foundation.

Tilly, Charles, and Arthur L. Stinchcombe. 1997. *Roads from Past to Future, Legacies of Social Thought*. Lanham, MD: Rowman & Littlefield.

Tilly, Charles, and Sidney G. Tarrow. 2007. *Contentious Politics*. Boulder, CO: Paradigm.

Tinker, Hugh. 1958. "1857 and 1957: The Mutiny and Modern India." *International Affairs* Royal Institute of International Affairs 34, no. 1: 57–65.

Tomlins, Christopher, and John Comaroff. 2011. "'Law as . . .': Theory and Practice in Legal History." 1 *UC Irvine Law Review* 1039.

Turner, Bryan. 1974. *Weber and Islam: A Critical Study*. Routledge & Kegan Paul.

Unger, Roberto. 1976. *Law in Modern Society*. New York: Free Press.

Vetch, R. H. 1905. *Life of Lieut-General the Hon. Sir Andrew Clarke*. London: John Murray.

Vikør, Knut S. 2000. "The Shari'a and the Nation State: Who Can Codify the Divine Law?" In *The Middle East in a Globalized World*, edited by Bjørn Olav Utvik and Knut Vikør, 220–50. Bergen.

———. 2005. *Between God and the Sultan: A History of Islamic Law*. New York: Oxford University Press.

Vogel, Frank E., and Samuel L. Hayes. 1998. *Islamic Law and Finance: Religion, Risk, and Return*. Arab and Islamic Laws Series. The Hague: Kluwer Law International.

Voll, John. 1994. "Islam as a Special World System." *Journal of World History* 5, no. 2: 213–26.

———. 2005. "Sufi Brotherhoods: TransCultural/Transstate Networks in the Muslim World." In *Interactions: Transregional Perspectives on World History*, edited by Jerry H. Bentley, Renate Bridenthal, and Anand A. Yang. Honolulu: University of Hawai'i Press: 30–47.

Washbrook, D. 1999. "India 1818–1860: The Two Faces of Colonialism." In *The Oxford History of the British Empire*, vol. 3, edited by Andrew Porter and W. Roger Louis, 395–421. Oxford: Oxford University Press.

Webster, Anthony. 1998. *Gentlemen Capitalists: British Imperialism in South East Asia, 1770–1890*. International Library of Historical Studies. New York: Tauris Academic Studies.

Wedeen, Lisa. 1999. *Ambiguities of Domination: Politics, Rhetoric, and Symbols in Contemporary Syria*. Chicago: University of Chicago Press.

———. 2008. *Peripheral Visions: Publics, Power, and Performance in Yemen*. Chicago: University of Chicago Press.

Weeks, Emily. 1998. "About Face: Sir David Wilkie's Portraits of Mehmet Ali, Pasha of Egypt." In *Orientalism Transposed: The Impact of the Colonies on British Culture*, edited by Julie Codell and D. S. Macleod, 46–. Vermont: Ashgate.

Wilkinson, R. J., Cuthbert Woodville Harrison, and Perak Council. 1907. *Papers on Malay Subjects History*. Kuala Lumpur: F.M.S. Gov't. Press.

Wilkinson, R. J., and J. Rigby. 1922. *Papers on Malay Subjects Law*. Kuala Lumpur: F.M.S. Gov't. Press.

Wilkinson, R. J., and Richard Olof Winstedt. 1920. *Papers on Malay Subjects Life and Customs*. Singapore: Kelly and Welsh.

Wink, André. 1990. *Al-Hind, the Making of the Indo-Islamic World*. Leiden: Brill.

Wink, André, and Consiglio nazionale delle ricerche (Italy). Committee 9. 1991. *Islam, Politics, and Society in South Asia*. New Delhi: Manohar.

Winstedt, Richard Olof. 1931. *The Constitution of the Colony of the Straits Settlements and of the Federated and Unfederated Malay States*. London: Royal Institute of International Affairs.

———. 1944. *Britain and Malaya, 1786–1941*. London: Longmans.

———. 1950a. *Malay Proverbs*. 1st ed. London: Murray.

———. 1950b. *The Malays: A Cultural History*. New York: Philosophical Library.

———. 1955. *An Unabridged Malay-English Dictionary*. Singapore: Kelly & Walsh.

———. 1958. *Malaya and Its History*. 5th ed. London: Hutchinson University Library.

———. 1969. *Start from Alif: Count from One: an Autobiographical Mémoire*. Kuala Lumpur: Oxford University Press.

———. 1982. *The Malay Magician: Being Shaman, Saiva and Sufi*. Oxford in Asia Paperbacks. Kuala Lumpur: Oxford University Press.

Winstedt, Richard Olof, Kay Kim Khoo, and Hussein Ismail. 1992. *A History of Johore, 1365–1941*. M.B.R.A.S. Reprints. Kuala Lumpur: Malaysian Branch of the Royal Asiatic Society by Academe Art & Printing Services Sdn. Bhd.

Winstedt, Richard Olof, and R. J. Wilkinson. 1952. *An English-Malay Dictionary: Roman Characters*. 3rd. ed. Singapore: Kelley & Walsh.

Winstedt, Richard Olof, R. J. Wilkinson, and William Edward Maxwell. 1974. *A History of Perak*. Kuala Lumpur: Malaysian Branch of the Royal Asiatic Society.

Wood, Leonard. 2011. *Islamic Legal Revivalism in Egypt: The Reception of European Law and Foundations of Modern Arab Legal Thought*. PhD diss., Harvard University.

Yengoyan, Aram, and A. Becker. 1981. *Imagination of Reality: Essays in South East Asian Coherence Systems*. Norwood, NJ: Ablex.

Zainuddin, Abdul Majid, and William R. Roff. 1978. *The Wandering Thoughts of a Dying Man: The Life and Times of Haji Abdul Majid Bin Zainuddin*. Kuala Lumpur: Oxford University Press.

Zeghal, Malika. 2013a. "Competing Ways of Life: Islamism, Secularism and Public Order in the Tunisian Tradition." *Constellations* 20, no. 2: 254–74.

———. 2013b. "Veiling and Unveiling Muslim Women: State Coercion, Islam, and the Disciplines of the Heart." *The Construction of Belief: Reflections on the Thought of Mohamed Arkoun*, 127–49. London: Saqi.

Ziadeh, Farhat Jacob. 1968. *Lawyers, the Rule of Law and Liberalism in Modern Egypt*. Palo Alto, CA: Hoover Institution on War, Revolution, and Peace, Stanford University.

———. 1979. *Property Law in the Arab World: Real Rights in Egypt, Iraq, Jordan, Lebanon, Libya, Syria, Saudi Arabia and the Gulf States*. London: Graham & Trotman.

Primary Documents

Colonial Office Records, London

C3285. Federated Malay States Residents Report 1883.
C4192. Perak Council Minute.
CO 273/70. Testimony of Mr. Dorville, British-appointed tax collector, June 21, 1876.
CO 273/87. Transcripts of the Inquiry into the Murder of J. W. W. Birch: Testimony of Native Witnesses.
CO 273/88. Birch to Colonial Office, December 14, 1874 and April 2, 1875.
CO 882/4/22. Supplementary Correspondence Straits Settlements 1873–1884.
CO 883/3/72. Straits Settlements Government Gazette Extraordinary: Singapore, Saturday, March 25, 1876.
CO Secret 39. 1878. Letter to Governor of Straits Settlements re: Maharaja of Johor.
CO Secret 41. 1878. Letter from Governor of Straits Settlements.
Correspondence relating to the Land Revenue System of the Straits Settlements, 1837–1844. No. 36: Letter from Commissioner of Lands to the Colonial Secretary. Singapore, October 3, 1883.
Parliament. "Reports from Committees of the House of Commons." Great Britain: House of Commons, East Indies, 1772–73; reprinted 1804.
Perak. 1899. The Laws of Perak: Orders in Council and Enactments Passed by the State Council 1877–1896. Taiping: Printed at the Perak Government Printing Office 1899.
———. 1905. Laws of Perak: 1:1877–01, 2:1901–03. Kuala Lumpur.
Punjab Government Record Office. "The Trial of Muhammed Bahadur Shah." Lahore: Punjab Government Record Office, 1932.
Victoria's Proclamation, 1 November 1858. British Library: BL/Mss_Eur_D620.

Arkib Negara Malaysia, Kuala Lumpur

Panduan Sumber- Sumber Bahan Mengenai Islam.
Panduan Sumber-Sumber Bahan Mengenai Kebudayaan Melayu.
Senarai Penerimaan Arkib Diraja: Acquisitions/1957–1967.
Senarai Surat Persendirian Pelbagai.
Suratan Hervey.
Suratan Swettenham.

S. Penerimaan William Roff.
Warisan Sejarah Kedah Darul Aman: KL: Arkib Negara Malaysia, 2003.
Panduan Sumber-Sumber Sejarah Malaysia: Jilid 5.1: Panduan Rekod-Rekod Cawangan Arkib Negara Malaysia Cawang Johor/Melaka.
Pejabat Tengku Besar Pahang (Majlis Anggota Islam Pahang) 1920–1936 (jilid 1).
SUK Kedah 1326–1329: (1907–1910): setiausaha kerajaan kedah.
Majlis Ugama Islam Kelantan 1922–1929.
Selangor Secretariat: British Resident's Office 1880–1920s.
1957/ 0004363: (16.07.1885.) Enquiring whether the kadi has power to imprison the Mahomedans, and if the gaol is to be opened for their execution etc.
British Resident's Office Negeri Sembilan 1889–1895.
Senarai Fail Mahkamah Tinggi Alor Setar K.5B: 1332, 13341–44, 4653, 55.
Senarai Fail Mahkamah Tinggo Selangor (FMS) 1910–1963.
N/PU 1: Laws of Negeri Sembilan, 1883–1902.
D/MH 1: Mahkamah files.
D/Misc: Satu Risalah Pengajaran bagi Hakim-Hakim.
K/PU 1: Kedah Enactments 1925, Laws of Kedah (Ondang-Ondang Kedah 1893)
K/PU 1/2: Kedah Courts Enactment Procedure Code 1327.
K/SUK 1: Annual Reports of the Sec of State 1905–1908.
K/SUK 2: Govt Gazettes 1925.
K/SUK 7: Konvensyen Sejarah Negeri Kedah 28.11–1.12.1981.
RS/K/SM (1): Buku Cenderamata Jubli Intan Maktab Sultan Abdul Hamid 1908–1968.
P124 Agreement with the King of Quedah for the Cession of the Prince of Wales Island 1786.
P123 Treaty with the King of Quedah 1791.
P125 Treaty with the King of Quedah 1800.
J/PU 1: Laws of Johore 1918–1935.
J/Misc: Report on Johore 1879.
A/PU 1: SS Penal Code adopte din Perak 1884, Orders of the Sultan in Council 1877–1895.
A/SUK 5: Government Gazettes.

Private Papers

Mohammad Hassan, Abdul Hamid b., Tuan Haji. 1874–1962. SP 66.
Hervey, Dudley Francis Amelius. 1869–1939.
SP 16/2/1: Notes on the Constitution of Jelebu 10.6.1884.
SP 16/2/4: Constitution of Johol 1.11.1884.
SP 16/2/5: Origin of Penghulu of Johol 1.11.1884.
SP16/2/8: Naning Customs of Inheritance July 1892.
Sp16/2/13: Rights of the Chiefs of Rembau.

SP16/2/14: Customary Laws of Sri Menanti 23–27.1. 1886.

SP16/4/4: Notes on Johore.

SP16/4/5: Story on the death of Raja Haji as told by E Wasterhout.

SP16/5/1: Short Treatise on Muhammdan Law of Inheritance 23.8.1892.

SP 16/5/2 Correspondence to and from Kathi Wan Omar of Malacca and oficial papers regarding the Muhammdan Law of inheritance 17–25.3.1893.

SP/16/5/3: Muhammadan Law of Inheritance.

SP 16/5/4: Translation of a Malay account of the spread of Muhammadanisn in Eastern Sumatra.

SP 16/5/5: Notes on an aspect of religion.

SP16/6/2: Miscellaneous correspondence between FA Swettenham and the rulers and dignitaries of Acheh, Kedah, Kelantan, Perak, Siak and Terengganu.

SP16/7/3: Straits Settlements Legislative Council Paper regarding the Administration of Native States.

SP 16/7/6: Minute by British Resident Perak on a Draft Land Code for Perak 13.6.1894.

SP 16/7/7: Malayan Information Agency reports on the Administration.

SP 38. Sheppard, Mubin, Tan Sri, Dato, Haji. 1895–1982.

SP 9/6/76. Raja Mansur, Raja Kamaralzaman b., Raja Dihilir Perak. 1862–1970.

SP 60. Syed Sheikh al-Hady, Syed Alwi b. 1919–1970.

SP 24. SP24/1/1: Riwayat Hidup Syed Sheikh b Ahmad b Hassan al-Hady, oleh anaknya Alwi b Sheikh al-Hady. Syed Ahmad al-Hadi, Syed Sheikh b. 1835–1967.

SP 4/1. Sir Hugh Low, diary, 1877, vol 1.

SP 2/1. Sir Hugh Clifford, diary 1893.

SP109/E/3. Sultan Abdullah, Gambar-gambar sulit: Gambar menunjukkan Istana Sultan Abdullah di Seychelles.

SP12/2/1. Swettenham. Report of the Commissioner under Clause XIII, of the 'Perak Engagement' dated 20th January, 1874 and Journal of their expedition to Perak.

SP 12/8/2. Frank Swettenham. Daily Journal Entires during FAS stay on the langat river 13 aug-2 sept 1874.

SP12/64. Breach of Promise in Malaya. Translations of two letters of Aminah binti Awang Jah and Imam Prang Indra Setia Raja.

SP 10/196/16. Sheikh Tahir Perjanjian Inggeris Belanda 1824.

SP 10/11/1. Sheikh Tahir. Pembangunan Umat.

SP 176/8/5. William Roff: Indirect rule in Kedah 1910–1915.

SP43/6/1. Nik Ahmad Kamal.

SP6/53:Baginda Sultan Omar ibnu Sultan Ahmad Shah (1839–1876) Terengganu: Ikrar persahabatan dpd Raja Kelantan (1844).

SP6/6: Membawa balek ka-Terengganu Tuan Sheikh Abdul-Rahman anak beranak supaya di-hukom dengan hukom shara', dpd Sultan Mahmud Mudzaffar Shah Lingga, 1850.

SP6/51: Kenyataan berkenaan kedudokan dan kuasa Sultan, dpd Resident Councillor Spore 1858.

SP6/55: Nasehat jangan membuat kesalahan lagi, dpd Bendahara Seri Maharaja Pahang kdp Enche Wan Ahmad 1858.

SP6/30: Pergaduhan Wan Embong, dpd Bendahara Seri Maharaja Pahang.

SP66/31: Tuan Hj Abdul Hamid,—Al-Ikhwan, 1928; 24: Rengkasan Penyata Surohanjaya atas Pelajaran 1947.

SPP/A/1: Susunan Surat Kuasa daripada Kerajaan Perak.

2: Riwayat negeri Perak dan Raja2 serta orang besar-besar.

3: Why Resident JWW Birch was murdered.

4: Surat-surat Kadhi kepada Residen Perak.

5: Surat-surat Sultan Abdullah Mohd Shah.

6: Dokumen mengenai Negeri Perak dalam Bahasa Arab.

7: Salasilah keturunan Syed di Perak.

8: Adat lembaga Orang-Orang Melayu didalam Negeri Perak.

Negeri Sembilan

SPP/N/2: Adat Perpateh Naning.

SPP/N/3: Sejarah dan Adat Negri Sembilan.

SPP/N/4: Riwayat hidup Dato' Shahbandar tunggal Khatib Maharaja Kepayang.

SPP/N/5: Kejatuhan Kota Lukut.

SPP/N/6: Asal usul Adat Perpateh.

Kelantan

SPP/D/11: Geran tanah lama, Mukim of Mahang West, Daerah Pangkal Kalong GTL: no. 1526.

SPP/D/15–17: Surat-surat Tengku Chik Abdullah.

Kedah

SPP/K/10: Surat-surat Yang Dipertuan Majlis Negeri Kedah 1897–1904. SPP/K/T/2: Correspondence between Kedah and Siam 1887–1895.

Johore

SPP/J/3: Perkara Pasal 15 dalam Undang-Undang Tubuh Kerajaan Johor.

SPP/J/4: Surat tauliah mengangkat dan melantik ahli Majlis Mesyuarat Negeri Johor 1.7.54.

SPP/J/7: Hukum Syariat Johor 1939–1958.

Terengganu

SPP/T/3: surat nikah kerajaan terengganu 1324
SPP/9: surat beranak dan surat pengakuan En Pakiri (20.11.1897, oct 1905)
SPP/26: sijil cungkil, sijil akuan beranak dan tiga surat. 18.5.17, 22.9.53
SPP/44: buku daftar nikah kahwain negeri pesut tahun hijrah 1311.
SPP/48: undang-undang 99
SPP/57a: Kitab hukum/hakam syed ahmad (b arab)
SPP /62: isu mengenai istana kg glam dan hak waris2 sultan hussain

JMBRAS

Kempe, J.E. "Malay Legal Digest Compiled for 'Abd al Ghafur Muhayudin Shah, Sultan of Pahang." MB 21, no. 1: 1–67 (April 1948).
———. "A Malay Legal Miscellany." MB 25, no. 1: 1–19 (Aug 1952).
Peletz, M. "Malaya Social History." MB 54, no. 3: 73–74 (Dis 1981).
Wakeman, R. W. "The 'Pahang Kanun.'" MB 24, no. 3: 150–51 (October 1951).
Winstedt, R.O. Kitab Seribu Masalah. MB 3, no. 1: 84–85 (April 1925).
———. The early Muhammedan missionaries. SB 81, nos. 5–6 (March 1920).

Malaya in History

Abdullah Alwi Haji Hassan. "Kelantan: Islamic Legal History before 1909." AP/56/C/Vol 23, 1980 ms10.
Fawzi Basri. "Perkembangan: Peranan Jabatan Agama Johor 1895–1940." AP/56/D, vol 18, no. June 1, 1975, ms 10.
Muhammad Sarim Haji Mustajab. "Sheikh Muhammad Tahir." AP/56/D vol. 10, no. 2 (December 1977), ms 1.
Nik Abdul Aziz Nik Hassan. "Pendekatan Pengajaran Islam do N Sembilan." AP/56/C, Bil 11, 1982, ms 50.

Theses

Abol, Ai'sah. "Pentadbiran Mahkamah Syariah Negero Perak." UIA 1987.
Ahmad, Hazlina bt. "Perkembangan pendidikan di Tanah Melayu." Maktab Perguruan Seri Kota.
A. Karim, Zulkeflee b. "Madrasah Idrisiah Bukit Chandan." UM 1988.
Cha, Haliza bt. "Tokoh Islam Perlis." UKM 1988.
Has Zanah Mehat. "Sejarah Perundangan di Kedah sehingga 1957." UM 1980.
Jaid, Ariza bt. "Sejarah dan peranan Bahagian Agama Jabatan Perdana Menteri (Pusat Islam)." UKM 1988.

Latif, Jamlah bt. "Melaka: Istana. Maktan Perguruan Raja Melewar." NS 1987.
McDonnell, Mary Byrne. "The Conduct of Hajj." Columbia 1987.
Mohammad Bisri, Nurul Huda bt. "Pentadbiran Undang-Undang Keluarga Islam Negeri Selangor." UM 1990.
Suaidi b. Otek. "Undang-Undang Kedah: Gambaran Masyarakat Melayu Lama dan Sebagai Hasil Sastera." UPM Serdang: 1988.
Wan Embong, Wan Azizah bt. "Majalah-2 yang diterbitkan oleh Institusi Pentadbiran Agama Islam." UKM 1988.

Law Reports

P/PEG 7: Legal Reports on Ordinances 1896–1910
A Digest of Reported Cases, FMS
Legal Reports
P/Peg: Commentaries of the Indian Penal Code 1860
Conference of Rulers:
P/MR1: Minutes of the Session of Chiefs, FMS 1897
P/MR2: Proceedings of Durbar, FMS, 1939
P/KH 3: Privy Council Practice in relation to the Federation of Malaya 1958
P/PTG 6: Instructions to Land Officers (cd also be 4): 1911
P/PTG 4: A short treatise on registration of titles in FMS, JK Innes 1907–1913
P/P 3: Federal Council Records
P/P 4: Federal Legislative Council Records
P/SP 2: Annual Departmental Reports FMS, UFMS
P/PER 2: Census Malaya 1891–1957
SS13: Acts and Ordiances of Legis Council 1867–
W/Misc: The Penang Riots Reports 1867
Arkib Diraja:
ARA/1/3: Proclamation of the Perak State Council
ARA/1/6: Award of an Honorary Companion of the Most Distinguished order of St Miachel and St George by Queen Victoria to Raja Idris of Perak. 22.10.1884
ARA/1/7: "Hon Knight Comdr" to Sultan Idris of Perak 1.6.1892
ARA/1/8: "Hon Grand Cross" by King Edwrad to Sultan Idris of Perak. 20.3.1901
ARA/1/9: Letter appointing WE Maxwell to the Perak State Council
ARA/1/10: "Perkahwinan Puteri Sulong Sultan Perak": Khutbah nikah YAM Raja Nazhatul Shima Ibnati Sultan Idris Almutawakil Shah dgn YM Syed Oman bin Ali Alsagoff
ARA/1/58: Salasilah Datok Changkat Piatu Orang Kaya Kaya Panglima Kinta Seri Amar Bangsa Diraja
ARA/1/59: Surat Asal Kuasa Penghulu Perak 21.4.57
ARB/1: Commission granted by HH Sultan Abdul Samad to the Selangor State Council delivered in 1876

ARB/18: Surat kuasa dpd Sultan Abd Samad kdp Raja Kahar (I:his son) untuk memrima wang dari taukeh Chan sebanayak $8960.64 (1881)

ARB/19: Surat dpd Gov Jervois kpd Raja Kahar, anakanda Sultan Abdul Samad Selangor meminta supaya Raja Mahadi tidak diberi pertolongan atau kebenaran masuk ke Selangor

ARB/119: Kenyataan cadangan Sultan Selangor kep Majlis Raja-Raja Melayu Bersekutu dlm tahum 1936 bagi mengadakan kapal terbang perang

ARB/129: Surat dpd Sultan Abd Samad Selangor kpd Sir Andrew Clark untuk melantik Frank Swettenham sbg Penolong Residen di Selangor. 18.6.1875.

ARC/8: Hikayat Pahang

ARD/1–9: Catitan harian Tengku Zainal Abidin b Tengku Kundor (1894–1912)

ARD/13: Salinan surat dpd Raja Kelantan kpd Robert W Duff; Slainan surat dpd Abdul Mutalib ibni raja kadir (raja negeri thai) kpd Robert william duff 6hb rejab 1320

ARD/14: Satu catitian mengenai masalah sengketa atas takhta kelantan dlm abad ke18–20

ARD/15: Satu salinan surat yang telah dihantar oleh Raja Kelantan (tuan Long Senik b tuan Kundor) kpd Gov Inggeris di singapura kira2 dlm tahun 1908/9 membantah diatas perjanjian "Anglo Siamese Treaty" of 1909 yang dibuat oleh Inggeris dan Siam dgn tidak terlebeh dahulu berunding dengan baginda sbg Raja pemerentah negeri kelantan kpd kerajaan inggeris dlm tahun 1909

ARD/16: Ucapan DYMM Sultan Kelantan (Tuan Long Senik b Tuan Kundor) bergelar Sultan Mahmud IV Kelantan di upacara penubuhan Majlis Ugama Islam Kelantan. 24.12.15

ARD/20: Surat, gov spore kep raja kelantan 7.7.1893

ARD/22: SP43/6/1

ARD/24: Undang2 perlembagaan tubuh kerajaan kelantan bhg ke2: fasal viii: keputusan mesyuarat majlis kerajaan n kelantan

ARN/2: Copies of misc notes, records and correspondence btw 1773 and 1961 extracted (with permission of his son) from the personal note book of the late Yang Teramat Mulia Tunku Besar Burhanuddin Ibni Yam Tuan Antah, Tunku Besar Sri Menanti.

ARK/4: Photostat copies of correspondence relating to the gift of the "Bunga Mas" to the King of England from the Sultan of Kedah and the Raja of Perlis (1909)

ARK/5/1 and 2: Surat daripada Sultan Muhd Jiwa Muazzam Shah kpd Capt Francis Light, dan kembali, dan juga ARK/6 (1773)

ART/16: Surat2 perisytiharan oleh Sultan Omar Ibni Almarhum Sultan Ahmad

ART/17: Surat dpd sultan zainal abidin kp FA Swettenham

ARP/5: Celebration in Perak of the Diamond Jubilee 1897

Arkib Johor

Salinan surat-surat Dato Menteri dan Setiausaha Kerajaan Johor 1891–1899.

Arkib Kedah

K/PU 1: Undang-Undang Kedah 1893.

S104: Ishak Mohd Rejab: Working Paper Wisma Negeri Alor Setar 1981. Peranan Ulama' Dalam Masyarakat di Kedah dengan diberi penekanan kepada Tuan Husain b Muhd Nasir al-Mas'udi dan Hj Wan Sulaiman Wan Sidek.

S342. Islam di Kedah Darul Aman. Konvensyen Sejarah N KDA, 29–30.9.1996, Alor Setar KDA. Majlis Kebudayaan Negeri.

S364: Surat Menyurat Zaman Sultan Abdul Hamid Halim Shah Negeri Kedah 1882–1943. Dato Hj Wan Shamsudin Mohd Yusof 2001: Bengkel Kajian Naskhah Kesultanan Melayu (DBP: Bahagian Kesusasteraan Tradisional KL 2–5 Julai 2001).

TS022. Fisal Haji Hussain. "Haji Hussain Che Dol 1904–1967: Satu Aspek Perjuangan Ulamak dalam bidang Agama dan Politik Melayu Kedah." UM 1979.

TS056. Muhd Isa Othman. "Kedudukan dan Perkembangan Golongan Politik Elit Tradisional di Negeri Kedah Sebelum dan Semasa pemerintahan Sultan Abdul Hamid Halim Shah 1881–1943." Univ Sains Msia P Pinang 1986.

TS088: Masrina bt Jasin. "Jabatan Zakat Neg Kedah: Satu Kajian Tentang Sejarah Penubuhan dan Peranannya terhadap Masyarakat Islam Kedah." UKM Bangi 1994.

TS0113. "Warkah Sosial and Warkah Undang-Undang SAH Hilm Syah: Satu Analisis Bandingan dari Sudut Struktur." Mohd Nasir b Tahir Mahfor. UM 2001.

Mariyam Salim, ed. "Undang-undang Kedah." DBP: 2005.

Wan Shamsuddin bin Mohd Yusof. "Perkembangan Dakwah Islamiah dan Penulis2 dari Golongan Agama di Utara-Barat Malaysia: Tumpuan di Negeri Kedah Darul Aman (Kertas kerja disediakan untul dialog utara VIII 1–4.12.1999 di Narathiwat, Yala dan Patani." Anjuran GAPENA.

Interviews

Discussion at Arkib Negari Kedah, 7.1.2007 and 9.1.2007.

Film, Arkib Kedah, 9.1.2007. Majlis Istiadat Perarakan Surat Diraja, 1995.

Datuk Wan Shamsuddin bin Mohd Yusof, 9.1.2007.

Pejabat Mufti Negeri Kedah. Mufti Besar, previous Mufti, Datuk Paduka Shaikh Abdul Majid, January 2007.

Muhammad Hashim Kamali, December 2005.

Nik Noriani, 1.12.05.

William Roff, January 2006.

Index